BOTSWANA TRAVEL GUIDE 2023:

Discovering Botswana's hidden gems with safety advice and helpful phrases

Dave C. Albert

All rights reserved. No part of this publication may be reproduced, distributed, or transmitted in any form or by any means, including photocopying, recording, or other electronic or mechanical methods, without the prior written permission of the publisher, except in the case of brief quotations embodied in critical reviews and certain other noncommercial uses permitted by copyright law.

Copyright © 2023 by Dave C. Albert

Table of Contents

Introduction to Botswana
Making travel plans for Botswana
Means of Getting to Botswana
Accommodations and Restaurants
Top Places to Visit in Botswana
Botswana's Wildlife and Nature
Experiences in Botswana's Culture
Botswana's Outdoor Adventures
Safari Camps and Lodges in Botswana
Taking pictures in Botswana
Sampling Botswana's regional cuisine
Botswana's Festivals and Events
Conservation and ethical travel
Language and Cultural Etiquette

Chapter 1

Introduction to Botswana

Botswana, the jewel of Southern Africa

Welcome to Southern Africa's real treasure, Botswana! This engaging nation provides an enthralling fusion of varied landscapes, lively fauna, and rich cultural experiences. Botswana's natural splendor will astound you, from the enormous Kalahari Desert to the calm waters of the Okavango Delta.

Entertain the grandeur of elephants, lions, and other majestic animals in their native habitats by setting out on exhilarating safari expeditions in internationally recognized national parks like Chobe and Moremi. With its distinctive habitat and the chance to travel by traditional mokoro boats, the Okavango Delta, a UNESCO World Heritage Site, beckons.

Absorb yourself in the friendly demeanor of the people as they impart their traditions and rituals, giving your tour a unique touch. The soul-stirring dance and music performances honoring Botswana's traditional history should not be missed.

Botswana has something spectacular to offer for everyone, whether you like the outdoors, animals, or culture. So, in this gorgeous treasure of Southern Africa, let your heart wander and make memories that will last a lifetime.

Overview of Botswana

Botswana is a landlocked nation in southern Africa that is renowned for its amazing wildlife, breathtaking scenery, and rich cultural history. It is a nation with a relatively low population density—2.3 million people—allowing for significant areas of uninhabited wilderness.

The varied and alluring terrain of the nation includes everything from the parched plains of the Kalahari Desert in the south to the lush wetlands of the Okavango Delta in the northwest. With its distinctive environment and an abundance of animals, the Okavango Delta, one of the biggest inland deltas in the world, draws tourists.

Botswana is a popular safari destination because of the astounding variety of wildlife that calls it home. While the Moremi Game Reserve provides an opportunity to see predators like lions and leopards, Chobe National Park is well known for its vast elephant herds. The Makgadikgadi Pans, sizable salt pans in the Kalahari, also play home to breathtaking zebra and wildebeest migrations.

Botswana is known for its vast cultural diversity in addition to its natural beauty. A diversified and thriving civilization is a result of the nation's many ethnic groupings, including the Tswana, San, and Herero. They showcase their culture via traditional music, dance, and crafts.

Botswana's dedication to sustainable tourism and wildlife preservation is one of its outstanding accomplishments. Due to the government's emphasis on environmental preservation, there are now organized national parks and privately owned reserves that provide ethical and responsible opportunities to see animals.

An important component of Botswana's economy is tourism, which draws visitors from all over the globe looking for outstanding services in the heart of Africa. Botswana guarantees a memorable trip that will make a deep impact on your heart, whether you're exploring nature on safari, engaging with kind people, or learning about the historical rock art of the Tsodilo Hills.

Climate and geography

The topography and climate of Botswana are both fascinating and varied. Located in southern Africa, the nation is primarily distinguished by a semi-arid to arid geography, which includes a mixture of flat plains, savannas, and desert areas.

The southern and central areas are dominated by the Kalahari Desert, which spans a significant chunk of the nation. Contrary to common opinion, the Kalahari doesn't qualify as a real desert since it gets a little bit more rain than other desert regions do. As a consequence, a variety of animals are supported by grasslands and scant but hardy flora, such as acacia trees.

A magnificent interior delta nourished by the Okavango River, the Okavango Delta is located to the north of the Kalahari. It creates a verdant paradise rich with animals and aquatic vegetation that contrasts sharply with the nearby desert. Due to the abundance of wildlife it draws, the delta is a top location for safaris and birding.

The Chobe River and Chobe National Park are located farther northeast. These natural areas are home to a variety of habitats along the riverbanks and floodplains, which serve as crucial water supplies for wildlife during the dry season.

There are different rainy and dry seasons in Botswana. Typically, the rainy season lasts from November through March, when high temperatures bring cooling showers. These rains renew the soil, filling lakes and waterholes and luring a plethora of animals to the area.

The dry season lasts from April to October in Botswana. Temperatures spike during this period, and the surroundings dry up. Since animals are more likely to concentrate near sources of standing water, it's a great time to go game-watching.

The temperature in Botswana may vary a lot from day to night throughout the year. While summer days may reach temperatures above

40°C (104°F), winter nights can be quite cold, particularly in desert areas.

Travelers may enjoy both the splendor of dry desert landscapes and lush, wildlife-rich wetlands in Botswana because of the country's geology and climate, which create an amazing patchwork of habitats. Every explorer and admirer of nature will find something genuinely special at this location.

Heritage and Cultural Diversity

As compelling as Botswana's natural beauty is its rich cultural variety and tradition. The nation is home to several ethnic groups, each of which adds to the complex fabric of cultures, traditions, and beliefs.

The Tswana, who make up a significant share of the population, are the biggest ethnic group in Botswana. The native language is Setswana, and their culture is fundamental to the character of the nation. A passionate "dumela" (hello) and "pula" (rain), which stand for blessings and good fortune, are often used to welcome guests. The Tswana people are renowned for their great hospitality.

An indigenous population that has lived in the area for thousands of years is the San, also known as the Basarwa or Bushmen. They have a strong connection with the earth and have maintained their hunter-gatherer way of life, depending on their understanding of nature. The rock art of the San people, which may be seen in areas like the Tsodilo Hills, provides a window into their illustrious past and mystical practices.

Another important ethnic group is the Herero, who came from Namibia to Botswana in the 19th century. They are renowned for their unusual Victorian-era clothing, which is proudly shown at social gatherings and festivals.

Botswana's cultural holidays are lively, joyful events that highlight the variety of the nation. A feast for the senses is created by the rhythmic rhythms and vibrant clothing that are a part of the traditional music and dance that are performed on these occasions. You could see some mesmerizing performances, such as the "Ditshomo" dance of the Tswana people or the "Setapa" dance of the Herero.

Storytelling is a vital part of Botswana's cultural legacy as a nation with a strong oral tradition foundation. Through the transmission of storytelling, elders preserve history and teach younger community members important lessons about life.

Even though Botswana has embraced growth and modernity, the preservation of its cultural heritage is still a top concern. To ensure that the nation's cultural variety thrives, efforts are undertaken to safeguard and promote traditional customs.

An exceptional chance to get immersed in the customs and procedures of a people is provided by traveling to Botswana. Travelers who interact with the local population and take part in cultural activities will definitely get a deep appreciation for the vast cultural diversity that pervades this captivating country.

Chapter 2

Making travel plans for Botswana

Ideal Season to Visit

The dry season in Botswana, which normally lasts from April to October, is the ideal time to go there. The weather is good at this time, with a bright sky and little humidity. Additionally, since animals congregate around water sources, wildlife watching is fantastic. However, be aware that it may become rather chilly in the mornings and nights during the winter months (June to August), so dress appropriately. Visit during the wet season, which lasts from November to March, if you love lush landscapes and bird viewing, but be ready for sporadic severe rains and restricted access to certain regions due to floods. The time of your visit will ultimately depend on your choices and interests.

Entry requirements and visas

Most visitors need a visa to enter Botswana. The country does not, however, need a visa for nationals of several nations to enter for a limited time. Before making travel arrangements, it is crucial to confirm the precise visa requirements, depending on your nationality.

Botswana provides a visa-on-arrival service for numerous nations, enabling visitors to get their visas at the port of entry. The visa-on-arrival is often good for a brief visit, such as one for travel or business. Make sure your passport is valid for at least six more months than the length of time you want to spend in Botswana.

You may apply for a visa via the Botswana diplomatic missions or embassies in your home country if you'd like to get one in advance. To prevent any possible delays, it is advised to apply for the visa well in advance of your trip dates.

You should always double-check the most recent information with the Botswana government's official website or call their embassy before making travel plans since visa and entrance requirements might change over time. Travel safely!

Tips for health and safety

Consider your health and safety a top priority while visiting Botswana. Observe the following advice:

1. Vaccinations: Before visiting Botswana, speak with your doctor about the required shots for diseases including typhoid, hepatitis A and B, yellow fever, and hepatitis A and C. Additionally, it's a good idea to keep up with normal immunizations like those for rubella, mumps, and measles.

2. Malaria Precautions: Due to Botswana's prevalent malaria, take the necessary safety measures. To reduce the risk of mosquito bites, talk to your doctor about taking a malaria prophylactic drug, using insect repellent, dressing in long sleeves, and sleeping beneath a mosquito net.

3. Drinking water: To prevent waterborne illnesses, stick to bottled or boiled water. Ice cubes and raw food purchased from street sellers should be avoided.

4. Heat protection: Given how hot Botswana may become, shield your skin from the heat by using sunscreen, sunglasses, and a hat with a broad brim. Drink lots of water to stay hydrated, particularly when engaging in outdoor activities.

5. Wildlife Safety: Although Botswana provides incredible opportunities to see wildlife, it's important to always keep a safe distance from animals, particularly in parks and reserves. During safaris, adhere to the instructions of

knowledgeable guides to protect both your safety and the welfare of the animals.

6. Respect Local Customs: To respect the culture of the people in Botswana, get familiar with the regional customs and traditions. When visiting religious or cultural institutions, keep tabs on clothing regulations and steer clear of sensitive subjects.

7. Travel Insurance: Invest in comprehensive travel insurance that includes evacuation and medical situations. You'll feel more secure knowing this in the event of unanticipated occurrences.

8. Driving Safety: If you want to drive in Botswana, use caution since the state of the roads may vary. When feasible, drive during the daytime instead of at night, obey speed restrictions, and keep an eye out for animals crossing the road.

9. Protect Your Property: Keep your property safe, particularly in busy areas and in tourist

destinations. Carry your valuables in a money belt or a safe bag; do not expose pricey goods to public view.

You may have a more joyful and worry-free time while experiencing Botswana's stunning landscapes and animals by heeding these health and safety recommendations. Always put your health first, and before and throughout your vacation, keep yourself informed about the local circumstances. Travel safely!

Chapter 3

Means of Getting to Botswana

Botswana flights from abroad

The capital city of Gaborone's Sir Seretse Khama International Airport (IATA: GBE) is where most visitors arriving from outside to Botswana will land. Ethiopian carriers, South African Airways, and Air Botswana are just a few of the carriers that fly internationally to Botswana.

Checking the flight times and accessible routes from your starting point to Gaborone is crucial. When planning your trip, be careful to take stopovers, distance traveled, and ticket costs into account. Additionally, before reserving a global trip to Botswana, make sure you have all the appropriate travel documentation, such as a current passport and any relevant visas. Please inquire if you need more information or if you have any special queries.

Travel Options Overland

In terms of overland travel possibilities in Botswana, there are a number of ways to discover this lovely nation and its varied landscapes:

1. Self-Drive Safaris: Renting a 4x4 and going on a self-drive safari is a well-liked option for tourists looking for freedom and adventure. The national parks and reserves of Botswana include well-kept gravel roads that let you travel into the bush and get up close to animals.

2. Guided Safaris: If you'd want a more accompanied experience, there are several tour

companies that provide guided overland safaris. These excursions provide knowledgeable guides who are familiar with the finest routes and animal locations, ensuring you don't miss any noteworthy sightings.

3. Mokoro trips: In the Okavango Delta, conventional mokoro trips provide a distinctive and tranquil opportunity to explore the convoluted waterways and take in the rich birds and aquatic life of the delta.

4. Public Buses: For transportation within significant towns and cities, public buses are provided. Despite not being intended for tourists, they may be an affordable method to get about town and cover small distances.

5. Private transportation: A few lodges and safari camps provide private transportation for its visitors, making it simple to go from one place to another and explore neighborhood sites.

6. Domestic Flights: Domestic flights are a practical choice for visiting rural locations or traveling across great distances. Major cities and wildlife locations are connected domestically by Air Botswana's aircraft service.

7. Guided Walking and Cycling Safaris: In certain regions, guided walking or cycling safaris are planned, enabling you to have a more personal relationship with nature while being accompanied by expert guides.

8. Organized Overland Tours: If you want a hassle-free vacation, going on an overland trip might be a terrific option. These excursions often include a variety of locations and pursuits, giving guests a complete safari experience.

Plan your Botswana overland excursion by taking into account variables like the season, the areas you wish to visit, and how comfortable you want to be in the environment. No matter whatever route you choose, you'll get to see amazing animals, breathtaking scenery, and Botswana's special charm.

Transportation Within Botswana

Certainly! There are a number of ways to move across Botswana in terms of transportation:

1. Minibusses and Buses: Minibuses, sometimes referred to as "combis," and buses run in major towns and cities, offering both residents and tourists a cheap means of transportation. They are a popular option for short- to medium-distance travel even though they may be congested.

2. Taxis: In metropolitan areas, taxis are accessible and may be located at authorized taxi stands or by hailing one on the street. Metered taxis are prevalent in cities like Francistown and Gaborone, whereas smaller towns sometimes need fee negotiation.

3. Shared Taxis: Shared taxis, commonly referred to as "shared combis," are minivans that travel along predetermined routes in cities and villages. The car has many stops along the trip as passengers share it. This approach could be more adaptable than buses and could reach places where there isn't as much bus service.

4. Car rentals: If you want to travel alone and explore distant locations or national parks in Botswana, renting a car is a great alternative. Car rental companies with a variety of vehicles are located in major cities and airports.

5. Trains: Botswana has a small rail system, with the main line running from Lobatse to Gaborone, Francistown, and Ramokgwebana (close to the Zimbabwean border). Trains are slower than other modes of transportation, but they provide a distinctive kind of transportation and an opportunity to observe the countryside.

6. Domestic Flights: Between large cities and towns, domestic flights are accessible for vast

distances or when time is an issue. The country's internal flights are run by the national airline, Air Botswana.

7. Walking and Cycling: In certain cities and rural places, walking and cycling may be convenient and fun forms of transportation. You may get a close-up view of the local landscape and culture.

It is essential to be informed of the routes and timetables while using public transit since they might change based on the location and time of day. Furthermore, it's a good idea to research transportation choices in advance if you want to go to rural locations or national parks since they could be less frequent or call for more preparation. Overall, Botswana's transportation options come in a variety to suit a range of travel needs and price ranges.

Chapter 4

Accommodations and Restaurants

Hotels and Resorts

Botswana is a top choice for travelers looking for an exceptional hotel or resort stay because of its stunning natural scenery, rich wildlife, and distinctive safari opportunities. Let's set off on a quest to discover some of the best lodgings in this magical nation.

In addition to Sandibe Okavango Safari Lodge:
1. The Beyond Sandibe Lodge: This is located in the gorgeous Okavango Delta, is a gem of sustainability and design. Its construction effortlessly melds with the surrounding scenery, giving visitors an opportunity to experience nature in opulent luxury. The resort offers

private game drives and escorted walks so you can see the diverse wildlife of Botswana up close.

2. Jack's Camp: Jack's Camp in the Makgadikgadi Pans is a haven of luxury and culture for a distinctive desert experience. It's a veritable oasis in the middle of the Kalahari Desert, with tastefully furnished tents and a captivating starbed for stargazing at night. With the assistance of knowledgeable guides, visitors may explore the pans, interact with habituated meerkats, or learn about the history and culture of the area.

3. Belmond Savute Elephant Lodge: One of the greatest populations of elephants may be seen up close at Belmond Savute Elephant Lodge, which is located in Chobe National Park. Each room at the lodge has its own terrace with a view of the renowned Savute Channel, which is often teeming with animals. The lodge's decor emphasizes the rustic appeal of the locale. Close encounters with elephants, big cats, and other

animals are common on game drives in this region.

4. Nkasa Lupala Tented Lodge: The tranquil Nkasa Lupala Tented Lodge in the Caprivi Strip is situated in the isolated Wuparo Conservancy. You may enjoy the views and sounds of the African environment while staying in the simple but cozy tented lodgings. In this less-traveled area of Botswana, you may go on boat safaris, nature walks, and birding excursions.

5. Sanctuary Chief's Camp: A classic example of luxury in the middle of the wilderness is Chief's Camp, which is situated on Chief's Island in the Moremi Game Reserve. The luxurious pavilions at the camp have private plunge pools and breathtaking views of the Okavango Delta. Both exciting game drives and serene mokoro (dugout canoe) trips provide visitors the opportunity to see the renowned "Big Five."

In Botswana, the outstanding service and experiences provided by these hotels and resorts are the only things that can compare to the beauty of your surroundings. Whatever draws you to the Okavango Delta's lush wetlands, the Makgadikgadi Pans' bleak vastness, or the Moremi and Chobe regions' wildlife-rich environments, there is opulent lodging ready to make your visit memorable. For those looking for an elegant fusion of nature and luxury in the heart of Africa, Botswana is undoubtedly a jewel.

Guesthouses and hostels

While luxury lodges and upscale safari camps are often associated with Botswana, the country also has a variety of lodgings that are more affordable, including hostels and guesthouses. With these choices, visitors may enjoy the nation's scenic splendor and kind people at a lower cost. In Botswana, a few notable hostels and guesthouses include the following:

1. Starting with The Old Bridge Backpackers (Maun): Budget tourists often choose The Old

Bridge Backpackers in Maun, which serves as the entrance to the Okavango Delta. Along the Thamalakane River, this hostel provides camping options as well as dorm-style accommodations. It's a great starting point for planning safari trips and visiting the neighboring wildlife preserves.

2. The Ghanzi Trail Blazers: In Ghanzi, a town close to the Kalahari Desert, there is a resort that welcomes backpackers called Ghanzi Trail Blazers. This economical choice offers lodging in conventional huts and cultural activities like bushman treks and dances, giving it a distinctive and affordable stay.

3. The Big Five Lodge in Kasane: The Big Five Lodge in Kasane, close to Chobe National Park, provides welcoming and moderately priced accommodations. It's the perfect option for those who want to see the magnificent wildlife of Chobe without breaking the bank.

4. The Maun Rest Camp (Maun): The Maun Rest Camp is yet another inexpensive choice in

Maun. It offers a range of lodging options, such as camping and chalets with full kitchens. If you want to schedule safaris or see the Okavango Delta, it's a practical spot to stay.

5. Khwai Guest House: It's located on the outskirts of the Moremi Game Reserve, in Khwai Village, lies the guesthouse-style lodging known as Khwai Guest House. It provides cozy rooms with private toilets and is an excellent option for those seeking a more genuine and local experience.

While these hostels and guesthouses may not provide the same degree of comfort as upscale resorts, they do provide an inexpensive option to see Botswana's wildlife and natural beauty. They are often managed by kind and competent hosts who can assist you in organizing your travels in this amazing nation. Botswana offers choices to meet different visitor tastes, regardless of whether you're on a limited budget or just want a more authentic experience.

Botswana's top restaurants

Botswana has a distinctive culinary landscape that combines regional cuisines with global influences. There are nevertheless a number of eateries that stand out for their delectable food and pleasant ambience, despite the fact that they may not be as renowned for their restaurants as some other locations. Some of Botswana's top eateries are listed below:

1. The Meat Company, located in Gaborone: The Meat Company in Gaborone is a local and tourist favorite because of its superb steaks and grilled meats. They offer a range of cuts on their menu, including excellent Botswana beef, as well as lamb and chicken selections. A variety of wines are also available at the restaurant to go with your meal.

2. Sanitas Tea Garden in Maun: Sanitas Tea Garden is a beautiful eatery with a lush garden setting that is situated in Maun. They provide a variety of regional and international cuisine, with their traditional Botswana meal standing

out in particular. For a genuine sense of the food in your area, try the mokoro beef or chicken stew.

3. Chutney Restaurant in Gaborone: Chutney Restaurant in Gaborone is a must-visit if you like Indian food. They provide a large selection of Indian food, including tandoori specialties and tasty curries. The welcoming atmosphere and excellent service at the restaurant enhance the dining experience.

4. Marina Café in Maun: Both residents and tourists frequent the Marina Café in Maun. The Thamalakane River's serene waterfront location and reputation for serving fresh seafood dishes make for an excellent dining experience. While savoring meals like grilled tiger prawns, take in the tranquil surroundings.

5. The Courtyard (Kasane): A delicious dining experience with a cuisine that mixes international and regional tastes is available at The Courtyard in Kasane. They have a great outdoor dining area where you can dine beneath

the stars. Never pass up the chance to sample regional specialties like seswaa (pounded beef) and sadza (maize porridge).

6. The Fig Tree (Kasane) (number six): The Fig Tree, a fantastic alternative in Kasane, is situated at Chobe Safari Lodge. With an emphasis on using foods that are fresh and easily obtained locally, this restaurant serves a blend of African and international cuisine. After a day of safari experiences in Chobe National Park, it's a great spot to eat.

7. Stopover at Woodlands (Francistown): The Woodlands Stopover is a warm restaurant that serves a range of foods, including steaks, burgers, and traditional Botswana fare, for visitors traveling through Francistown. It's a well-liked option for a casual supper because of the laid-back ambiance and helpful personnel.

While Botswana's eating options may not be as vast as those in some other countries, these establishments provide visitors with the opportunity to enjoy delectable cuisine and the welcoming atmosphere of the host nation. There are restaurants in Botswana that can accommodate a variety of tastes and preferences, whether you're in the nation's capital of Gaborone, the safari capital of Maun, or another area.

Chapter 5

Top Places to Visit in Botswana

Exploring the capital city of Gaborone

Gaborone, a bustling and fast-growing city, has a distinctive fusion of modernism and traditional African culture. Botswana's political, economic, and cultural center provides a wealth of thrilling activities for tourists.

The Three Leaders Monument, which celebrates three tribal leaders who made a major contribution to the history of the nation, is among the must-see attractions in Gaborone. The National Assembly building, a stunning architectural masterpiece that exemplifies the country's democratic character, is another well-known monument.

The National Museum and Art Gallery is a fantastic place to visit if you're interested in art and history. It is home to a varied collection of antiquities, works of art, and exhibitions that explore the rich history and cultural variety of Botswana.

Gaborone Game Reserve, conveniently situated inside the city boundaries, is a delight for nature lovers. With the background of the city, you may see a variety of animal species here, including zebras, wildebeests, and numerous bird species.

Visit the Main Mall, a lively area with stores, cafés, and marketplaces where you can buy crafts and souvenirs and enjoy Botswana's traditional food, to get a sense of the native way of life.

In addition, Gaborone has a thriving nightlife with a wide variety of pubs, clubs, and eateries.

It's a wonderful way to relax after a day of city exploration.

While visiting Gaborone, you may like to put on some traditional attire made of the 'dikgobe' or's shweshwe' fabrics, which are significant in Botswana culture. Don't forget to socialize with the hospitable locals, who will surely enhance your stay there.

Travelers seeking to immerse themselves in the heart of Botswana will find Gaborone to be an outstanding trip thanks to its beautiful blend of urban attractions, cultural insights, and natural beauty.

The Okavango Delta exploration

A magical adventure that immerses you in the center of one of Africa's most remarkable natural beauties is exploring the Okavango Delta in Botswana.

The biggest inland delta in the world and a UNESCO World Heritage Site is the Okavango Delta. It is a massive system of islands, lagoons, and rivers that spring to life every year during the flood season. The best way to see this untainted environment is on a mokoro trip, which involves paddling a traditional dugout canoe under the expert guidance of native guides. The plentiful fauna and breathtaking scenery will captivate you as you softly glide between the reeds and water channels.

Elephants, buffalo, hippos, and other antelope species are just a few of the amazing animals that can be found in the Delta. Consider going on a walking safari with knowledgeable guides who can share their expertise of the flora and animals with you for a really immersive experience.

With over 400 kinds of birds identified in the Delta, birdwatchers will be in awe of its diversity. Every bend in the canal exposes a different bird marvel, from the spectacular

African fish eagle to the colorful malachite kingfisher.

Away from the rush of contemporary life, exploring the Delta offers an opportunity to get in touch with nature in its most unadulterated state. You may camp out at night beneath a canopy of stars and enjoy the tranquil sounds of nature.

Some hotels and campers provide superb lodging for those looking for a little more luxury, enabling you to comfortably take in the magnificence of the Delta.

The Okavango Delta is a vulnerable environment; therefore, it's important to keep in mind that, in order to preserve its beauty and animals, ethical tourism is vital. During your vacation, it is crucial that you respect the environment and the customs of the locals.

In conclusion, visiting the Okavango Delta is a breathtaking excursion into the unspoiled interior of Africa. It is a must-visit location for nature enthusiasts and adventure seekers alike because of the region's abundant animals, quiet streams, and unspoiled beauty.

The splendor of wildlife in Chobe National Park

The animal magnificence of Chobe National Park is a unique experience that immerses you in the midst of untamed nature and offers a stunning display of African species.

Chobe, in northern Botswana, is well known for having a large and diversified population of animals, making it one of the best safari locations in Africa. The Chobe River, a vital lifeblood that attracts species from all around, particularly during the dry season, is the focal point of the park.

An exceptional chance to see one of Africa's highest densities of elephants is provided by a Chobe safari. You'll be in amazement as herds of these gorgeous animals graze freely and are often spotted swimming or cooling off in the river.

In addition to elephants, Chobe is home to a wide range of other animals, such as buffalo, lions, leopards, and the critically endangered African wild dog. The park is home to approximately 450 different kinds of birds, which will thrill bird aficionados.

The Chobe River boat safaris are a must-do because they provide you with a close-up view of wildlife as it comes to drinking or playing in the water. The river tours provide a unique viewpoint and an opportunity to see hippos, crocodiles, and a variety of bird species that live near the water.

For those looking to view lions and leopards in their native environment, the Savuti area of Chobe is known for frequent predator sightings, making it an exhilarating location.

Some resorts and camps inside the park provide superb lodging and top-notch service, enabling you to rest after thrilling days spent exploring the area's animals.

A trip to Chobe National Park is not only about seeing rare species; it's also about getting in touch with the unadulterated beauty of the African wilderness and feeling the energy of the natural world all around you.

Responsible tourism is essential to maintaining the ecosystem's delicate balance, just as it is for any natural area. The beauty of Chobe's wildlife will be preserved for future generations if people respect animals and adhere to park rules.

In conclusion, Chobe National Park is a haven for both wildlife and environmental lovers. Anyone wanting an outstanding safari experience should be sure to visit this region because of its remarkable wildlife encounters, beautiful scenery, and the unadulterated enchantment of the African bush.

The amazing Makgadikgadi Pans

An experience unlike any other in Africa, marveling at the Makgadikgadi Pans takes you to an ethereal setting.

The Makgadikgadi Pans, one of the world's biggest salt flats, are situated in northeastern Botswana and span a total area of more than 6,000 square miles. Thousands of years ago, an ancient lake that formerly covered these wide, shimmering stretches dried up, leaving behind a bizarre and hauntingly beautiful desert-like landscape.

The dry season, which runs from April to October, is the best time to explore the Makgadikgadi Pans because the parched white surface then spreads out as far as the eye can see, giving the area a captivating, mirage-like appearance. The seclusion and silence of the pans are very humbling and provide a feeling of tranquility that is difficult to obtain anywhere.

The yearly zebra migration is one of the most stunning natural occurrences to see here. Thousands of zebras congregate in the region as the dry season intensifies, traveling along historic migration routes in search of water and grazing options. A photographer's fantasy and a really unique sight, these striped herds against the stark white background are a sight to see.

Additionally, the Makgadikgadi Pans provide a unique chance for stargazing unmatched anywhere else. When the sun sets, the sky becomes a huge canvas of sparkling stars that is unobstructed by light pollution. It's the perfect location for a surreal encounter among the cosmic marvels.

An exhilarating way to see this unique environment up close is to explore the pans on guided hikes or quad bike tours. You could come across unusual plant life that has evolved to thrive in this dry climate, as well as tough desert fauna like meerkats and springboks.

For those looking for cultural interactions, seeing surrounding traditional villages will give you an understanding of the native people who have coexisted peacefully with this area for countless centuries.

It's essential to conduct responsible tourism while visiting the Makgadikgadi Pans to protect this fragile habitat. By abiding by the rules and protecting the environment, you can guarantee that future generations will be able to awe at the natural beauty of this alluring location.

In conclusion, for those looking to commune with nature's unadulterated splendor, the Makgadikgadi Pans provide a unique and captivating experience. Whether you are lured to these isolated and otherworldly places by the stunning landscapes, the yearly zebra migration, or the starry night sky, a trip there ensures that you will have memories to last a lifetime.

Chapter 6

Botswana's Wildlife and Nature

Game drives and wildlife safaris

Botswana is a popular travel destination for wildlife photographers and environment lovers due to its rich fauna and unspoiled terrain. The chance to see some of Africa's most recognizable creatures, such as elephants, lions, leopards, giraffes, and many more, in their native habitats is unmatched by anything else. A wildlife safari in Botswana provides this opportunity.

Selecting a trustworthy tour company or resort with knowledgeable guides who are well-versed in the regional flora and fauna is crucial when going on a wildlife safari or game drive in Botswana. These professionals will not only guarantee your safety but will also improve your whole experience thanks to their expertise and insights.

One of the most popular locations for safari lovers is the Okavango Delta, a UNESCO World Heritage Site. During the dry season, when wildlife is abundant due to the transformation of the environment by this enormous inland delta, game watching is at its best. A distinctive and relaxing way to see the delta and take in its rich birds and aquatic inhabitants is to take a mokoro ride (traditional canoe) along the water channels.

Chobe National Park, renowned for its vast herds of elephants and abundant wildlife, is another fascinating destination. Safaris on both land and in boats are available in Chobe, enabling guests to see wildlife along the Chobe River from various angles.

Within the Okavango Delta, the Moremi Game Reserve is renowned for its various habitats and great predator sightings. A lot of large cats may be found there, including the elusive leopard.

Wildlife is preserved and permitted to flourish in its natural habitat because of Botswana's dedication to ecotourism and low-impact safari techniques. Visitors must respect the wildlife and their habitats by keeping a safe distance and following the instructions of their guides.

In conclusion, a wildlife safari or game drive in Botswana guarantees spectacular experiences with some of the most beautiful animals in the world, enveloping you in the beauty of the African wilderness and leaving you with memories that will last a lifetime.

Observing birds in Botswana's wetlands

Bird lovers and wildlife enthusiasts alike find birdwatching in Botswana's wetlands to be an exceptional experience. It is a home for many different bird species, making the nation's various wetland ecosystems a delight for birdwatchers throughout.

The Okavango Delta is a top location for birding because of its lush floodplains, reed beds, and rivers. More than 400 different bird species, including colorful kingfishers, graceful herons, dazzling fish eagles, and magnificent African fish owls, may be seen at this UNESCO World Heritage Site. Popular methods to experience the tranquility of the surroundings while getting up close and personal with the avian marvels of the delta are guided boat cruises or mokoro tours.

Wetlands in Chobe National Park, especially those near the Chobe River, are excellent places to see birds. Here, you could see the recognizable African fish eagle resting in the trees and the vibrant bee-eaters elegantly darting through the air. For any ardent birder, the incredible variety of waterbirds, such as storks, spoonbills, and pelicans, makes for an enthralling display.

Given that the Moremi Game Reserve has wetlands and savanna ecosystems, birdwatching there is equally enjoyable. Numerous bird species are drawn to the thick foliage along the water channels, including uncommon wattled cranes and lilac-breasted rollers that display their vibrant plumage.

The birds and their habitats must be respected, just like with any wildlife excursion. More natural actions and greater possibilities for observation may be seen when respect is maintained and disruption is kept to a minimum.

Botswana's wetlands provide an adventure of discovery and amazement, whether you are an experienced birder or a novice to the world of birding. A very enriching experience that will leave you with priceless memories and a greater love for nature is the joy of discovering new species and seeing the stunning majesty of these winged animals in their natural habitat.

Exploring The Moremi Game Reserve

The untamed grandeur of the African environment is revealed during an exciting exploration of Moremi Game Reserve. This protected region is a top destination for nature and animal lovers and is situated right in the middle of the Okavango Delta.

The varied landscapes of Moremi, which include wide grasslands, lush floodplains, flowing canals, and mopane woods, are one of the region's distinctive features. Every game drive or safari is an exciting and surprising event because of the incredible diversity of species that these areas sustain.

Throughout the reserve, you will come across recognizable African wildlife, such as mighty elephants, attractive giraffes, sly leopards, and the magnificent African lion. A highlight for many tourists is the ability to see elusive predators in the wild and observe their behavior.

Over 500 different bird species may be found in Moremi, which has an equally outstanding birdlife. The reserve provides unlimited opportunity for birding aficionados to study and admire the avian marvels, including graceful herons, vividly colorful kingfishers, and majestic raptors flying above.

You may explore the wetlands of the delta in a more quiet and personal manner by traveling through the rivers in a traditional mokoro. This will bring you closer to aquatic life and give you an opportunity to see more elusive animals that live there.

Because of Moremi's dedication to conservation and responsible tourism, the ecology is preserved, enabling animals to flourish in their native habitat. Visitors must adhere to the rules established by the park's management and the qualified guides who go on safari with them.

The dry season (May to October), when wildlife congregates near water sources and provides superb game-watching possibilities, is the optimum time to explore Moremi Game Reserve. The delta turns into a verdant paradise during the green season (November to April), when migrating birds arrive and the environment is bursting with fresh growth.

A soul-stirring trip connecting you with nature in its most basic form is exploring Moremi Game Reserve. The sights, sounds, and feelings you encounter in this wilderness will leave you with lifelong memories that will deepen your understanding of the need to preserve these priceless environments for future generations as well as the delicate balance of life.

Chapter 7

Experiences in Botswana's Culture

Looking closely at San Bushman culture

Learning about the San Bushman culture in Botswana is a humbling yet fascinating journey. This long-extinct indigenous people's customs, habits, and way of life may be completely experienced, which is a really one-of-a-kind opportunity. As you go into the vast Kalahari Desert, they will greet you with open arms and make you feel as if you are an integral part of their community.

By living with them, you may see the particular way of life of the San Bushmen, which is deeply ingrained in the culture of the nation. By learning how to observe animals, identify medicinal plants, and do so, you may emulate their hunting and gathering practices that have kept them alive for thousands of years. By taking in the fascinating stories they share around the campfire, you may discover their history and in-depth knowledge of the environment.

Since there is mutual cultural exchange going on, they are just as interested in your way of life as you are in theirs. By sharing your experiences, stories, and skills, you have the chance to encourage respect and understanding among individuals.

While you're with them, you may see their mesmerizing dances and take in their folk music to witness the San Bushmen's abilities in action. These performances not only display their culture but also provide an insight into their spiritual values and beliefs. By taking part in these rituals, one may develop a deep appreciation for the simplicity and wisdom of their way of life, as well as a sense of harmony with nature.

The more you integrate into the community, the more you'll realize how broad the concept of family and community is. Everyone looks out for one another, and it is really fascinating to observe how they divide up the tasks and resources. You can come to the conclusion that your own life's aims and ambitions need to be reevaluated.

But you must approach this event with respect and humility. Always remember that you are a guest in their home and that you must show respect for their customs and regulations. Respecting their culture and not interfering with their daily routine will lead to a more meaningful and real encounter.

In conclusion, immersing yourself in the San Bushman culture of Botswana is an incredible experience that will have a significant impact on your soul. You will always treasure the opportunity to learn from these amazing people and get insights into their timeless way of life. It is a one-of-a-kind, valuable experience.

Music and Dance from the Past

Traditional dance and music in Botswana are vibrant expressions of the country's rich cultural heritage. These artistic endeavors are vital to the people's way of life because they enable storytelling, celebration, and the maintenance of their predecessors' traditions.

The locals of Botswana have a close bond with their native music. There are many different instruments in it, each with its own sound and purpose. The "segaba," a stringed instrument with a violin-like sound that is fashioned from animal skin and features a calabash resonator, is the most well-known instrument. When the segaba is played by skilled musicians, beautiful melodies are produced that captivate listeners and transport them to the heart of Botswana's cultural legacy.

Traditional Botswana music is often accompanied by joyful singing, the lyrics of which represent the people's experiences, beliefs, and ideals. The songs may be joyful and express gratitude for plentiful harvests or rain, or they may narrate tales of mythical figures and significant historical events. The music also often participates in social commentary by addressing contemporary issues while maintaining a link to traditional wisdom.

Without a discussion of dancing, Botswana's culture cannot be understood. In different parts of the country, different traditional dances are connected to different occasions and customs. Some dances are performed during harvest celebrations, weddings, and initiation rites, while others are done for amusement or to strengthen links within the community. The dance movements are characterized by a blend of grace, agility, and rhythmic precision, which mirrors the dancers' close connection to the surrounding natural world.

Participating in traditional dance and music performances in Botswana is a fantastic experience. The musicians and dancers engage the crowd with such passion and intensity that the ambience is captivating and unforgettable. As a spectator, you can't help but be moved by the performers' infectious joy and pride as they share their cultural heritage with you.

In Botswana, there has been an upsurge in recent years in the protection and advancement of traditional music and dance. The beauty and significance of this intangible cultural inheritance are made visible through festivals and cultural events that promote these creative manifestations.

The country of Botswana's traditional music and dance are also powerful representations of the country's cultural diversity and identity. They serve as a bridge between the past and the present by keeping the wisdom, values, and traditions of the ancestors alive. Experiencing and engaging in these vibrant artistic forms may help one have a deeper understanding of the spirit of Botswana and its people.

Handicrafts and Homemade Products

Crafts and artisanal products made in Botswana are a true reflection of the country's inventiveness and cultural diversity. Local artisans skillfully meld traditional techniques with contemporary materials to produce a wide variety of superb handicrafts that precisely reflect the essence of Botswana's history.

In Botswana, one of the most well-known artisanal crafts is basket weaving. The intricate designs and embellishments on these baskets are not only visually attractive but also have significant symbolic meaning. The art of basket weaving has been passed down through the years, and each piece reflects the attention to detail and craftsmanship of the crafters.

Ceramics are given special importance in the artistic history of Botswana. Aesthetic clay pots and jars are created by artists, who often cover them with exquisite carvings or vibrant paints. These ceramic creations harmoniously blend shape and beauty in the manner of Botswana's indigenous arts. They are both beautiful and utilitarian.

The craft of beading is a significant aspect of Botswana's artisan culture. A vast range of colors and patterns may be seen in the carefully created beaded clothing, accessories, and jewelry. Each beaded item often has a cultural significance, and the exceptional workmanship required to create them reveals the craftsmen's close links to their society.

Leatherworking is another highly valued profession in Botswana. Local artisans turn animal skins into gorgeous leather goods, including shoes, belts, and handbags, with skill. By using ancient tanning techniques and hand-stitching techniques, these handmade products' durability and authenticity are ensured.

Wood carving is an important creative material used by artisans to make intricate sculptures and masks in Botswana. The intricate ties the country has with the outside world and its long history of oral storytelling are reflected in these carvings, which often include old symbols, animals, or figures from local folklore.

Outside of Botswana, there is a widespread appreciation for handmade products and crafts. These unique objects are greatly sought after by tourists and collectors as souvenirs or works of art that represent the essence of Botswana's culture and resourcefulness.

The local government and organizations further strongly support and promote them as a consequence of their realization of the importance of these historic crafts in preserving cultural heritage and providing local artists with a means of subsistence.

In conclusion, Botswana's handicrafts and handcrafted products provide a glimpse into the vibrant cultural landscape of the country and the artistic prowess of its people. Modern concepts and traditional techniques are blended to provide a broad range of well-crafted products with cultural and aesthetic significance. Accepting and valuing these handmade products is a way to respect and encourage the ongoing spirit of Botswana's creative tradition.

Chapter 8

Botswana's Outdoor Adventures

Canoeing in the Delta with a mokoro

In Botswana's Delta, mokoro canoeing is a magical experience that gives you a special chance to peacefully connect with nature. An up-close look at the rich environment of the delta may be had while floating across the river in a traditional dugout canoe called a mokoro. The beautiful flora, many birds, and possibly even some animals grazing at the water's side will be all around you.

Local experts who are often local to the area are quite informed about the flora and animals and provide intriguing anecdotes and observations while expertly navigating the serene waters. As the mokoro's gentle rocking soothes your senses and the sounds of nature create a calming symphony, the tranquility of the trip provides for reflective periods.

The sensation of being completely enveloped by nature is one of the most breathtaking features of Mokoro canoeing. When you leave behind any technological distractions and embrace the simplicity of life on the river, there is a feeling of peace as you blend in with the surroundings. The Delta is one of the most beautiful places on earth, and every turn reveals something new, whether it's a secret lagoon covered in lilies or a troop of elephants relaxing in the distance.

For your experience to be sustainable and have a beneficial effect on the environment and local populations, you must adopt responsible ecotourism techniques in this fragile area. The Delta will help you get a greater understanding of the value of conservation efforts and the relevance of protecting such pure natural regions.

Mokoro canoeing in the Delta is a soul-stirring experience that offers a chance to break away from the bustle of contemporary life and immerse yourself in the enduring beauty of nature. It's an encounter that will always have a special place in your heart and leave you with priceless memories and a strong bond with Botswana's alluring environment.

Bush guides on walking safaris

A real and thrilling way to see the African environment is via walking safaris with bush rangers in Botswana. Instead of taking a standard game drive, you may experience the sights, sounds, and smells of the savannah up close and personally on foot with these safaris.

Leading the journey and imparting their extensive knowledge of the area flora and animals are trained and experienced bush guides. They can follow animals with astonishing precision and have a thorough grasp of wildlife behavior, making the safari both safe and educational. You'll be in awe of the amazing wildlife that calls the area home as you stroll alongside these specialists.

It is humbling to stroll across Botswana's enormous landscapes because you start to feel like a part of the place rather than just an observer. A strong connection to nature is formed when people get the chance to see animals in their natural environment, untouched by the presence of cars. You could come across quietly grazing herds of elephants, beautiful giraffes perusing from the treetops, or perhaps get a glimpse of a pride of lions in motion.

You'll also have a chance to take in some of the lesser bush marvels as you walk through the wilderness, such the complex animal trace patterns, the variety of birds, and the intriguing insects that flourish in this habitat.

Because they encourage little environmental effect and help the preservation of species and their habitats, walking safaris place a high priority on conservation and sustainability. The encounter cultivates an understanding of the need to protect these beautiful landscapes for future generations and the fragile balance of nature.

During walking safaris, safety is of the utmost importance. The guides are trained to deal with any possible wildlife interactions, ensuring that both you and the animals stay safe. You may totally immerse yourself in the woods while being certain that you are in excellent hands thanks to their knowledge and alertness.

In general, Botswana's walking safaris with bush guides give a life-changing and memorable trip. It's an experience that not only gives you the chance to see Africa's wildlife in all its splendor up close, but also leaves you with a renewed feeling of amazement and appreciation for the natural world.

Desert of the Kalahari for stargazing

Awe-inspiring and enchanting stargazing may be had in Botswana's Kalahari Desert. The desert provides a clear and unhindered view of the night sky, showing a spectacular tapestry of stars that appear to extend eternally above. Being far from the bright lights of towns, the desert also offers a peaceful and serene environment.

When the sun sets, the desert becomes a mystical world of darkness, and the first stars gradually start to appear. With stars and constellations glowing brilliantly and creating beautiful patterns across the cosmic canvas, the Kalahari's pristine and unpolluted sky provide for superb stargazing.

You'll have an intense sensation of connectedness to the cosmos while lying on a blanket under the expansive night sky. The desert's utter stillness enriches the experience, engulfing you in a serene tranquility that enables you to completely immerse yourself in the splendor of the universe.

You could have the opportunity to see other celestial beauties than the stars, such as meteor showers or the Milky Way's brilliant radiance. Low humidity and little light pollution make the desert an excellent place to see these unusual occurrences.

Stargazing tours are often accompanied by local tour guides and astronomy specialists, who add to the experience by sharing their expertise on the night sky and its legends. They will identify stars, narrate old tales, and provide information on the cultural importance of astronomical events.

It's difficult to avoid feeling insignificant when you look up at the sparkling stars because of how big the cosmos is and where you are in relation to it. A time of introspection, stargazing in the Kalahari Desert allows you to think on the riddles of life and admire the grandeur of our galaxy.

Warm clothes are a good idea to pack, since desert evenings may grow cool, and binoculars or a telescope can make stargazing more enjoyable. Whether you're an expert astronomer or just someone who enjoys the beauty of the night sky, stargazing in the Kalahari Desert is an incredible voyage into the depths of space that will leave you with memories that will shine in your heart for a lifetime.

Chapter 9

Safari Camps and Lodges in Botswana

The finest safari lodges in Botswana

Botswana is a popular travel destination for people looking for an amazing safari because of its pristine nature and variety of species. The nation has a wide selection of opulent safari resorts that blend luxury with an actual African safari trip.

The renowned Mombo Camp, which is located in the Moremi Game Reserve, is one such hotel. Mombo Camp provides amazing views and chances to see the Big Five up close and in their natural environment thanks to its opulent tents that fit in with the surroundings.

Zarafa Camp in the Selinda Reserve is a great option for those looking for a little seclusion. Spacious accommodations, private plunge pools, and skillfully guided game drives are all available at Zarafa, a safari lodge renowned for its cozy atmosphere and ecologically friendly construction.

With its exquisite apartments and private verandas overlooking the Linyanti River, the King's Pool Camp in the Linyanti Wildlife Reserve provides an opulent hideaway farther north. Visitors may enjoy game drives, walking safaris, and boat cruises, all of which are conducted by expert guides who are passionate about Botswana's animals and scenery.

Consider the Okavango Delta's Duba Plains Camp if you're looking for a genuinely solitary and remote safari experience. This opulent resort is famed for its extraordinary animal encounters, particularly with lions and buffalo, as well as its lovely tented rooms affording breathtaking views over the floodplains of the Delta.

Luxury safari lodges in Botswana will unquestionably provide an unmatched combination of luxury and wildness, helping you to create experiences that will last a lifetime, whether you decide to visit the verdant Okavango Delta, the sizable Chobe National Park, or the captivating Makgadikgadi Pans.

Tented camps and eco-friendly campsites

Due to its dedication to the preservation of wildlife and environmentally responsible tourism, Botswana provides a variety of eco-friendly campsites and tented camps that let tourists take in the country's natural beauty while having the least amount of an effect on the environment.

The Sanctuary Stanley's Camp, which is situated in the Okavango Delta, serves as a prime example. By using solar energy, recycling programs, and low-impact building methods to lessen its carbon footprint, this camp has made tremendous progress toward sustainability. The fact that they are staying in luxurious tents with contemporary conveniences fosters ethical tourism.

The Khwai Tented Camp in the Moremi Game Reserve is a shining example of a firm commitment to environmentally friendly methods. Solar energy is used to power this little camp, and the selection of environmentally friendly materials guarantees that the surrounding nature is hardly impacted. While enjoying the camp's dedication to safeguarding the sensitive environment, visitors may immerse themselves in nature.

Meno A Kwena Tented Camp, situated on the edge of the Makgadikgadi Pans, is a noteworthy alternative. Offering a distinctive mix of luxury and authenticity, this eco-aware camp places a strong emphasis on responsible tourism. The knowledge that their visit directly supports conservation initiatives and improves the neighborhood allows guests to experience animal interactions.

Eco-friendly camping options in Botswana also include Chobe National Park, where establishments like Chobe Under Canvas are models of sustainability. These transient, non-permanent camps are made with the intention of leaving little to no trace following their removal, enabling the ecosystem to flourish undisturbed.

Additionally, several campgrounds in Botswana that are part of the local community work to support and advance ecotourism projects. These camps make sure that a percentage of their earnings supports neighborhood businesses and environmental initiatives, giving visitors the chance to practice responsible tourism.

Overall, Botswana's dedication to eco-friendly methods makes it a great place to visit for tourists who want to enjoy the natural beauty of the country while being considerate of the environment. Visitors may help ensure that the natural legacy of Botswana is preserved for future generations by selecting these eco-friendly campsites and tented camps.

Gaze at the stars during the night

An awe-inspiring experience that will live with you for a lifetime is sleeping beneath the stars in Botswana. Words can scarcely express the wonder that is created when the sun sets over the wide desert and the African sky turns into a stunning tapestry of glittering stars.

The Makgadikgadi Pans, a large, flat area that appears to go on forever into the distance, is one of the greatest spots to see this celestial show. Due to the absence of vegetation and little light pollution, the pans provide a weird and otherworldly experience during the dry season, making them ideal for stargazing.

The Milky Way sends its magnificent glory over the night sky as you relax around a campfire, listening to the calm sounds of nature. It is a humbling and spiritual experience because of the solitude and expanse of the African bush at night, which inspire awe and a feeling of connection with the cosmos.

In a few upscale safari hotels and tented camps in Botswana, guests may choose to stay in open-air suites or elevated platforms where they can sleep under the stars. An experience that will kindle your sense of adventure and make you feel more alive than ever is drifting off to sleep under the cosmic canopy, with the distant animal noises serving as your lullaby.

The start of a new day in the African bush is marked by the sky's slow transformation from a canopy of stars to a canvas of gentle pastel hues as dawn draws near. A reminder of the beauty and simplicity of nature, seeing the dawn in such a quiet environment is equally mesmerizing.

As a getaway from the rush of contemporary life, spending the night in Botswana beneath the stars enables you to reestablish contact with nature in its most unadulterated state. A once-in-a-lifetime chance to be engulfed in the cosmos' marvels and the natural beauty of Africa's bush, making memories that will last with you long after your trip is over.

Chapter 10

Taking pictures in Botswana

Wildlife and landscape photography

In Botswana, it's crucial to approach the assignment with respect for nature and the animals in order to capture wildlife and landscapes. It's important to have patience; give yourself time to study and comprehend the activities of the animals without causing any disturbance. To keep a safe distance and prevent interfering with their normal activities, use long lenses.

Try to incorporate Botswana's breathtaking natural settings into your compositions. To emphasize the animals' surroundings and tell a more interesting tale in your photos, place the animals in the middle of expansive savannas, marshes, or beautiful woods.

Early in the morning and late in the day, when the light is soft and golden, are the greatest periods for wildlife photography. This creates a cozy environment and brings out the colors and textures of the surroundings and the animals. Utilize the "golden hour" to get those beautiful pictures.

If you want to depict the immensity of Botswana's many terrains in your landscape photos, think about employing wide-angle lenses. To produce aesthetically appealing photos that capture the magnificence of the landscapes, pay attention to factors like leading lines, foreground interest, and balance.

Recall to be kind and patient, letting the animals act in their natural ways. The use of flashes or any other intrusive techniques that can disturb the animals should be avoided.

Last but not least, really enjoy your time in Botswana. Let the natural beauty of your surroundings and the variety of animals inspire you, and use your photography to attempt to capture that sensation of awe and connection. Not only are images taken, but stories about the extraordinary and magnificent world of Botswana are also told.

Photographing Wildlife: Some Advice

In order to capture those magnificent moments when photographing wildlife in Botswana, it is important to keep the following in mind:

1. Be Prepared: Botswana's animals may be unexpected, so have your camera set up and ready to go at all times. To prevent missing out on great photographs, keep extra batteries and memory cards close at hand.

2. Recognize that you are a visitor to the habitat of wildlife and respect it. Maintain a safe distance from animals and refrain from

interfering with their normal activities. To prevent generating tension, keep your distance and use long lenses while observing.

3. Research animal behavior: It's important to know how the wildlife you want to shoot behaves. Knowing this will enable you to foresee their behavior and be ready to capture special moments.

4. Golden Hour Magic: The ideal lighting for wildlife photography occurs during the "golden hour" in the early morning and late afternoon. Your photos will have a magical quality because of the gentle, warm light, which also brings out the colors and textures.

5. Use quick shutter speeds: Because wildlife is often in motion, it's crucial to use quick shutter speeds to capture their movements and prevent blur. Test out several speeds to find the ideal balance.

6. Time Pays Off: It takes time to capture wildlife in a shot. Spend some time monitoring

the animals and watching for the ideal opportunity to record their interactions or natural behavior.

7. Tell a Story: A compelling wildlife image conveys a narrative. Find compositions that are appealing by including the animal's surroundings, highlighting the habitat, and evoking a feeling of location.

8. Refrain from disturbing nocturnal animals: Some of Botswana's flora and fauna are active at night. Use a flashlight with a red filter if you wish to take pictures of these animals, so as not to startle them.

9. Consider employing camouflage or blinds: To approach wary animals, think about employing camouflage or erecting a temporary blind. This boosts your chances of taking amazing pictures and helps you blend in with the surroundings.

10. Engage in ethical photography: Steer clear of any behaviors that might endanger animals or their environment, such as baiting or invasive

behavior. Keep the environment natural so that future generations may enjoy it.

The beauty and variety of Botswana's natural wonders may be beautifully and meaningfully captured in wildlife photography by adhering to these suggestions and being aware of your activities' effects on species and ecosystems. Cheers to the gun!

Chapter 11

Sampling Botswana's regional cuisine

Trying the Local Delights

In Botswana, you're in for a treat when it comes to sampling regional cuisine! The wide variety of traditional foods available in Botswana is a reflection of the nation's rich natural resources and cultural legacy. Seswaa is a delicious stew prepared from diced beef or goat that is slow-cooked with onions and spices until it is soft and tasty. It is one of the must-try foods. Pap, a hearty maize porridge that goes well with the meal, is often served with it.

Morogo, a variety of spinach that is popular in Botswana, is another delectable meal you should try. It often has a great and distinctive flavor since it is cooked with onions, tomatoes, and even peanuts. The phane worm is a treat worth trying for individuals who like hot tastes. These protein-rich edible caterpillars are usually dried or fried to give them a crunchy texture and tangy taste.

Don't pass up eating magwinya, which are deep-fried dough balls with a crispy outside and a fluffy inside, if you have a sweet craving. They make a delicious breakfast alternative or snack when paired with a spoonful of jam or peanut butter.

You'll also come across a variety of meals in Botswana that are made using sorghum, millet, and other grains, highlighting the significance of agriculture in their cuisine. No culinary excursion in Botswana would be complete, of course, until you had some of the country's cool indigenous drinks, such as palm wine and ginger beer, which will add a cool touch to your culinary voyage.

In addition to satisfying your taste buds, discovering the regional specialties of Botswana lets you fully experience the lively culture and customs of the region. In this stunning African country, don't forget to have an open mind and enjoy the gastronomic pleasures that lie ahead. Enjoy your culinary trip!

Typical meat dishes

There is a delectable selection of traditional meat dishes to choose from in Botswana, which reflects the nation's enjoyment of flavorful and filling meals. Seswaa, as I already said, is one of the most well-known foods. It takes a lot of work to cook, shred, and pound the flesh, which is often beef or goat, until it is smooth and soft. The end product is a flavorful stew that is rich and meaty. It is often salted and eaten with pap or sorghum flour.

The always wonderful beef stew is another preferred meat meal. This stew is a representation of Botswana's passion for beef, a country that takes pride in its meat. A delicious and fragrant meal is made by simmering tender beef chunks with a mixture of spices, veggies, and sometimes sorghum.

The phane worm is a must-try for individuals who want a more daring gastronomic experience. These substantial caterpillars, which are high in protein, are prized in Botswana. Typically, they are boiled first, then cooked with onions, tomatoes, and spices to produce a flavorful and distinctive meal.

At numerous parties and festivals, you may often discover excellent grilled meats in Botswana due to the country's robust barbecue scene. The locals take great pleasure in their grilling prowess, so you can anticipate enjoying mouthwatering pieces of beef, goat, and even game meat that have been marinated and grilled to perfection over open flames.

In addition to these recipes, you may find a variety of different meat-based stews and curries that differ from area to region, each with its own unique tastes and ingredients, inspired by the nation's vast cultural background.

The traditional meat dishes of Botswana are not only a pleasure for the palate but also a window into their culinary culture and respect for fine ingredients. So, if you ever have the opportunity to eat these dishes, I would suggest doing so to embrace the flavors and appreciate the rich culinary legacy of this lovely African country.

Having meals at camps and lodges

The finest of nature, comfort, and delectable food come together at Botswana's camps and lodges for a memorable dining experience. A lot of camps and lodges in the nation provide an all-inclusive package that includes plush lodging as well as scrumptious meals and dining experiences that suit a range of tastes and preferences.

These camps often provide a big breakfast that includes hot items like eggs, bacon, sausages, and pancakes, along with fresh fruit, cereal, pastries, and hot cereal. The energy you need for a day of thrilling safari activities and discovery is provided by this filling meal.

Some camps provide packed lunches so you can remain energized and fully enjoy the wildlife and natural marvels of Botswana when you're out on game drives or other excursions throughout the day.

The traditional boma meal experience is one of the pleasures of eating in Botswana's camps and lodges. For a lavish buffet-style meal beneath the stars, guests congregate in a boma, an open enclosure that often has a fire pit in the middle. It's a wonderful chance to sample regional specialties, such as the traditional meat meals we previously discussed as well as other savory selections that highlight the finest of Botswana's culinary history.

Often with stunning views of the surrounding landscapes, the dining spaces at these camps and lodges are intended to provide a combination of rustic charm and comfort. It's not unusual to have your meals while looking out over a river or waterhole, giving you the opportunity to see wildlife in its natural setting.

To ensure that every visitor has a memorable and gratifying eating experience, camps and lodges in Botswana can accommodate dietary preferences and limitations.

In summary, eating at camps and lodges in Botswana is more than just about the cuisine; it's an entire culinary trip that lets you connect with the outdoors and taste the real tastes of this amazing nation. Consequently, if you're considering going on a safari or visiting Botswana, be ready to savor a pleasant mix of wildlife excursions and top-notch eating opportunities!

Chapter 12

Botswana's Festivals and Events

International Arts Festival in Maun

Here are some details on the Botswana-based Maun International Arts Festival:

A lively and culturally enlightening occasion, the Maun International Arts Festival takes place in Maun, Botswana. It honors the variety of artwork, music, and performances by both domestic and foreign artists. The event often takes place in Maun, a charming hamlet in northern Botswana next to the well-known Okavango Delta.

Visitors to the festival may immerse themselves in a wide variety of cultural expressions, including modern theater, poetry, and visual arts, as well as traditional music, dance, and storytelling. While encouraging cross-cultural connections and exchanges, the festival provides artists with a stage on which to display their skills and originality.

Locals, visitors, art aficionados, and performers from across the globe are among the festival's varied audience. It not only amuses but also significantly contributes to the preservation and promotion of Botswana's rich cultural legacy.

The Maun International Arts Festival often includes workshops, seminars, and conversations in addition to the artistic performances to promote learning and knowledge-sharing within the creative community. These events give budding artists the chance to learn from seasoned experts and encourage the development of their craft.

The Maun International Arts Festival is a must-attend occasion for everyone interested in discovering Botswana's thriving arts sector since it is, in general, a celebration of culture, creativity, and harmony.

Celebrations for Botswana Day

The Botswana Day Celebrations honor the Republic of Botswana's independence and are a meaningful and happy event. Every year on September 30, celebrations and events are organized around the nation to celebrate the occasion.

On Botswana Day, people gather to honor the history, culture, and accomplishments of their country. People from many backgrounds participate in the celebrations since it is a time of national pride and solidarity, regardless of their nationality or religious views.

The festivities often begin with a large ceremony that is attended by dignitaries, government representatives, and members of the general public. The national anthem is sung enthusiastically when the flag is raised. Speeches are given that discuss the nation's development and the future.

During the festivities, cultural performances take center stage, exhibiting customary music, dance, and storytelling that represent the rich legacy of Botswana's several tribes. The vivid and colorful exhibits provide a window into the nation's cultural tapestry.

Sports activities, exhibits of arts and crafts, and culinary fairs are also held in addition to cultural shows to occupy and amuse the visitors. These events give local talent, innovation, and gastronomy a chance to shine, highlighting a sense of pride and identity.

The Botswana Day Celebrations are not simply held in the capital; they also take place in a number of other areas of the nation, allowing citizens from all parts of Botswana to join in on the fun.

The occasion serves as a reminder of Botswana's struggle for independence, a chance to consider the nation's development through the years, and a chance to envision its further expansion and prosperity. It's a time for celebration, camaraderie, and thanksgiving for the accomplishments that have formed the country and its people.

Festival of Culture, Domboshaba

Botswana hosts the engaging and culturally significant Domboshaba Festival of Culture. It happens at the Domboshaba historical site, which is close to the community of Lentsweletau in the northeastern region of the nation.

The event pays honor to the nation's indigenous origins and customs and offers a special chance for residents and guests to appreciate the richness and splendor of Botswana's cultural legacy.

The festival grounds of Domboshaba come alive with a variety of cultural performances, visual arts exhibits, and customary rites. It's a time when several ethnic groups from Botswana and surrounding nations assemble to commemorate their common heritage and present their distinctive cultures and rituals.

The event features spellbinding storytelling, enchanting traditional dances, and beautiful music that capture the essence of the surrounding towns. Visitors are drawn into the center of Botswana's rich cultural tapestry by the performers' rhythmic motions and vibrant costumes.

The event also provides a forum for intercultural dialogue and education. To provide an enjoyable experience for everyone, workshops and interactive sessions are scheduled to teach participants about traditional crafts, musical instruments, and culinary methods.

The Domboshaba Festival of Culture serves as a vehicle for advancing cultural sustainability and preservation. It highlights the value of preserving historical customs and knowledge so that they may be transmitted to future generations.

The festival includes a lively marketplace where local craftsmen and merchants sell their wares, including crafts, artwork, and regional specialties, in addition to the cultural events. This helps the local economy while also enabling tourists to bring home distinctive mementos of their cultural adventure.

The Domboshaba Festival of Culture is an alluring celebration of the nation's identity and variety that brings people together to commemorate their ancestry, enjoy their customs, and take in the vibrant cultural diversity that genuinely distinguishes Botswana.

Chapter 13

Conservation and ethical travel

Supporting locally-focused tourism

In order to promote sustainable development and give local communities more clout, community-based tourism must be supported in Botswana. Visitors who practice responsible tourism may immediately improve the lives of the people who call Botswana home while also helping to preserve the nation's natural and cultural heritage.

It is crucial to promote community participation in planning and decision-making processes for the tourism industry. As a result, local viewpoints are taken into account, and activities are in line with the needs and goals of the communities. The ability of people to actively engage in the tourism sector also enables them to demonstrate their distinctive customs, crafts, and ways of life, improving the overall experience for tourists.

Building the community's ability to handle tourism-related activities successfully depends heavily on education and training programs. Giving them training in hospitality, environmental protection, and business helps them provide guests with genuine and memorable experiences while protecting the environment and being mindful of cultural sensitivities.

To develop a framework for community-based tourism that is inclusive and sustainable, cooperation between the public and commercial sectors and local communities is crucial. In order to achieve a win-win scenario for both visitors and communities, partnerships that support ethical revenue-sharing procedures, responsible tourism practices, and environmental preservation may develop a cordial connection among all stakeholders.

Beyond the recognizable wildlife experiences, promoting community-based tourism might help broaden Botswana's tourist offerings. Visitors may discover lesser-known cultural treasures, go on tours organized by the local community, and take part in neighborhood celebrations and activities. Both the towns, which get new sources of revenue, and the tourists, who have a deeper and more genuine experience, win from this diversity.

Continuous monitoring and assessment are crucial to the long-term viability of community-based tourism programs. To improve the socioeconomic effect on communities and preserve ecological balance, continuous input and evaluation are important.

In conclusion, encouraging community-based tourism in Botswana is a potent method to promote sustainable development, protect cultural assets, and give local groups more clout.

Travelers may positively impact the health of Botswana's people and environment while taking part in meaningful and unforgettable experiences by encouraging responsible tourism practices, developing collaborations, and offering opportunities for education and training.

Initiatives to protect wildlife

In order to safeguard the nation's abundant biodiversity and iconic species, wildlife conservation projects in Botswana are of the utmost significance. A healthy balance between human activity and the environment has been maintained through the implementation of several measures by the government and other organizations to protect animals and their habitats.

The creation of national parks and animal reserves, including Chobe National Park and the Okavango Delta, is one such initiative. Numerous animal species, including elephants, lions, leopards, rhinoceroses, and many different bird species, enjoy safe havens in these protected regions. To limit human influence and protect these areas' natural integrity, strict laws are implemented.

To stop the illicit hunting of endangered species and the trafficking of such animals, anti-poaching efforts and law enforcement have been stepped up. Rangers and law enforcement organizations put in a lot of effort to thwart poachers and save animals from being hunted for their priceless body parts or trophies.

Local communities' participation in wildlife preservation has been greatly aided by community-based conservation initiatives. Communities are enticed to actively engage in conservation initiatives by including them in eco-tourism endeavors and revenue-sharing plans. This strategy helps with the sustainable management of natural resources and instills a sense of ownership and accountability among the community.

Understanding animal behavior, migratory patterns, and population dynamics also requires extensive study and observation. Together, scientists and conservationists collect information and insights that help decision-makers create plans for the management and protection of wildlife.

Initiatives like community-driven crop security and predator deterrents have been created to alleviate conflicts between humans and animals. These projects attempt to lessen human-wildlife conflicts and promote cooperation by offering assistance and training to farmers and communities.

Wildlife is seriously threatened by climate change, and Botswana understands the need for environmental preservation. To lessen the effects of climate change on animal habitats and ecosystems, initiatives are being made to cut carbon emissions and encourage sustainable lifestyles.

Campaigns for public education and awareness are also essential for advancing animal conservation. The public is informed about the need to conserve wildlife and the negative effects of unlawful activity via educational institutions, the media, and outreach programs that promote ethical conduct and support for conservation efforts.

Finally, protected areas, anti-poaching measures, community involvement, research, climate action, and public awareness are all part of Botswana's wildlife conservation projects. This comprehensive approach to conservation is reflected in the country's wildlife management policies. These coordinated efforts show how dedicated the nation is to protecting its unique animals and maintaining its natural legacy for future generations.

Practices for Sustainable Safari

In order to protect Botswana's distinctive species and landscapes and to ensure the welfare of the surrounding people, sustainable safari techniques are crucial. Safari tourism may lessen its negative environmental effects and contribute to the biodiversity of the area's long-term preservation by using ethical and environmentally friendly practices.

The reduction of the ecological footprint is one of the fundamental tenets of sustainable safaris. The management of garbage, energy efficiency, and water consumption are strictly regulated by tour companies and hotels. To lessen their influence on the environment and support sustainable operations, they use eco-friendly technology like solar energy and energy-saving equipment.

Safari companies adhere to regulated access and guest limitations in vulnerable regions to avoid congestion and reduce disruption to animals. This contributes to the general health of the ecosystem by preserving the normal behaviors of animals and guaranteeing the preservation of their habitats.

Another important step is educating visitors about ethical safari techniques. Visitors are taught the proper way to interact with wildlife before going on a safari, including keeping a safe distance from animals and not feeding or petting them. This promotes a culture of care for the natural environment while ensuring the safety of both visitors and animals.

Sustainability also heavily emphasizes including local people in safari tourism. Community-based tourism programs enable locals to engage in the tourist sector and get a direct financial benefit from it. Communities are encouraged to participate actively in animal conservation activities as a result of this, which also improves their economic well-being.

Sustainable safaris must prioritize promoting moral wildlife watching. Operators place a high priority on watching animals in their natural environments and refrain from anything that might hurt or exploit wildlife. Safaris are managed with the highest consideration for the care of the animals, making sure that their needs come first above all other considerations.

Safari companies work with conservation groups to assist anti-poaching initiatives and conservation studies in an attempt to save threatened animals like rhinos and elephants. The safari business helps to safeguard these threatened species by actively taking part in wildlife conservation programs.

Sustainable safaris include the promotion of ethical travel via the Leave No Trace philosophy. Visitors are urged to leave the area in pristine condition with no signs of their presence, such as trash or harmed natural ecosystems.

In general, sustainable safari methods in Botswana seek to achieve a harmonic balance between travel and environmental protection. Botswana's safari sector can flourish while preserving its priceless wildlife and environment for future generations by implementing eco-friendly practices, including including local people, educating visitors, and emphasizing ethical wildlife watching.

Chapter 14

Language and Cultural Etiquette

Common Setswana greetings and phrases

Given that Setswana is the official language of Botswana, below are a few expressions and salutations that residents often use:

1. **Dumela** (doo-meh-lah)- Hello/Hi.
2. **Le kae? (leh kah-eh?)** - How are you?
3. **Ke teng (keh tehng)**- I am fine.
4. **Kea leboga (keh-ah leh-boh-gah)**- Thank you.
5. **Sala sentle (sah-lah sehn-tleh)**- Goodbye.
6. **O tsogile jang? (Oh, tsoh-ghee-leh jahng?)** - How was your day?

7. **O tlaa gola jang? (Oh, tlah goh-lah jahng?)**- What are your plans?
8. **Mma (mmah)**- used to address an older woman, similar to "ma'am."
9. **Rra (rrah)**- used to address an older man, similar to "sir."

You are welcome to greet and converse with the people of Botswana using these words and phrases!

Cultural customs and etiquette

To demonstrate respect for and awareness of the local traditions in Botswana, it is crucial to be knowledgeable about cultural etiquette and customs. You should have the following in mind in order to remember:

1. Greeting: The Batswana customarily shake hands with new acquaintances. Elders are traditionally greeted with a little bow or head nod as a symbol of respect.

2. Courtesy: Batswana cherish humility and courtesies. In social encounters, it is courteous to use words like "Dumela" (Hello) and "Ke a leboga" (Thank you).

3. Giving gifts: It's considerate to bring a sign of gratitude or a modest present when you pay someone a visit at their house. Using both hands to present the gift is a display of respect.

4. Timeliness: While most Batswana value timeliness, occasions and gatherings sometimes begin a little later than expected. For formal events, it is still preferable to be on time.

5. Conversation: Before starting a more serious conversation, make a courteous small chat. If your local host doesn't bring up a difficult subject, such as politics or religion, stay away from it.

6. Personal space: In general, Batswana appreciate their privacy, so keep your distance while talking to people.

7. Attire: It's polite to wear modest clothing in more formal situations or while attending traditional rituals. Don't dress provocatively, particularly in rural places.

8. Accepting food: It's polite to take food or drink when provided, even if you don't want it. This action is seen as a display of respect and hospitality.

9. When photographing individuals, particularly in rural locations or at cultural events, they always get their consent. Some people could object to being photographed.

10. Foot and hand gestures: In Batswana culture, it is considered rude to point your feet in someone's direction or to present or receive anything with your left hand. Always engage in these exchanges with your right hand.

It's important to keep in mind that respecting regional traditions and customs will enrich your cultural experience and make a good impression on the people you encounter in Botswana.

Printed in Great Britain
by Amazon

The Big Black Motorbike Ride

The Big Black Motorbike Ride

A Motorcycle, a Wife and a 3,000(ish) Mile Road Journey through Europe and Time

John H. Lewis

The Big Black Motorbike Ride
A Motorcycle, a Wife and a 3,000(ish) Mile Road Journey through Europe and Time
By John H. Lewis

FIRST EDITION

Leonaur is an imprint of Oakpast Ltd
Copyright in this form © 2024 Oakpast Ltd
John H. Lewis identifies himself as the author of this book for copyright purposes

ISBN: 978-1-916535-76-3 (hardcover)
ISBN: 978-1-916535-77-0 (softcover)

http://www.leonaur.com

Publisher's Notes

The views expressed in this book are not necessarily those of the publisher.

Contents

IMPORTANT:	9
INTRODUCTION: About How This Book Came Into Being	13
1. Ignition on: In which we virtually meet, greet, establish the 'rules' and leave	16
2. Neutral: In which we have a brief interlude as we tumble back through time and space	26
3. First Gear: In which a little reassessment is required, but we have a nice big surprise	32
4. Second Gear: In which 'Her Ladyship' makes her entrance onto to our stage	43
5. Still in Second Gear: In which we get ready to hit the road and very nearly do	54
6. Third Gear: In which we take ship, with some trepidation, for the Continent	65
7. First Gear again: In which having disembarked, we set off for Normandy	80
8. Second Gear: In which we ride to Mont Saint Michel and then ride away again	91
9. Third Gear: In which we reach Saumur, drink, eat, cough, sneeze and go to bed	101
10. Fourth Gear: In which we ride to between Rocamadour and another hard place	107
11. Still in Fourth Gear: In which we head south towards the Pyrenees, like pilgrims do	120
12. Several Low Gears: In which we ride over the top, stop, and ride down the other side	131
13. A Stall: In which it all goes horribly wrong, but we get there in the end	141
14. Mostly Neutral: In which we wine, dine and ride the hot plain	151
15. Fifth and Sixth Gear: In which we hang around where the hanging houses are	162

16. Third Gear again: In which we enter Andalucia and encounter several of its wonders — 171

17. Second Gear: In which we ride into a mountain range I didn't know was there — 182

18. Fifth & Sixth Gear: In which we come down from the mountain and reach the blue sea — 193

19. Ignition Temporarily off: In which we rest before turning to the west — 202

20. Fourth Gear: In which we ride north of the Sierra Nevada across Andalucia — 212

21. Still in Fourth Gear: In which we visit a wonder of the world and ride the road to Rome — 224

22. Fifth Gear: In which we ride over the hills and far away — 233

23. Neutral: In which we go back in time for walls and invisible balls — 241

24. Another Interlude: In which there are definitely things that go bump in the night — 250

25. First Gear: In which we visit a battlefield of the Peninsular War and its postman — 259

26. Definitely still First Gear: In which we are outsmarted by a 'burro' — 271

27. Fifth Gear: In which we ride to somewhere quiet in hopes of a nice dinner — 280

28. More Fifth Gear: In which, after a bumpy start, we follow the Camino route — 290

29. Third Gear: In which we see fantasy palaces and high peaks — 300

30. Several Low Gears: In which we have a most peculiar experience up a mountain — 308

31. Parked in Gear: In which we ride to the sea and board ship — 317

32. Headlights on: In which we disembark, shiver and head back to the North — 326

Epilogue: In which we say goodbye and farewell — 333

Dedication

This one is for ladies on motorcycles.
The pillion passengers and the riders
For those of them who enjoy biking
And for those who tolerate it for love
May they always come safe home, every one.
And for my own true love, of course, as always and forever

★★★★★★★★★★★★★★★★

A motorcyclist's sigh of contentment

A motorcycle journey
A sunset
A bottle of something special
A companion to share
A sunrise
Happiness!
Aaaaah!

J.H.L.

IMPORTANT:
About this book, with essential warnings to the wise and not so wise

I wrote this book as an entertainment. Just that. A light read for those who like reading, motorcycles, travel, interesting historical background (in moderation) and a little bit of whimsical marital romance. I may possibly chuck in some magical realism to spice it up—perhaps not—we will see how we go.

Please, do not be tempted to burden it (or me) with anything more weighty like 'inspiration'. The book is not intended to be an authoritative (or even a mediocre) guide to overseas motorcycling or indeed, any kind of 'travel guide' that it might be advisable to assiduously follow.

It is written from a British motorcyclist's perspective, describing 'two-up' riding experiences in Europe with a pillion wife, together with impressions on various other subjects as the impulse takes me. I have never ridden a motorcycle elsewhere, so nothing I have written has any bearing on motorcycling matters on other continents. Actually, that is not strictly true. I had a go on one in India many years ago, but everything on that bike was somewhere I wasn't expecting it to be, so I gave up on it after about 100 yards.

This tale doesn't contain an infallible route for the journey which it principally describes. Some roads and their conditions have probably changed in the years since our association with them. I haven't thoroughly checked them all recently to report one way or the other. Furthermore, I cannot precisely confirm what some of those roads were—most particularly some minor ones—because I didn't make a note of them in detail at the time.

So, in fairness to everyone, you will not be getting a map.

This book is absolutely NOT a recommendation or encouragement for anyone to follow our route (once someone has more or less worked it out, if they must) which, as you will discover as you read, on occasion transpired to be an ill-advised one, and sometimes possibly an out and out blunder on my part. When I describe somewhere as perilous in these pages—that means it seemed that way to me at the time, balanced against my evaluation of my own abilities on our motorcycle, which was possibly not always the most appropriate one for the places I took her, especially with a passenger and heavy luggage on board.

Those descriptions are not intended to be 'thrown down gauntlets' to encourage anyone to ride those roads themselves or pit themselves against them, so they can say they were not that bad after all. If anyone is inclined to go ahead in that frame of mind, this discouragement notwithstanding, on their own head be it. The writer accepts no responsibility. Once you are out there in the 'wide blue yonder'—you are your own. I know, because I've been.

My opinions on any subject are my own and not intended to influence anyone, except to always ride safely, considerately and legally. Anyone who is contemplating riding a motorbike or improving their motorbike riding should seek training from those who are qualified to provide it and those qualified to adjudicate whether they have learned enough.

It is also only fair that I admit, for those who get excited about engine fins and such like, that this isn't a book full of insights into the mechanical workings of motorcycles—a subject about which I remain for the most part, blissfully (or woefully—it depends how well or otherwise the one I am sitting on is behaving) ignorant.

Our motorcycle for this ride was made, in my opinion, with the precision of a fine time-piece by a company with an enviable reputation for quality and reliability and it could go like Billy-O (given the encouragement) to the degree that—for a time, with the right rider—it was acknowledged as a production bike, to be unbeatable at top speed.

I wasn't that variety of right rider, incidentally and didn't particularly want to be. I just do the best I can on two-wheels—whatever that is on the great scale. The chances are I will not transpire to be the motorcyclist some readers might prefer me to be, because I am not, unfortunately, the motorcyclist I would prefer me to be.

Nevertheless, I thank the higher powers, IIIIII REDACTE-DIIIII and every wonderful talented designer and engineer that was involved in creating my IIIII REDACTEDIIIII from concept to manufacture because, as you will discover, I am fairly sure, that on one occasion at least, it significantly contributed to saving our lives, when I didn't feel—on sober and honest reflection—I could entirely take all the credit myself.

★★★★★★★★★★★★★★★★

I offer my sincerest apologies that this book has come to a screeching halt—an emergency stop if you will—so early in its proceedings. The reason for this previously unforeseen circumstance is this: The version of my tale you are now reading does not represent my first attempt at crafting this book. In fact, I had completed the entire thing and was preparing to publish when I became aware of the stringent rules that surround trademarks and their like. In short, one should not, as I understand it, ideally employ them in one's text without prior permission from their legal owners. It has been suggested to me that the rules on this matter may not be so 'cut and dried', but I am persuaded—given subjectivity might become involved—to ere on the side of caution.

Need it be said, this book contained any number of references to brands and models because it consistently (if not entirely) concerns comparatively modern motorcycles. They, in fact, provide the thread that holds this story together, so this development was to say the least, problematic, especially since I genuinely believed I had—so to speak—'finally put the baby to bed'.

I could, of course, have then gone about requesting the required permissions, but after some deliberation, decided not to do so, since that seemed to me likely to be a long process with uncertain outcomes required from several organisations before I would be able to conclude the project, notwithstanding that this book, within its pages, has nothing unkind to say about any company or its products or services.

So, somewhat disconsolately, back to my keyboard I went to institute necessary changes. We shall proceed henceforth, therefore, without (hopefully) infringing upon anyone's rightful commercial domains and trust that development will not transpire to be a spoiler for the reader. Don't worry, you will not find the word, 'Redacted' littering every page.

I shall do my best to be careful regarding this matter and apologise in advance if I have not been careful enough. However, if I innocently describe a creature that has a bill, webbed feet and spends most its time in a stream, I hope I am not held to account if someone (well informed on the habits of various waterway dwellers) draws the conclusion that I must inevitably be talking about a platypus.

★★★★★★★★★★★★★★★★

That motorcycle never let us down—not once. No one has paid me to say that by the way, (given, let's face it, anyone in the know will shortly deduce model and manufacturer both), that's just the way I feel about it.

John H. Lewis, 2024

INTRODUCTION:
About How This Book Came Into Being

This book came about by accident. I know—how often have we heard that one? In this case, though, it is more or less true. Actually, as I think about it, 'accident' is not such a good word in a motorcycling journey book. Let's go with 'by happen stance'.

What happened was this. I always intended to keep a personal photographic record of the journey this book describes and so I made photographs as we travelled along. The original aim was to put these colour photographs in one of those online albums that are so easy to create these days and to support the images with a short narrative: A bit more than a caption per picture, but much less than a full book of text. So, I took a notebook with me on the journey to jot down the most interesting occurrences at the close of each day and when we returned home again I typed up my notes and printed them out onto A4 sheets of paper.

Well, I started work on that book quite soon after we returned home, intending to have a small quantity of the finished book printed to distribute to our family as a keepsake that Christmas time. I wrote the copy directly into the online program from the notes as I went along, which probably wasn't the smartest thing to do. I suppose I was about 40% through the work (which also included processing the images) when—Horrors!—I turned on the computer one morning and it had disappeared. Don't ask me how. Try as I might I couldn't get it back again. Someone competent probably could have retrieved it easily, but not me, because even now I'm a digital dinosaur—then I was a digital garden gnome.

I had put a fair amount of time into the project so I was, you will understand, quite cross and downcast at this point. I brought to mind that classic story of the medieval Scottish king, Robert the Bruce who, having suffered half a dozen battlefield defeats at the hands of the English, was sitting gloomily in a damp cave, burning cakes, for some reason. There he noticed a spider attempting to build its web and though it failed, time after time, it persevered until it finally succeeded. Inspired, the motivated Robert rose once more to his challenges. Shortly thereafter he defeated the English and never ate a burnt cake again. Well, he was a king, so could be picky with his food.*

Anyway, putting the finer details aside, it's a wonderful uplifting story and a life lesson for us all. Unfortunately, I don't like spiders much, so I thumped my irritating metaphorical one with a metaphorical rolled-up newspaper and in a petulant temper, rammed the notes into a folder and slung them into the back of a desk drawer where they could fester, gathering dust forever and good riddance. And the moral of this story (though not necessarily one anybody should follow, in keeping with much of the contents of this book) is 'if at first you don't succeed—do something else you might actually be good at, for life is short'. If you don't believe me, just ask Jorge Manrique, who you will meet later in these pages.

The years zipped by. I was poking around in a desk drawer, when I found the folder of notes. The quite amazing surprise was that as I read them many details flooded back into my mind, as a consequence of these prompts, that I am certain I would not have otherwise recalled. I had recently finished writing and publishing a history book (which very few people, apparently, were inclined to read, irrespective of how impressed with it I was myself) and was feeling a bit in withdrawal, so I thought to myself—forget the photo-book idea—write the notes up as a yarn.

Is everything recounted in these pages the unvarnished truth? Well, no its not, varnish has been applied, but the narrative is framed more or less as I was able to perceive and remember events and places. All those can change in fact and memory with the passage of time, of course. However, readers may be wondering whether I would lace my prose with advantages and fictions simply for something so cheap as enhanced thrill or comedic effect. That is a perfectly outrageous suggestion. So, naturally, of course I would, and now you know. It's a tale written for entertainment remember, not a statement made under caution. Do not, therefore, be in a rush to take what I have written entirely literally: A modicum of common sense will keep you on the right track, if just accepting it for what it is will not suffice.

I will confirm one aspect for the curious. Anything I attribute to my wife—in spirit, sentiment, deed or speech is, so far as I am able to remember and capable to judge, accurate. Please do not imagine her character in these pages is in any way an alter-ego of mine. I appreciate, of course, having told you this, that if you had not even considered such a possibility, my qualification might seem a trifle disarming. Could he do that? Yes, he could, but I haven't—honest.

Is the manner in which I have characterised myself accurate? Well, really, that is entirely a different matter. Could anyone genuinely be that hopeless? I found the digital work for my original idea incidentally—it was there all the time. By the point of discovery, however, this book had been all but completed. Still, a significant admission on my part, I have to confess.

So that's it, I think, and here it is. I shall be content if, having read it, you say to yourself,

'Well, someone had to write the definitive motorcycle journey book. It wasn't this bloke obviously, but it was alright and it passed some time'.

JOHN H LEWIS, 2023

*If you have a mind to contact me about the authenticity of this story, please feel free not to do so—I do know my 'Alfs' from my 'Bobs'!

1. Ignition on:
In which we virtually meet, greet, establish the 'rules' and leave

So you've turned up for the ride have you?

It's a rhetorical question, I know. You are, after all, holding the 'ticket' in your hand which means you paid for the trip or it's been given to you as a gift, which amounts to the same thing so far as I am concerned. So, we should get down to business. As Patsie would doubtless say, 'If we are going sightseeing and doing a bit of shopping, I'll do that and you can buy me lunch somewhere nice, but if we are going to ride, then I want to ride and I don't want to get off again until I really have to—so let's get on with it'.

What a girl! You will be hearing more from Patsie—as she will mostly henceforth be known—in due course. Wife, ally, partner, friend, confidante and pillion rider, she is central (and indeed, essential) to this ride. You will probably like her—most people do, I find. Me, to be honest, despite my best efforts to be amenable, they usually don't like so much. I don't know why that is, because I am absolutely delightful, really.

Where were we? That's it, 'getting on with it'.

The reassuring news is I am not going to drag you through the first thirty pages of this odyssey with tales of when I was a lad. I know that's not what you signed on for.

We will be travelling for some time and many miles together on a 1137 cc motorcycle of a type frequently referred to as a 'sports-tourer'. She has the appearance of a very fast, substantial machine to have between your legs as I trust, before the fact, you will agree (She does and is, in my informed opinion anyway, even if you don't agree and that should count for something, because she's mine). That could be a small motorcar engine, right there—but with no car wrapped around it, (162 bhp/125 nm torque at some revs or other). So, I know what her capabilities are and much more to the point, as far as you are concerned, the limits of my own abilities when I'm the one mounted upon her.

That bike—magnificent lady that she is—is more of a motorcycle than I am a motorcyclist. I know that to my bones and never forget it. Laugh if you like, but it's a silent mantra I say to myself every time I put my leg over any motorcycle together with, 'When you are riding the bike, don't think about anything but riding the bike'. That rarely works as well as it should, to be honest, distractions coming my way inevitably, but I say it anyway. In fact, I suppose you could say that consideration has applied to practically every motorcycle I have ever ridden. Yes, including that old German moped—top speed 30 mph with a following wind, because before that one I was peddling, wearing bicycle-clips round my trouser-leg bottoms.

Possibly, with substantiated reasons I hope, you don't feel the same way about motorcycles. That admission on my part is, nevertheless, one of the reasons I, having assumed the status of veteran, am able to speak to you instead (so far) of quietly languishing in a small urn, gathering dust on the mantle. Anyway, the bottom line is I tried to give 'Madam'—an indisputable 'Empress of Motorcycles'—all the respect she was due. I loved her, but her kind and their works have the potential to be problematic for the inattentive. That is not in any way their fault, of course. One must properly deal with everything in a way commensurate to its nature. To be clear, I am referring to motorcycles generally—not the wife—on this occasion. I don't claim to have much of a handle on how to effectively negotiate with that lady, as you will shortly discover.

So how shall we get through this first bit? Setting the scene so to speak. Establishing the rules: Because there are going to be rules. Like it or not, I am at the pointy end on this venture in every way. This is my narrative, those are my hands on the grips, my foot on the gear lever pedal and hovering—possibly pointlessly most of the time on this bike—near the rear brake. My eyes will be checking the mirrors and my head will be turning around all the time like a fighter pilot heading into a dogfight— left and right—never mind who is supposed to have right of way, who is supposed to overtake on whichever side or indeed who might decide to do absolutely anything, whether it makes any sense to me or not, that might end us. Now you have it. I am looking out for you, because I am definitely looking out for me.

The first piece of good news is that I am no stranger to riding with a pillion behind me and if this was my first 'two-up' outing it definitely would not be on a journey of this magnitude nor anything remotely like it. You see this trip bears no relationship to riding solo. It is not going to be a Sunday afternoon scratch round the green lanes and back home for tea and crumpets. It's not going to be a track-day, knee and (possibly) elbow down, where you can pretend there's a podium place beckoning and nothing coming along in the opposite direction. This will be the long haul: Day after day. We will be riding on roads we don't know. Those roads won't be hundreds of miles of dead straight, but within countries not our own, over terrain that is not always going to be as flat as a dining table.

You might well be a better rider than I am, but let's face it—you are a passenger this time. It will be just me, you and the bike on our own. There's no support vehicle with mechanics, a comprehensive tool kit, spare wheels and a medic on board. We are going to be, more or less, welded together— riders and motorbike in one homogeneous lump. Whatever happens to one of us, happens to all of us, though you have a part to play and I'm going to tell you what it's going to be.

This is a big powerful bike to be sure, but likewise carrying a big load. There's the two of us on board (one of us, at least, no light-weight) with big panniers on the sides and a large top-box at the back; all of them full of our stuff and heavy. I will also have a magnetic tank bag in front of me, between my arms, filled with the things I am going to need as we go along, together with the 'bits and bobs' my paranoia (or understandable caution—it's all a matter of perspective) won't allow to be out of my sight or far from my hand wherever we are.

'If you don't want to lose it—don't leave it lying around'. Just one of several tedious maxims about being at large in the world you will probably be hearing from me before we are done. A mighty relief that will be to you too, I expect, when the time comes.

Where was I? Oh yes, 'getting on with it'. The Rules.

How about this? Imagine, if you will, that you have stepped through the open door of my well-appointed workshop and there I am, spannering away, surrounded by a modest, but impeccable and well maintained (by me, obviously) collection of motorcycles. Look now. One of them is up on the bench (you can choose what it is to coincide with your own tastes) having been in need of a bit of fettling. It was a carburettor issue—probably. It might have been something more complicated, but regardless of what it was, a mere trifle for a man of my mechanical engineering capabilities.

(Stop that sniggering, you lot in the cheap seats).

I ask, casually flinging aside a slightly oily rag, 'Are you ready to go?'

Now you might mumble something I am not very interested to hear along the lines of, 'I don't like being a *blanky* pillion, me. I like to be in control'. I know exactly what you mean. I don't like riding pillion myself, but it's the only way you are going anywhere with me. Mind you, given your own preferences on the matter, please bear that in mind the next time you have someone sitting behind you.

I well recall being overtaken—at who knows what speed—by some jockey on a sports bike who was apparently playing at being whoever had won a TT somewhere that year. There, glued to his back, perched on one of those elevated, tiny seats, possibly designed I imagine for transporting a pet gerbil in his little cage, was a diminutive, leathered pillion. So, the girlfriend, I assume, since long tresses were streaming from the rear of her helmet. She was gamely hanging on for dear life, knees up to her elbows;

'Anything for her man', and all that love-blind folly.

Now I knew that road intimately, so I also knew these two were precipitately heading for a sharp dip, followed by a tight, steeply rising Z-bend and I thought to myself, 'Oh dear, this has the potential to end quite unfortunately'. And sure enough, not so long afterwards, when I arrived on the scene, there was their bike, inelegantly spread down the tarmac. It might have been asphalt. What do I know? The road, anyway.

I didn't stop to offer assistance for two reasons. Firstly, because —thank goodness—both rider and passenger were on the green verge and more or less on their feet. So, they had a slide, no one else was about and nothing heavy ran over them. Not such a bad outcome then, in my view, by motorcycling 'off' standards. I say 'more or less on their feet', because the pillion rider was screaming abuses at her *beau*, whilst vigorously 'paddling the tar out of him', so he wasn't quite on his feet per normal. They were both still wearing crash helmets, so not much damage would be done, I expect.

She was displaying, furthermore I thought, a really impressive enthusiasm and stamina for the task, given her *petite* proportions. Quite transparently unhappy, she was past the point of perpetuating the delusion, on his part, that she had ever enjoyed her lot. I could tell, because I am sensitive that way. His status as an imaginary championship contender and his stock as a caring, sharing partner, by contrast, had taken some knocks—including some of them, quite literally.

And all the aforementioned was the second reason I didn't stop. I wasn't riding a motorcycle myself at the time, but was driving my motorcar. That section of road was not ideally the place to be pulling over and if I climbed out 'booted and suited' (I had been to a meeting), I probably could not expect much empathy, given emotions were running high, from them. So there was a fair chance any intercession on my part (no matter how well intentioned) might not—just then—have been so welcome with potentially unfortunate consequences for me. So, I left them to it; discretion being the better part of valour, as they say, marginally misquoting the Bard.

Several valuable lessons therein, I hope you will agree, especially since these affairs don't always conclude so satisfactorily. Not condoning violence, myself, of course. The girlfriend, despite extenuating circumstances, should have simply, very calmly and quietly explained how terribly disappointed she was that he might have killed her and left it at that. The moral of the tale, in my judgement—if you need one and some do—is 'Passengers are always responsibility—never inconvenient incidental luggage.'

So, coming back to our imminent departure. I smile reassuringly, because I can see—given my recently divulged views on the matter—you are feeling much more confident in me and so I say, 'First—Getting on and off the motorcycle'.

Now you may well be tempted to straight away protest that you '*blankety* know fine-well how to get on a bike and off one too', but don't say that, because you don't. Not on this particular bike, juiced up to the filler-cap, fully laden, with me on it into the bargain. You don't get on this bike or off it until you see me nod my head positively—that's *positively*—up and down which means 'I am ready'. None of that 'you twitched a bit, so I thought' nonsense. Oh yes, I've had that together with all its perils.

Why this performance? I will share, since you are asking. Everything we do henceforth is a partnership. As you get yourself sorted back there, I am holding the whole shebang steady-feet, side-stand, brake on and body-braced and if—perish the thought—she goes over we can be in several kinds of trouble and none of them any we need.

When she starts to tip from standing there will be an irresistible attempt on my part to right her by heaving the bars in the opposite direction. I can tell you, laden or not, once that bike passes her centre of gravity, she is going over all the way. I'm not strong enough to stop her. Before I let her go indescribable parts of me will be painfully popping. If I am astride her when she hits the ground, she will—need it be said—be on top of me. You, caught up in the shambles, might be on your face.

For all we know this could happen when we are far from

home in the *campo*, it's Sunday, it's raining 'stair-rods' and everyone (if there actually was anyone to help us) only speaks Basque. So, then we need to think about the motorcycle, because she is part of this team and we need her every day and all the time. She can easily break anything protruding: A mirror, a light, an indicator, snap or bend a clutch or brake lever, burst open a pannier and all the other inconveniences of a minor 'off'. Those things can not only blight our day, they will impact our ability to carry on legally, delay us and so destroy the schedule of the whole trip.

Well, it was like this, officer. Ah, no English, is it? Ydych ch'in siarad Cymraeg? No, me neither, to my eternal regret and shame. I have no excuses. Still, what were the chances? Ha, Ha.

Before you tell me I worry too much or I am over thinking all this, I may as well tell you I have seen those things happen to others and most of them have happened to me. So, I trust that settles that hypothesis. We are embarking upon a modest adventure. Events will occur we didn't plan for and that's good, because it would not be an adventure if they didn't, but we don't need to ask for trouble by being careless. That goes as much for when we are stationary as it does when we are moving. So, remember—a positive nod from me—on and off.

If you are experienced at riding on motorcycles, then you do not need to be told to keep your arms inside the line of the bike, because vehicles will sometimes shave us closely and sometimes, (the little tinkers), it seems deliberately. When I put my foot down at traffic lights and junctions—you keep yours on your pegs. Take a quick stretch if you must, but feet back on the pegs fairly promptly. When I lean as we take bends—you follow the line of my body. No more—no less, but definitely no more. Do not under any circumstance lean the other way to keep yourself upright, because that can end messily for both of us.

Don't worry, I will not be breaking any sound barriers. It's supposed to be a journey we should both enjoy, not a race. Try not to lean out too much to look forward over my shoulder or fidget and if you catch a cramp, must have the toilet, need to stretch your legs or just fancy a cup of coffee, then let me know and I will—I promise—pull over for you as soon as possible.

I am wearing a pillion belt which has two handles on it. Normally, I wear it back-to-front, because it's what Patsie prefers since, given her smaller size, so shorter reach, the revised handle position means she is not bending too far forward for her comfort. I think—but more importantly she thinks—these belts are a good idea, but also use the handles on the panniers or bike rail behind you to suit yourself. There's a back support pad on your side of the top/back-box.

Most of the time we are going to roll along steadily, but if for whatever reason I think I have to open her up—and you need to trust me on this—I will let you know with the verbal alert, 'Going' (If we have lost 'comms'—which has happened—I give Patsie an unambiguous quick knee-tap). Then we are going to accelerate quickly and I will keep that up until we are out of potential trouble and can come back to a usual cruising speed as the road, traffic and weather dictates.

A good example of this kind of occurrence is on the continent where exit lanes on some motorways (autoroutes) are from the fast lane, not the slow one as they invariably are in the UK. In those cases (mercifully few in my opinion) we have to be at a speed comparable to other exiting traffic and not dither in making the manoeuvre. I will also use this signal for overtaking, because we do not want to spend too much time on the 'wrong side' of the road or on motorways (especially on the continent) where overtaking traffic can appear behind us from practically nowhere at terrific speeds in outside lanes. So, remember—come the word—to brace yourself to avoid lurching (which can bang your helmet into the back of mine) and hold on tightly with everything you have that grips, because we are going to be shifting!

If you see anything—I mean *anything*—you think I should know about that bears on our safety—please, tell me without hesitation. There is no bad call and it doesn't matter if I have already seen whatever it is. I will reply, 'Thank you' or 'I have seen it'. Four invested eyes are better than two. 'Eyes like gimlets' as Patsie would doubtless say; honestly you have no idea! It's not the gin cocktail, obviously, but the needle-sharp woodworking tool, so makes some kind of abstract sense. My more prosaic perspective is any precaution or procedure that would be essential to sailing a yacht or flying a light aircraft, from the perspectives of their crews, has to be useful on a motorcycle. The reason for that is simple enough. They can't afford to make mistakes and neither can we.

★★★★★★★★★★★★★★★★★

As an aside, I must disclose my wife will alert the presence of a chaffinch that is sitting in the road when we are 75 yards away from it, but which has no intention of abstaining from flight when we are 10 yards distant. I do not fault her for that. Firstly, on the grounds that this is just one more indication that her heart is in the right place and secondly, because it demonstrates an adherence to a principle which would be equally applied had the obstacle been a velociraptor. Should the occasion arise, I would prefer you accept my word regarding the chaffinch. It *will* fly away. If you spot a velociraptor, feel free to alert me at the earliest opportunity by whatever method seems good to you. Refrain from waving your arms about if you can though, since this will not only draw the attention of the creature, but also destabilise the bike.

★★★★★★★★★★★★★★★★★

As for the motorcycle—she needs as much daily consideration as a saddle-horse, because in her way that is what she is; a very lively mechanical palfrey.

Will this experience test our patience, our ability to work together and even question whether we actually like each other very much? Oh yes, definitely, but if we are worth it—we will work it out. If you want to be more casual than any or all of this when you are on your own motorbike—well, that's up to you and yours. I can't say I am a fan of assumptions on two motorised wheels myself, but good luck with it!

Right. Are we fit to go? We are. That's *the* nod from me. You can get on her now. I'll fire her up, though she purrs rather than roars, don't you *cariad*. So are we sitting comfortably? We are. Then I'll begin. Oh yes, there is something I haven't mentioned.

The first journey we have to make is to the past, because 'The Big Black Motorbike Ride' didn't happen last week and even if it did, practically everything is history beyond the fleeting moment, isn't it? So, it all depends on when 'this' is. How long ago? You will be able to work it out if you are inclined, but it doesn't seem that long ago to me, though someone wearing short trousers at the time could be married with an infant as I write this. Anyway, that is why everything before us is going wobbly and why that smoke is spiralling around a circle in the air. That's the way we are going—right down the old rabbit-hole.

Mind the GAP! All aboard for the Skylark ! And we're off!

2. Neutral:
In which we have a brief interlude as we tumble back through time and space

I know I recently promised—actually it would be at some point in the future if we need to be strictly accurate about it—that there would be no long-ago recollections from me. However, since here we are in this space and time wormhole with not much to occupy our attention, but a tedious all-embracing vortex of melding colours, I may as well clarify my relationship with that previously (or to be much later on) mentioned old moped. I appreciate, of course, that in so doing, a harsh critic may conclude my word is worth next to nothing.

Anyway, I plead my case for the legitimacy of this modest recollection since it is at least—if a bit of a stretch—more or less 'on subject'. Furthermore, I hope you will find this interlude informative, because if you judge Patsie and I solely on the snapshot of our lives that the larger account will reveal, you might find you are judgemental about us in some ways that are quite wide of the mark.

The moped was actually my late father's ride. Dear old Dad; he was a swarthy, flint-eyed, little North Welshman, (Lord knows where I came from. It must have been a foggy night.) with a hair-trigger temper and a penchant for domestic violence. I was not infrequently on the sharp end of that proclivity as a boy and once he got into his stride, he displayed every evidence of being unable to rein himself in which, alas, indelibly taints my fonder memories of him. Someone said—I cannot remember who—that when his father came in through the front door, 'joy' departed by the door at the back. Our house could be like that.

That having been said, Dad knew his duty as the man of the household and that is why, for several years, he held down two jobs. One was as a wages clerk for a brick-making company during the daytime and thereafter at the city telephone exchange (this is dating me, isn't it?) where he worked as a switchboard operator in the evenings. Little wonder then, if you think about it, that he had a short fuse. The man hardly slept and he had a duodenal ulcer, which some family members (not me) gleefully attributed to divine judgement and retribution.

Only now do I consider how he got himself to his work before the moped came along. It had to be on that big framed (to me anyway, at the time) old bicycle that was kept in the shed, because there was nothing else by way of transport in the family and no other options open to him, bar the time-table impracticalities of local buses. That brick company clocking-in machine must have been at least five to six miles away from our home, so with all his comings and goings, in all weathers, he did his share of peddling on our behalves (Mum, my sister and I) before he ever began earning the crust that fed us all.

Then he purchased the moped and, to be fair to him, he did give thought to me (if perhaps incidentally) and how he could spend some quality time with his only son and heir. The little bike had just a single seat (which is why I know I was an after-thought) and behind it there was a kind of super-structure which featured a narrow metal shelf over the rear wheel, that may have been intended for carrying a lunchbox or something of that sort. I have recently examined some photographs of the various models of this machine which were manufactured over the years and, perhaps predictably, none of them exactly square with my memory of it, though the model that bore a suffix that possibly implied 'luxury' looks the closest, excepting his one definitely didn't have leg-shields. However, they were optional, so that is possible.

If I was going to be travelling anywhere at all on that moped it had to be sitting on that parcel shelf. So, what Dad did was find some old carpet underlay which he cut into a rectangle to the dimensions of the shelf. This was not—need it be said—the dimensions of any known motorcycle seat. It was the possible, driven by what was available and affordable. In fact, he cut five or six like-sized underlay pieces which he sandwiched to create a deeper pad, thereafter sewing them together using a leather working needle and red twine. The issue then was how to keep the pad on the seat. There were metal fastenings for securing a parcel on the super-structure, so he attached a couple of thick, elasticated bungee cords with hooks on their ends to them. These cords ran right through the centre and over the underlay pad. And that, believe it or not, was my perch. Where I put my feet, bearing in mind there was originally no provision for them on the moped, I cannot now remember.

To be clear, these moped excursions we took together were comparatively local. Just as well too, because I could not sit for long on that pad before the bungee cords made their presence felt right on and up my personal lower centre line. So, there were frequent stops as I begged to be let off for some respite. I do not recall that we were ever pulled over by police, but these were different times, because in our council-owned avenue only two families had motorcars and no one—for that reason—had a driveway, much less a garage in which the vehicle we didn't own could be securely sheltered at night from the predations of thieves who probably couldn't drive.

Dad enjoyed coarse fishing as a hobby and for that pursuit there was our local river bank (three and more miles of discomfort on my part) or at flooded clay-pits, which involved slightly less suffering for me, because they were nearer. He made himself a stout wooden fishing-box complete with a seat, bait storage and drawers for reels, bait, floats, line, shot and the like. It was a sizeable, robust piece of kit. To make it portable (in name only) he fashioned a wide webbing shoulder strap. So, it weighed 'heavy' to me. When we were on the moped it was my responsibility and it bore down on my shoulder and the strap cut into my neck. The fishing rods were strapped lengthways down the moped, so I suppose, but can't remember, they must have been behind our legs. But we went fishing, all these obstacles overcome and once he caught a 2lb bream that made his year—little pleasures being big pleasures, if they are the ones you have.

One day Dad decided he needed peat for some gardening project. Needless to say, no one was sensitive about digging up peat to dig into their gardens in those days, because in our version of reality, in keeping with most natural resources, peat was infinite and made no difference to anything if it was removed or used for something else. He said he knew where there was some peat available free, because it was in common land, somewhere nearby, but he told me he couldn't manage the job alone, so I was to go with him. He would dig up the peat, putting it in a sack which I would hold for the return trip. Off we puttered on the moped. I cannot remember how he carried the spade, I just know I didn't have it.

So eventually—it wasn't *that* nearby, as my rear-end could testify—we arrived at a sparsely wooded area and he began digging. He was a bit furtive about it too, now I think about it—you know—given this peat was free and all that. Anyway, he filled his sack with peat and then we had to resolve the problem of positioning a boy, a sack of wet peat, a man and his spade upon our moped in preparation for the return journey, without the boy and peat promptly (or even at some future point) falling off the back. We failed utterly in that endeavour and we came home empty handed. Mightily grumpy Dad was too at being foiled in his horticultural machinations.

I know you may be considering, 'What was this dreadful man thinking?' and so forth. Well, I don't blame him for any of it. We were a working-class family living in austere times. We didn't have much income irrespective of how hard he and Mum worked. He did his best, including in the early days, cobbling our shoes on an old last. Once, when my feet grew and the shoes fitted too tightly he cut slits in their sides like fish-gills. Patsie was a country girl, incidentally, and she and her folks—inconceivable as it may seem these days—didn't have electricity or mains water for a time and were simply happy.

So, of course, we made the best use of the family wheels and if you think that was remarkable then you have never been to points East and the sub-continent in particular. There are men—very many of them too, I wager—who would consider our peaty problems to be so insignificant as to be unworthy of mention. I know this because we have been to India several times and have seen, on more than one occasion, a man progressing effortlessly on a small motorcycle, carrying his wife, serenely seated side-saddle, wearing a spotless *sari*, their three children of various sizes and ages and—I kid you not (no pun intended)—a goat.

So on that basis, there must be a way (disregarding—as we certainly must not—legal and safety considerations—so don't try this, folks!) to carry a man, a spade, a boy and a sack of peat on a moped. It was simply that we lacked the ingenuity or the genuine imperative of necessity to discover what that was.

The day eventually came, of course, when Dad decided we could afford our own motorcar. It was a smart saloon for its day, two-tone with subtle fins at the back-end suggestive of 'sporti-ness'. It wasn't very sporty actually, but Dad wore his brown suede and pale crochet, knuckle-less driving gloves when he was sitting behind it's steering wheel and was as happy as he could ever manage to be.

That meant that his moped was surplus to his requirements. The time had long past when I could have ridden on the back of it, even if I been inclined to do so. So I was given the moped as a 'hand-me-down' and I practised riding it around a nearby field. It was my first motor powered bike and initially thrilling. It wasn't very stylish, but it was an indisputable advance over peddle-powered propulsion.

My disappointments came when I was riding in the company of my peers, because every one of them by then was riding something with a motor in it that sent them along faster than I could go. For a while, on outings, they would hang back for me in a comradely way, but these were teenagers with throttles in their fists. So they abandoned me eventually, flying away ahead, leaving me to putter along on my own, bouncing up and down on the seat in frustration, willing my reluctant steed to greater exertions with imprecations and prayers.

This moped had a model name that was suggestive—not of

blistering speed it's fair to say—but of a certain sprightliness. That may well have been true too, from several perspectives, but was like most things, entirely relative. I am sure I must have rocketed past herds of stampeding field-mice as though they were quietly grazing, but that was meagre consolation to me. Apparently, the moped had a 49cc engine and a declared top speed of 25 mph, so my previous claims of a staggering 30 mph were, it seems, just rose-tinted hindsight.

Naturally, this state of affairs could not abide and I soon had my eye on what I thought, at the time, were more glamorous personal wheels, rightly befitting a young devil who imagined he urgently had places to go and special people to meet when he arrived there. So I sold the moped to a former school classmate for twenty pounds sterling and thought I had done rather well on the deal.

Apparently, during the Second World War, the company responsible for my moped manufactured a wonderful contraption for the German Army which combined a motorcycle front end with a tracked rear unit. Now, had my ride been one of those I would have certainly kept it, which would have been a sound idea, because they feature comfortable seating for two, are able to transport full sacks in quantity containing practically anything without soiling or burdening children and, these days, are worth a small fortune.

I'll never forget the old moped we had of course, because, in the imagination, I can still feel her between my legs—you know, down and up there. Great Scott! Enough gibber-jabber! We appear to be approaching our destination.

Steady as she goes. Flaps down—we don't want a prang, wizard or otherwise! Chuck out the anchor, there's a good fellow. How quickly time passes when one is reminiscing. Happy Days—sometimes. I loved Dad, in spite of everything, of course I did. Don't doubt it. He was my Father.

3. First Gear:
In which a little reassessment is required, but we have a nice big surprise

Here we are! *Nous sommes arrivés* as the French would say, though with a hyphen buzzing around somewhere like a blowfly, I shouldn't wonder. Hold on, when I say 'we'—where have you gone? That time jump didn't quite go according to plan. You, pillion, have metamorphosed into a disembodied observer in the process, though it's probably for the best in consideration of Mrs. Lewis's impending entrance on to the stage of this story. You were occupying her seat on the bike after all and that was never going to play well for long, especially for me.

I too, it seems, have changed. I now have two characters within me—the one from the last chapter who knew a thing or two about long-distance motorcycling and this one—who, unfortunately, does not know so much. Never mind, I doubt that you will have much difficulty in differentiating one from the other, because one of them is making all the mistakes.

I am as disinclined to address you henceforth as, 'Ethereal Sprite' as you are to have me do it, so I am rarely going to address you directly, other than as 'reader'. I shall confine myself to telling our tale and you can pay more or less attention as you please. To continue, though now you can take a break to put a girdle round the earth if you want. Or make yourself a pot of tea, which will take far less than forty minutes before you can come back to our story. *Adieu!*

★★★★★★★★★★★★★★★★

This journey began, if full disclosure is necessary, (and I begrudgingly suppose that it is) exactly where I am now sitting and doing what I am doing right now—which is tapping away at my PC in our home in Yorkshire. That's a large (the largest, actually) English county, in the United Kingdom, if anyone reading this needs to be told. At this distance in time, I cannot remember what I was writing about and it probably doesn't matter. Something I thought was clever, I expect. It's usually that, until I have read it again.

I was alone in the room. Patsie's desk is situated behind mine, but when couples have been together as long as we have, they can feel each other's presence infallibly—so she wasn't there. I am fairly sure this would have been late May or possibly early June. It was a good bright day with enough blue in the sky between scattered clouds to 'make a pair of sailor's trousers'. Don't ask me—it's something Mrs. L says—picked it up from her mother, probably. Patsie came into the room and folded her arms: Rarely a good sign in a Northern woman in my considerable experience, even if they barely top 5ft—toes to tip—as my one does. So I stopped typing with some trepidation and turned on my swivel to hear what was coming next from 'the light of my life'.

'There is something I want to talk to you about', she announced. *(Oh dear, another bad sign. What have I done now, what is the latest blow life has dealt us or what catastrophe has befallen someone in the family?).* You see the trend developing here. I can be a worrier. Fortunately, she quickly put me out of my misery.

'It's nothing bad' (*Phew, that's alright then. Bullet dodged this time—for now.*) She came straight to the point, I'll give her that, 'How would you like to ride the bike down to Mojacar and back?'

Oh, she can do it, my girl. She's not really 'my girl', by the way—she is her own independent woman. I know that and that fact is an essential consideration as to why she is mine, if you follow me. Nevertheless, in my view, if you have a partner of your own that never loses the capacity to surprise you in a good way—then try never ever to do anything to provoke her/him to leave you.

Boom!—there it was, right out of that 'sailor's trousers' blue sky. A very long motorcycle ride—more of an adventure expedition really—over land, south bound across Europe and back again. How long had she been cooking that one? Never a hint was there and I do pay attention, despite numerous accusations and calumnies to the contrary. I gaped silently and then gaped a little more. I can see myself doing it, but my racing mind was thinking, 'WHAT!!?SERIOUSLY!' She laughed. Of course, she laughed, my face must have been a picture, but I finally managed to blurt a response.

'I beg your pardon? Are you SURE? Are you coming?'

'Yes, of course I am coming. You don't think I would let you go alone, do you? What would be the fun in that?'

'Well, of course I want to go and with you—so long as you are sure you are really up for it.'

Mojacar, incidentally is a village on the Mediterranean coast of Andalucia in southern Spain. More on that later. The significant part of that particular stipulated destination is that a road trip in the round, from our front door in Yorkshire would be an absolute minimum of between 2,500 and 3,000 miles by road without counting sea distances or inevitable diversions and convolutions, even if we came back again by a different, though shorter, route. And that is a long way on two wheels and potentially out in all weathers. Actually, altogether including the seagoing element, I believe it is just shy of 4,000 miles. Maybe that isn't such a long way for some riders, but it would be a long way for us, because we had attempted nothing like it before. Undaunted by any of that, she had it all figured out, of course.

'We can ride down to Mojacar as I've said but. . . .(*Oh, Hello, here we go—there is a 'but'*) you have got to be fitter than you are now and you have to lose some weight'. I instinctively sucked back my stomach I expect, and, of course, she spotted it, because she went on, 'There's no point doing that. You can't keep it sucked in all the time and you don't try, do you? When we are on the bike you are always telling me to shift backwards, because you say you don't have enough room, but I can't go back any further, because then I am off the end of the seat pressed against the top-box. It's just not comfortable. I'm not the problem. The problem is your bum and back and they are a problem because your tummy is too big.' She is a lady by the traditional definition. She says, 'bum' and 'tummy' and so forth. It is, what it is.

'OK, you've got a deal'. I said without prevarication or procrastination. What else was I going to say? *I think you are being a trifle harsh within your critique of my physique, madam. Let us bide a while whilst we discuss the issue in a more balanced way that may reveal a mutually acceptable consensus.* I don't think so. Serious matters were at stake here.

'Not so fast, John Lewis', Her little forefinger came up and began to wag ominously in my direction. *(Oh no, not THE finger AND my full name. She means business then.)* 'If you think you can fob me off with a promise you don't intend to keep, you can forget it. *IF* you are no fitter, no matter how much money you've spent or how organised it is—I'm not going. Are we clear?'

'Crystal,' I demurred, 'still I am not going to get fitter and thinner in five minutes, am I? When are you suggesting we set off on this jaunt?'

She had that clear in her mind too. 'We leave third week in September,' she said in a manner that denied any possibility for negotiation.

'What say! This September coming? Won't it be getting a bit chilly round the old wotsit by then?'

Good Lord, I thought this was going to be happening in the following Springtime.

'Yes, this September. That gives you more than three months to get the job done on yourself and organise everything for the journey. The weather might be a bit cold out there to begin with, but it will alright the farther south we go. Anyway, never mind the problems. If you can't resolve them, you don't want to go enough. Do you want to go or not?' she demanded.

'Yes, of course I do, absolutely' I replied hurriedly, lest she changed her mind. Moreover, I thought now was about the right time to show some appreciation for this wonderful gift, so I said with genuine sincerity, 'I really want to thank you for this, love'

'Huh, you're not on the boat, YET!', she huffed adorably, giving me a *faux* hard look. Then she turned on her heel and flounced out of the room. Thank our stars we never arrived at 'hands on hips', which is reserved for when I am really 'catching it' or some other scenario I wouldn't want to be around to experience.

My wife has a disorienting talent for doing something really special for me, whilst giving the impression that she is angry. It might be because she's small, auburn haired and Northern English; possibly all three considerations put together. Bizarrely though, as time has gone on, I have come to the conclusion that one of the principal benefits of being married is the presence of someone you know very well cares about you, but who will tell you 'what for' occasionally. It's a counter-point that probably prevents us from becoming unhinged, because our own inner-voice is mostly telling us how marvellous and right we are when, of course, quite often we're not.

So that was that. Bless her. Rubicon crossed. *Alea Iacta Est* and all that Latin jazz. It is a well-known saying that, 'A good marriage is a matter of give and take'. That is not my experience. A good marriage is more a matter of 'give and give'. It is as simple as that. The only consideration in making that philosophy workable is that both parties have to feel the same way about it more or less consistently and if (well, 'when', practically speaking) someone lapses then that individual will always come back in line, because anything else is inconceivable. Apparently half us who attempt the married life can't do that though, so there is not much point in confining circumspection to those far fewer of us who also like motorcycling.

As I believe it has been succinctly observed—everything good in the world is kindness—and I invite anyone to give that proposition its due consideration and arrive at a different conclusion. On this occasion I was fortunate enough to be on the receiving end, so very happy to accept that which was offered.

I will not go into the details of the diet I put myself through or the hours I spent on a rowing machine. Both subjects make uninteresting reading, (though probably not for some people these days, now I think about it, sad though that is) and were not very engaging in the undertaking either from my sloth-like perspective.

Patsie had laid down the conditions for going ahead with this trip, I had agreed to them and I stuck to the deal. After all it was not as though she wasn't perfectly correct (as annoyingly usual) in everything she had said about me. So, I was going to be the beneficiary, any way I wanted to look at it. What is more, I knew better than to call her bluff. She would keep to her position, whichever way it went. I did, I confess, very diplomatically suggest it would be a help to me, if she supported me with a bit of dieting and exercise herself. Indeed, I reasoned, it would do no harm for her to be a little slimmer and fitter for our forthcoming experience. I felt like I was offering a full-grown lioness a titbit when I made this proposal, given what started all this, but I must have caught her at the right moment, because she agreed readily and that cooperation worked out fairly well.

There will be some sceptics, no doubt, who may say, 'Oh come on, admit you are at root just another selfish male 'so and so'. You know your good wife is doing this for you, despite her own inclinations and yet here you are latching onto on this tenuous pretext like an irresponsible leech, intending to drag her across Europe on a *blanking* motorbike'. Do not think the notion never occurred to me. I cannot now remember if I double (or even triple) checked whether Patsie truly wanted to go through with the venture, but I probably did.

So, I can only say it would be disrespectful to Patsie (and a serious underestimation of her) to imply she didn't know her own mind and wouldn't be pressured by me—or anyone—against her wishes, on any subject. However, I also know, if one day I said something along the lines of, 'I have read a book written by a man who shot man-eating tigers, before becoming a conservationist in somewhere called Kumaon in the foothills of the Himalayas, so I would like to see the place', I guarantee she would reply with no hesitation or querying the finer details, 'Right, let's go'. I know that for a fact, because I did say that and she did say that and we went. She is actually up for it. It's that simple, thank goodness.

Travel on boats, aeroplanes and motorcars is not, of course, the same thing as riding on motorcycles. Without going too far into the recesses of our relationship, it's probably worth explaining how we came to be sharing the same motorcycle seat. I shall pick a point in time. It's not the very beginning, because Patsie had already ridden pillion on proper British motorcycles before we met and had also been riding on her own motorised wheels after that.

There came a point—and unkind people would probably call it a 'mid-life crisis'—that I decided that I had lost myself within my many obligations and that, frankly speaking, it was about time I had something to call my own—just for me. Selfish, narcissistic or quite understandable and reasonable: I don't know. I wasn't a subsistence farmer with his concerns to occupy my mind, so any of the foregoing self-indulgences would be possible. It was not that I was holding on to lost youth, either. I can assert that honestly, because I remember when the revelation that I was no longer young struck. That was two years afterwards and I've always been grateful for the extra time spent in that particular delusion. We all stand on an unreliable platform when it comes to self-analysis, it seems to me, which is why there are psychiatrists to help us out—not that I've ever consulted one myself thus far.

I recall, however, that as a couple, a marriage, relationship or however one could define us as a unit—we were also going through a time, commonly referred to as a 'bad patch'. At home we were uncompromising, snarling and perpetually grumpy with each other. Whose fault was it? Mine, probably. Small children and stray animals sometimes uncannily gravitate towards Patsie, like iron-filings to a magnet. Once an unknown elderly lady approached her in a department store and said, 'Do you know, my dear you have the most beautiful purple aura'. I don't have those gifts and I dare not speculate what colour my aura might be, if I actually possess one. Like something old, drained out of a sump, probably. What was all the furore about? I have absolutely no idea at this distance in time and I suppose that is why it's called a 'patch'. Anyway, I was feeling sorry for myself. Boo hoo! Poor me.

Whilst, as I made clear in my preface, I am not going to use names that may be registered as trademarks in this narrative, there can surely be little doubt regarding the identity of the company and its products that I am now about to describe quite simply because, for anyone who knows anything about motorcycles, the options that I could be referring to anything else are (or certainly were at the time) so far as I know, limited to one.

Around this period, I was taking particular interest in the progress of a British company that had comparatively recently revived a revered motorcycle marque, returning fine examples of proper engineering and heritage to the English Midlands in the process.

I may as well say I felt and feel immensely proud of this company, I admired the man who founded it, I wanted to 'fly the flag' by supporting it, I have visited its factory, purchased several of its bikes and I have worn its brand emblazoned across my chest for decades up to and including this date. In fact, I once heard a motorcycle dealer tell a representative of this company that I had that name running through me like 'letters in a stick of seaside rock', and he was not that far wide of the mark!

However, for now we are concerned with my earliest association with all of that which was when (if my memory serves me correctly), I first saw a double page magazine advertisement for a new cruiser which I thought looked so fantastic that I was prepared to purchase one just I could sit on a stool and gaze upon it at my leisure. Actually, riding one was simply a fantasy in which I could only vaguely visualise myself eventually taking a leading role at some future time.

That was then. Later, I fell out of love with chrome and wirewheels, when the essential cleaning and polishing of them became a reality. I wasn't all that keen on single-disc front brakes in practice either, whether anyone thinks that's enough for 68 bhp or not, though maybe it is these days for all I know. Anyway, I wasn't thinking that far ahead, so I decided to purchase one of these 900 cc beauties, but I said nothing about it to Patsie for the very good reason that I was, as far as my feelings towards her went, dedicatedly focussed on being objectionable at the time .

I already had my full-bike licence, but had not ridden regularly for some time, so I thought it would be wise to take a refresher tutorial to ease myself back into the swing. Since my new bike had yet to arrive, I took part in a motorcycle course created for absolute beginners. At the time I intended to thereafter undertake some advanced tutorial, but that never happened once I took possession of my own bike.

I cannot say I needed the obligatory explanation of what the front and back lights were for, but never mind. I knew how to make a motorbike go well enough, but it was good to be back on a bike in the company of experienced riders who were able to cast a constructive eye over my riding. Things do inevitably change over time—with developments in machines and in road conditions. So, I was glad that I did it. Furthermore, the instructor in the theoretical part of the lesson said something at one point that really hit home and has stayed with me (though decades have gone by) as a tenet. It was this and I shall share.

'In the event of an accident, whose fault is it?' he demanded. Then he peered at us intently for an answer, which I am fairly sure he had never received from anyone. There was a gaggle of us before him—young and not so young—and we looked at each other with 'insufficient information' expressions on our jointly confused faces. 'The answer is. . . . ' he paused for dramatic effect, no doubt having delivered this line multiple times. . . . 'Yours! Why? Because you are the one most likely to be leaving the scene in an ambulance or worse'.

I know this man was not suggesting anything so ludicrous as that there are no innocent victims or entirely culpable perpetrators. Mind you, it's not a bad maxim generally, even for drinking a mug of hot cocoa. He was making a point that as motorcyclists our own safety (since no one cared for our well-beings quite as acutely as we did ourselves) was best served by constant vigilance and forethought, given practically everything else, from multi-wheeled vehicles to immobile solid objects was more robust than we were. The point would not, to be fair to him, have been so emphatic had he just then qualified the matter with all the exceptions to the rule including being perpetually mindful of pedestrians of all stripes and cyclists.

    He was right too, in my opinion, in his further tactical views on defensive riding. He also said that we should never sail past a T-junction, which had a car waiting at it, if we could only see the back of the driver's head. If they did not turn our way so we could see them full-face, before we crossed in front of them, we should slow down and sound our horns if need be so they did turn our way because, although they would invariably have angry expressions on their faces, they would have seen us which was what mattered.

    Its true, I have found, I always slow down and, on occasions, give a quick beep if I must. Those drivers usually do look cross (because they have been inattentive and caught, I suspect), but they *have* seen me and thus far I've not been T-boned. Time enough yet though, I suppose. I take nothing for granted. It will happen the day I forget to look or slow or beep. I believe, but may possibly be mistaken, that the following (or something very like it) originally appeared on an ancient headstone:

> *Here lies the body of William Jay,*
> *Who died maintaining his right of way*
> *He was right as he sped along,*
> *But he's just as dead as if he'd been wrong*

    So, times do not change so much, since poor Bill was possibly speeding along in charge of his handcart and was mown down, whacked in the flank, by a careless carter driving a horse-drawn hay-wain. Anyway, with no concern in my mind for any such potential future hazards, I secretly purchased my new wheels together with the riding gear to go with them, and one fine Saturday morning, without telling Patsie where I was going, set off to a nearby city to collect it from the dealer and ride it back to our home. I know—what a cad! All that went well and as I rode into our courtyard, I could see Patsie looking out of the kitchen window at my arrival.

    I may as well admit it (though I am discovering this autobiographical stuff is a bit inconvenient), I was thinking to myself, 'Yes, that's right, I have bought a motorcycle for ME. Yes, ME for a change, because this is ME and has always been ME, not just some damned, dull, domestic drudge, working all-hours of the clock, now just you dare say anything about it and I will tell you some home truths, my lady' and so on and so forth. There was quite a lot more in a similar vein, which I shall spare the reader. So I sat there in my shiny new leather trousers, whilst the bike thrummed between my taut masculine thighs menacingly (or so I imagined), steaming with self-righteous indignation, ready, willing and able to do battle. I didn't rev it though, because I knew that wouldn't be cool, since it almost never is.

Well, the back door opened. Patsie came outside wearing her little, fluffy turquoise mules, and she wandered over, lethally smelling of clean woman, talcum powder and (bizarrely since her father had selected it for her as a signature fragrance) that perfume she wore that had the potential to utterly confuse me in unguarded moments. She slowly, silently appraised me, up and down. She then examined the bike from end to end and back again and do you know what she eventually said?

She said, 'Where's my helmet?'

To which I replied, 'Oh'.

I didn't rev it. I honestly didn't. Not even a little bit. I didn't give her the tiniest excuse or opportunity to whittle me down by increments and she took me down anyway, just like that from a standing start in three words. Well, four words strictly speaking, but you know what I mean.

So that is how that 'bad patch' ended and how we became a motorcycling partnership. There were other 'bad patches', of varying degrees and dimensions along the way as you will discover in these pages, need it be said. This was real life, not a fairy tale, though witches do, as I know, actually exist.

4. Second Gear:
In which 'Her Ladyship' makes her entrance onto to our stage

It occurs to me that all my enthusiasm concerning this impending journey may have given the impression that we had rarely ventured out into the world before. That wasn't the case. We had undertaken our share of globe-trotting, including independently. Before you think, 'Oh, they were wealthy, then', I will remind you of that rectangle of underlay on the parcel shelf of that moped. In the early days we usually travelled on one of those metaphorical rectangles of carpet underlay—substituting currency with resolve. For one trip to the Greek Islands, we came to the conclusion we could only afford to go if we only ate cooked food every other day. We went, need it be said, existing on saved breakfast scraps.

Our finances incrementally improved over time, as they can sometimes when you work hard, so we could afford to venture farther afield. We even indulged ourselves with the occasional hotel luxury, but would usually elect a night as a reward at the end of a week or more of sweat and grime, when air-conditioning, a deep bath of clean hot water, a huge bed with spotless sheets and room-service seemed like a very good—if not absolutely essential—idea.

We had driven a motorcar to southern Spain several times (though taking the shortest direct routes) and farther away in Europe than that. Incidentally, whilst I would not draw breath to persuade anyone to become a motorcyclist, I am confident being one myself has made me a more considerate and careful motorcar driver. I look behind more often than most, I think. On consideration, since practically everything in the natural world that runs, flies or swims seeking lunch (by eating other runners, fliers and swimmers), does so at top speed and from the rear, looking over one's shoulder fairly regularly is not such a bad habit to foster, practically everywhere. So, I shall take this opportunity to commend it.

We had also ridden motorcycles extensively in the UK and abroad for long weekends and week-long breaks, but nothing to date on the scale of what Patsie was now proposing. As it transpired, other long motorcycle tours would come along later, but this one was something new to be sure.

I owned a couple of bikes from the same manufacturer as my original purchase during this period. Actually, I am proud to say I own one of them at time of writing, but it is not one I purchased during that era. Mine currently is a 1998, 900cc classically styled model—a big machine and one of the last made with the sweeping flank and elliptical tail light.

It remains my idea of a business-like British motorcycle. Design relevant to its time, though a small, but logical step-forward from her heritage, she is not trying to be anything but herself. Not over-designed or a pastiche, just honest, very solid engineering with no pose to her and a minimum of shiny or prissy details and no wire-wheels. Big traditional lines, a huge fuel tank (if slightly too long for comfort for me), a massive headlight, no-nonsense analogue gauges, big double exhausts and 'clip-on' style grips, not a single pipe-bar. She starts, these days, when so inclined, with a key at the front end.

Admittedly, the bike (I think, anyway) is idiosyncratic, somewhat long-legged, and its gear-box is positively agricultural by today's standards, but if she isn't a classic yet, then she will be one day before long and they are not so easy to come by already. These matters are subjective, of course, but to me she is the real deal, turning heads still, with the unmistakable sound of that triple, despite her weight and age.

As it became clear Patsie and I would tour more frequently on two-wheels and for longer periods of time, I realised we ideally needed a ride that did the job—in all of its aspects—better. One of the main issues was that none of my bikes had featured full fairings and so we suffered from being sucked backwards at speed or in strong headwinds. In poor weather and upon fouled roads we invariably climbed off the bike looking as though we had been Enduro riding. This wasn't so much of a problem (for me) at the end of a day, but for mid-run breaks, in 'Ye Olde Tea-Rooms' and the like, our appearance caused some issues, especially for Patsie who did not respond well to her lower extremities being sprayed with slimy road dirt and farmyard slurry.

That problem was exacerbated because we regularly rode in company with a couple who had a fully faired model—a big comfortable tourer from the same company as our one—and so they climbed off their machine in good order, whilst we could appear to be veritable tramps by comparison. We gentlemen must be mindful of the eccentricities of our ladies regarding these matters, or weeping and gnashing of teeth will surely follow. And we don't want that, especially since some of it will be indisputably be our own.

At about that time this motorcycle company announced a new model was about to be launched and that development, since I wanted to continue supporting the marque, suited me very well, because it was to be a sports-tourer.

That motorcycle suggested it was just what we needed, though at that time I had never actually seen one in the 'nuts and bolts.' So, I was irrationally giving it advantages, especially regarding its size, so it aligned with my hopes and aspirations. On that basis I was quite excited about the prospect of owning one and put in a provisional order with the dealer. For some reason the process didn't go smoothly. At the beginning of the launch, I recall there was some minor issue with delivering the bike with colour co-ordinated panniers, though that was not the reason we didn't eventually purchase one.

The time came when the dealership had a bike available for a test ride. The friend of ours, who had been riding the before mentioned big tourer, was also proposing to purchase one of these new models. Patsie came along for the test ride, because two-up long-distance riding was the principal, if not the only, consideration so far as I was concerned. So, we both climbed aboard and away we went.

We soon realised this motorcycle was not going to work for us. I could not make myself comfortable upon it. There did not seem to be enough room for my legs and before long I developed a cramp at the hip. We were hoping for more space for the two of us, but instead we felt jammed together. So, we came to the conclusion that the bike, irrespective of any other merits it might possess, was not simply big enough for us.

As it transpired, in 2010 this motorcycle was revised and given a new suffix together with a longer wheel base and slightly increased cubic capacity, which no doubt would have done the trick, but obviously that was some years beyond the time of our immediate need. That development, nevertheless, revealed our own concerns had some legitimacy, given the idea was to be aboard for longer periods of time, not least because the bike then—to me, anyway—did bear a marked resemblance to the bike we eventually purchased.

None of the above constitutes a criticism of that bike we test rode or any motorcycle in its own right. These matters require an equation of several factors to work at their best, but also align with our own subjectivity. Two of those considerations were Patsie and I individually, followed by Patsie and I together on that particular motorcycle—indeed—on that particular day combined with my abilities as a rider at that time.

Having established that the answer for us lay in another motorcycle entirely and I could not see how, much to my disappointment, it could be another model from my favoured marque. What then would it be? The principal consideration in my mind was that if we were going to be travelling together over distance for long periods of time, the arrangement had to be built on a foundation of fairness and equality. What does endure in the absence of those essential ingredients?

I have heard discourse on how to ride with pillions from those who apparently ignored the fact that their passengers were required to perch on a seat disproportionate in size and position to the one they were sitting on themselves. Before a mile has gone by the message to the pillion rider is surely. 'You do not count for so very much'. A smaller seat might be acceptable for a quick run to a coffee bar, but not for a journey of far longer duration. That activity demonstrably requires a bike built for the task. In my view pillion riding requires an objective appreciation of what the word 'partner' means especially since, unlike a front seat motorcar passenger (who so far as I know never is required to sit in a differently proportioned seat), the person behind the rider contributes positively or negatively to the experience in every way. For synergy, in an equation of three constituent parts, *all* of them need to be fit for purpose. In the best design form follows function without detriment to either consideration.

In my mind this essential qualification discounted a significant number of motorcycles from the outset. Some of the remaining contenders butted up to my prejudices against marques and styles so they were the next to be crossed off the list, followed by those motorcycles that fell to my probably misinformed judgements as to their qualities and capabilities. No one has ever claimed these decisions were made entirely scientifically or objectively.

Finally, there were those motorcycles which were dismissed simply because I didn't (quite subjectively) like the 'cut of their jib'. Among the latter group was the motorcycle eventually selected by my friend who had also found—for reasons of his own—that he didn't get on with the bike we had both believed would be our next rides. He purchased a sports tourer made by a German manufacturer. I knew that this company had a fine motorcycle history, but was not sure their bikes necessarily equated to their very highly regarded motorcars. So genuine unfamiliarity and ignorance on my part, possibly, for that rejection combined with a trivial dislike of what I considered to be fat plastic switches some of which, if my memory serves me well, were yellow.

Our friend later, having ridden on a fabulous tour in the USA across the West with motorcycling friends he knew there, moved on to the kind of motorcycle one would imagine to be perfect for the job when he returned to the UK. Though I understand why that was in the circumstances, he lost me with that choice, because I could not readily identify with the undeniable cultural heritage of that bike. I can see what that is of course, because it is, in my opinion, as American as, 'Old Glory'.

Motorcycling heritage to me looks like 'ton up boys' with thick white socks over their high boots riding their British Classics (except they weren't classics then, of course, they were just what those guys were riding) on the A1—The Great North Road. I can remember them, because as a youngster I lived close by to one of their meeting *cafés*. I went to this place once in its hey-day, intimidated by its piratical clientele and their machines, if I am honest.

Each to their own, though. Moreover, let it be noted that I have 'gone without' enough times to know that the privilege of actually having a choice on any subject is a blessing. So in that spirit I would ride any motorcycle in preference to riding no motorcycle. Well, I had that old German moped as we know, so my credentials are solid on that score.

Before long, Mrs. Lewis began dropping hints and casting covetous eyes in the direction of a very substantial machine, long well-regarded for wafting its riders effortlessly across great distances. Rather, she coveted the pillion seat of that bike. I don't believe she cared a fig about the rest of the motorcycle. That could have been powered by clockwork for all she cared. I wager she could see herself in that armchair, listening to the stereo whilst reading a book, weaving a rug and drinking tea.

From my own perspective, I felt that option was not what I wanted in a motorcycle during that period of my life. There was, furthermore, I thought, some danger (given the demonstrable ease with which tables could be turned upon me by the 'Flower of my Oasis') in my becoming a motorcycling chauffeur. That was never the plan and whilst I wanted to tour with Patsie, I also knew there would times when I would be riding alone or with motorcyclist friends without luggage and her idea of a dream ride would not do for me, for that. That bike's slightly less imposing stable-mate (which made no bones in its name as to its potentials) was rejected for the same reason. At the time, the notion of owning another bike for my own indulgence never occurred to me, quite simply because I thought we couldn't afford two of them.

So, the choice eventually came down to two contenders, so far as I was concerned. For the purposes of avoiding treading on anyone's motorcycle trademark preserves, but liberating me from having to fabricate numerous sentence reconstructions I shall refer to them simply as Bike A and Bike B. The most obvious consideration was that Bike A was a much newer development, the initial version having been released in the previous year. Bike B had been around for some time by that point with few changes and rumoured to be coming to the end of its form. On the subject of appearance, I thought Bike A had the edge on elegance of design and that Bike B did, indeed, appear to me by this point, blunt-nosed and, perhaps, rather dated by comparison.

I suspect Bike A had been introduced to compete with Bike B. So, it wasn't so surprising that if one was to compare specifications: brake horsepower, weight, torque etc., Bike A consistently nudged ahead. However, those margins, in practically every instance, were insignificant to my way of considering them and even smaller than that, bearing in mind the pilot was going to me and much of the time with a passenger and luggage aboard. I knew I could not possibly be making a mistake with up to date engineering from the manufacturer of Bike A, should I select it, as seemed for the above reasons, to be the most probable outcome.

Looking back from the perspective of later years it almost seems foolish to admit that I was intimidated by both of these bikes, because they were bigger, heavier and more powerful than any I had been riding. Surely, everyone can remember how very large a large motorcycle can appear to be if you have never ridden one before. I know I can, anyway, on more than one occasion and vividly. That one of them was the fastest production motorcycle in existence at the time and (presumably) named after a military jet aeroplane was no marketing draw for me, because I didn't want it for that reason—by implication or association. In any event, it would never do 170 mph plus with me and mine on board, even if that was what I had wanted. My principal objective for any vehicle has always been that I never want to be anywhere I don't want to be for very long, before I can get back to where I do want to be.

I had been speaking about the other contender with one of the younger motorcycle dealership staff and expressing my concerns honestly and candidly. I recall he said something like, 'Well, you know John, I have ridden that bike and I can tell you the world can go by pretty fast. Perhaps you should consider something tamer'. He then gave me some statistics of his experiences, which, if I remember correctly, included the phrase, 'curve of the earth', that didn't really help me very much either.

I was rescued from my indecision by one of those experienced motorcyclists who are so calm and laid back that they give the impression they are about to fall asleep and yet transpire to be very competent riders, indeed. So henceforth I shall refer to him as, 'The Motorcycling Sadhu'. When I asked him the same question regarding Bike A he quietly said, 'It is my understanding that every motorcycle increases and decreases its speed directly in relation to the amount you turn your wrist'. And he left it at that with no elaboration, as was his way. This declaration is both obvious and a truism, but what he was actually saying was 'you are in charge, so the bike will do your bidding based on your own wisdom or lack thereof—not the other way around'. That made me feel better anyway, not least because he knew me and I believed he was also saying I was the measure, capable enough, being neither particularly timid nor reckless.

I took what looked like being the winner of the competition for a test ride alone, because pillion comfort would transparently not be an issue. It had a well sized seat for two and would readily accept and cope with carrying three good-sized pieces of bolt-on hard luggage. I know that some journalists and riders speak of 'lack of character' when it comes to motorcycles of this kind. My perspective was somewhat different, because up to that point I had ridden nothing for years, but bikes that some would typify as 'characterful', though they were at the time comparatively modern motorcycles. They had gears that audibly went 'clunk' and 'click', when one changed them, anyway, if that was a qualifying consideration.

So, when I rode this bike for the first time, surging forward on a velvet band of power, changing gears smoothly and effortlessly—feeling the sophistication of the engineering and poise of the bike in every manoeuvre, frankly, it was a revelation. Was I pleased? Was I satisfied? Mine was more of a great aerial light and celestial choir experience. In short, I was absolutely flipping elated!

I recall returning the bike to the dealer who was waiting for me and my decision—not anxiously I hope, though I had come off one of his courtesy bikes in the past. It wasn't my fault. I won't go into the details here, but it really wasn't and he was compensated by those who were responsible. Nevertheless, I felt, thereafter, I had a 'blot on my copy-book'.

'So', he enquired as I climbed off the bike and removed my helmet, 'how did that go?'

I believe I hesitated so I could compose a sentence that accurately reflected my feelings. 'Sex on wheels', if my memory serves me correctly, was what came first to mind, but what I actually said was, 'I have only one question to ask and it is this. If *that* is a motorcycle, what on earth have I been riding?'

'They are all different,' he replied succinctly, and possibly diplomatically given he had sold me my previous rides—chosen by me—in good faith, but on reflection I don't think so. *'They'* are all different in truth and one does not necessarily want the same experience every time one rides. Equally, some riders do perpetually want one experience—others something entirely different. Some consider riding a sport (even in situations, in some cases, when they absolutely shouldn't) and for some it actually is a legitimate sport of one kind or another. For others it is liberation: a way to intimately enjoy progressing through and engaging with a landscape, whilst for others there are cultural and camaraderie considerations, the pleasure of mechanical tinkering and combinations thereof. That's a large part of the appeal of motorcycling, I suppose. The rider is in a unique, intimate and exclusive connection with the bike, so the experience can be practically anything one needs it to be.

The issue didn't feel that expansive to me at the time however, because I was simply ready to move on with what my new ride had to offer, just as later on I was ready for the retrospective experience of another bike and what it had to offer and so forth. Anyway, it is no revelation at this point in this narrative that we purchased a well, let's face it, you know what it was by now or you are probably reading the wrong book. As the order was placed, the dealer asked me what colourway I would like.

'Why,' I replied, 'black, to be sure. What other colour could it be?'

'Hmm', he mused. 'I am not sure we can get you a black one. I can get you a blue one'.

'Well.' I recall saying, 'that would rather make it some manner of blue bird, wouldn't it? What is the point of having one of these that's not black?'

I knew that was nonsense, of course, but one must make some kind of attempt to have one's way. My previous ride had been a kind of lilac-blue, so I was ready for some implied 'attitude' with my new impressive cubic capacity. He said he would see what he could do on that score and we know how that issue resolved itself, because you are not now holding, 'The Big Blue Motorbike Ride', which just does not have quite the same ring to it, in my view, especially for a bike of this one's name. That having been said, both the blue and red colourways admittedly also look very well.

She was to be *my* principal motorcycle for a very long time from that point onwards, because I never for a moment dreamed that I had outgrown her or that she would not or could not deliver anything I asked of her which would mean I needed a change. So, I suppose, that being the case, I was henceforth *her* principal rider instead, which sounds about right, actually. I could never claim any kind of mastery as far as she was concerned—not to myself nor deceitfully to anyone else. Eventually I wasn't intimidated by her, but I always treated her with respect and ultimately that was, I think, no bad thing in a practical sense. Furthermore, it was not the case that I took her home and promptly began planning the trip this book describes. That came along several years later.

For the record, I also never considered it to be comparable to an ouzel, or any other darkly plumaged avian species, nor yet to a super-sonic war plane; a link I personally considered to be a bit of a stretch given the aircraft blitzed along at 2,200 mph. The bike—whilst unsurpassed at the time as a production motorcycle—had a top whack (presumably carrying the right, slight jockey and not much else) of 178 mph or thereabouts, I believe. A notable German sports car of that period and on the same track, I understand, would have topped out at around 198 mph.

Do not consider I am disrespecting my new purchase in any sense. I know better than that. It was to me, if I anthropomorphised it in my mind a powerful, mature feline creature in the manner of Rudyard Kipling's, admittedly male, 'Bagheera'—the wise, capable, dependable panther of the Jungle Books. As I said at the outset, motorcycle royalty in my opinion, a veritable, 'Empress of Motorcycles'. Although our relationship was intimate, I may occasionally refer to her respectfully as, 'Madam'. I could no more give her a pet-name in the manner of 'Molly', 'Dolly' or 'Rosie' and the like, than I could fly unaided to the moon.

The real world stayed the same, of course—on the highways and off them—it was always a jungle to me in all its complexities, wonders and perils and it still is. So, the years rolled along bringing some peaks and sometimes, as it happens for most of us, appalling tragic troughs. We had our share, believe me. They were not part of the focus of this tale, but that does not mean they didn't happen.

5. Still in Second Gear:
In which we get ready to hit the road and very nearly do

I suspect I know why Patsie devised the surprise suggestion of the run to Andalucia, because that year marked one of my own decade anniversaries and, though she didn't say as much, it was probably her imaginative way of celebrating it with me in a way she knew I would really enjoy.

The departure date was fast approaching. As I had promised, there was a little less of me in some places and some of the parts of me I retained were a bit firmer than they once were. That having been said, when I was stripped down to my boxers, it would have required more imagination than Patsie possessed to discover an abdominal 'six-pack' on my midriff. Nevertheless, there had apparently been enough improvement to satisfy her. She may have called me 'my Adonis', but the ironic inclusion of the possessive, 'my', (thus excluding the possibility of any other potentially interested party), did not pass me by unnoticed. We were going to Mojacar and back, nevertheless, which was what mattered.

I was understandably very excited that we would be soon on our way, but—in my usual dynamic style as a dauntless road warrior—also apprehensive. This trip seemed like a pretty big deal to me at the time. We had not been disabused of that impression by anyone we knew who rode motorcycles, because none of them had undertaken a bike journey of this scale either. In reality, as a journey, it wasn't that great shakes in the grand scheme, as we subsequently discovered in conversation with other bikers on the continent who had undertaken at least—if not more—ambitious journeys. The story remains worth the telling, perhaps for that reason. If we could do it then experienced riders who were moderately capable and more than moderately careful could do it. We know there are some riders who set off for Outer Mongolia and so forth and whilst we are all impressed, most of us know we won't be doing that ourselves, so will most likely not be sharing their extreme challenges.

Readers will, I am sure, recall that at the beginning of this account I referenced an imaginary motorcycle workshop. It may come as some surprise that this place is not imaginary at all, but exists. In fact, I could reach it in a stroll of a few minutes from my own front door. It isn't my workshop though, which is probably a less surprising revelation. It belongs to the proprietor of a motorcycle business. Therein abides GB—A Great British long time good friend, advisor and motorcycle mechanic extraordinaire, who expertly attends to all my requirements in that regard.

It is to him that a 'new to me bike' first goes for a thorough examination—top to bottom—before I ever put my leg over it. And it is GB who will give any motorcycle of mine another thorough examination before we embark on a long journey, including (in the case of this bike) adjusting the mono-shock and forks to accommodate extra weight and filling the tyres with a gooey substance that apparently will instantly re-establish their integrity in the event a puncture: An essential precaution for a long road trip, in my opinion, though so far as I know I have yet to put its effectiveness to the test and am in no rush to do so.

I cannot claim I am mechanically minded. As I child, I shall never forget the look of disappointment on my father's face having presented me with a well-known juvenile metal construction set one Christmas. I had screwed a flat rectangular piece to the end of a long thin piece and said, 'Look Daddy, a tomahawk!'. I was keen on Hawkeye, Chingachgook, 'The Last of the Mohicans' and so forth at the time. Any hopes he had been fostering that I might grow up to be an engineer drained out of his face with his blood.

I like looking at motorcycles and I like riding them, but don't see why that means I must take them apart and put them back together again. After all, equestrian types don't give Dobbin a whiff of anaesthetic, haul him up on the kitchen table and set about his exhaust pipe, do they? They have veterinarians—we have mechanics and everyone happily earns a living. Do I actually own a toolbox? Of course I do—the very idea! What on earth do you take me for? Well, to be honest, I don't. WE have a toolbox, but it's mostly Patsie's. I know, shameful isn't it? She purchased the box and she filled it with the tools.

I am not completely domestically useless, though. I am, allow me to emphasise, entirely responsible for the 'too heavy', 'too high', 'follow my instructions without deviation', 'don't pull up anything growing, until I have given permission' and 'stand here, because there is a wicked draught coming through that crack', work, so don't you dare knock me, because I can be useful, can't I, dear? *I said, can't I, dear?* Anyway, you may give me a hammer, if you must, so long as you appreciate the first thing I am going to hit with it, is probably going to be me.

I know all that sounds outrageous and can only claim, in my own defence, that I am, by way of compensation, possessed of several rare and enviable abilities and talents. I won't list them in the interests of humility (or avoidance of derision), though most of the time, in the everyday working world, it's fair to say none of them are particularly practical or useful.

Perhaps I might marginally redeem myself if I reveal that once, a very long time ago, my parents made enquiry of a gentleman who was training me—it doesn't matter what for. They asked him how I was progressing to which he replied, 'John gets himself into more scrapes than anyone in my experience, but then he gets out of them faster than anyone in my experience'. It's not much of a plaudit, I know, but given an inevitability of the first consideration, the second one has come in very useful. Should the reader be inclined to imagine this is merely braggadocio on my part—reserve final judgement, if you will, until the latter pages of this book.

I had taken the motorcycle to GB's workshop, as usual, for a thorough pre-run overhaul of 'all things oily' and perhaps predictably, since I tried to keep her in good trim as a matter of course, all was well with her mechanically. When I arrived to collect her, he and his team, aware of our imminent departure, seemed very pleased for us, but I told him I was frankly anxious, considering the scale of this adventure.

'No! You'll be right,' he said promptly. He was not a man to be nonplussed on any subject, based on my experience of him, so useful to know when one is feeling timorous.

'It is a very, very long way,' I persisted.

'No, you'll be right.' he repeated, 'Look at it this way, if you were going out for a day trip—would that bother you?'

'No, of course not,' I replied, since that was no more nor less than the truth

'Right, then', he said 'it's exactly the same as that. You ride a day trip, then you go to bed and the next day you get up and just a ride a day trip'

'By Jove,' I exclaimed, gasping with relief and grasping at this insight like a drowning man at a floating drinking straw, 'You're absolutely right!' Genius. *Voilà! Allora!* A wave of relief washed over me. Why had I not seen it was so simple? I was completely buoyed up by this incisive rationale, though I suspect, if truth be told, any affirmation he might have come up with was exactly what I was hoping to hear from him, because he would have said it. This was a man who really knew his motorcycles and could ride them too—including competitively. He wasn't, 'The Motorcycling Sadhu' though, in case you were wondering.

It was not until much later that the theoretical notion occurred to me that if I played Russian roulette with a revolver that had just one bullet in it and it didn't blow my brains out when I pulled the trigger for the first time, that was no indicator, that if I tried it again immediately afterwards, it wouldn't, whether I spun the cylinder or not, blow out my brains. In fact, the more often I pulled the trigger in the shortest time frame, the more that would significantly bear on my prospects for longevity, simply because I was playing Russian roulette.

However, before we become mired in such nonsense, it's also worth pointing out that we both knew very well that I was going on that trip anyway, no matter what he had said, including-though he would never have said it *'It's been nice knowing you, but let's face it you are doomed, so what's it to be—flowers or charity contribution?'*

I will not be going into too much detail about how I planned the route of the journey, because that will reveal itself as this story unfolds. I did, however, plan it from beginning to end accounting for days of riding, days of taking a break and places to stay where there would be something interesting for us to see during the short time we were there. On that basis I booked all our accommodation in advance, because looking for somewhere to stay each day at the end of a ride takes too much time and if the search doesn't work out fairly quickly is particularly stressful at the time when you need stress least. Actually, finding the place you *have* booked can take time enough, if truth be told, possessed of modern gizmos designed for the task, notwithstanding. Our camping days were behind us by this point and we were looking for some creature comforts, so we usually booked into hotels, pensions and the like.

There is no single 'right' way to handle the daily riding planning so far as I know. It depends whether one is alone or how many motorcycles there are in the group, what those motorcycles are, the distances, roads and terrain to be traversed, the personal riding tastes of the riders and, in my opinion, if there are pillion riders—then especially their views. As passengers, I think it's so easy for pillions to become marginalised. That is not fair to them given how intimate 'two-up' motorcycling is, but irrespective of whether one is inclined to be selfish on the subject, it is also not very tactically astute if one hopes for a happy companion (rather than a miserable, complaining one) or if there is any expectation of cooperation and approval for another ride at a later date. There are a number of other things one may be doing without too, but readers can compile that list for themselves.

We eventually, over time, developed a pattern for motorcycling travel that fairly much corresponded with what we found we were doing that worked best without contrivance. In short, we took each day easily and we didn't push our luck. There is no correlation between riding fast wheels and the way one deals with everything else, practically and mentally. I know some people think there is, but they are kidding themselves, if no one else.

By the time we have climbed out of bed, taken a shower, eaten some breakfast, undertaken some re-packing, checked out and paid our bill, loaded the bike and were ready go—it was invariably between 10 am and half past. We would then ride for between two and three hours dependent on where we might come across what we thought looked promising for a light bite and a toilet break.

I am minded at this point of that 'The Motorcycling Sadhu' of my acquaintance, who quietly commented, 'Was there ever a motorcycle invented that one did not want to climb off, after two hours?' I can stay on board for a little longer than a couple of hours given the option myself, but I absolutely understand, as usual, what he meant. A paragraph on the subject could follow, but will not do so, because by this point readers have doubtless grasped how the man 'rolled'. Never imagine he was actually me, incidentally. How I wish that might be true!

After a break we would ride—maybe with another break or possibly not—until between 4 pm and half past. In hot weather, at that time, we found it best to be off the bike for the day throughout most of Europe, because the sun—contrary to what one might think of high-noon—is then at its zenith, has been stoking up the earth for a long time and can be very unpleasant. Riding can become progressively harder for a number reasons including the heat generally, discomfort in the rear and legs, tiredness leading to lack of focus, increasing traffic (people are going home after work) and eventually that potentially treacherous violet/grey, dusk light that comes before full dark.

So by checking in for an overnight in the late afternoon, there was time to take a shower, change into lighter clothes, take a rest with your legs up, see to mails, attend to battery charging, take a stroll to scope the town and get ready to go out in the evening for something to eat. After that, if our luck was in, there might be an atmospheric bar with a dimly lit corner where the drinks are cheap, the music is good and the table-tops sticky.

Goodnight and repeat. Happy days. Need it be said this plan, like all plans, is just a plan. Sometimes, for one reason or another it may not work, but it includes a margin for error. As this story progresses examples of getting it 'right' and getting it 'wrong' abound.

I could write an entire chapter on what one should and should not pack and where one should put it when travelling by motorcycle. Once again, these matters are subjective. I have known people who would buy a inexpensive collection of clothing to be worn for the duration of the trip and upon returning home, simply dispose of it all in a bin. Some riders dump and re-purchase as they go—arriving home with nothing but what they are wearing.

Likewise, these days, apparently very high quality, 'fashion' motorcycling apparel exists, purchasable at some premium. Everyone is at liberty to wear whatever they please. Still, when riding a motorcycle I think it is best to leave all expectations, illusions and delusions about what other people will think or see when they look at you at home. All riders have (or should have) more practical and vital considerations to occupy their minds. It's all about being realistic with ones priorities.

Our own first consideration had to be the outer-clothing to be worn when riding. In the early days Patsie and I would wear leathers which was fine when actually riding, especially in temperate climes, but on those occasions when we were afoot, we were uncomfortable, ungainly leather-clad medieval knights. In hot weather, 'all leather' in our opinion is not ideal and impractical when one is wearing the same garment day after day—on and off the bike. A compromise solution to account for both situations was needed. So, we moved to breathable, water resistant, fabric jackets. Leather trousers gave way to bespoke (custom-made for comfort) strong motorcycling denim jeans and our dedicated bike footwear changed to tactical boots.

On this journey we had to take account of the fact that we would be heading south initially, but conversely coming north again to return home in the UK, by which time November would be knocking at the door, which is why we also carried a tightly rolled one piece water-proof suit each.

So, we had two jackets each—one of them light weight for inevitable very hot weather. Hot weather is not so bad when moving on the bike, but at higher temperatures when stationary—irrespective of the duration of the halt—one begins to forthwith cook.

At the end of some days of riding we have had to—without any exaggeration—laboriously peel the sticking, wet clothes off each other, until we both stood naked in our hotel bedroom, dripping with perspiration. Try not to dwell too long on that vision. I know I don't. It lacks any conceivable glamour, though, admittedly included a fair amount of humour—now and at the time. For the other end of the weather scale, we also each carried a full set of thermal underwear (with long legs) each, including glove inners and were glad that we took the precaution, as you will discover later, not least because south is not always hot when it is also early in the day and at higher altitudes.

We had known a fine young motorcyclist who had a collision with a dry-stone wall that resulted in a broken back. Thank goodness, he wasn't paralysed, but it was a sobering event and a nasty injury, nevertheless, which could very easily have been much worse. So taking this as a salutary lesson and motivation, we always wore sleeveless waistcoats with integral protective turtle-back, spine-protectors under our jackets when riding. These items are comparatively bulky, but of course, are also an extra layer of clothing which contributes to warmth or overheating and so must be taken into account as any other top garment one might wear.

Later on, we wore the obligatory hi-visibility gilets. We stuck the stipulated reflective strips on our helmets and I went so far, with long trips in mind, to purchase and wear a fluorescent yellow helmet. My appearance was a cause for mirth for some people actually, which disappointed me mightily as one may imagine, because possibly in consequence of wearing this giant lemon on my head, we were not splattered all over the highway.

Our off-wheels clothing followed a simple principle, which was that it never needed ironing and that most of it was so thin that it would fold up to occupy the least space possible. So, we tended to buy and wear dedicated tropical travel or other performance garments. Variety of choice is not so important when one is constantly moving on, if a small pack hand laundry cleaner is kept in the luggage. This is no issue for men, but if a lady is on the back seat there has to be, in my opinion and possibly Patsie's though I didn't ask, the opportunity for her to wear something to her taste in the evenings. She possibly wouldn't want to be the only woman in a restaurant concerned that she gave the impression she spent all her days in an inspection pit, though that's not a 'one rule fits all' perspective, of course.

Regardless of all of these considerations we had already made our first blunder before we set off on this journey. In fact, we began that error not so very long after we knew we were going. I can see now how it happened. We had not ridden together very much that year and we certainly had not ridden together that year with cold-weather kit, spine-protectors, a full tank and a full luggage complement. Tellingly, since we had an objective in mind, we also didn't do any of those things during the three months leading up to our departure. All of that put together was potentially a serious mistake. We definitely should have undertaken a few fully laden short practice runs in the manner of the main event.

So, cutting to the chase, the day and hour came when we were about to set off. The motorcycle was fully loaded with fuel and all our luggage. We were wearing our cold weather gear and our destination was the ferry terminal at Hull on the English north-east coast, because we were booked for the overnight cruise to Zeebrugge in Belgium. Since we live in the North of England, this was the most convenient port of exit to Europe at the time, if one intended to turn west or south once upon the continental shore.

The weather wasn't awful, but we had a ride before us to arrive at the ferry terminal and we knew, from experience, that there would be an interlude—possibly an hour or more—before we were boarded. As motorcyclists, of course, we would be corralled together with the other bikes and their riders, waiting outside in a concentration zone with our machines and the temperature, at that time of year, would become progressively colder as evening drew on. Furthermore, comparatively early on the following morning we would be riding off the ferry onto the continent and we would then have a day of riding westwards before us along the English Channel coast before arriving at our night stop. As it transpired the weather forecast for that part of Europe was comparatively encouraging, but not so reliable that it would be wise to change into hot weather clothing so early in the venture.

It was evident that all was not well from the moment that Patsie climbed onto the bike. That old problem of discomfort and lack of room asserted itself immediately and a squabble of accusations and denials broke out. We had arranged to visit a good friend immediately before our departure and the ungainly hulk that wobbled away from the kerb seemed unlikely to be able to remain upright and out of trouble for the first afternoon, much less for the thousands of miles that lay ahead. We were in mid-domestic dispute when we met him and that bickering continued until we bade him farewell. I looked in a mirror as we tottered away and I can still see the very unhappy expression on his face which seemed to me to say, 'I think I shall never see you again'.

This was a very disheartening moment and so certain was I that we were heading for disaster somewhere down the road that I said to Patsie (through our headsets), 'Look, this just isn't working. I have made the decision that if we are doing no better than this by the time we reach the port, we are not going. To board that ship would be just foolish, because, if this is the best we can manage, we are bound to have a spill before a day is out,'. I had never been more serious. She said nothing.

The ride lapsed into a tense uneasy silence. Bizarrely, it was at about the point that we entered the outskirts of the City of Hull, that I noticed we were doing rather better and had acquired some space and balance. If I must put myself on the spot for an explanation as to why that was, I can offer only this. Rain or shine, good times and bad, Hell or high water—we are together.

You know, properly married. No one has ever packed a bag to leave, so far as I know. Not me, anyway. We were tense, anxious and then we sorted ourselves out. That, hopelessly lacking in qualifications, is all I have on the subject.

6. Third Gear:
In which we take ship, with some trepidation, for the Continent

Eventually we rode into the ferry terminal from which our ship would take its southwards route, following the English east coast, down the North Sea towards the Low Countries. We were familiar with the check-in and customs procedures, having travelled on this ferry regularly. Ours appeared to be the first motorcycle to check-in and after the usual border protocols we were directed to the spot on the pre-boarding holding area where we motorcyclists are habitually gathered, so we could be boarded at the same time and positioned for the crossing—more or less—in the same part of the ship's garage deck.

I quite enjoyed those pre-boarding waiting periods, because numbers of riders and pillions incrementally arrived and were all together in a companionable crowd that usually turned itself into a minor social event. That was not immediately happening on this occasion for obvious reasons. So, we waited and waited for company to arrive. No other motorcycles ever arrived. This was the first time and indeed, the only time, accounting for all the journeys we made subsequently on any ferry as motorcyclists, when we were completely alone.

As it dawned on me that ours would be the only motorcycle on the ship, I was not a little taken aback. Given the way the day had begun, I took this development as an ill omen. What on earth did the motorcycling fraternity know about this day and being at sea that I did not know? Was Hurricane, 'Arbuthnot', or whatever it might be called, at that very moment raging out in the North Sea unbeknown to us, despite all my weather forecast checking? Before long, it was too late to worry about that or anything else, because our singularity soon brought a dock marshal in our direction and he waved us forward and onwards to the open vehicle deck doors of the ship. So away we went.

I think the most important aspect of motorised ship boarding, I personally try to remember, is not to be intimidated by the angle of metal ramps, but to ensure I move onwards, upwards and off them at their further end under a steady level of sufficient and consistent power. That might sound obvious enough, were it not for the number of vehicle drivers who, presented with this slope, have felt the need to rush up it at speed and upon arriving at the point where 'angle' meets 'level' have grounded their vehicles rear-ends noisily. In one instance I witnessed, a driver left his exhaust pipe behind him, which is rarely a good start for a vacation.

I try, furthermore, to never begin a climb on a ramp (be that the main one into the vessel or most particularly those within it) unless I can see my way clear of it and not be stuck half-way along it (on brakes and gears) with other vehicles stacked up on the incline close behind me. So, I give a modicum of tactical thought on that likelihood when it comes round to our turn to climb and hold back for a moment if I must. That manoeuvre, on this occasion, safely accomplished we were ushered to the bow of the vessel to an area reserved for motorcycles and there, as expected, were all the ropes, belts, ratchets and wheel-chocks needed to secure dozens of motor bikes.

I shall digress ever-so slightly. When the airline cabin crew give the safety announcement before an aircraft takes off, am I the only one who is not that sure that in the 'unlikely' event of the aircraft landing on water, having managed to get my life-vest over my head, I will then have the ability to swiftly tie those tapes in a double knot on my hip? I can imagine myself sinking beneath the waves, an object of curiosity for shoals of passing haddock, ineptly fumbling with those damned tapes all the way down to the sea-floor. It took me forever to learn the knot tying component of the Boy Scout badge and then forgot everything

I had learned immediately.

How does any of that concern riding a motorcycle or being a motorcyclist? Evening is drawing on, so I shall elaborate. We had arrived at that point where normally, surrounded by our peers, we must make our motorcycle secure for sea. On some European ferries the crew attends to that procedure, but in my time to and from the UK from this port, each rider secured his own bike. Of course, if a vehicle on a ferry is a four wheeled one, that is no more complicated than putting it in gear, applying the hand brake and disarming the alarm. If all the motorcars are going to be shifting about very much after that precaution, then everyone onboard, I assume, has a substantial problem.

The bikes, however, are left, gear engaged, leaning on their side stands. So, at this time there were capable motorcycling men (not indulging stereotypes, usually they were men) busy everywhere, deftly securing their machines with slip-knots, half-hitches, bowlines and Lord knows what else, as though they did it every day for a living. It was comforting for me to imagine some of them were professionals. Perhaps they were—on every sailing we took, based upon the evidence—by bizarre coincidence, all sailors, mountain climbers, rope makers, boy scout troop leaders or hang-men.

I by way of contrast, was trying to remember the difference between a 'Reef' and a 'Granny', which was a pointless conundrum, because having tied my knot, I wouldn't know which one it was anyway. Once, additionally, as I blundered through this farce, there was a couple next to us who were riding a motorcycle that was so ancient that originally someone must have walked in front of it with a red flag. These two adventurers were proposing to tour around Europe on this antique. Strapped upon its rear was a wooden toolbox also containing, apparently, most likely needed spare parts, because the rider knew—actually knew—his ride was going to break down, probably up an Alp, and he would be required to fix it by the side of the road. This certainty would be no problem to him at all or to his confident wife who was smiling beatifically, without a care in the world, as this was revealed.

He didn't have any knotty problems either, needless to say. If I thought we were destined to break down, I would employ the expedient of riding another motorbike where that eventuality was so far less likely as to be totally improbable.

★★★★★★★★★★★★★★★★

Before I leave this subject altogether, I will touch on the consternation I felt when I had to load 'Madam' on to motorcycle railway rolling stock for an overnight run across Europe. Yes, such a thing does exist. This wagon looked like an open motorcar transporter, such as one would see on the highways. The bikes were parked two-abreast, cheek by jowl, and coincidentally, ours was placed next to a bike all but identical to our own (except it was a red one) whose rider was a confident Dutchman, who assured me as he deposited his own ride that all would be well. The bike's wheels were clamped by metal 'shoes' attached to a stout rigid metal pole. Then over-straps were applied. Our bike appeared to be positioned perilously close to his ride to me—even before the train began to move. I hovered uncertainly as the loading crew went about their business.

'Are you sure', I asked them, 'this is secure?' I know, it was a stupid question, so I deserved what came next. They were also Dutch, by the way, so not above 'leg-pulling' or quickly taking advantage of an opportunity to do it.

'We think so,' one of them replied in good English, examining their work in feigned uncertainty and rubbing his chin, 'I tell you what. If you are unhappy about it, you can stay with your bike, if you want. It does get cold and windy at night though, even if it doesn't rain'. For a split second I actually considered it. Their howls of laughter sent me on my way.

At a certain point on that train journey, I looked out of our cabin window as the train was taking a long curve at speed. To my dismay, I could see the line of wagons leaning at what seemed to me to be a horrendously acute angle. My heart sank. I was so certain that we would be returning to collect a jumble of scrap, that when I saw the red bike rider again over dinner, I apologised to him in advance in case our bike transpired to have mangled his. He laughed and told me this, if memory serves, was the sixth time he had loaded his own bike onto a similar train without mishap. He was right, of course.

★★★★★★★★★★★★★★★★★

None of these kinds of experiences are particularly good for my self-confidence, as I have, on more than one occasion, attempted to explain to my shrewd wife. She listens to my ramblings for a little while then, relying on Kismet presumably, simply flips her personal 'OFF' switch.

On the subject of mechanical competence, I do envy those kinds of outstanding amateur and professional engineers who will go about disassembling, repairing (even crafting new components from scratch) and then reassembling everything perfectly, so that the finished motorcycle, not only looks marvellous, but starts upon demand, purring like a contented kitten. Instruction manual? Pah! such things are apparently for small children and furred creatures which lack opposable thumbs. I would love to be able to do all that stuff, though ideally with the flourish of a wizard's wand and a short, easily remembered incantation—not with grime covered hands, accompanied by broken fingernails and bleeding knuckles.

I am fairly certain I over secured our poor motorcycle. Normally one has the use of ones share of ropes, belts and chocks, whereas on this occasion I had access to all of them. If we were bound for a rough crossing, I was determined 'Madam' was not going to suffer for it, though by the time I had finished with her she looked a very sorry sight, chocked, strapped and roped, covered in Granny knots and lonely in bondage. I quietly whispered my apologies for her humiliation, of course, then took our small overnight bag from the back-box and sheepishly left her, slinking away to find our cabin.

There was a time when we opted, for obvious financial reasons, to occupy the least expensive cabin available on ferry boats in the bowels of the vessel with all that implies. That choice changed to a cabin for two without a window, then to a cabin for two with a window. One of the problems with that style of cabin meant someone—well, not *someone* really—had to occupy the top bunk, creating issues in the middle of the night if calls of nature came. So, I had to then come down a metal ladder in bare feet or take my shoes up to bed with me—neither of which was ideal in a swell and less practical incrementally with the increasing size of the waves outside for a man of my limited agility.

By this point in our maritime careers, we booked cabins for four occupants with a window and so we both had beds at floor level, which reduced the probability of early-hours flying accidents and offered more room for metaphorical 'cat swinging' generally. We are not fans of motorcycling on full stomachs, so we ate a light meal of quiche washed down with a couple of bottles of Belgian beer.

I recall that Patsie and I sat on our bunks, opposite each other as the ship rumbled its way into the Humber estuary, until one of us—I cannot remember now who it was—said, 'Well, that's it, we've done it now!' There was not much more to say, though the tone suggested this excursion might not have been one of our most astute decisions. We had, indisputably and irreversibly 'done it', so turned in for an early night to be as sharp-witted as we could manage for our first full day of riding *sur le continent* on the following morning.

Needless to say, I spent much time lying there, staring into the dark, pointlessly debating with myself whether I was up to the task ahead. I had never been sure whether the fact that I owned a motorcycle and rode one was enough justification for me to assume I was anything close to what motorcyclists I had seen, could be. By my own estimation, my credentials were consistently sub-standard in that regard. I wasn't reluctant to admit any of those concerns in conversations with other motorcyclists, though I consistently had the impression that none of them really believed me. Maybe that was because of the manner in which I explained myself (which often raised a laugh or two for some reason) or that I was prepared to say anything on the subject at all.

When I was gliding down an urban road on the bike in those days, small boys would sometimes run to the curb to look at my passing in obvious awe, occasionally calling out, 'Give us a wheelie, mister'. I would wave a nonchalant gloved paw, of course, and ride on. Give them a wheelie? I had no idea how to execute a wheelie. And I certainly would not have attempted one on that particular motorcycle of all options, so certain was I that it would end horribly in an expensive mess of me and motorbike in the road.

I have seen photographs of bikes like ours performing wheelies, of course; they appear rather undignified to me, like bullied big cats in a circus ring that have been prodded to rear up on their hind legs. Anyway, as a matter of fact, I can't do a wheelie to this day, even on a bike suitable for one, not that impressing small boys—or behaving like one—comes very high on my agenda.

I am slightly consoled that 'The Motorcycling Sadhu' once commented, in his inimitable style, that, 'wheelies' were, 'An accomplishment unworthy of the effort expended to acquire'. That sober judgement would satisfy me forever, were it not for the fact that he regularly manoeuvred 'live' motorcycles about whilst standing on just one peg and side of them. What baffles me is how he eventually acquired that skill, without having first dropped motorcycles all over the deck in quantity. However, I have always had the suspicion that he could have thrown up a wheelie whenever he liked, riding whatever anyone liked and I also suspect he could put his knee and his elbow down if he wanted to—even though he didn't want to. If there can possibly be any readers by this point contemplating whether I can put my knee down the answer is, 'No'. Well, not intentionally, as you will later discover.

I once, long ago, attempted to ride with a motorcycling group which met at the weekends. Actually, there were two groups, tellingly identified as, 'The Fast Group' and, 'The Slow Group'. That differentiation seemed quite reasonable to me at the time, though less so now. Sober heads may ponder, 'How slow or fast, that it requires dividing, can a group ride motorcycles on English roads?' Need it be said, being new to this kind of experience, I elected to go with 'The Slow Group' and was about to find out. Both groups would meet at the same location and then we would split again to ride separately for about about 40 miles to a motorcycling race event.

Anyway, we all congregated at a specified car park at the appointed time and there was the usual companionable chatting among us, until the group leader called out, 'Right lads, are we all clear where we are going to meet? (scattered nodding assents) Good, then its about time for the Fast Group to set o.........'. and it seemed to me, before he got the 'ff' out of his mouth, six or eight of 'us' were not just already at the next roundabout, but some of 'us' were powering up the straight beyond it.

I began frantically fumbling with my helmet to get it on my head and properly fastened, if this was going to be the way things would be done, and sure enough it was not very long before 'The Slow Group' was barrelling away. I came along at the rear. I didn't intend to be there. It just happened, probably because I was, 'Johnny come lately': The one rider who hadn't yet considered someone had to be, 'last man—slow group'. I think that day I was expecting 'Hares' and 'Tortoises', but actually soon discovered we were all 'Hares' from my perspective—some of us marginally more of the 'mad March' variety than others.

Actually, I took no issue with the 'Fast Group', whose intentions were declared unambiguously. The 'Slow Group', it seemed to me by contrast, was prepared to accept the epithet, so felt no compulsion to be demonstrably fast, whilst at the same time were determined not to be considered among themselves, for reasons we may imagine, remotely slow.

Being at the back of a speeding group is not a great place to be, because one finds oneself recklessly intent on catching up with the pack. I felt that if I fell behind noticeably, I would be identified as incapable of being in the group at all, which would been humiliating even had there been a 'Really Shamefully Slow Group', which there wasn't. So, it seemed to me the price to be paid to be a member of 'The Slow Group' was an immediate abandonment of the full and proper attention to the quality of my own riding. On balance, I wouldn't recommend that mind set to anyone. I did keep up, more or less, hating myself all the while for feeling the weight of the juvenile compulsion to do it. So, for me honestly, it was a miserable experience.

When we arrived at our destination there was no sign, curiously given they had set off first, of 'The Fast Group'. They weren't all dead though. They showed up, with no one missing in action, about ten minutes afterwards and they parked their bikes, engine-blocks pinking and tinking as they cooled among us, their riders laughing like drains.

Their story, I believe, was this. It transpired, none of them had bothered to consider the route between point A and point B. The first rider away, it seems, was principally concerned with being the first rider away and had no clear idea where he was going specifically. The rest of 'Fast Group' just chased him. So, they had ridden many more miles than were necessary to arrive, until they found themselves more or less in the right vicinity and had spotted some advertising posters promoting the event on a hoarding. All of which was apparently hilarious to themselves and everyone present and judged one of the triumphs of the day because, of course, they gained a longer ride out of it.

'So', enquired the group leader to me later in a quieter moment, 'did you enjoy that, John?'

'Well,' I replied, politicly and nearly honestly, 'it wasn't quite what I was expecting. I mean, it appeared to me anyway, that no-one seemed to slow down or take very much notice of the usual road signs and signals and so forth.' Maybe some did. I had no idea, as 'Tail-end Charlie', what was going on at the front of the pack or in the middle, for that matter.

'Oh', he laughed, 'Is that what all those pretty lights and pictures mean?'

He was probably joking to be fair, though perhaps there was a 'Tortoise' out on the road that day in more ways than one. Slow on the throttle—slow on the uptake, as it were.

I felt rather foolish, as though I had signed up for an afternoon pleasure boat cruise around the bay, when a monotone Hollywood swashbuckler, had sidled over, and, leaning on the taffrail, languidly enquired, 'Faith, Johnny, you *do* know we're all buccaneers, do ye not?', 'Well, no, actually, Cap'n, I really didn't'.

To be fair to them all, they weren't maniacs, they were indisputably experts. Whether they should have been employing their expertise in those circumstances is another discussion.

They were, let it be admitted, operating on a different level to me. I wanted to be more or maybe, like the 'The Motorcycling Sadhu', I just wanted to be able to be more if I chose to be—which I probably wouldn't. Ability combined with restraint as it were—like a Wushu monk. Anyway, I couldn't do it and so didn't go again. I can get into the 'brown and foaming' (as my late father would say) without much assistance from anyone.

On the subject of 'Fast Groups', 'Slow Groups' and, 'Shamefully Slow Groups' it has occurred to me that if that scale continued downwards to its inevitable conclusion there would eventually be a 'Parked while drinking Cappuccinos Group', though that is possibly a fantasy too far.

They were great lads, every one of them, genuinely the 'salt of the earth' and I have no complaints of them. I can honestly say we have received overwhelming kindness, consideration, comradeship, assistance and generosity from motorcyclists both at home and abroad almost without exception. I didn't expect to be embraced into a community I had shown no inclination to join and this aspect of motorcycling solidarity initially surprised me, because I have never been particularly clubbable. So, we have never been members of an MC of any persuasion.

To be identified as a biker has been my honour for all these years though, it really has, so thank you all. Never was anything so touching as the consistently reliable support of complete strangers. I didn't take it for granted, because it was special and I still feel the same way about it, because they have been—as an identifiable group—the kindest of people.

★★★★★★★★★★★★★★★★★★

Before we leave that subject, there is this incident which for me was educational. A few of us had taken, on one fine morning, a short run out to the city of York: Fifty or so miles—round trip. On Micklegate, if Fortuna smiled, there was parking by the curb. She was in a good mood on this morning, so we were going for a cup of coffee and a bun before returning home. I was taking off my helmet sorting out the bike (and this was many, many years ago) in preparation for leaving it for a short while, when a man's voice behind us asked, 'Can you let me have the price of a breakfast and a cup of tea, Guv'nor?'

There was a raggedy, elderly man—a 'gentleman of the road'. He looked as though he could benefit from something inside him, so we gave him a few pounds. That was no big amount nor big deal, so I am not trying to suggest it was. Anyone who can nay-say evident need on those few occasions when it's standing right at their toe-caps has a damned hard heart, in my view. So, there are no prizes for not being horrible, nor should there be. The old fellow was inclined to chat, so we spent a few minutes with him mulling over this and that.

When it was time to say goodbye he said, 'You know, I knew very well you lot (meaning bikers, of course and I was barely familiar with being identified as one then) would help me out'.

'Oh, aye,' we laughed (we were in Yorkshire, remember—it's 'up North'), 'How could you know that?' You old rogue, I thought, you had us down for 'soft touches' from the get-go, but it wasn't that, good gentlefolk all. It was this.

'Well', he said, 'you always do, don't you?' And off he went on his way. Pardon me? Always? Do we? That was news to me.

It's all a bit complicated really, in a chicken and egg kind of way, isn't it? Is there something about being a biker that motivates one towards basic empathy or are empathetic people also possessed of something that possibly motivates them to become bikers? Internationally, as most know, there are motorcyclist groups who are supporting veterans, mental health awareness, children and young adults issues and a host of other worthwhile and creditable causes. Whilst I know very well motorcyclists are not alone as collectives engaged in these activities—our own cabbies and their support for veterans being a shining example, I cannot say, in all honesty that I am ever very surprised to hear about them when they are motorcyclists. To paraphrase our own old 'gentleman of the road', 'Well, they always would, wouldn't they?'

✶✶✶✶✶✶✶✶✶✶✶✶✶✶✶

On that positive—if somewhat confusing note—so to sleep. As it turned out, any concerns I might have had regarding our sea passage or the security of our motorcycle were entirely unfounded, because the North Sea had been kind that night. The crossing had felt as though we were within a slowly rolling billiard ball traversing a faultless, level green baize covered table. We skipped the on-board breakfast to avoid riding over full stomachs and predictably found 'Madam' in the good order we had left her.

The great metal doors of the ferry's vehicle deck eventually opened and we had our first glimpse of the continental shore. Despite a forecast of fine weather, the morning was misty grey with a chill in the air, so I took the opportunity to growl pointlessly. Patsie by contrast was feeling really rather cheerful, upbeat and positive, so I suppose the balance of our Ying and Yang was working splendidly, irrespective of which one of us should rightly have been contributing which part of it.

So, after unravelling the bike and going through the usual formalities, we set off, down initially familiar roads—beyond the enormous sign reminding us, 'To drive on the RIGHT'—from the Zeebrugge port.

Almost uncannily, there now seemed 'all the room in the world' aboard the bike. It felt nothing like it had done during the previous day, being easy, light and biddable. One's state of mind apparently translates into ability and sensation on a motorcycle, as it does in so many other things in life. We were, all three, back in sync and feeling good to be on the road again.

Incidentally, for those who may be nervous about the prospect of riding on the 'wrong' side of the road, the *aide memoire* I employ is a whimsical one and it is this: 'Remember John, the gutter is your friend, so if you look down and its by your right foot—all is well'. I don't have particularly strong affiliations with gutters as it happens, but it's useful to have this ritual, because one can find oneself, in an unguarded moment, setting off into the face of oncoming traffic. Fatalities have resulted among those who have made that error. Readers are at liberty to invent their own ditty as it suits them. My point is that it's worth having a reminder for British bikers, because there is, need it be said, no steering wheel in front of us as a constant prompt. Put a fluorescent sticker on a right bar; whatever or wherever seems useful.

As the reader is aware our ultimate outward, destination was Andalucia in Spain, but the principal purpose of this adventure was always intended to be the journey itself. Our first overnight destination would be in Normandy, which was why we were riding westwards from Belgium into France along the coastline. In the past we had driven due South which almost unavoidably meant tackling Paris and its ring road, the *Périphérique*. The less said, in my view, about that road the better. I would avoid that particular experience, if at all possible, irrespective of our reasons for travelling, though we have driven it on five or six occasions. Of course, I know Parisians hurtle round the *Périphérique* all the time, but for them, familiarly and not on the 'wrong' side of the road. However, in a ride designed for the pleasure of riding, all of the reasons why one might avoid driving around Paris were academic. We would be nowhere near the place.

Equally, we did not want to spend too much time on autoroutes, for fairly obvious reasons which I may elaborate upon later on. However, we felt that at the outset we should get some riding under our belts and so would press on in the early part of the run, not least because we would be in the North where the weather would be most likely to be inclement.

★★★★★★★★★★★★★★★★

Actually, as we eventually became wise to the occasional potentials of ferry travel throughout Europe, we would only begin a journey if our scheduled arrival was before mid-day. If it was after that time, we always booked accommodation comparatively near the port of arrival (no hardship since these were often new or rarely visited places for us) and began the serious business of moving on the following morning. That way we would never again be concerned that we had docked two hours late, be unable to disembark (which takes its own time, irrespective of delays) because the vehicle bay doors were stuck (or something like it) or when we did get ashore, find ourselves grid-locked in Derby-day football match traffic. Thus, in consequence of any of these things and several others, singularly or combined, we would not find ourselves up a mountain at night, battling with a Biblical thunderstorm, instead of leaning against a friendly bar, drinking 'Boilermakers' as planned. The reader may imagine that the afore-written examples were exaggerated fictions, laced with gallows humour, constructed by me simply to emphasise a point. Alas, they were not.

However once, after we had learned our hard lessons on that subject, we were stuck on an arriving ferry that was unable to dock in the appointed place and had to be moved—after some hiatus—elsewhere in the port. The evening wore on, the light faded to total darkness and the temperature plummeted. We were, as usual, among the gathered bunch of motorcyclists waiting to disembark, though we had not, thus far, been allowed onto the garage deck.

By this time most of them were in poor humour, as they lamented that they were that evening scheduled to be in this place or that place and few of their destinations, close-by. One rider and his lady pillion rider bemoaned they were booked into a hotel in a city 111 miles away. I knew that road and it went through some high bleak terrain, so I didn't envy them their coming ordeal. Had that been the travel-wise version of us, having been through a similar experience, I would have abandoned 'Plan A' and checked in somewhere locally without a second thought.

For once I prudently kept my counsel, motivated, I expect, by some clandestine head-shaking and a stony glance of caution from my wife. So, I suppose that silence wasn't prudence at all— I was just doing as I was told. Eventually though, after everyone had chipped in a contribution, eyes turned in our direction. 'So where are you going?' someone asked. As it happened, the ship was being towed in the direction of the distinctively designed (so easy to identify) hotel into which were booked for that night. In fact, we had stayed in the same place before as an insurance policy which was, on this occasion, about to pay out and it hove into sight. So, I pointed out of the window and simply replied, 'There'.

I probably, on reflection, should have told them a diplomatic falsehood, because there was, understandably, no ensuing round of applause nor even an odd ironic chuckle. Still, the point is well made and taken, I trust. Need it be emphasised we didn't learn all of this by being smarter than usual from the get-go, but (as dear old Dad would have said) by spending our own time in the 'brown and foaming'.

7. First Gear again:
In which having disembarked, we set off for Normandy

Our ride had begun and we were in a good place which meant the next order of the morning had to be coffee. As we pulled into a Belgian service station the rising sun began to burn away the mist and warm the morning from chill to crisp.

Those two coffees were made to a predictably high continental standard and we drank them together contentedly outside, leaning against the bike. It is, in my opinion based on personal experience, surely one of the last great mysteries that acquiring a good cup of coffee in an English hotel for breakfast is an odds against bet, whilst obtaining one from a continental service station at any time is an odds on certainty. Be that as it may, signs of forthcoming motorcycling enjoyment were beginning to appear more auspicious.

From that service station car park, towards the east swept the expanse of the mighty Himalayas and, before us, rose the goddess mountain, Nanda Devi. From her wind-kissed, white crown, there constantly peeled a long, fine plume of coruscating snow, waving gracefully in a clear lapis lazuli sky, like a magnificent egret feather.

Well, no, we couldn't see any of that. I just thought that since this was the first true travelling day of this adventure, we ought to be able to kick off this chapter with a description of some impressive scenery. Unfortunately, the landscape of coastal Flanders and Northern France is superficially rather flat and unprepossessing, which is not to say the area is without interest. I ask the reader, in that regard, to bear with me now with a little patience because I am going to park us for short while, so far as the story of this ride is concerned, to explain how I am tackling writing it and how that will bear on what you will read.

It seems to me that what we take out of life depends on how much we open ourselves to see and experience (or even, no less importantly, imagine) whatever comes our way because that receptivity will invariably deliver dividends. As a former colleague of mine once astutely commented, though on the subject of making photographs from the photographers perspective, 'Its not so much about what there is to see, its more about *how* you see what there is to see'.

All of life is comprised of these prompts, I suppose, if we remain constantly on the lookout for them, though we all become mired in the routines of necessity—so concentrate on those instead. Travel is inevitably multi-aspected and fresh which is, of course, much of its appeal. So, a motorcycle journey can certainly be like that if we allow it to be. Beyond the riding sensation, we can see and engage in a time, season and country in terms of landscape, its people and their cultures, its architecture, its wildlife, its history, its cuisine—all or some of them according to taste. It's a big old wonderful world out there. Cards on the table—Patsie and I are sponges for all of it.

Certainly, one can blaze across the continent, concentrating on the sensations of the bike and road, taking in an available track if it presents itself and then enjoying dinner and drinks each evening. There are those who do that exclusively and good for them. I will not say Patsie and I have shunned those things ourselves within our own journeys, including this one, because we have embraced them wholeheartedly for the pleasures they bring. This book, however, would be inevitably a shorter one and our journey less interesting from our own perspectives and to recount, if that was all there was to it. So that is not all you are going to get.

Motorcycling is, thankfully, a very broad church with room in it for everyone. We once had a very enjoyable evening on board ship with one of the redoubtable, 'Iron Butt', non-stop, long-distance riders, who coincidentally lived quite close to us in the UK. He regaled us with tales of staggering journeys on his double-tanked adventure bike, including one effort that had him hammering up to the Arctic Circle. I almost understand what it's all about and admire the determination and fortitude of those guys, but we don't want to do that kind of riding ourselves, not least because he often rode autoroutes as a consequence of the strictures of time constraints.

No one should be too alarmed by my declaration (made in the introduction of this book in fairness) that I write and edit history books. I also read them, so know something about the subject, if generally. The present passes in less time than it takes to consider it, whereas the future is yet to be revealed and so capable of any potential—especially useful to note, if there are many c.c's at work between your knees. History is absolutely everything else, so was in a time when you started reading this chapter. There is no escaping history therefore, irrespective of one's inclinations on the subject.

That having been said, readers may be relieved that I have absolutely no intention of turning this tale into a history book on two wheels, overburdened with unwanted detail. Nevertheless, history informs landscape and often the other way about. Flanders and Northern France were ever battlegrounds and one rides over the bones of conflicts that were fought there over centuries and the names of places that we rode past on our route could fill volumes (and have filled libraries) with their stories. Where they are particularly notable, I shall very briefly mention them now and henceforth.

One cannot ride for too long from Zeebrugge, westwards along the E40, before on the right, Nieuwpoort, which stands at the mouth of the River Yser appears. This was a region of bloody conflict in 1914 in the first months of the First World War. In fact, sign posted to the left is Diksmuide where the French Marin Fusiliers fought a desperate stand against the advancing German Army, sometimes battling across the width of a narrow canal that runs through the town. Beyond is Ypres renowned for its place in the carnage of trench warfare and then very soon upon the right, on the Channel *(La Manche)* coast,

Dunkirk, known to practically everyone as the site of the momentous evacuation of the defeated British Army in 1940 during the early stages of the Second World War. A short distance ahead stands Calais, where 600 years ago, King Henry V, after Agincourt, (that battlefield itself just 75 miles distant) defeated a French Army leaving 7,000 of them dead upon the ground.

What can I say? That 80 mile stretch of flat road either has very little to commend it or it has all of this and certainly much more within its history, irrespective of its indisputably interesting natural world. We simply, without pause, rode by and beyond them all on that morning, though in later years on other trips also visited them, including their museums and visitor centres, and so we can recommend them to the interested. I will leave this theme by mentioning that the battlefield of Waterloo was also just 80 miles away and that the shades of the principal players of that final drama in Europe's struggles with Napoleon Bonaparte and his armies during the early years of the 19th century would be unavoidably tied by a thread to this journey all the way through France and into Spain and Portugal.

After a few hours of riding, we pulled into an *'aire de service'* to stretch our legs. We had not been there long before a solo British motorcyclist riding a faired 600cc job (I cannot recall which one it was—just as well since I wouldn't be able to say!) pulled in and parked beside us. Need it be said, we soon fell into a conversation with this young man during which—if only by pure coincidence given the foregoing—he revealed that he was a British Army, serving soldier who was taking a break to visit the D-Day landing sites in Normandy, having recently ridden, not from a ferry or the Channel tunnel, but from Ypres and a tour of the scenes of the Western Front. He outlined his plans for his Normandy excursion and we thought they sounded really interesting. In fact, so impressed were we that we undertook that journey ourselves later, though not on that occasion in company with 'Madam', but riding another highly regarded sports-tourer that was a little easier on my wrists and pulled like a train with its 1300 cc lump.

As an aside, a tour of Normandy including the D-Day invasion sites of 1944, war cemeteries enough to break your heart, of course, and the Bayeaux Tapestry which chronicles the Norman Invasion of Britain in 1066 (both huge and stunning) is recommended. The countryside is enjoyable and the food and drink excellent. Even a brief description of our experiences on that trip would easily fill a chapter, though that may be a digression too far for this book. It must be chronicled, however, that we visited the Pegasus Bridge at Ranville (in pouring rain) and were treated most kindly by the lady who operated the *café* there—who was, as many know—as a small child present when the bridges over the River Orne and Caen Canal were assaulted by British glider-borne troops in a precursor operation to the sea-borne landings. Fabulous though that all was, that wasn't my most vivid memory of that time, however, which was, perhaps predictably, another of my blunders. What happened was this.

On the first day of that trip, we had been riding westwards on the same road we travelled for this journey. On that day, however, by the time we were on the A29 Autoroute, heavy clouds were gathering and Patsie's infallible, country-girl nose for impending rain, informed her that a deluge was on its way. We know very well that to ride a motorcycle is to elect to be wet and not complain about it, since the remedy is simple enough—don't ride a motorcycle.

That having been said, at that time two considerations were paramount in my mind. The first was that our overnight accommodation was not so very far ahead and the second was that I had for some time—for the reasons given—been pushing our luck on the matter of fuel and we were perilously close to riding on fumes. What should I have done? Pulled in for petrol when we needed it, obviously, not least because this was a dual carriageway. Hey, ho! I didn't. I risked it instead and the rain came down upon us like a monsoon anyway, rendering my irresponsible stratagems soggily irrelevant.

Never mind, I thought, now there is such a very, very little way to go before we reach Honfleur and it was then that I saw **it** for the very first time, the Pont de Normandie over the estuary of the River Seine. What a fright! My heart all but dropped out of my chest, because I had no idea that it lay between us and our destination: A lesson there in itself about relying only on road maps without checking the details.

End-on, from our viewpoint, the core of this massive structure appeared to my shocked and uninformed eye as a vertical ribbon of road, shooting upwards, raised against logic and the forces of gravity. Motor vehicles appeared to move upon it implausibly, like beetles crawling up and down a plank. And there we were, 'two-up' as usual, on a fully laden motorcycle which had virtually no fuel in its tank. Such was my despair and first panicked impression, in that driving rain, of the Pont de Normandie.

I slowed in confusion to the toll gates, but an official waved us straight through, since apparently motorcycles were not to be charged. So, what then to do, but push ahead, willing, praying and hoping for the best. Filled with misgivings, my mind raced. What if the motorcycle coughed its last effort half way up this daunting climb? Would we be stranded in the wet at some perilous height, blocking traffic, beside an expired motorbike, needing to be rescued, amid sirens and flashing lights, by a squadron of justifiably annoyed *gendarmes* and *sapeurs pompiers?*

Had I been inclined to rationality at the time, I might have considered that challenging autoroute bridges are not actually constructed, much less opened and employed by quantities of everyday traffic. But then I was tired, drenched and stressfully prone to imagining impossible scenarios. The visual effect I described is presumably an optical illusion created by the condensing effect of perspective. Viewed from a side elevation the bridge appears to be, perhaps disappointingly for some, simply a bridge, though an impressive example of design and engineering to be sure and a credit to everyone who brought it into being.

We crossed the Pont de Normandie, *bien sûr,* without incident, not least because in the actual crossing it is fine, not as steep as I believed or dramatic in the least but, far more importantly than any of those considerations, what remained of the vapours in the bike's fuel tank held out and kept her pistons working, thank goodness. Immediately after leaving the bridge we swung into Honfleur, where I gratefully rode into the first petrol station I saw, silently promising myself, Patsie and any familiar spirits that might still be listening, that I would not make a mistake of such magnitude again. It was a hollow gesture, mind you, because none of them wisely would have believed me and I could have then solved our fuel issue with a can.

So back, some years previously, to the 'Big Black Motorbike Ride' which, appropriately, was about to reveal another—though in reality a previous—shortcoming in my planning abilities. Need it be said, it is best to calculate each day's ride by hours to be ridden, rather than by the number of miles it comprises, because one has to take into account the terrain over which one will ride and the kind of roads involved to do it. Demonstrably it is easy to make a mistake with that kind of calculation because, given this was our first day, I had purposely planned for an easy ride which was to deliver us by mid-afternoon to our overnight accommodation in Fontaine le Soret, about an hour of riding beyond the city of Rouen. Regardless of how straightforward that objective may have seemed, that was not what happened.

It is also worth knowing (though I did not consider this at the time, obvious though it is) that one's Sat Nav results will not necessarily correspond with—for example—a convenient for planning, though different online routing program, so if one needs the two to be virtually calibrated one must allow for 'via' or by-passing points along the way on one's motorcycle instrument or one may be routed through a town or city which was only intended to be circumnavigated.

On this occasion I found we were following the Sat Nav attached to our handle bars into the heart of Rouen when I had, of course intended, using the other program, to by-pass it. Does that matter? It matters at what point of your riding day that kind of set-back may occur and, indeed, how long you had planned to ride on that day, and how long it takes to find your way through urban traffic. We still crossed the River Seine, of course, but some way from where it joins the sea, so that was something of a non-event and it never occurred to me, at the time, it could be anything else.

These days there are those who use their smart phones for practically everything, including installing them on their motorcycles as Sat Navs. I know some of those GPS apps are excellent, but I would not do that, unless I had another and principal smart phone securely padded and kept elsewhere, applying the proverb of 'eggs' and 'one basket'. But then, we also always carry two sets of every essential document copied on paper in separate places. Few petty thieves are prepared to mug anyone for a sheet of A4, so far as I know.

Before you smile at such quaintness, I shall point out that once, whilst driving in Switzerland we were simultaneously struck by a large articulated lorry and another motorcar. I thought, as that lorry's enormous bumper came through the window beside me, spraying us with shattered glass, that it was all over that time. So, no one has much to tell me, that I would care to consider, about far from home road disasters and their consequences.

Lest some remain inclined to disregard me, the quiet 'Motorcycling Sadhu', of impeccable credentials, tellingly asserted, 'There are just two kinds of people when it comes to motorcycling: Those who come off motorcycles and those who don't ride motorcycles'. That is a sweeping statement, it's fair to say, so I don't take it literally or definitively, though I know what he meant. So, my duty is done for I have passed his wisdom forward. 'Send not to know for whom the bell tolls, it tolls for thee' etc. A chilling clarion call from me (well, John Donne wrote it several centuries ago, but you take my point), since I know all this, yet managed to frequently embroil us in troubles.

In the event, my idea of a first easy day of riding resulted in our being on the road for seven hours, when it should have been closer to five hours. I do not recall that we stopped for much of a proper break after that encounter with the young soldier—not even to eat a sandwich. To put the business in perspective, the distance we rode on the continent was longer, because the distance we rode in the UK was shorter, since we left from a northern port. Had we elected to enter France via Calais—through the tunnel or by ferry—the continental ride (entirely dependent on traffic, road accident delays etc) would have been in the region of four hours and if we had caught a ferry from the south coast of England to Le Havre, probably one hour or so at the most.

Clearly, both choices would have required a longer period of UK riding for us and so we would have been unlikely to have overnighted at this particular place, but farther on, though we might also have had an initial overnight stay in England. So all depends on the starting point. All that having been said, we had been on the bike longer than I thought we would be or was entirely enjoyable, which made me concerned for the remainder of my daily riding estimations, because all our destinations were now set. I would have to change them on our mini laptop PC—which would be a chore—should I prove to be consistently wrong.

The final stretch of road passed through a vaulted archway of trees in full, bright green leaf, despite the first day of October only being a couple of days away. We pulled over outside the front door of our hotel which was an attractive half-timbered traditional building by the roadside, then gratefully (and somewhat stiffly) climbed off the bike. I pushed at the entrance door. It was only when it didn't budge that I noticed the *'Ferme'* until 5pm sign upon the other side of its glass panel. So we wouldn't have been able to gain entry even if, as planned, we had arrived earlier.

I was initially quite annoyed by this development, so I checked the booking confirmation readying myself to make a complaint. The document clearly stated opening time was 5pm—I just hadn't bothered to read it; another lesson. By this point it was about 4.15 pm, so not a disaster, though we could have sunk a beer or two about then, it's fair to say. Patsie was kind about our situation, which was what mattered most. There was some seating considerately positioned outside the place, so we stripped off our jackets with some relief (bearing in mind we were wearing cold weather gear) and stretched out to enjoy the late afternoon sun.

The motorcycle was to spend the night outside in the car park at the rear of the hotel so we removed all the hard luggage, so it could be stored safely inside the building. One can simply remove the fabric luggage inners, of course, but the thief who bursts your panniers open will not discover that until he has done his dirty deed and damage which will then be an unnecessary problem to resolve and a hindrance that could have been avoided.

At 5pm, 'on the button', we heard the sound of activity from within the hotel and the sign on the door was flipped to *'Ouverte'*. My old notes inform me that, 'we were welcomed inside by the proprietor and his wife, who were the epitome of Norman hospitality'. I am not sure how I came to that conclusion, since this was the first Norman hospitality we had ever experienced, though to be fair to my former self, Norman hospitality sounds as though it ought to be good for some reason.

It was a relief to shed our riding gear, wash and put on something more comfortable. In Patsie's case that also meant something more feminine. The interior of this hotel was decorated to the owners', perhaps idiosyncratic, taste. The walls were decorated with prints and original artwork of contemporary illustrations, especially French comic book art, some of it absolutely fabulous if one has a taste for that kind of thing and I do. The atmosphere of the interior was muted, inviting and cosy under beamed ceilings. Comfortable sofas were surrounded by tables and shelves piled high with books on art and photographic monographs, whilst scattered around there were funny, whimsical and peculiar objects to be investigated. Some good jazz was being played quietly in the background and the bar served a selection of local draft beers. The dinner menu was an imaginative fusion of west and east and the wine list was impressive too.

We were, let it be admitted, in our version of chill-out paradise. So, we enjoyed it all in full measure and eventually staggered off to our comfortable bedroom contented, replete and ready for sleep. The day may have had its small setbacks, but that hotel made up for it in spades. I suggested to Patsie that the only attraction that had been lacking was a stripper, but for some reason, she didn't agree. Oh well, one can't have matrimonial harmony all the time, as I well know.

★★★★★★★★★★★★★★★★★

'No, you didn't say that at all, John!' 'It's just a joke, a minor quip if you will, dear.' 'What on earth will people think of you?' 'Well, they might just smile at the contextual incongruity of it, as it were. You remember humour, surely?' 'Take it out, this minute,' 'No, shan't, this chapter needs a bit of levity, the rest of it makes me seem like a total idiot,' 'Nonsense, you are not an idiot, as I have repeatedly told you. You ACT like an idiot, which is something quite different and what is more you don't like watching strippers any more than you like watching boxing. Anyway, I'm going to change the bed linen now, so if you want some stripping you can come with me and help me take off the sheets.'!
★★★★★★★★★★★★★★★★★

For those who may be curious, I have no idea whether it is preferable or otherwise to be an idiot or to act like an idiot and I am not going to ask 'you know who', because I'm not usually that much of either option.

Incidentally, I will not directly identify the specific lodgings we stayed at, because they may be now closed, have new owners, have changed their style or policies or indeed any number of differences since our time. As I said at the outset this is not intended to be a guide book. I do not think, however, we had a bad experience with accommodation or with the very pleasant, welcoming and helpful people that owned or worked in those places throughout the entire journey. Wherever they are and whatever they are doing, we genuinely wish them well.

8. Second Gear:
In which we ride to Mont Saint Michel and then ride away again

The previous day of miscalculations on my part had shaken my confidence, by reacquainting me with the ancient lesson that there is a world of difference between theory and practice. Oddly, although this was only our second day on the road, on this day that potential for error would matter the most in practically the whole journey, because we would not be moving towards our ultimate most southerly destination. We would be taking something of a diversion.

Our destination was Ducey on the Normandy coast and it was only about 130 miles or so distant, which we should have been able to cover—all things being equal—in less than three hours. The reason we had to ride those miles in the morning was because, that afternoon we planned to visit Mont Saint Michel, which was why we had chosen a hotel nearby to it for the night.

The margin of error we had experienced regarding ride times on the previous day was so wide, that I persuaded Patsie that we should rise early and, to be on the safe side, be on our way as soon as possible. I had come to the conclusion that every daily run was almost certain to take longer that I originally believed it would.

This point in our narrative is the time to reveal that one of Patsie's talents is to remember poems, often from her childhood, and at moments when she feels they are appropriate, recite them. I well recall the very first time she delivered one of these treats. It was early in our time together, so it came as a surprise (popping out of nowhere) and was rather charming. The character of these pieces is in consequence of a certain time and kind of education, no doubt. State, by the way, not private. Things change, not always for the better and we can become accepting of 'less' after a time to the degree that 'more' in certain instances can seem preposterous.

This morning, she opened our first floor, bedroom window and leaning out, Normandy, no one in particular or anyone who cared to listen received John Keats', 'To Autumn'. I will give just a taster of it, since we have places to be.

Seasons of mists and mellow fruitfulness.
Close bosom-friend of the maturing sun;
Conspiring with him how to load and bless
With fruit the vines that round the thatch-eves run;
To bend with apples the moss'd cottage trees,
And fill all fruit with ripeness to the core.

.....and so on and so forth, though I am fairly certain we must have had an abbreviated version at the time because it is quite long in its entirety.

In the interests of full disclosure, listening to that particular poem on that occasion was no new experience for me. I will hear it at least once a year, because, obviously, there is certain to be one English morning that will ideally accompany the verses and so inspire the rendition. In the same spirit of disclosure, I have to reveal I also hear the poem, 'Lepanto' by G.K Chesterton from her, fairly regularly. That one begins like this,

White founts falling in the courts of the sun,
And the Soldan of Byzantium is smiling as they run;
There is laughter like the fountain in that face of all men feared,
It curls the blood-red crescent, the crescent of his lips
*For the inmost sea of all the earth is shaken with his ship*s.

...... and once more, so on and so forth.

I am not quite sure why we have that one, if truth be told, because it concerns a naval engagement fought in 1571, between the Ottoman Turks and the navies of certain European states in the Gulf of Patras, which for those who legitimately might not know (including me, once) is in the Ionian Sea not so far off the western coast of Greece. Motivations for the revival of that topic, in the normal scheme of things, remain few and far between these days. They don't come around like Autumn anyway, that's for sure, but I get the poem anyway and don't complain. We are not particularly aficionados of poetry, by the way. Please, don't jump to any conclusions on that score. It's just an example of one of those things that happen to keep the days interesting. As someone wisely commented about gardening, 'The more you put into it—the more you take out in pretty much equal measure'.

Before we leave this subject altogether—and I imagine for the remainder of this book—it has to be admitted that given at some point Patsie was going to recite, 'To Autumn', she could not have chosen a more appropriate time or place. The Normans are well known to be big on their *pommes,* so the hotel predictably had its own apple orchard at the rear and the boughs of its many trees were heavy with soon to be harvested bright red fruit. I know apples are not always bright red, so that sounds like a *cliché,* but these ones actually were. An early morning mist clung about the apple trees and lapped up to the crimson leafed Virginia Creeper that framed our bedroom window. The air was sharp and clean as it can only be in the countryside and the day was promising to be fine as the sun climbed.

We went downstairs for some breakfast, which transpired to be a new culinary experience for us, comprised of fresh baguettes, Norman ham, an apple sauce accompaniment, hard boiled eggs, natural yoghurt and strong coffee—all of which seemed entirely appropriate as local fare invariably does. Breakfast complete, we reloaded the bike with our luggage and were on our way.

The first part of our journey could not be described as interesting, because it crossed a flat landscape, reminiscent of the fenland of the English counties of Lincolnshire and Norfolk. These places can have big dramatic skies rather than notable topography, but on this day the firmament was broad, clear and blue.

So we cruised along making good speeds, down miles of almost perfectly straight undemanding roads, rarely meeting other traffic which was exactly what we needed on this morning, after the previous fraught day, any way one wanted to consider the matter.

Eventually, the open farmland became rolling hills, often thickly covered with woodland among which small villages nestled, whilst occasionally the roofs of pretty *châteaux* broke through and above the arboreal canopy. The bending road sank between high banks crowned with tall thick hedgerows. This, though it was our first personal experience of it, we recognised from old Battle of Normandy newsreel footage as the *'bocage'*, made notorious in 1944, because these formidable barriers were so easy to defend by the German Army and difficult and deadly to assault for the advancing Allies.

Despite its violent past the countryside was quite beautiful that morning and we took a break in a small lay-by among the trees and rested for a few minutes in the sunshine. Patsie put her legs up on a decrepit bench, whilst above us inquisitive woodland birds bobbed compulsively closer to see what we were about. We knew that despite this idyllic setting, Falaise, site of dreadful violence and carnage within the retreating German Army, not so long ago during the battles for Normandy, lay close by to our North. If one didn't know the history, there was no way to suspect, on that fine morning, how dreadful it had once been.

How quickly the most momentous affairs of humankind are diminished, engulfed and healed by the tides of time and nature. One might imagine, in one's most hopeful moments, that this simple lesson, repeated so frequently over time and practically everywhere, might have illuminated the dimmest spark that war is not simply bloody, but bloody pointless. Need it be said, we haven't arrived at that enlightenment at time of writing, nor I suspect at time of reading, whenever that might transpire to be.

We were by this point in a better position than on schedule and nearing our destination. So, I began to feel relaxed about our prospects. The woodland thinned then ceased and we rode once again among open farmland. Ahead I could see signs for the village of Barenton. By the side of the roadside to our right stood the flag of the United States of America upon its staff. We rode by it initially, but curiosity motivated me to turn around and we rode back to where it stood to discover why it was there.

I have since that time attempted to find out more information about this site, but have not succeeded, so I apologise without reservation, to anyone better informed, for anything I may now recount which may be less than accurate. No disrespect is intended on our part. Nothing could be further from our minds, because we were both moved by this encounter.

Upon this crossroads stood a tall Second World War memorial. Patsie and I have visited war cemeteries practically everywhere we have travelled in Europe, Africa and the Far East where our own people and their allies have made the ultimate sacrifice. I won't make more of that here, other than to affirm that we consider those visits to be our duty, for we owe all these people, beyond debate, the benefits of the lives we live in a free society. Though every cross or marker represents a life tragically lost, in some of the larger cemeteries they overwhelm the senses with their numbers.

This was a far more intimate memorial and the more poignant by its solitary location in the landscape. A young soldier of the American forces who had served during the Battle of Normandy, having survived the war, had fifty-five years later privately commissioned this monolith in memory of three of his comrades and friends who had been killed, whilst manning a light armoured vehicle (the memorial bore an image of it; a Greyhound or M3 possibly, I am no expert on these matters) belonging to the 82nd Reconnaissance Battalion, in an ambush laid by German Army forces

The names of these young men which were inscribed upon the memorial seemed to us to suggest French family connections. Perhaps, we speculated, they were the descendants of French families who had emigrated to the New World and in due course had returned to the homeland of their forebears to lay down their lives in its liberation. It was impossible not to be touched by the tragedy of war encapsulated in this one small area and single violent event that had snatched away the potentials of young lives and crushed the aspirations of their loved ones.

The commemoration of these lives lost among so many and the unerring fidelity of their friend who had felt it essential, in later life, to create this lasting testament, spoke of enormous personal loss and the lifetime defining consequences of war. We paid our own proper respects to these young fallen warriors.

Honour can only be awarded to those who give and most honour is due to those who give their all.

We remounted and rode on a short distance, arriving in Ducey in good time. This was a pretty, quiet typical small market town and our hotel, which was easy to locate, had formerly been a flour-mill and so was pleasantly situated upon a stream bank. The proprietors were a charming husband and wife team who greeted us warmly. We established ourselves in our bedroom and then prepared to travel to Mont Saint Michel, which was only nine miles distant. The day was glorious, so we shed most of our travelling clothing and removed the hard luggage from the bike.

Almost everyone has seen images of Mont Saint Michel. It is one of the most stunning and recognisable sites in Europe; a towering abbey begun in the 8th century, surrounded by fortifications, on an island in a bay. This isn't the place to go into an historical description of the place, because it will come as no surprise that this occasion for us did not go according to plan.

To tell it simply—it was heaving with people and vehicles and we could get nowhere near the place. Actually, sometimes that outcome is not the disaster it may initially seem, because the views of some iconic places do not improve the closer one comes to them. In my opinion, the Taj Mahal and the Pyramids of Giza come readily to mind in that respect. I am hoping that Mont Saint Michel is another example, because it is very impressive from a distance and we have never visited it to this day.

As we drew closer to the monument, we discovered its approach road was under maintenance with half of it excavated to create a contra-flow. The road is flanked by numerous large hotels. The romantic in me (which is a big part) was hoping for an expanse of marsh-grassed isolation, the plaintive cry of the curlew and perhaps a lone, cloaked and helmeted paladin galloping across the sands, the pennon at his lance tip whipping in the wind. I know, some chance of that, though everything but the knight would have been nice.

My heart sank. The car parks were full to overflowing and patrolled by attendants determined to do their jobs properly. Even good viewing points were out of reach and cordoned off with yellow and black striped tape. We rode to within a half mile from the island wedged in snail-paced traffic. Eventually the opportunity came where there was enough room to turn the bike around, so I took it and we headed back the way we had come, thanking our stars—as we have done many times before and since—that we were riding a motorcycle. Without panniers it was even easier to wriggle and weave through the grid-lock.

★★★★★★★★★★★★★★★

So, our excursion was something of a disappointment, though I appreciate, for some, the notion of exploring Mont Saint Michel would not have had much appeal in the first place. For example, once, having arrived at a hotel in Luxor, waiting in the lobby for our room keys, a man sat down beside me. He asked if we had stayed at this place before. I confessed that we had not. By way of making conversation, I asked him if this was his first visit, to which he replied—to my astonishment—it was his fifth. I, not unreasonably surely, assumed I had fallen in with an amateur Egyptologist, so began to enthuse about the many archaeological sites of the Theban Necropolis on the west bank of the River Nile—The Colossi of Memnon, Hatshepsut's Mortuary Temple, The tombs of the Valley's of the Kings and Queens and so forth.

'Oh', he recoiled, cutting me off in midstream enthusiasm, 'we don't ever go over *there*. We just come here for the sun. If I want to see a pile of old stones, I've got some lying about in the back of my garage'. So much for 3,000 years of incredible civilization. It takes all sorts to make a world and whilst everyone is entitled to their own opinion to be sure, I may as well run up our standard and say his was a perspective incomprehensible to us, so we don't correspond.

★★★★★★★★★★★★★★★★★

We rode away with regret. I pulled over to make some images that featured the island from afar, because it can be seen for miles around. As I was making these photographs, I noticed that a large military transport aircraft was circling over Mont Saint Michel and then, quite suddenly, a scattering of parachute canopies blossomed open and began to drift down towards the island. Who these parachutists may have been I cannot say. Possibly a crack cadre of para-padres on a training exercise or more likely, a group of desperate, but resourceful, tourists who had astutely calculated the only uncongested way they could gain access into Mont Saint Michel on that day.

Upon our return to the hotel, our amiable host enquired how our afternoon had gone without, perhaps diplomatically, alluding to the extraordinarily short time we had been absent. We recounted our woes and he—to be fair to him—seemed very sympathetic. He then told us that he had heard on the local radio station that on that day alone there had been 30,000 visitors to Mont Saint Michel. Well, that would explain it! Of course, we understood he had no complaints on that score himself, because those were the kind of figures that kept him perpetually in business.

We decided a couple of stiff drinks might improve the day and our host, eager to oblige, suggested we might like to have some Calvados, since we were in the right part of the world for it. As initiatives went, we thought this one had something going for it. We had never before tasted Calvados, so knew nothing about it except it was a brandy made from apples. On that basis one might imagine it would not be very expensive, but apparently it can be dependent on its quality. We thought ours was anyway, so presumably it was a good one. As far as I can recall that was our first and only foray into the pleasures of Calvados, so I am in no position to credibly judge.

That evening we wandered into Ducey and discovered a husband and wife run *café* that specialised in traditional Norman *galettes* which, for the uninitiated, are savoury crepes made from buckwheat, folded over and stuffed with all manner of good and gooey things. It was still warm in the evenings in Normandy that year at the end of September, so we ate outside on the pavement terrace and fittingly washed the meal down with copious amounts of cold, pale Norman cider served in handle-less pottery *boules*. Memory is extraordinary in its selections, because I can now recall that at the next table there sat three diners. All were Americans, two of them were an older couple who, it was my impression, were visiting a very tall, handsome young priest, who looked very smart in his spotless, full length black cassock. One cannot restrain one's thoughts and mine, unbidden at the time, were that it was to be hoped he was a careful eater, because that cassock would take some cleaning.

Towards the end of the evening a pizza-van rolled up outside the *café* and for a moment I thought our hosts might take some exception to it as competition to their *galette* business, but in fact they greeted its arrival with some enthusiasm and rushed over to order their own dinners. This struck me as quite odd at the time, but of course, it's not. *Galettes* were, no doubt the last thing they would have chosen to eat, being no novelty to them at all.

So back to our water-mill and bed, arm in arm, we went. The next day of riding beckoned and was, once again, to be a special one because it was the anniversary of the Battle of Salamis wherein the Greeks under Themistocles gave King Xerxes and his Persian lads a sound thrashing at sea (also off the coast of Greece) in 480 BC—so we might, in consideration of this comparatively tenuous connection, yet have 'Lepanto', from Patsie after all, if I gave her the 'heads up'.

Actually, I have since discovered there is also a poem about the Battle of Salamis itself, but Patsie apparently doesn't know that one, so the reader will be spared an extract. Oh well, never mind, one must be reasonable. How many naval engagement poems can one's wife be expected to learn? At least she knew one and there must have been many marriages, I wager, that have foundered on the rocks for want of a recitation of 'The Rime of the Ancient Mariner' or 'Casabianca' and the like. Anyway, broad-sides, boarding parties and boys standing on burning decks put aside, far more importantly for us—the morrow also happened to be our wedding anniversary.

9. Third Gear:
In which we reach Saumur, drink, eat, cough, sneeze and go to bed

Our destination on this day was the beautiful, historic town of Saumur, a fairly easy, two to three hour ride due south. The morning was fine and bright and for riders like us, familiar with English countryside, the terrain not unlike the undulating, verdant fields and occasional woodlands of Leicestershire though—as can be said of most of Europe—with considerably less traffic. Motorcyclists, perhaps uniquely, among those moving along on motorised transport can report with authority that Normandy on a hot Autumn day can smell of thyme and rosemary, until one passes through its villages, when the fragrance of herbs gives way to the tantalising odours of fresh, warm baking brioche dough.

I drive a motorcar and I don't think of one as a 'cage'. For transporting all your family, collecting eight bags of (note) peat-free compost or carting away Aunt Millie's sideboard, a motorcycle is not much use. We could—more or less—do this journey in a car, unconcerned about that downpour that has washed over us because we are snug and dry or comfortable and cool with the 'air-con' on full choke when the sun is beating down mercilessly. Our motorcar is a cosy home extension on wheels; a small private bubble—a familiar lounge with our own armchairs. If we drove a thousand miles (and we have), upon reaching our destination we would still be in the same place we were on our own driveway. Until we stepped out of the motorcar, at which point we would be pedestrians like everyone else.

We may persuade ourselves as we drive that we are out in the world, but actually the world is remote—a simulation; a flat projection on the other side of the window glass. On a motorcycle we move through a fully dimensioned world with which we are totally engaged as we are with our motorcycles. As we ride it could be said that we are removed from a sense of 'place' because we leave it behind in a moment. While that may be true, the sensation of 'free flight' is irresistible and beyond comparison. For me it all comes together when I stop, even momentarily. In that moment when my boot comes off the peg and plants on the ground I am 'right there'—far from my every day connections, really on that spot—present in time and place. I can't get motorcycling out of my system and don't try because it liberates me—body and spirit.

As we rode through Meslay du Maine we noticed a little *café* with tables outside it. Time was getting on so we pulled over and enquired about the possibility of some lunch. The amiable owner explained that choice was limited to *omelette aux fines herbes et frites*. That was no problem to us, so his equally pleasant wife set to work. We ate like royalty for a very modest price. Never had we eaten better omelettes. What is it that the French know about eggs that remains a mystery to most of the rest of us? Need it be said, I never drink any alcoholic beverage when riding a motorcycle. The coffee was pretty good too, though one comes to expect that.

★★★★★★★★★★★★★★★★★

The reader has probably grasped by now that I am fascinated by how one subject can be inexorably connected to another. It came as something as a surprise to me, nevertheless, that might also apply to omelettes. Apparently, the finest omelettes in France, a country renowned for superlative omelettes, were made by a particular woman during the later years of the 19th century and early 20th century in her kitchen on, would the reader credit it, Mont Saint Michel. Her name was Annette Poulard. She and her husband kept a hotel on the island which is periodically cut off by the tides. So, diners had to be served a good dish that could be prepared quickly. So was created the legendary, *'Omlette du la mère Poulard'*.

Apparently, this culinary wonder remains, unknown to us at the time for the reasons already given, served on Mont Saint Michel. So, we have never eaten one made to that specific recipe and cooked in that unique manner.

Furthermore, I have read, but cannot vouch for the accuracy of the source, that the classic French omelette did not originate in France at all, but came from Spain. This account stated that during the French siege of Cadiz during the Peninsular War, those beleaguered within the walls ran out of potatoes which are an essential ingredient of the Spanish *'tortilla'*. However, by good fortune Spanish chickens were still laying like patriots and so a version of that Spanish dish was created—out of necessity—minus the requisite 'spuds'. Accordingly, I suppose—given the authenticity of this tale—the French were notionally responsible for the recipe (if only indirectly) by lobbing inspirational cannonballs at Gaditano chefs—as folks from Cadiz are known. I will not give the reader the impression I already knew that denomyn, because I didn't.

All that having been said, it occurs to me that beating an egg is not much of a stretch of innovation, so it wouldn't surprise me if Neanderthals made and then ate them, if only by accident which is most likely the way several recipes have come about.

★★★★★★★★★★★★★★★★★

Since this was our wedding anniversary, I had booked us, intending it to be a treat, into a premium grade hotel situated on an island in the River Loire. The shine, unfortunately, had been taken off our expectations of a special time together, because as the afternoon developed it was soon apparent that we were both feeling somewhat under the weather and were coming down with colds. 'The best laid plans of mice and men often go awry' etc. I am not sure whether that consideration discoloured my view of the landscape, but the last leg was ridden along the bank of the River Loire which I expected, based on its reputation, to be particularly attractive, wasn't. Nevertheless, we arrived in

Saumur in good time and stashed the motorcycle in the hotel's underground car park.

If there is a chance for a secure undercover car park in an urban area (especially with CCTV) I would always elect to take it, for obvious reasons, and because that means we would not have to detach the hard luggage to lug it into the hotel. We must always be mindful, furthermore, that our transport can be physically lifted off the ground by the number of big, bold men it takes for the task, loaded into a van and be gone in moments.

I was once present when that happened from a motorcycle dealership forecourt in broad daylight, so it's not an alarmist's flight of fancy. In fact, I once returned to my own bike (a stripped-down 750c.c four cylinder number, so a comparative light-weight) in a car park to find a white van next to it and by its open rear doors a man holding a substantial, metal single-wheel ramp in his hands. Apparently, the only reason he had for being there was to enquire after the state of my health when I eventually returned, which was jolly nice of him considering that up to that moment we had never before set eyes upon one another. Why he held the ramp I cannot imagine—some manner of family totem, possibly.

Our room at this hotel was comfortable, though its most outstanding feature was its enormous picture window which overlooked the river and the old town beyond, dominated by the impressive Château de Saumur. We did not really make the best use of our time in Saumur, electing instead to recuperate in our room for a time.

As I emphasised at the beginning of this book, we came on this journey primarily to ride. If one composes the journey to include more sight-seeing then it will inevitably be less of a ride. So, we find it best to stick to the plan. That having been said, if this was not a ride, if we had more time, if were not feeling unwell and possibly, it was not our wedding anniversary, there was much to keep us entertained in Saumur. The town is a military one with an emphasis on the *arme blanche* and contains a large museum covering the history of the French cavalry and another featuring tanks and other armoured vehicles. It is also the home of the performances of the riders and horses of the 'Cadre Noir', which is a spectacular display of equitation.

So, determined to make the best of our day, in the later afternoon we made ourselves presentable and strolled across the bridge for an evening in the old town which was, it seemed to us, peculiarly, for a town in the middle of France, quite Belgic in character. Pavement *cafés* and restaurants offered, '*moules et frites*' and numerous bars, frequented by a lively looking young clientele, served Trappist beers in their multifarious varieties which, need it be said, we sampled with as much enthusiasm as we could muster given our physical conditions. One of them tasted of forest fruits (a quite traditional recipe, apparently) which was better than it sounded it might be—not least because it had a respectable alcoholic kick and we could actually taste it despite our fur-covered tongues.

The truth was we were progressively only going through the motions. We ordered dinner at a recommended restaurant, which was either quite average after all or innocently suffered as a consequence of our virus. In any event, we discussed our respective meals and agreed that whilst they both were well presented and had interesting textures—expanded polystyrene, stuffed-toy filling, breakfast cereal box cardboard and so forth—they were, for both of us, more or less, devoid of any flavour. In the end we reluctantly decided to give the evening up as a failure and wandered, snuffling and coughing, back towards our hotel.

By this time it was dark, of course, but still quite warm and a few pedestrians were about as we approached the long bridge over the Loire (Pont Cessart) that led to the island upon which our hotel stood.

Little Gulls—they are small, but that is their proper name—then in winter plumage; pure white with a black cheek spot, occupied the skies over the river during the day, but roosted in large numbers, each one close by another, all along the balustrade of this bridge during the hours of darkness. The pavement of this bridge was, I suspect, a busy pedestrian thoroughfare throughout most of the night. Being wild things, as someone approached on foot, each gull took to the air over the river, looped briefly before flying to resume its place facing the water. As each bird took off, its nearest neighbour alighted behind it, so a fragmented, white, aerial Mexican wave perpetually rippled along the parapet and out into the night. Before long, and often no more than seconds between each disturbance, another walker would cross the bridge and so the whole performance was repeated all through the night and, presumably, every night.

There was a nightmarish quality to the way these dainty creatures constantly endured disturbance in their attempts to secure some rest. We are not especially informed birdwatchers, incidentally. It's all there to see though, as I have said, if you tune in to see it. As to Little Gulls—I checked their appearance. They may have been Bonaparte Gulls, if it makes a difference to anyone, but I don't think so.

We were more fortunate than those poor creatures as we collapsed into our bed, of course, though feeling quite sorry for ourselves, because to accompany our coughs and sneezes we were now feeling the effects of our days of continual riding. So lying down and getting up again was accompanied by groans of complaint as previously underworked muscles made their presence felt. I reassured Patsie by prophesying that all these aches and pains would become easier as the days progressed. Oracle that I am, that proved to be true, resolving themselves to an almost complete absence of discomfort beyond the end of our journey and about a week—possibly ten days or so—after we returned home to England.

Before sleep on this very special day (we were married in Hong Kong by the way; another story entirely, though not one that included a sea battle. We had dinner at a floating restaurant though, if that counts as coming close.) I hope I apologised to my wife for our predicament. I told her how much I loved her and she definitely told me (between a cough, sneeze or groan) that she loved me too, though possibly followed by an ironic single arched eyebrow, which would speak of much, but in the final analysis, mean practically nothing.

There definitely would have been no recriminations from the 'get on with it, girl'. I don't need memory to know that.

10. Fourth Gear:
In which we ride to between Rocamadour and another hard place

We slept well, but were predictably not on our top form the following morning when we climbed aboard the bike for the day's riding. Furthermore, this day was about to offer its share of challenges as a result of my poor destination planning. Patsie had suggested we take a rest day following this ride and that would have been in Souillac in the Lot, where we have a very good friend, a lady, who operates a small hotel there. That plan had become compromised by the disappointing news that our friend would not be at home during the time we would visit, so I booked us into another small hotel for a two-night stay in nearby and picturesque, Rocamadour.

We always knew that this day of riding was going to be a longer one than usual. However, we were now discovering it would be certain to take even longer than anticipated, because that phenomenon had applied to every daily journey thus far. I knew I could have solved the problem, on this particular occasion, by joining the Paris-Toulouse motorway as soon as possible, but—as I have already pointed out—Patsie does not like riding multi-lane motorways, if they can be avoided.

I understand that preference perfectly, because they lack the variety of interesting scenery and enjoyment, especially from a pillion rider's perspective, since upon them one's choices are far from one's own. It is essential to be more than usually on the *Qui Vive* as regards fast moving, instantly appearing vehicles, driven by occasionally bullying drivers and especially for long 'high-siders', the draught of which can suck the bike into their flanks if they are too close.

So, the riding can be stressful. I try to keep ahead, not overtake until I can see nothing at all behind us in the mirrors and when I overtake, take two consecutive over the shoulder 'look-sees', stay wide of other vehicles and go like blazes to be within a manoeuvre for the least time, pulling in afterwards only when there is a very good gap behind us. That may not be the best methodology, but I have seen many worse. We can cope with all those situations, of course, but would prefer not to do so, if possible. I suppose the fact is that if our objective was to get from point A to point B in the shortest and most comfortable time, we would not be riding a motorcycle at all.

So, we set out on a diagonal course across country as we had planned, but having ridden a short distance, stopped at a small supermarket where Patsie purchased the necessary provisions for a picnic lunch, which we could eat comparatively quickly, wherever we found a convenient spot. She returned with the food in a fabric 'tote' bag which had an image of that most iconic of motion picture motorcyclists printed upon it and which we somehow managed to lose at some point.

The good news was that the weather was becoming increasingly warmer to the degree that, at speed, the air we breathed in through our snoods made our noses drier and breathing easier. Lunch time had come around when we noticed a large grassed area planted with young trees under which tables and benches were scattered. So, I pulled in and we dismounted, lodging our ride next to the only other motorcycle present, which was another sports-tourer, a comfortable looking Japanese 1300 c.c number, only to discover, on closer examination, that every table on the site was already occupied by diners.

We stood for moment forlornly with our lunch in our hands, but soon spied a man and woman dressed in motorcycling gear, busily clearing space around their table and benches, whilst energetically waving at us to join them. Of course, they did, bless them always—one could have put money on it. Our picnic partners transpired to be a mature, French motorcycle policeman and his wife from Lorient, who were returning home after a biking tour of Corsica.

Our French was rudimentary and their English was to about the same standard, so naturally, we got along together famously, because we shared closer bonds than language. Our new companions extolled the virtues of their bike and riding the *Haute et Basse Corse* and we listened to them. Actually, though they will probably never know it, we did more than listen, because eventually we owned that very same model (blue, the same colourway as their bike, now I think on it) and toured Corsica and Sardinia, though we were riding 'Madam' again for that trip. We also spoke of motorcycle engineering and if he realised, I was in good measure out of my depth on that subject, he was polite enough never to reveal that he knew.

Actually, this interlude featured its share of mirth, because the trees under which we were sitting, were Horse Chestnuts and it was the season of the dropping 'conkers'. It was hilarious to attempt dodging them, have them bouncing off one's head or notably sploshing into a full coffee cup. Simple pleasures. Good comradeship and kindness are priceless. I do not claim these qualities are only possessed by motorcyclists, but they are typical of motorcyclists.

Lunch over, we said our goodbyes and *bonne routes* to our French friends and pressed onwards. By 4.30 in the afternoon, we had arrived in the region of Limoges and it was by that time absolutely clear that, if we stuck to ordinary roads, it would be after dark—even if all went well—before we arrived in Rocamadour. In fact, we knew that the motorway passed very close to both our current location and our destination and so, if we took to it, a deliberate hour and a half ride at most would deliver us to our hotel. We discussed the matter briefly. So, the decision made, we dropped into the outskirts of Limoges for a fuel refill because 'Madam' needed a drink if we were moving non-stop and fast, because she is then at her thirstiest. The weather had turned from warm to hot and at this, the hottest part of the day, we were sweltering.

I had no idea where we would find a filling station, so when we stopped at a traffic light and a sports bike rider pulled up beside us, I attracted his attention and made the universally understood filler-pump nozzle sign at our tank. The rider gave me a short nod down (OK) and another to the right (follow me) and when he took off, I tucked in behind him. A few turns later he rode into a filling station, waved a gloved hand and was gone. As I have said before and will re-emphasise evermore—priceless and not a word spoken.

★★★★★★★★★★★★★★★★★

For the second time that day, French motorcyclists had come through for us in the time-honoured fashion. Mind you, much the same can be said for the bikers from many of the European countries in our experience and I could, by the time of writing this, present an enormous list of favours and considerations—both large and small—that have come our way that reveal what fine folk they are. Apart from that foot wiggling thing. I am sorry, but I just can't get my head around that.

The first time I saw the foot wiggling, I thought the passing rider simply had circulation problems. It was only when I saw it more frequently that I realised what it was. In fact, though I did eventually realise it was communication, I wasn't that certain, initially, that it was well meant. The Brit curt, sideways nod, (an invisible wink, if you like), by contrast suggests, 'I know that you share our mysteries, for we are tribe'. There is nothing audible, of course, passing between us, though I assume, if there was, we would be mumbling, 'Alright, mate', (not especially profound, I know, but that is what it would be) whereas the wigglers would, it seems to me, be making some kind of exuberant sound effect, because foot wiggling surely doesn't really segue with, 'Alright, mate' in any language.

I declare myself truly ignorant about what habitually goes on between passing motorcycle riders on other continents. My heart, however, is both open and hopeful on that subject. So were I ever to be on the receiving end of whatever it is, I would respond with a well-intentioned acknowledgement—as I do, indeed, to the foot wigglers. My own foot, nevertheless, will always remain on the peg.

Before we leave this general subject altogether, we can do no less than disclose Patsie's distinctive take on the business of motorcycling nodding and waving. As a pillion passenger, it's fair to say, she was always aware of the rider's nod/wink. It was, however, a revelation when another pillion rider specifically waved to her. People were actually prepared to wave to her—a pillion rider—in a spirit of friendship? Really? That was all she needed to know. The genie was out of the bottle, never to be returned.

Did she wave back? She did. Did she wave first? She did. She waved to those sitting on pillion seats. She waved to riders. She waved to people riding scooters, people riding bicycles, people riding tricycles and whatever they are that have two little wheels at the front. She waved to small children riding anything on the pavement, even if it was pink, plastic and fitted with stabilisers. She waved to despatch couriers, pizza deliverers, motorcycle cops and post-persons on mopeds. She waved to girls riding ponies and jockeys exercising thoroughbreds. She waved to anyone on top of a donkey. She waved at everyone leading a donkey. She waved to those who had 'L' (Learner) plates affixed to their bikes ('because it's encouraging for them'). She waved to people who, because of their sub-cultures, usually only waved to each other and she waved to miserabilists who never waved to anyone at all. I would like to claim Patsie drew the line at waving to pedestrians, but if they showed any interest in us, especially if there were pointing small children present—well—I would be misleading the reader.

Patsie was goodwill on two wheels. If anyone's day could be improved by a wave, then Patsie was very happy to oblige with one. I tried to imagine something outrageous to claim that Patsie would wave to and the first thing to come to my mind was a column of marching nuns, but that won't work, because she definitely would wave to one of those and, odds on, they would all enthusiastically wave back in unison whilst gleefully singing that song for which nuns are famous. If we came across a black coach driven by a headless coachman and pulled by four headless black horses, Patsie would send forth a wave and if the bleached, forlorn face of an irredeemably damned passenger appeared at the coach window as it went by us, she would wave to him too—you know, 'to perk him up a little, because perdition might not be that bad after all'.

I did once attempt to explain to her that when it came to waving there were certain protocols to be observed; the included and the excluded, rights of passage, honours to be earned and so forth, but she looked at me as though I was a miserable, soul-less, bottom-feeder who would begrudge a fellow traveller on the hard, 'Wheel of Life' so meagre a consideration as a wave. She was, as I should have known before I uttered a syllable, never going to buy into the nuances of the ritual. So, I gave up on the subject as far as she was concerned in short order.

If you, reader, find folks waving to you as you ride by and you have no idea why—don't dwell upon whether their gestures were appropriate. They are after all, irrespective of any other consideration, just other travellers on the 'Wheel'. So why not give them the nod, (observing every safety consideration, of course) because—as usual and I have given this some thought—Patsie has the right of it. That doesn't mean I am going to be initiating any waving to all and sundry, let it be noted, but she is right.

Patsie also incidentally, quite rightly, keeps her feet on the pegs, where they should be and no wiggling.

★★★★★★★★★★★★★★★★

We re-fuelled hurriedly, pulled over to the filling station's grass surround, opened our panniers, peeled off anything that was thick or heavy and—not before time—changed into our light, warm-weather gear. Exclamations of relief and gratitude rose towards the heavens.

Temperatures had reached a point where one could feel one's head baking inside the helmet, but until we were on the move there was nothing to be done about that. So, we got underway again and I took the nearest slip-road onto the southbound motorway, released the clasp from 'Madam's' collar and away she went (as they say around our parts), 'like a long dog': A Greyhound or possibly a coursing lurcher to make sense of it, not a

Dachshund, presumably.

It wasn't as though we had committed to a full day of motorway riding. We had an objective in mind and a short time frame in which to accomplish it. Patsie knew she must endure higher speeds for a short while and did her job whilst I, perhaps a little guiltily, was doing mine and enjoying myself. The speeds we were travelling and the change of clothing not only cooled us, but definitely lifted our morale, because the end of the day in the saddle was within our grasp. Nevertheless, by the time we rode into Rocamadour we knew and felt we had done enough riding for one day.

We were, yet again, in luck with our choice of hotel (*'No John, what we are is astute'*, as my wife would almost invariably correct me. Well, we *are* astute sometimes, but lucky with it.). This was a small modern, clean, informal place run by a friendly young couple who had returned to their home region having learned their trade in Paris. Our host was strolling around in a rugby shirt and shorts having promised himself he would not again wear a suit, shirt and tie for work.

He had been a biker and ushered us into a secure bike-sized parking place within the hotel compound that he used himself. His next comment, having given us a quick appraisal, was that he thought we were about ready for some ice cold beers. So, realising we were exhausted, he thoughtfully brought them up to our room which featured a vine covered pergola over a spacious private terrace. We were liking him more with every passing minute. After draining two bottles of beer each without much ceremony, we began to really wilt. It had been a long, tough, hot day on the road, so we surrendered to our fatigue, passed on dinner and went to bed early where we 'went out' like someone had flipped a switch.

Rocamadour is another one of the iconic sites of France. It is situated in a gorge through which runs the River Alzou, but what makes it noteworthy to the eye is that its principal buildings do not only crown the cliff top, but adhere in steps to the cliff-face on their way down to the quaint old village below. It is a place (named for St. Amadour, a Christian hermit whose tomb it contains—hence Rock of Amadour) steeped in history particularly from the early 12th century as a religious location and place of pilgrimage with links to the Knights Templar. Wedged into the cliff is said to be a fragment of the sword, 'Durendal' formerly belonging the hero, Roland about whom we shall hear more later in this tale. These days of course, Rocamadour is a tourist attraction though surprisingly unspoilt, so well worth visiting, though we wouldn't need parachutes to get into it this time, which was something of a relief.

We then had a full day at leisure so we decided to discard our motorcycling clothes, remove all the luggage including the tank bag and take a short ride into Souillac, which sits alongside the River Dordogne, and have lunch at one of our favourite restaurants in the town. There is a municipal car park directly behind this place. We would need to leave the bike unattended, so I put the wheel-lock and the florescent yellow spiral-reminder wire (which connects to the brake lever) in my pocket and off we went, burdened only by our crash helmets. The weather was glorious, the short ride had been enjoyable, free of all our habitual excess weight, we were feeling quite over our colds and the lunch had been up to its usual high standard. Life was looking pretty good, so it couldn't possibly last.

We wandered out to the bike after that lunch in good spirits and climbed aboard. I put her into gear, let out the clutch and then I have to report that no one who has not actually experienced 'instantaneous' has any idea what it really feels like. I fancy I heard a '*Chuck!*' sound, but then (and this is going to take far longer to recount than the time of the actual event) I was on the ground, an intimate view of asphalt on the other side of my visor, with the bike partially on top of me, trapping one of my legs, which hurt. I was, in fact virtually sitting on the bike in the usual vertical position, except now both bike and rider were horizontal. I turned my head to see Patsie, who of course, was also down, but since she had been sitting on the narrow part of the bike and as the side luggage was off, had fallen clear and rolled away.

I had, obviously, fitted—but forgotten—the wheel-lock which had hit the front fork, the moment we moved forward, as it is intended to do. Where then was the lock-fitted, fluorescent yellow alert wire? Stolen by some unknown spiteful miscreant intent on bringing about our ruin? Was it rather removed by some dastardly foreign agent of the Anti-British Motorcyclist League? No, it was in my pocket, that's where, because I had neglected to attach it before we left the bike.

I am prepared to say nothing that might ameliorate my actions. Absolutely nothing. I had never made this error before or since (for this was my 'fire burns, don't you know' moment) if it makes any difference and it doesn't, because I had been riding for a long time and absolutely should not have made that rookie error. What would 'The Motorcycling Sadhu' have said? He would shake his head slowly and philosophically whisper to himself, 'Wasn't the first—won't be the last'. That is not supposition on my part incidentally, because I have heard him say those words exactly after a similar incident involving another rider we both witnessed.

My trapped leg was, in one sense thankfully, keeping the bike off the ground and the same could be said for my fore-arm and shoulder. Events at this point over took us. Before I could say or do anything more, we were surrounded by a bustling trio of concerned, diminutive French ladies who first lifted Patsie to her feet, examined her thoroughly and dusted her down. Then —and I can barely credit this part even now—the three of them, (fairy godmothers possibly?), effortlessly hoisted 'Madam' upright onto her wheels, as though she weighed no more than a double feather duvet.

Thankfully, Patsie, though shaken, had only one small scratch on her forearm and a couple of pains that threatened to come out as bruises. My leg was bleeding a bit, having a shallow five-inch groove cut into my calf, though strangely, without tearing the fabric of my trousers, though they were not my habitually worn when riding, strong motorcycle jeans. We were both wearing gloves. Whilst I try not to include the word, 'insist' in any subject when dealing with Patsie, always wearing gloves on the bike is an exception. Everyone puts their hands down in a fall. I didn't on this occasion, but usually everyone does.

Approaching danger, unfortunately, does not come with a warning musical accompaniment, as the infamous fictional shark does. How useful that would be. All is well and then, usually at one's least guarded, it bites. I don't remember Patsie speaking much in these brief moments, though I recall repeatedly thanking and apologising to the three French ladies in English for some reason. I don't think they understood a word I gabbled, though they probably understood the sentiment of what I was saying well enough. From the way they cast their eyes empathetically in my wife's direction, I am fairly sure that nothing I could say or do was going to impress them and I don't blame them.

Insensitive though it may seem, my next task was to check poor 'Madam', because even a minor breakage would seriously put a 'spanner in the works' of our schedule and I had, in the past, seen compromising damage caused to other bikes that had merely toppled over from standing. She had, it transpired and to my relief, nothing more than a minimal scuff on her paintwork. The intercession of my body—which is not slight—had prevented an impact with the ground, and the miracle of the three ladies meant I was not forced to crawl from underneath the bike allowing it to crunch that problematic small distance to *terra very firma*, which was a mercy. I wasn't particularly happy about her little graze, if truth be told, and felt awful having dropped 'Madam' so ignominiously, (actually, I didn't drop her in reality, because I still had my hands on the grips when my shoulder hit the ground!) but everything could have easily been very much worse.

A car park wasn't the place for Patsie and I to review all of this drama, particularly since my leg needed some attention, so having removed the wheel-lock (of course), we rode back to our hotel at Rocamadour. Our hosts were initially alarmed when we walked through the door—one of us with a bloody leg—and offered us bandages and the like, but Patsie attended to me well enough from our own first aid kit. We did accept their kind offer of clothes washing facilities, which was useful given our limited wardrobe.

The time came for my reckoning with Patsie and I promised

her I would never make the same mistake again. I was genuinely upset at having put her at risk through carelessness; an abdication of my responsibilities to her. Patsie didn't give me the lecture or the dressing down I expected or deserved. She told me quite sternly, however, that she, henceforth, fully intended to personally ensure that this mistake was not repeated, then generously suggested that the accident had only occurred because I was very tired and had been ill. That was very kind of her, but had I believed that was the case, I should not have been riding a motorcycle, especially with her on board. *Mea Culpa,* an idiot acting like an idiot and that was all there was to it. On balance, of the three of us, I was the one who had fared worst in the incident. So, some kind of universal justice had prevailed.

So, October 1st memorably drew to a close. That warm evening, we were more inclined to have a good dinner than we had been in Saumur. So we wandered out in the evening and decided to eat on the terrace of a restaurant at L'Hospitalet, which was a short stroll away from our hotel (thankfully, so far as my leg was concerned, though I thought it politic to say nothing to my date for the evening on that subject), on the cliff top overlooking the village of Rocamadour below. We picked out a table that would enable us so to see the lights of the place coming on in the gathering dusk and finish our meal in darkness.

This view of Rocamadour, from the top, is the most impressive one, I think. It resembles, as detail is incrementally enveloped in shadow, an enormous presbytery candle set upon the edge of a chest. The wax, repeatedly melted by the candle's flame, has run copiously down to cover the chest's face to pool outwards at its foot. In the colours of twilight and at night the scene is a beautiful and romantic one, sparkling with pin-point lights and floodlit features—a faerie realm brought to life in our world. So not an indifferent location for a dinner with a special person, as one may imagine. I cannot remember what we ate, though if the meal featured *pate de foie gras* and glasses of Montbazillac (a pairing made in Heaven, which thousands of people certainly knew about before we were enlightened) I would not be surprised, because they are regionally typical.

Patsie and I are comparatively familiar with this part of France, so I could spend several paragraphs describing its countryside and notable sites including dwellings of prehistoric mankind which feature some of the most notable cave paintings discovered in Europe. However, it occurs to me that there is nothing I can relate in that regard that anyone could not find in a guide-book. Apart from all of that, it is incredibly beautiful countryside and well worth visiting.

One local place, quite rarely visited so far as I can tell compared to other attractions, resonates with us particularly. That is the village of Labastide-Murat. Once called Labastide-Fortuniere, it changed its name because it was the birthplace in 1767, of Joachim Murat, whose father ran and owned the local inn. Murat, grew to maturity in the time of revolution, becoming the flamboyant and fearless leader of his nation's cavalry during the Napoleonic Wars. Eventually, he became a general, a marshal, a duke, married Napoleon's sister, Caroline, a prince and finally, King of Naples—a throne given to him by the emperor because he needed his unexceptional brother, Joseph—who also had no legitimate claim to it—to park himself on the throne of Spain.

His father's inn has been preserved and one could visit it accompanied by a custodian. Within there was an exhibit of Murat's incredible life, including a large glass cabinet which contained an excellent reproduction of one of Murat's uniforms. I was surprised to see it there, because I recognised it instantly. I had seen it before, many years previously, as a young man, worn by an English Napoleonic period re-enactor, as we both stood among numbers of his group, who were dressed as the emperor's blue-coated, infantry soldiers, in a Yorkshire field. We had a short conversation and, with his permission, I took several photographs of him. The cabinet held a similar photograph of him to those I took, so there could be no mistake. He had, presumably, donated his creation to its most appropriate spiritual home. It really can be a small world.

The actual Murat, a courageous chancer on a grand scale, having turned against Napoleon after his brother-in-law's defeat at Leipzig in 1813, then foolishly declared war on Austria, was in his turn defeated and ended his days, shot to death in 1815 by a firing squad comprised of his former Neapolitan subjects. The man—pot boy to king—was undeniably short on wisdom, but had what it took to live his life with the throttle permanently wide open, one has to give him that.

My other notable memory of Labastide-Murat comes from a lively debate I had with a Frenchman in a bar there. This discussion must have turned to the Napoleonic Wars, because this man said, 'You English have nothing to brag about, because you burned this countryside to the ground, destroying villages and killed hundreds of ordinary people'. He had me on the back foot there, because I knew that Wellington's army was under iron discipline after Napoleon's abdication. Furthermore, I couldn't square that accusation with anything that might have happened in the First or Second World Wars in that region. So, I began to furiously think backwards, until I could discover what on earth he could be talking about. When I eventually arrived in the 14th century, I realised he meant the medieval army of Edward, the Black Prince! Crecy, Poitiers and so forth. This Frenchman was right in his accusation, incidentally, on that basis. So, we Brits are still on the hook and unforgiven for that one, 600 years later, whether we knew it or not.

11. Still in Fourth Gear:
In which we head south towards the Pyrenees, like pilgrims do

So, this day was to be our seventh on the road, though it felt to us as though we had been travelling for considerably longer than that. Our own time doesn't move along the steady and consistent course of a clock and calendar, but is entirely subject to perception. That is why the summers of childhood seemed interminable, whereas in later life, six weeks slip past in an eyelid blink. Furthermore, variety absolutely is the 'spice of life' and, indeed, 'travel broadens the mind'. For longer life from one's own perspective, if we can—do more and be more diverse in what we do, because perpetual routine will drain life away like water going down a pipe. On our death beds I suspect few of us will bring to mind that really excellent refrigerator we once saved for, at the expense of financing new experiences.

★★★★★★★★★★★★★★★★★

I am reminded of a story told to me in India by my Rajput friend in Gwalior. He may have undertaken some moustache twirling as a preliminary, I expect, but I shall leave that to the imagination. The tale he told me one evening was this: There was a very devout young man—let's name our fictitious character, Ajay, because its short. One night, in his dreams, a deity appeared to him and said, 'Ajay, you are living an exemplary life and I am well pleased, so I have decided to reward you with everything you desire.'

Whilst initially flabbergasted, in his dream Ajay eventually had enough presence of mind to reply, 'Lord, I ask for a long and healthy life for myself and my future wife who will be beautiful, as will be the three wonderful children she will give me. I also wish for a good, reliable profession with an uninterrupted stream of dependable clients, a fine house, abundant prosperity and to be free from all earthly concerns'.

'Granted', said the deity and Ajay awoke. All those things came to pass, though by what agency, including Ajay's own inspired choices and motivated hard work, we may never truly know. Eventually, however, after very many years had elapsed, in another dream, the deity once more appeared and said, 'Ajay, now your span has almost ended. It is soon time to go, so prepare yourself'.

'Wait!' exclaimed an alarmed, Ajay, 'I'm not ready to die—it's not fair!'

'Not fair,' queried the perplexed deity in his dream, 'how can you say that, have I not given you everything you wanted?'

'That is true, Lord,' replied Ajay, 'but apart from all that stuff, when do I get my actual life?'

You can think about this for a bit, before moving on, if you like, though I am of the conviction, as I have said before, that there is no adventure if nothing ever goes wrong. As a matter of fact, I may as well confess I quite like it when things go a bit wonky, because then one can play with the new options. Every life step, is surely essentially a step in the dark and no one can do anything about that, so it is pointless to be anxious about it.

However, in my opinion, having acknowledged that reality, the second step is to learn not to care and the third is to try to enjoy it. Needless to say, one needs the potential and ability for manoeuvre to make this navigation workable. It's perfectly useless as a methodology if a grand piano unexpectedly lands on top of you from a great height, though of course, part of the game is to attempt to ensure that doesn't happen.

★★★★★★★★★★★★★★★★

This was to be another diagonal course headed towards the south-west so we could align ourselves with our route to cross the Pyrenees mountain range which divides France and Spain in a narrow neck of land of about 300 miles between the Atlantic Ocean to the Mediterranean Sea. One has the option to use a tunnel through the mountains for the most efficient passage, but we were here for the experience of the ride, so following advice from a friend of ours, the late, Ian Robertson who was both an historian of the Iberian Peninsula and at one time, author of a renowned and well-regarded guide book to Spain, we were going over the top using the Pass of Roncesvalles. All of that was later. First, we had to ride to a point from where we could then tackle the mountains, within a single ride, and be ensconced in a night stop within Spain at its conclusion.

We had not ridden over the Pyrenees before, so were not sure what lay ahead of us particularly with regard to the foothills of the mountain range on the French side. I had driven a commercial vehicle over the col, because a tunnel was closed (and shudder at the memory), but not by this route. If these mountains were to prove challenging, I did not want to find myself riding over and through them at the close of the day, particularly, as was likely, if my journey timing was once more awry. So, our destination was to be Saint Cricq Chalosse near the town of Amou in the Landes department of Nouvelle-Aquitaine.

Our ride was supposed to take about four and a half hours, so we could reckon, if matters ran true to form it would be at least an hour longer. Nevertheless, this was not going to be a particularly taxing day, if all went well, since its principal purpose was to position us for the day following. Although we had travelled around the Lot, we had never taken the road from Rocamadour which was now indicated by our Sat Nav.

That first section proved to be incredibly beautiful with narrow roads, falling and rising, passing fern covered crags or through tunnels of densely packed oak trees which typify this region of France. The road was moderately rising, twisting and demanding with focussed riding required constantly and no possibility for speeds in excess of 40 mph and most often considerably less than that. The day was bright and the riding, though slow, was fabulous in every respect for both of us. I cannot claim, in all honesty, that 'Madam' liked chugging along at urban speeds for a long period of time, but there was nothing for it and she had to do as she was told.

Most British riders familiar with 'twisties' are aware of the riding style often known as, 'crown of the road/cutting daisies'. For the uninitiated, it means the rider can see farthest around approaching bends by appropriate positioning, including the safest lean, dependent on whether the bends are left or right handers. I hesitate to attribute national characteristics to everyone, since there are good and bad riders and drivers everywhere. Nevertheless, I have noticed a more than usual propensity for several distinct driving behaviours, detrimental to motorcyclists, in different countries.

So, I will simply say that in rural France I found it prudent to keep my speed cautiously down, tuck in, be very alert and principally 'cut daisies'. Regrettably, it often did not seem to matter how small the oncoming car was (and it usually was small), its driver perpetually found it impossible to moderate its speed, so that on bends it remained on its own side of the centre line. No one, who has the right to be riding or driving, should need me to explain the consequences of a head-on collision. Still, this paragraph would be pointless if some people didn't need enlightening, so I shall elaborate. Everyone involved can die horribly. That having been said, how many times have I ridden behind riders—silver-haired ones too—in my own country who were prone to riding the crown and then leaning *into* oncoming traffic space? I am aware that there are creatures which can re-grow lost parts of themselves, but so far as I know, all of them are in trouble if that lost part is a head.

We stopped for coffee at a log cabin kiosk, beside a charming lake beyond Gourmand before riding on through the pleasant, if undemanding landscapes of Gascony.

Since we were cruising along easily, this might be time to mention a couple of motorcycling practicalities. Do not feel the necessity to learn lessons from me, I am simply explaining what I did then and sometimes later with my tank bag that worked for us. On the clear window on its top was a map folded to show the route of the day, so I could double check against the

Sat Nav or get a wider view easily. A map is essential, of course, if for whatever reason one no longer has a functioning GPS device. The bag had side and front pockets on the outside and net pockets on the inside. In the front pocket (though not on this trip) we carried a compact battery charger and a set of different charging connectors. So, if our Sat Nav died, I connected this for a power substitute. Actually, at this point in this journey I was charging off the bike battery, but we will return to that subject later on. Still, these small chargers are invaluable in my opinion.

The bag contained a mini-laptop PC with a keyboard (preferable so far I am concerned to a pad and no comparison to a phone), the mobile phones, a small camera, one paper set of all bookings, tickets etc. in a waterproof plastic wallet, all copies of insurance, ownership, accident recovery service documents in a similar wallet, the passports in a sealed wallet, room to put the Sat Nav when we were away from the bike, room for my travel wallet (with neck cord) with some of the main cash, my credit cards etc, the wheel lock and its alert wire, a soft cloth and *chamoix,* some visor clearing fluid, a small first aid kit, a bottle and can opener, a plastic picnic cutlery set for two, spare fuses and bulbs, a breathalyser test kit, pens, notepad, a soft cap, a headscarf and a waterproof cover for the whole bag.

Essentially this bag, kept at hand always, contained anything we could not afford to lose, would not leave unattended, would need if we had an incident or were required to provide documentation on the spot for whomsoever in authority. If one is stopped by law enforcement, it's best to be efficient and not waste their time. I don't put my small water-bottle in this bag, because of all the things I do put in this bag. Patsie had the operating cash (including coins for tolls and incidentals) with her among other vital things, because she had two free hands.

On the route we were riding, there was the occasional road sign warning of the potential for comparatively large mammals to suddenly cross the road in one's path, but that didn't happen to us. I take those signs seriously. Some people don't and have paid for it. Once, at night in a sunken road a small herd of deer jumped from cover into my path and streamed out the other side. A fortunate escape. Nevertheless, *sans* collision with a wapiti or whatever it might be, we arrived at our hotel—predictably an hour later than I had originally planned. This hotel was configured quite unusually—comprising separate buildings set over a good sized plot of land operated by a personable young Dutch couple who, they told us, had decided to opt out of the rat-race for a better life, to raise their family in the rolling countryside of the Chalosse.

Their hotel was modern, clean and stylish with accommodation in cabins amid a landscaped garden filled with tall decorative grasses and bright flowers including a fine display of multi-coloured Cosmos which was still in bloom. Most usefully, the motorcycle could be parked right outside our door, which meant I could take off the luggage, carrying it into our room over the shortest possible distance and in least time. I had hoped that as I became used to the weight of our full panniers, the easier carrying them would become, but that was not, thus far, going to plan any better than most of my plans.

Our kindly host intuitively understood that ideally, we would prefer not to take the motorcycle out again for the evening, so he offered to drive us into Amou for dinner. Furthermore, having asked us what kind of meal we would prefer, he delivered us to a delightful, but very reasonably priced restaurant, where we sat comfortably outside in the warm evening under a pergola draped with vines. The meal was a simple, but very well prepared, regional menu of warm goat's cheese salad followed by sliced duck breast, fried potatoes and mushrooms, which we washed down with two bottles of an inexpensive, but eminently quaff-able local Landes *blanc*. It is usually worthwhile trying the local wine because often it is better, in shorter supply or both and sometimes cheaper, so never finds its way farther afield. Our hotelier had arranged with the restaurant proprietor to be notified when we had finished our meal and he collected us, returning us to our comfortable bed, grateful, replete, tired and slightly tipsy. Could one possibly ask for better hospitality?

I subsequently researched the wine of Landes, since we had enjoyed it so much and was surprised to read that, by some at least, it is not particularly highly regarded. We, admittedly no experts, enjoyed it, though it is possible that the taste of anything is substantially influenced by time, place and the company one is keeping. In fact, I now recall drinking a local beer with Patsie in the East African bush, at sunset whilst a herd of elephants progressed before us and thinking at the time, that it was the nectar of the gods. Sometime later I found the same brand in the UK, purchased several bottles, brought them home, chilled them thoroughly and we drank them together in our lounge, full of anticipation at reliving our safari experience. It was lager.

When we awoke the following morning we were greeted with yet another fine sunny day, though there had been a heavy fall of dew during the night which refreshed the countryside in colours and fragrances. It also left 'Madam' sparkling in a sequinned gown, which looked very nice, but necessitated some work with my chamois leather before we could leave. I looked forward to every day on the bike, but this day, I hoped, would be a particular highlight and I was really excited about it. Patsie, to be fair, doesn't really want her motorcycling to be exciting. She wants it to be interesting.

I recall on one of our longer trips we kept company for a time with another man and wife couple (hailing from one of the Balkan countries I believe, though cannot remember which one) who were also riding a sports tourer with an emphasis on the 'sports'. There came a point—and it wasn't on a motorway—when the rider suddenly opened his throttle and accelerated away at some considerable speed ahead of us. Of course, I don't know if the lady hanging on the back approved of that style of riding and it wasn't my business to make enquiries. Patsie, however, through our intercom, promptly made her own views on the subject known—as if I needed any clarification.

'I don't come away on the bike,' she huffed, as our companion's bike disappeared into the distance, 'to look at the world going by as a flipping blur. I want to have a look around and if you try any of that nonsense there will be trouble at t'Mill, I can tell you'.

She is a Northern lady, as I have mentioned, though so far as

I know has never set foot in an industrial mill in her life, far less organised a labour rebellion in one. Nevertheless, she is typically direct and so one is never left in much doubt for very long how she feels about things. Anyway, I try to do my best for her on balance—inadequate as that, demonstrably, can be.

At its most straightforward we intended to ride over the Pyrenees to stay the night in Olite, which was the medieval capital of Navarre, during the time when Spain was comprised of different kingdoms. Several of the north-western European countries may appear to meld into one another, but there can be few barriers (with the possible exception of a 20 something miles of cold sea water) between countries as significant as a shore to shore mountain range to guarantee that there will be huge differences of language, culture, history and food. The ride was less than 120 miles long, the Sat Nav system indicated it could be completed in just over three hours, but there was a mountain range to traverse in the middle which would be certain to contribute its own issues. So I was reckoning we would do well if we arrived in the late afternoon.

The ride began based upon a misapprehension regarding the location of St. Jean Pied de Port ('port' in this case meaning 'pass'), the last French town on this route. When I had examined the map, taking the mountain range as a broad swathe, it was clear the town was comparatively far across the width of the range in the direction of Spain and so I had it in my mind that it would be located in some high place. That being the case, before we arrived at St. Jean Pied de Port we would ride foothills, followed by steep climbs. That didn't happen and threw my thinking off balance. I later realised that this confusion in my expectations had, in measure, marred my full enjoyment and appreciation of the actual ride. Once again, a lesson as old as time: Take everything as it comes. If one cannot live in the moment on a motorcycle then when?

However, that was not my frame of mind, so I can only recount this journey as I perceived it. The first section was, of course, not dissimilar to the countryside that brought us to Amou. Gradually, however, it transformed to a gentle alpine landscape of rotund hills, through which the road rolled in a seamless stream of deep, easy curves which could be clearly seen stretching before us. I should have enjoyed that road in full measure, because it offered biker's joy, and would have done so, had my mind not been reaching for something more immediately dramatic.

Patsie, without any doubt whatever, would have said, *'That is just typical of you, John. You can't be content with anything—always going after the next thing and the next thing—whatever it is—before you have given us the opportunity to enjoy what we have'*. I know my faults, so have nothing to say in my own defence, other than this was coming from a woman who would begin building a nest at a bus stop. On balance, though, she had the right of it, notwithstanding she can rationalise making the same claim about something we have owned for a decade and more.

The route we were travelling had been used by those crossing the Pyrenees since anyone and probably anything crossed that mountain range. It is certainly a principal 'Camino' route which has been walked for a thousand years by Christian pilgrims bound for Santiago de Compostella (where the cathedral contains the shrine of the apostle, Saint James) on the north-western tip of the Iberian Peninsula. We would ride the 'Camino' routes regularly on this journey. Indeed, it is difficult not to do so in the hearts of France and Spain and the 'scallop shell' symbol can often be seen by the side of the road to assure wayfarers they are on the right path both literally and spiritually.

As one may imagine where the spirit moves, the profane is never far behind and, in common with all significant passes, this one has been a route for armies in both directions and conflicts have been fought upon and around it for aeons. We saw our share of pilgrims and the reader will meet them again in more detail later in this story. The armies had marched away, though—hopefully forever.

So, without going into too much detail on the subject, we were, nevertheless, passing through countryside over which was contested the closing struggles of the Peninsular War. I will give a little background to that conflict with as few words as I can manage. The French Revolution in the later 18th century facilitated the rise to power of Napoleon Bonaparte. He demonstrated genius as a soldier, rose to the rank of general, became the First Consul of his nation and by 1804 he had crowned himself Emperor of the First Empire of the French. The wars of revolution that made him evolved into his own imperial wars fought against the nations of Europe.

In 1807, Napoleon deposed the Spanish royal family, sent an invading army into Spain and placed his unexceptional brother, Joseph on the throne—renaming him King José, as if that was going to fool anybody. If the emperor was expecting this usurpation to be a push-over, he was soon to be disabused. By 1808 the invading French were facing armed opposition by Spanish, Portuguese and British forces. This was known as the Peninsular War, since it was fought primarily within the Iberian Peninsula.

Having fought the French armies of Napoleon throughout Spain, allied forces under the command of the Duke of Wellington pushed their stubbornly retiring enemy over the border back into their own motherland in 1813. There were battles fought at Orthez, just 16 miles from our starting point this day, and at Bayonne where the last deadly shots were fired, tragically after the war had concluded, which lay to the west of our course.

From my own perspective and notably, this was the first time, having read the history of that conflict, I had actually seen the infamous *gaves*. Accounts of the fighting from that period and place, make much of the difficulties posed by *gaves* for the advancing British Army and I could then see why that was so, because they are deeply cut, very steep sided, shallow gorges containing fast flowing white water. So, in offence and defence, in their way, they were as problematic or useful as the *bocage* of Normandy we had seen during the first days of our ride.

About mid-day we entered the outskirts of an attractive French town. I didn't know what it was called, having not as usual, spotted a name sign as we entered it, but we did soon notice a bar which was busy with a young clientele (always a good augury) eating and drinking coffee outside in the sunshine, so we stopped for a sandwich.

We were about to order when we noticed what this place

called a sandwich, because there was a young, local artisan about to assault, in our regional parlance, a 'chip butty', though his was simply huge, a baguette full to overflowing with *frites* and mayonnaise. We put his healthy appetite down to hard physical labour combined with clean mountain air, but didn't order one (far less one each) ourselves. I can't remember what we ordered, which suggests it wasn't noteworthy, so probably right for us.

However, the enormity of their 'butties' was not the most significant thing about that sandwich bar, so far as we were concerned. Printed on a paper napkin was an address in St. Jean Pied de Port, identical to the street name sign outside. We had already arrived in the last town in France and were unaware of it, which threw me completely. Actually, it more than threw me, because I was really disappointed, having been I felt, rather cheated out of the drama on the ride I imagined was my due.

We could see some unimposing, blue-grey, rising ground ahead, but if these were mountains they did not seem so grand and furthermore, if those were the mountains we were to cross, there remained—it seemed to us—a fair distance of comparatively level ground to traverse before we reached them. So, we began to suspect that crossing the Pyrenees by this route—given how deeply, according to the map, we were within the range—was going to be something of a non-event.

I need not have worried on that score. That we had not yet met a mountain did not mean we were not destined to meet a mountain-or two or three.

12. Several Low Gears:
In which we ride over the top, stop, and ride down the other side

According to the Sat Nav we had less than 75 miles to travel to reach Olite and it was not yet an hour after noon. So, on the face of it, we were on good form. Irrespective of what lay ahead we decided it was time we got on with it, so remounted and set-off. Before many minutes had elapsed, we were riding into and through the old town, over the bridge that traversed the River Nive and beyond an imposing citadel.

Any mountain pass worthy of the name is likely to have an elderly fortress at either end of it for obvious reasons. This one, in more or less its present form, was commissioned by Cardinal Richelieu during the 17th century and improved upon by Vauban, a master of fortification. It is an imposing, comparatively modern fort with walls thick rather than high, reflecting developments in artillery. So, it was potentially difficult to assault during the Peninsular War by armies under Wellington, which would have had to slog their way over the pass from Spain, presumably opposed by the French Army the whole way had they attempted it.

The duke certainly knew that potential well, which was one of the reasons he made his principal advance into France along the Atlantic coastal plain some 50 miles to the west instead. That route involved reducing the fortifications at San Sebastian by siege and storm, another inevitable bloodbath, but thereafter he could then readily receive reinforcements and supplies directly from the sea, courtesy of the Royal Navy. The French defenders of the pass, aware of developments on the coast, retreated for fear of being cut off, which would have been a certainty. So, the Citadel of Mendiguren (to give it its proper name) never had its mettle tested, time passed it by and it stands redundant as a barrier of war, draped in moss.

I was bound for another surprise before much time had passed. No sooner had we left the town than we saw signs for the Spanish border and the terrain became entirely different to everything we had hitherto experienced as the road began to climb. When we were scouting our route in St. Jean, we must have been looking the wrong way, though it was my impression we scanned across the general direction we would be heading. I knew demanding riding would begin on the mountain, but it came sooner than that and almost immediately. On this road, beyond St Jean, there is one French village, the following one being Spanish. In my brief notes I referred to 'the first village in Spain', but I have researched photographs of both of these villages recently and I cannot square my memory of what happened next with the appearance of either of them. Things change, of course, and the Spaniards are notably no slouches at repairing or building new roads, in my experience.

Certainly, we shortly entered a village where a stretch of road appeared to have either suffered from severe subsidence or was in the first stages of major roadworks. If the latter was the case, it seemed as though a berserk excavator with a mind of its own had run amok, because there were random holes of varying sizes—some a metre long—scooped out of its surface. This instantaneous development caused Patsie to receive a loud unappreciated expletive in her ear-piece from me. It might have been, 'Gosh' or possibly, 'Bother'—something along those lines, anyway.

A number of these craters were filled with dirty water and we had no idea how deep they were and only the potential for a disaster as a way of finding out. So, we had to proceed very gingerly (in my case whilst being told via my own ear-piece to moderate my language) as we weaved slowly towards what I hoped would be clear and open road.

'There is no point in swearing at holes in the road, John.' Patsie scolded. 'They can't hear you. Only I can hear you and I didn't put them there. Now be careful or you will have us off, *AGAIN*'. That last word was delivered with emphasis. My wife can be cutting when she puts her mind to it, reminding me that in her court of justice, that which has been forgiven can be unforgiven at discretion. Not that I needed reminding on that subject or, indeed, the necessity of avoiding water filled holes.

We had not long cleared this village's precincts when the road began to climb steeply, the wall of rock at our right shoulders. From that point we were engaged in serious riding that needed constant attention on throttle, gears and brakes, because mountain roads are rarely especially wide and never, in my experience, straight, but comprised of a series of bends, more than usually acute, divided by stretches of road in varying lengths, none of which are ever particularly long. So, as I remember the event, the experience was far more intense than its description can ever be, because it was a sequence of the same kind of speedily taken actions for me. A thrill though, need it be said. Patsie, of course, was sight-seeing. Well, she could.

Turn followed turn in quick succession which demanded absolute focus. When I could take my eye away from the business in hand for a split second, I could see, beyond the opposite asphalt rim and barrier that the ground dropped away immediately into a void. Far away across the chasm, on our left, rose steep cliffs of bare rock. In their clefts, and upon outcrops, pine trees grew singly and in small clusters until they coalesced into a fringe of conifer forest upon a high ridge, spiking darkest green against the sky.

So, what was the sensation? I can only speak for myself, as I was then. We were by no means the first or last motorcyclists to ride over the Pyrenees by this route, so I hesitate to make more of it than I should. I am not a brilliant rider and though this was not my first mountain, it was my first on two wheels and those wheels belonged to our sports-tourer with all I have explained about her burdens. All of those considerations make for a singular experience and perspective, inevitably. I suppose it felt something like a solo game of skill. Except death or serious injury (including for a non-participant) were possibilities which were not academic, because a great drop of indeterminate depth, to our immediate left, was ever present.

We accelerated, climbed, twisted and turned. I was tense. I was careful and steady away. This was not a time or place to make mistakes. This was not a place to push our luck or be reckless. I was excited with, by turns, a frisson of apprehension and then smiling and pleased with myself. I made a good turn—everything as it should be and then I made a poor one that needed some correction and so on. On balance, we were OK. WE were doing this. This was not so bad. I could handle this. I—let it be admitted—was having a good time.

We climbed higher and higher. Patsie's voice in my ear said, 'Can you see them?'

'I can't really see much of anything, love,' I replied, 'because I'm a bit busy and I dare not take my eyes off this road'.

'Two eagles', her voice came quite dreamily, 'two eagles not far away from us, gliding out there on the thermals'. There was a short pause then she whispered, 'I'm with the eagles'. I didn't see those eagles myself. Hers was a quite different experience, uniquely her own and she enjoyed it, which meant she felt secure with me at that moment, even riding up a mountain on a motorcycle. I felt pretty good about that at the time from a couple of perspectives and still do.

Eventually we reached the top of the pass at Ibaneta where the ground levels out and we could stop. So, we pulled over, climbed off the bike and we were together, both happy. There stands a chapel, a tall cross and a lone monolith. A small group of people were using a metal detector around its base, no doubt scratching around to see what they could turn up from a millennia and more of history, based on the near certainty that every traveller over the mountain would have paused at Ibaneta. Of course, there is a *mirador* (a viewing platform) so one can gaze back through the range towards France and I made a photograph of the magnificent panoramic view of ragged ridges folding into the distance which, unsurprisingly, looked totally unimpressive in two dimensions as these photographs of views invariably do. One has to be there—atmosphere and all—to appreciate the full effect.

For those riders who have never had the experience themselves, it may seem likely that 'down' a mountain road has the same attributes as 'up' a mountain road, except the other way around. That is not the case. The former is a matter of creating or moderating thrust to ensure one does not over-shoot a bend into oblivion, whereas the latter concerns the application of brakes and gear changes so one does not over-shoot a bend bringing about much the same outcome. Granted, the potential for personal oblivion is a common denominator but, that not insignificant consideration aside, they are quite different. On balance one feels slightly more in control when climbing, since if one does nothing at all, progress ceases, whereas a descent requires only wheels and gravity to do its work or, indeed, its worst.

Most of the motorcyclists I have met have given me the impression they were at least 'capable'. In fact most of them have given me the impression they were more capable than me! I am quite certain many of them were, but based on the balance of probabilities, many were not as capable as the impression it pleased them to present to others. I have made the acquaintance of a retired motorcycle racer possessed of more trophies with his name upon them than space to display them and, unprompted by me, in one of our conversations he offered the same opinion. So, I suspect I may be right on that subject. Mountains, if I may interject a word of council, are not the best places to concern oneself with that kind of posturing. So, the rider is best advised to square those undeniable realities with his or her own genuine abilities. For those who must carry fantasy or ego with them on a motorcycle, my recommendation is, at the very least, to lock them in a pannier until they arrive at somewhere clear and flat.

We rode down towards Roncesvalles, which had been the site of a battlefield on more than one occasion. The pass is sometimes known as the French, Ronceveaux, though the Spanish name is strictly speaking more accurate I imagine, because it is situated entirely within Spain. Though I don't want to be a history bore, it occurs to me that ancient passes in a landscape are not simply routes for walkers and riders, but also funnels and barriers that have influenced the fortunes of civilisations and empires. In 778 AD, Charlemagne, then King of the Franks and Lombards, made a campaign into the Iberian Peninsula through this pass. Among his array was the hero, Roland (remember his sword planted into the cliff at Rocamadour) who was with the rearguard of the army when it was attacked and he was among the many slain by Vasconian forces. The event, more or less, became the subject of a renowned poem, written in the 11th century, 'The Song of Roland'. Fear not, you won't be getting a verse from it. However, we may imagine doomed Roland, the sword 'Durendal' in one fist, blowing the great horn 'Oliphant' as the enemy host advanced upon him in a dark rain of arrows and, presumably, not a giant eagle or elf in sight to come to the rescue.

In 824 AD a joint army of Basques and Islamic Quasawis defeated a Carolingian host coming through the pass. Charlemagne was by that point Emperor of the Romans, but that didn't mean he could expand his influence southwards beyond the Pyrenees into Iberia as he pleased. The Basques went on to create the Kingdom of Pamplona and as a people retain a strong sense of identity, place and language to this day.

The Quasawi forces held the northern frontier territory of the Umayyad Emirate of Cordoba during the period when much of Spain was dominated by the Moors, who had themselves already failed to expand their power, in the opposite direction, into Western Europe, north of the Pyrenees. The invading Moors nearly reached Paris in 732 AD, before they were comprehensively defeated at Tours (just 130 miles away from Paris in a straight line) by Charles Martel—'The Hammer'. He didn't earn that sobriquet, one may depend, because he was keen on DIY in his spare time. Those 'Dark Ages' really were dark. We may contemplate how different the history of the world would have been had the Moors been victorious.

In more modern times there was another conflict that bore

far more closely on our experience of crossing the Pyrenees, so stay with me a while reader, if you will, because this absolutely bears directly on our ride. The site was also one of the later battles of the Peninsular War. The pass we had ridden was constantly in use by Napoleon's French armies entering and leaving Spain. In 1813, Marshal Soult had concentrated his force at St. Jean Pied de Port, then marched it in two huge columns over the pass, via Ibaneta, following the same route we had ridden, of course.

It took the French considerably longer than Patsie and I to cross the range, but at least they would have taken in more of the scenery than I had managed, since they walked it, if that was any consolation to them given they knew, that before long, there would be people shooting at them. I recall we rode by a small, ancient roadside stone chapel which would probably have been standing at the time of the battle. One could readily imagine the shades of soldiers dressed in blue or red, milling about it, sleeping, leaning and resting against its walls or lying wounded as the beast drawn wagon traffic of those old armies rumbled past.

When the collision of armies came it was a hard contested affair which ultimately favoured the French, though the tide of the war to the west along the Atlantic coastline, which went against them, as I have touched upon, meant Soult couldn't make the most of his advantage and was compelled to retire.

The point, however, as far as Patsie and I were concerned was that this battle was fought in summertime, in late July and yet thick mountain mists came down and closed visibility to less than 20 yards, so that the protagonists, though they could not see each other, could hear everything that the other side said and did. This situation, notably, was in marked contrast to the weather conditions we had experienced in the same area some three months later in the year, when anyone might expect the weather to be more severe.

I have explained that we were in contact with Ian Robertson, one of our finest historians of the Peninsular War, who had, for his own amusement, been tracking our progress from his home in Arles, where he lived with his wife, who was a Basque lady.

So, he knew the country we were travelling over intimately on several counts, including that he had personally walked over the notable terrain of the war. When next we communicated with him about our Trans-Pyrenees ride by email, he sent us, in return, a photograph of the pass as it had been just 24 hours before our own crossing, accompanied by the wry comment, 'I bet you are glad you did not have this!'

Our jaws dropped at the sight of this image. It showed the front of a car, a road sign (which we recognised as one we rode by ourselves) and, immediately beyond it, an opaque 'white out', like a curtain wall of wet, dirty cotton wool. Candidly, visibility did not seem anything so far as 20 yards. What would have happened if, before we had begun our climb, we had been faced with this? One could barely walk safely within it in a straight line it seemed to me, far less travel at any speed up a switchback road bordered by a death-drop. We could have waited for better conditions, but we would not have known at that point how long the weather would have taken to clear.

The Bielsa Trans-Pyrenees Tunnel was an option, but a minimum of three hours ride eastwards to the French entrance, so practically would have been out of the question as an immediate remedy. St. Jean de Luz on the Atlantic coast, close to Irun on the Spanish border, was just over an hour to the west, but directly away from our line of travel. In either case the delay caused would have meant the remainder of the journey would need to be re-planned, hotels cancelled and new ones booked.

What if we had decided to push on up the mountain and take our chances, given this was our first Pyrenees crossing and we would not have known what awaited us? What if we were at Ibaneta before a 'white out' closed in around us? That prospect, given there would be other vehicles moving in both directions, (some of them possibly bikes coming from Spain, the chasm on their immediate right) does not bear dwelling upon. I am certain, given modern technology, one can check conditions in the pass before entering it, but ours was a sunny day in St Jean Pied de Port and that thought never once crossed my mind.

I wonder what we would have done and honestly don't

know. My own, well known, obdurate impulses (let's not dignify them with a name more noble) might, unfettered, have put us on that mountain. I know, because I have set off for places in awful conditions in the past, just because I refused to be hindered, not because there were puppies in snow drifts to be rescued. Thank goodness, Patsie would have been with me to clarify our priorities—the first of which, whether she raised it or not, was her well-being. So by chance, or the guiding hands of our better angels, we undertook our Pyrenees crossing, for all its demands, at its most straightforward. Of course, for all I know, the pass may well be closed once really poor conditions have been confirmed.

So that was our Pyrenees experience. We were glad to have undertaken it, would not have missed it 'for quids' and speaking for myself would not baulk at doing it again—though I probably never will, because I've done it. Besides, before we concluded this journey we would experience mountain riding that would make traversing the Pyrenees appear like a stroll in the park by comparison.

The mountains receded behind us and we rode once again into a gentle alpine landscape. However, we had not travelled far before the Sat Nav indicated an unexpected sharp left turn on to a lesser road. This instruction initially surprised me, since I had a sense that Olite was an uncomplicated due south, but I took the turn anyway, because I knew we had not so far to go, time to spare and the route might transpire to be interesting. Before long we found ourselves on one of the most enchanting stretches of road of our entire journey and, furthermore, we were quite alone to enjoy it.

The road dropped down gradually until cliffs and interesting rock formations began to crowd in upon it. There were bends, but they were slow curves that we could enjoy with only a slight lean. I deliberately kept our speed down, so we could enjoy the sight and sound of a broad ambling, shallow river which tumbled and eddied over stones and around rocks upon our right.

We revelled in the sunshine that filtered through the canopy of the heavily leafed trees that grew down to the water's edge. Many of those trees retained their vibrant leaves of summer, whilst others had turned to the exceptionally bright colours of autumn including primrose and marigold yellows, oranges and rich rubine reds. Shafts of light illuminated banks of bright ferns which grew abundantly across the floor of this woodland. Occasionally the road crossed a small hump-backed bridge, which jumped the water, so we rode the right bank before another little bridge skipped us back once again to the left bank and so on. It was a delight to ride this valley (as near to a New England Fall as we could imagine, never having seen one) and share it with someone special who could appreciate the experience.

So magical was this place that I determined to remember its name, in case we were ever able to return to spend more time in the area. Signs naming the river appeared several times, so I repeated that word to myself so as not to forget it. I forgot it, of course, and it's not in my prompt notes either, which suggests I forgot it fairly quickly. I did remember it sounded to me as though it could be named after a South American Indian tribe. So I have checked the map in the area I know it must be and there I have found the Irati, which sounds about right. Photographs I have found of that river certainly reflect our experience, especially those taken in the Autumn season.

In that photograph search, incidentally, I also discovered the area was a favourite one for fly-fishing trout by the author, Ernest Hemingway. I cannot say I am very surprised. Man, place and activity—from what I have read of him—could barely have been a better fit and he spent some time in Pamplona, the inspiration for his novel, 'The Sun Also Rises' of course, which is not too far distant.

This diversion was an unexpected bonus for us, though it had used up some of our surplus time. So, having benefited from the obverse side of the coin of fortune, according to the great ledger of checks and balances, we were now due for some of the reverse side.

13. A Stall:
In which it all goes horribly wrong, but we get there in the end

I cannot say, in all candour, that I know very much about the planet's mountain ranges or how they variously affect the lands on either side of them as regards rainfall, other weathers, soil qualities and the like. I shall also shamelessly declare, since this a book principally concerned with riding a big black motorbike about Europe, that just now I am not going to bother to find out.

However, I can share my impressions, which are that the folks who live on one side of the mountains appear to reap the benefits, whilst those on the other side appear to have drawn the short straw. That may not be typical of all mountain ranges, but it certainly seemed that way to us, so far as the Pyrenees are concerned.

Once we had ridden beyond the rolling green foothills, we dropped into a hot, dry, dust blown terrain dotted with unattractive industrial plants. To give the Spanish their due, and as little as I know about the subject, they seemed to be making more of the land and conditions they had than their neighbours over the mountains were doing with theirs. The French appeared to be proprietors of a great deal of uncultivated lush meadowland, whereas the Spanish appeared to be industriously growing something on most of their dust and dirt. It's just an impression from the genuinely ignorant. I am, need it be said, even less of a farmer than I am a motorcyclist.

The afternoon was now becoming predictably hot and uncomfortable as the sun climbed towards its zenith. The good news was that we were now very close to our destination. Any reader might reasonably ask why I chose Olite as a place to visit when Pamplona was nearer to our road having crossed the mountains. The answer was that Pamplona is a much larger city—home of the famous Running of the Bulls—not that I expected to bump into that event, because they hold the festival in July. That said, it would be just our luck.

(Example: 'July, Senor? Si, normally this is so. This year, first time, we are having a very special October Running of the Bulls for just a few mas largo y mas agresivo toros. Did you not see the policemen, warning signs and barriers, Senor? No! Incredible! A pity then, by San Fermin, you were coming in the wrong direction, otherwise on the moto you would have certainly outrun them'. Mrs. Lewis? She is doing reasonably well in the circumstances, but no, unfortunately the senora does not want to see or speak to you.)

In fact, the reason we did not go to Pamplona for the night is because cities are too large for a single evening and so not worth tackling potentially problematic busy traffic. I wanted to be able to enter and leave our overnight accommodation easily on the following morning. Additionally, when I researched images of Olite, not so much farther on from Pamplona, though it is comparatively small, it is picture postcard attractive with historical buildings and towers; the epitome of fantastic Spanish grandeur. Besides, smaller notably always equates to easy—in and easy—out, does it not?

Admittedly, I was beginning to worry about Olite. I imagined I would be able to see an imposing skyline of medieval architecture in the distance, when in fact we were amidst a decidedly unpromising industrial landscape—not a crenellation or castle tower in view nor likelihood of one, notwithstanding there was only 5 (more or less) miles yet to ride.

What happened next may well have been my mistake. I didn't know the answer to that possibility at the time and I still don't know. It may have been that the Sat Nav was not up to date (though I had updated it before leaving the UK) or that it had over-heated and, in the colloquial parlance of our world, had 'thrown a wobbly'. Anyway, I discovered we were on a motorway heading in the wrong direction and worse than that, the nearest correcting turning point, was 15 miles away. So, another 30 miles had been added onto the day's riding, in the heat of the day, when we were so close to a shower and a cold beer that we could almost see it, including the runnels of ice water on the glass. Could matters become any worse? Well, of course they could.

When we came off the motorway at the indicated exit, the Sat Nav directed us to a roundabout. When we arrived at that roundabout the Sat Nav directed us to another roundabout which directed us to the first one again and so on and so forth with no obvious access to the motorway going in the other direction.

As one may imagine I dealt with being confounded when success was within my grasp and the prospect of being damned to a Faustian Hell, eternally riding the Worm Ouroboros, whilst my head boiled in a crash helmet, with the equanimity for which I believe I am justifiably renowned. Yet, quite inexplicably, my wife chose that very moment to decide she didn't want to speak with me anymore that day and possibly, as she thought more on the subject, ever again for as long as she lived.

I pulled over to a kerb after two or three attempts to escape 'the Worm' and stewed in my juices for a while, until I came to the conclusion that matters could not be worse if I switched off the electronic wonder and relied instead on my innate senses of direction and common. That worked, as it transpired (Let's face it, Marco Polo didn't have one and he reached China), though when I knew we were very close to Olite, I switched the Sat Nav back on again so we could find the street we were seeking. When the instrument came alive, it reported we were less than a mile away and yet before me there were still no Spanish castles or anything else that might suggest a medieval capital. All we could still see was more industrial park Spain.

It is possible, at that moment, I may have calmly uttered something only mildly vexed and yet Mrs. Lewis insisted I stop the bike, whereupon she climbed off, declared her intention to find our hotel on foot, then stomped off, still wearing her helmet, heading for who knows where, given we couldn't see the town, she had no idea where it was or where she was and, in any case, she didn't have an address for it. Admittedly, she did initially turn left (which was luckily the correct direction) when normally she automatically turns right on ground unfamiliar to her, so with that track record, one may imagine how this initiative of hers would eventually have played out.

I will understand if the reader is imagining, based upon these entirely unbiased revelations, that Patsie can be, for no particularly good reasons surely, very difficult to live with sometimes. However, whilst you may have every legitimate sympathy for me, in her defence I can reveal that many people—who admittedly don't know us intimately—comment to me how well Patsie and I operate together. I always reply, 'Yes, and do you know, we have never had an argument (at this point I pause for dramatic effect, so they can become all wide-eyed and gasp 'Really?') And then I say with emphasis, 'Today, though the sun has yet to set!'

On occasion, when this kind of thing has been said, in my stock response, if truth be told, I have not always been entirely candid about the 'today' part. The reader will, I trust, appreciate that this performance would not work quite so well if I had said, 'Well, it's funny you should say that, because we have had two spats already this morning'.

I wouldn't exchange her for any other woman on earth and not solely because no other woman on earth would tolerate me. I have never asked her whether she feels the same way. However, I did once ask her, in the event of my early death, if she would remarry and she replied aghast, 'Good grief, (with quite a horrified expression on her dear little face, actually) you don't think I would have anything to do with another man after all these years with you, do you?' So apparently, I have set the bar quite high on the husbanding front. I was flattered, of course, though genuinely didn't intend to frighten her.

I pulled up beside my own true love and though she refused

to engage in an actual dialogue with me, I eventually persuaded her that she was accomplishing nothing, but delaying us from any release from this e*n passe*, together or separately. So, she reluctantly climbed back on the bike again. I think it was the potential of imminent separation that swung it for her. How 'The Motorcycling Sadhu' would have handled all this I cannot say, other than better than I had, no doubt. Well, he wouldn't have got himself stuck on 'the Worm' in the first place.

Astonishingly, though now in accord with the Sat Nav, we were within a few hundred yards of its forecast destination when a medieval city wall materialised before us. It wasn't as high as I was expecting, since these days it wouldn't have kept out anyone assaulting it having climbed a domestic window cleaner's ladder, but there it was with its main gate wide open and access permitted for local traffic. So, we rode through it into the town and found ourselves transported to another, if diminutive, world and a veritable gem of a destination. My usual error: I had somewhere really medievally impressive in mind, like Carcassonne, which one can see for miles. Unfortunately, Patsie remained in no mood to be impressed or forgiving and would not have been either had I taken her into a combination of the Hanging Gardens of Babylon and the Lost City of Atlantis.

Our hotel was set into the ancient wall itself and promised to be delightful for anyone open to the concept of delight. One of us was. I come around fairly quickly from my moody outbursts, though I suppose that is understandable given I am usually the source of the problem, rather than a member of the unwilling audience. Would it assist any readers if I revealed that I had once contemplated titling this book, 'Crab and Fish ride a Motorbike'? It is the kind of declaration quite revealing to some people, I know.

We climbed off the bike in front of our hotel. Tired and harassed, I walked through the entrance door and found myself facing a flight of stairs leading to a first-floor reception. So straight away I saw how this ascent was going to be a constituent element of my penance, because all the luggage would need to hauled up it and then possibly up further flights to our room.

That would also have unavoidably been my burden, let it be noted, had I been blessed with the temperament of a saint.

I wearily climbed the stairs and was greeted by a bright, cheerful young man who spoke passable English and, furthermore, seemed genuinely pleased to see me, which was a nice beginning. I had pre-booked secure parking for 'Madam', so I asked him if he would assist me to bring the luggage up to reception, before I transferred 'her ladyship' to the hotel's private garage. Bless him, he not only insisted in carrying all the luggage up the main stair, but he also installed it in our room.

I know what the suspicious reader may be thinking. I told him some sob story about how we had been knocked off the bike in France by rampaging orcs, showed him my wounded leg and even flapped a fictitiously strained wrist at him, callously taking advantage of the fact he was young, fit and willing. Well, I didn't do or say any of those things. So there.

****

(Why write that John? I was there and you actually didn't say or do any of those things,' 'I know that and I have said so, haven't I?,' 'You may well have said nothing at all on the subject which amounts to the same thing,' 'I don't know sweetheart, you know what people can be like'. 'I know what you can be like, which is having a version of that ridiculous orc story up your sleeve in case you thought you might at some point need it. And don't call me sweetheart when you don't mean it,' 'I always mean it, my love', 'Huh, then you have a peculiar way of showing it')

****

I established Patsie in our room with her legs up, so she could ruminate upon how much time she was going to need before I could be forgiven and set off back to the bike, accompanied by the receptionist, so he could guide me to the place where 'Madam' would spend the night.

Our motorcycle, standing in the pedestrian precinct was now a quite different creature. Stripped of all the hard luggage, she was big, sleek and seductively menacing; every inch the two-wheeled panther. She took my new young friend's breath away, anyway. What follows, incidentally, corresponds to our conversation as closely as I can remember it. No disrespect is intended. We both had accents, which the reader must imagine. He wasn't from Northamptonshire which fashioned mine and we were speaking in a language which was not his native tongue. Had it been the other way about the interchange would have been monosyllabic, accompanied by hand signals. In Spain I was barely fluent in draught beer and toilets and could transpose those sometimes, alarming bar staff when I have also requested a *'tubo'* glass.

'This, *Senor,*' proclaimed the young man, nodding appreciatively to himself as he walked around 'her ladyship', 'is a very nice bike'.

People made this kind of remark around 'Madam' quite often and, if truth be told, I have never really been certain how to respond. I invariably felt a bit of a fool, shuffling my feet to thank them modestly for their accolades, as though I had designed and built her myself, rather than, as was the case, simply purchasing her and then consistently riding her less proficiently than she deserved.

'Well, thank you,' I replied modestly, shuffling my feet as though I had designed and built her myself and so forth, 'I like her very much.' There I was again; impression of big biker with his big black bike. 'Madam' said nothing, of course, but I avoided looking at her directly, in case I was transfixed by a baleful, judgemental, yellow eye.

'So,' he nodded, 'you have come on it all the way from England. Fantastic. I also like to ride very much'.

Ah, we have a kindred spirit passing the time of day, then. We find them everywhere and one must always pay back into the common pool, for reasons that require no elaboration if the reader is a motorcyclist. 'Oh, I see,' I replied, 'so you have a bike yourself, do you?'

'*Si, senor,* a beautiful, blue (you know the rules by now), but she is not like this one'.

'Really?' I said, well, one has to keep the conversation moving along, 'How is she?'

'No, no', he said, shaking his head, 'she is—how do you say —knackered'.

That sent my eyebrows up, because 'knackered' is not a word one hears very often coming from the mouth of a Spaniard. In fact, I had never heard it before or since, but, I thought to myself, the poor lad's clearly had bike troubles and a modicum of empathetic concern is in order at this juncture, especially since he had been extraordinarily kind to us. Patsie rightly impresses upon me that the most valuable thing you can give to anyone is your time. It's true, by the way, and pays dividends in both directions practically and spiritually. So I said, sympathetically,

'Oh dear, I am very sorry to hear that. An old one is it?'

My friend furrowed his brow, 'It is the way she is made.'

'Oh, I dunno,' I said, but was thinking, 'Crumbs, that's a bit harsh', so then I said, 'Those bikes are usually very good, you know.'

'No, no' he said, and I could see he was warming to his subject, 'she is not like this', and he leant down towards 'Madam' and cupping both his hands, swept them over her, making a sculpture in the air that I took to be the one universally employed to signify a voluptuous, horizontal woman with full hips. He looked up at me, 'She has no dress, but she is very fast'.

By this point, I confess, I had ceased thinking about motorcycles altogether, though the conversation was not becoming any less interesting. In fact, I quite liked the way it was going, wherever that might be. It did not occur to me, until a moment or two had gone by, that as the recipient of this mime communication, I was the sole interpretor of its meaning. I should have known that straight away, possibly better than most, because it is 'Communication 1:01' and that has been a cornerstone of how I have made my daily dosh.

My interpretation, however, on this occasion was apparently flawed and influenced by a more lascivious frame of mind than I believed I possessed. By that, I mean right then on that particular day. Under normal circumstances, I can be lascivious to order after practically any tea-time, if Mrs. Lewis presents me with a modest bunch of flowers and a bag of chocolate covered raisins.

He pointed at the bike's fairings, which re-directed the train of my thought completely and it was then, good gentlefolk, that the proverbial penny dropped into the proverbial slot. It had been a long, hard, frustrating, sweaty day, if your inclinations run to sympathy in my direction. The bike's fairings were her 'dress'. Of course they were.

'NAKED!' I exclaimed, possibly a little too loudly. Fortunately there were no pedestrians wandering close by at that moment, 'You said naked!'.

'*Si*, naked,' he nodded in affirmation, 'and very fast'.

I assume that any reader who has persevered with me to this point in this book knows what a naked motorcycle is. I am aware that I have confessed to stretching the facts in this book on occasion, so I am going to leave this anecdote with the reader without comment except in one regard. For all my multitudinous faults, I can laugh at myself, even when I have been more than especially dim. Anyway, on that basis, this brief interlude did its share to improve my humour, whether I deserved any consolation from anyone on that day or not. I have a bike made by the same manufacturer these days, by the way, and it's blue and naked. Mine is a four-cylinder 750cc number now of some vintage, but a lively pony to be sure, though whether it is the same model my chum had, I couldn't say.

I trundled the bike in my friend's wake, as he walked down the street until we came to a massive, thick, double door that would have kept a gang of determined *desperadoes*, looters and pillagers at bay: Orcs too, on a good day. He inserted a key into an impressive padlock and hauled at half the door which opened ponderously to reveal a windowless, stone cavern with a vaulted ceiling. Its sole occupant was a substantial, darkly coloured, older model stately German saloon car, reduced in stature by its failure to occupy very much of the available space.

This place was as near to a garage as the Middle Ages had to offer, though presumably for most of its existence it had been a merchant's store. So, I pushed the motorcycle inside and parked her, the door was swung shut with a reassuring, '*Ba-dooom*,' and the padlock was refastened. We wandered back to the hotel together companionably. I cannot say I gave much thought as to whether 'Madam' was going to be where I had left her, when I came to collect her the following morning. As a matter of fact, had I known where she was going to spend the night less parked than incarcerated, I probably would not have bothered to remove all the luggage in the first place, but let us not dwell upon that detail or upon any of its consequences for anyone.

Olite, as one may expect, was as connected to its times as all the other places I have described in the Pyrenees region. It was founded by the Visigoths in the 7th century as a base to control and punish the Vascones—the same tribe that had caused trouble for Charlemagne's Carolingian Army. In fact, the Vascones essentially became the Basques and the kingdom they created after that second ancient battle at Roncesvalles became Navarre. That is history for you—it's not just times gone by, but relevant weft engaging relevant warp to eventually weave an expanding multi-aspected fabric that keeps expanding until its connectivity can arrive at you, reader, standing in the street licking on an ice-cream.

Olite's fabulous castle and palace has been associated with the King of Navarre since the 13th century, though the reader will not be surprised to learn that Spanish guerillas fighting their 'war to the knife', in 1813 set fire to the place so that it would be denied to Napoleon's French invaders who were by then losing their grip on the country to the advances of the Duke of Wellington and his lads.

All the dots, invariably and dependably, as I have said, connect one way or another. Deny or ignore them as you like, it doesn't really matter. The Norns will just keep spinning regardless.

14. Mostly Neutral:
In which we wine, dine and ride the hot plain

On returning to our hotel bedroom, I found Patsie, where I had left her, resting on our bed. She made it clear that she was in no mood or condition for tourism. In the circumstances that was easy to understand, but this was my only chance to see Olite and since it waited to be explored at the foot of the stairs, I was disinclined to waste the opportunity. No one would benefit if I sat silently in a room with someone who did not, irrespective of how legitimate her reasons were, at that moment, want to spend time with me. Early evening was not so far away, but there remained a warm tone to the light coming in through our window, so I quickly washed and changed into lighter clothes, picked up our camera, excused myself and departed.

As I passed reception, I noticed my young friend was no longer on duty. Having finished his shift, he had handed over to a young woman who also greeted me cheerfully and was helpful. I never saw that young man again—may he always ride safely and no harm come to him. I am sorry I didn't get the opportunity to say goodbye to him properly. Not only did his replacement give me a map of the town, but she also marked out a walking route on it that would take in principal sites, together with recommendations for three restaurants which she had marked with X's. Well informed as I could be in short order, I headed down the stairs and out onto the streets.

There was about an hour and a half to stroll before it became dark, so I cannot really provide much insightful information about the place. Olite is certainly very pretty, worth a visit and almost too much of practically everything it had to offer for me to assimilate. It is, of course, an almost perfectly preserved walled town of the later Middle Ages, distinctive in its architecture with its stone-walled streets, squares, palace and noble houses, crenellated walls and circular turrets with grey slate cone-shaped roofs that give it a fairy-tale quality.

I wandered around in the gathering dusk taking snapshots of its gregarious people. In the shade outside a bar a line of serious male drinkers, their backs to the wall, silently surveyed the scene, whilst at a table a couple of old men hunched intensively over a board game. In the sunshine a *viejo* animatedly argued with a mature, red-rinsed *senora* of the town. A bevy of weary young matrons sat on doorsteps, whilst their inexhaustible offspring raced about on tireless legs or furiously pedalled small bicycles fitted with stabilisers. These twilight impressions were seen from the perspective of a visitor to a 'Navarre World' theme attraction. I was barely an interloper. I wasn't there long enough to be one of those.

I made my way back to our hotel as the light of the day faded, peering into the illuminated windows of several small shops, which were exclusively offering the wines of Navarre. I love those kinds of speciality businesses that one finds regularly in the old towns on the continent. You know, little shops with names like, 'Lenez et Fils, purveyors of fine nose-hair clippers since 1856', and so forth. My knowledge of the wine of the Navarre region was that I knew I had drunk some before, because the name Navarra had been printed on the label and that it was 'alright'.

★★★★★★★★★★★★★★★★★

My knowledge of wine generally, whilst we are on the subject, can be summarised thus:

Category No.1: So awful as to be undrinkable, but I should have known better, because it was cheap and served from a cracked pottery jug, containing its very own expiring fly.

I won't mislead anyone. We have drunk our fair share of this undrinkable stuff, when there has been nothing else better or affordable. One made of orange-coloured cacti fluid comes to mind. With this 'wine', one must soldier on through a mug or two, at which point, it does markedly improve. Thereafter, one can actually laugh at its imperfections, as indeed, one can eventually laugh at several other tragedies that hitherto had not seemed particularly funny. Ultimately, that's not a panacea for anyone's woes, of course.

Category No. 2: The largest category—'Alright', by escalating degrees, beginning from 'Not bad', because I can drink it without grimacing (or otherwise steeling myself for a coming ordeal) and we are going to do so therefore, without much preamble.

Category No.3: The smallest category. 'Absolutely fabulous'. Probably, but not exclusively, because it cost far more than I usually countenance spending on a bottle of wine.

I promise myself to remember names and vintages of exceptional wines, but very rarely do. There are some worth remembering and on a good day I can basically classify them by most likely country of origin and grape variety if it's a common one, but that's it. I believe there are those whose palates are sophisticated enough to swig a mouthful of wine and taste chocolate, toasted almonds, apricots, pine nuts, truffles and last Wednesday's fish 'n' chip wrapper, but I can't.

The subject of wine is as complex or as simple as one needs it to be, which is why I stopped 'blagging it' some time ago. *'Would you like to taste the wine, Sir?', 'No, thanks, just pour it, but if at some point something dead drops out the bottle—I'll let you know'.* As a matter of fact, quite recently in Spain a *maître d'* asked me how much I wanted to spend on a bottle of wine. I told him there was not much point in my spending 'big bucks', because I lacked the palate to appreciate it. He leant forward conspiratorially and whispered, 'Neither have I, so have this one' and he pointed at a wine on the list that was so inexpensive at the table I began to visualise the dead fly that would accompany it. Still, I agreed with him, it came and we thought it was really excellent! Well, the top side of 'alright', anyway.

Pearls are apparently similar, by the way. They all look the same, until someone who knows about them, explains the various grades—which is how I know. That will ruin cheap pearls for you forever (if you can summon up the enthusiasm to care about them one way or the other) and possibly have you peering inappropriately (if innocently) at great-aunt Agatha's neckline to check if hers are any good or not.

★★★★★★★★★★★★★★★★

Anyway, I decided to take a bottle of Navarra back to the hotel room as a 'pick me up' before we ventured out for dinner and also on the off-chance that a nice wine would put Patsie in a slightly better, more mellow frame of mind. That development might also induce her to hasten my return into her better books, though of course, that selfish consideration didn't occur to me at the time: Much.

So, I entered a wine shop that had no customers within it, with the intention of seeking advice from the proprietor (at that moment reading a newspaper) since he would, given his uniform stock in trade, assuredly know his stuff. He peered at me over his spectacles as I entered and no doubt instantaneously knew I was going to be a complication. Did he speak English? *No hablas Ingles.* Given where I was, that was not a huge surprise.

I had a more than usual problem before me, because so far as I could tell, every wine in the shop (and there were a great many bottles there) was—on one level, *i.e.,* mine—the same. They were all 'Navarra'. I may not speak good Spanish (or bad Spanish), but I am fairly proficient at reading silences, so when he stood up, walked around the counter, fixed me in the eye and waved an arm expansively in the direction of walls of bottles bearing unfamiliar labels, I knew he was saying, 'Well, Englishman, what do you want?' I was in embarrassed trouble. I knew nothing and he knew I knew nothing, so was probably wasting his time. However, in a moment of inspiration I said, '*Tinto*' (Red) and was quite pleased with myself.

He replied, *'Si'*, though it came out as 'Seeeeeee', which I knew, (being also fairly proficient in understanding one word sentences), roughly translated as, 'Oh that's absolutely flipping marvellous, English bloke, we have made a beginning, so now I have only 98% of my wine stock remaining to consider by some other term of reference I might be able to understand'. Valid point, concisely made in two letters and modicum of tonal inflection. One has to credit him for that.

I recall another—though fluently English-speaking Spaniard—informing me that there was white wine, rose wine and 'real' wine, which unambiguously revealed how much of Spain views the subject. My confidence sagged and it seemed I was unlikely to be rescued. Then I had another idea. If the wine was intended to reflect the drinker, how about this: I drew myself up to my full height, put my hands on my hips, stuck out my chest and said, *'Como yo'*. Which meant, I hoped, 'Like me'.

Miraculously, that seemed to work because he laughed, quickly walked along his shelves, and without hesitation, selected a bottle and brought it back to the counter. It was a red (of course) and on the label was written, 'B——, 2008, Navarra'. This was already something of a relief, because I knew that B—— does not mean 'idiot' in Spanish, so he wasn't matching me to the product too literally. That word is *'Idiota',* so not difficult to remember.

The bottle cost me seven euros (it would be twice that now at the least, I expect) and, whilst I wasn't feeling mean at the time, (given I had a hole to climb out), I thought that price probably meant it was at the better end of, 'Alright'. I was purchasing a Navarra wine in Navarre after all, so it wasn't laden with transportation costs.

The vintner was still chuckling as he wrapped the bottle in tissue paper and put it in a paper bag. We parted on good terms and each of us came away with a tale, notwithstanding one would concern successful and ingenious enterprise and the other, possibly an encounter with a foreign buffoon. Flaubert wrote, 'There is no truth—only perspectives', which sounds as though it could be true, though—on the other hand, evaluated by its own principles—might not be.

★★★★★★★★★★★★★★★★★

As a personal example, we were once in Kandy, on the square before the Temple of the Tooth, one evening when the sky was striped pink and violet and swarming with very large bats. When I later spoke of this astonishing panorama to someone who was with us, he replied that he had no idea what I was talking about, having seen nothing of the kind. I do have a vivid imagination, it's fair to say, though not usually (so far as I know) as far removed from reality as giant bats. Bats; funny looking creatures if you think about them. There will be intriguingly more on the subject of what is real or otherwise from our perspectives, later in these pages.

★★★★★★★★★★★★★★★★★

When I arrived back in our hotel bedroom, Patsie had revived, was well on the path of forgiveness in my direction for the time being and very pleased to see my peace offering. So, we opened the bottle, probably didn't give it the time to breathe it warranted, but set to drinking it anyway from the bathroom glasses, after unceremoniously dumping out our toothbrushes. The wine was well chosen, definitely on the top end of 'Alright', big flavoured and full bodied. So, I like to assume my vintner and I were ultimately on the same wine-list. We made short work of that bottle of Navarra and, since we poured it onto our empty stomachs, were feeling fairly convivial as we went out, arm in arm like happily married folk do, to enjoy our dinner.

We wandered the streets visiting each one of the restaurants that our hotel receptionist had suggested, before opting for the one that she had told me was not only the best, but also the best value. This *Asador* combined a bar, pizzeria and traditional Spanish restaurant in one large room within a genuinely historical stone building, which would have been exceptional practically anywhere else, but in Olite, where the same could be said for the hairdressers and the greengrocers.

Dining in France for us can be about savouring well-prepared dishes—often in very nice locations. Much the same experience in Spain—particularly in places like this one—is regularly more warmly chaotic—surrounded by someone's legion of friends and family including numerous children, everybody talking at once, whilst eating well-prepared, uncomplicated food. This place had a great atmosphere and was demonstrably popular with the locals.

We were ready to eat and tucked into grilled chicken, eggs, peppers, Serrano ham with fried potatoes. It wasn't sophisticated cooking, but it was honestly prepared and flavoursome. We washed it all down with mineral water, because we were still feeling the effects of our bottle of Navarra, and finished the meal off with an exceptionally good *cortado* coffee. We know we are properly back in Spain when we have a *cortado*. French *noisettes* are supposed to be the same thing, but somehow manage not to be.

As we strolled through the stone walled streets back towards our bed, it seemed incredible that our dinner in Amou was eaten on the previous evening. Was that really only yesterday? That easy meal under the vines now seemed so long ago. We slept well as the weary do and the following morning I released 'Madam' from her cell.

I had actually planned for the day's ride to be a longer one, notwithstanding that long rides were becoming an unintended, though consistent, theme. My original calculation was based on the assumption that we would be riding over fairly straightforward roads across level terrain. The ride was always going to be over 4 hours long (so in reality certainly bound to be longer) and we were heading for an overnight stay in Cuenca in Castille-La Mancha.

Why did I chose Cuenca given it was so far away? I knew it was notable for its peculiar location, built to the very edge and beyond a cliff edge which dropped into a river, which is why it was also known for its 'hanging houses', novelly built, in part, over the void. Urban sprawl is bound to be problematic when one lives on a cliff. So, I suppose they are 'hanging *over* houses' or houses that hang over, strictly speaking as opposed to houses in which miscreants were hung. They possibly had one of those in days gone by, for all I know, though not necessarily in one of the houses that hang over.

Hair splitting aside, I hadn't been able to find another location that seemed worth a visit anywhere nearer, though far enough away, from our starting point in Olite. As regards moving the journey along, that night we would be deep in the Spanish interior, level though north-east of Madrid and more or less opposite Valencia, some distance away on the Mediterranean coast.

So, we set off. There is a well known phrase which declares that Spanish plains are more than usually subject to rainfall. I have no idea whether that is actually true. Presumably, one would need some time spent on the plain to know for certain, based on personal experience. We, by contrast, were not about to stick around long enough to gather meaningful data on the subject.

On this trip, thus far, the rain had not fallen anywhere at all and neither of us had any complaints on that score. In any event, it was my understanding that the meteorological content of that phrase was never the point of it, being exclusively concerned with elocution. I had, furthermore, never given much consideration as to whether Spain actually had a plain. It does and it seemed like a big one to us, but then we were from England which has some flat fields in Lincolnshire and couple of other counties. Some folks, I grant you, live in places that have plains with buffaloes roaming upon them.

It obviously hadn't rained on this plain for some long time and that state of affairs didn't look likely to change any time soon. Furthermore, as an unpleasant development, from the west, a hard hot wind was rising. Our route crossed parts of the country possibly not highly regarded for their natural beauty, notwithstanding we were in Aragon, which sounds as though it ought to be romantic. One can only take these things, as usual, as one finds them.

We took an unexceptional, but good enough *desayuno* in a dimly-lit bar by the side of a straight road, halfway down a low-built, ribbon development village. Eight *euros* bought us both *tostadas* with chopped tomatoes, olives, cucumber *tortilla* and strong black coffee, so there was no point in dwelling on the *décor*. We ate in silence. A few people came in the place and left again including a lottery ticket seller, who didn't bother to ask us if we wanted to buy any tickets, because he knew we wouldn't. Nobody was interested in who we were, where we had come from or where we were going. So, we paid our dues and went on our way. The day was beginning to feel as though we had stumbled onto the set of a Spaghetti Western.

I was also dealing with an irritating bike related issue which I kept to myself, lest I be condemned, by my *companera*, for belly-aching. I had been continually charging the Sat Nav from the motorcycle battery, which meant I had to disconnect the cable every time I removed the instrument. The previous night, whilst removing it, the connection attached to the cable had disintegrated in my hand and there was no way I could repair it or replace it. So, the Sat Nav's own full charge (recharged each night) would have to suffice for the entire day of riding and for every day henceforth.

I knew very well that an integral full charge wouldn't last a full day on the bike, if I left it permanently switched on. I also knew there would be occasions when it would be particularly important to have the Sat Nav operational (especially at ride's end when we might have urban detail to follow) and likewise times when it wasn't. So today and for the rest of the trip I kept my eye on the screen for upcoming long stretches of a straightforward road, which I cross referenced with our maps, so I could ensure we were on the right track. Then I turned the Sat Nav off, having an idea when to turn it on again. All of this was a distraction I could have lived without. The reader will recall I eventually solved this problem by purchasing a battery pack (invaluable for several purposes as it turned out) which I kept in the front pocket of the tank bag, but that solution didn't occur to me during this trip. Need it be admitted, we had undertaken plenty of road travelling before the age of Sat Navs, using only maps and thought nothing of it, since there was no alternative. I can't say we were never lost, but not that often. Conveniences can become necessities alarmingly quickly.

Try though I might, I cannot now bring to mind the gadgets I purchased for this journey which were promoted as being particularly useful aids for long distance motorcycling. All I can remember is later telling someone that four of them had not lasted longer than four days. The fifth was the exception (a GB recommendation, I believe) and was an ingenious little invention that clipped over the throttle grip, so one could set a cruising speed and hold it steady by the pressure of the heel of the hand, rather than a sustained twist of the wrist which would become strained over time. At some point I left this little clip on the bike when we went to lunch and when we returned someone had pinched it. I have characterised the thief in my mind as some weasel-faced, low-life for whom any petty larceny was a compulsion irrespective of the item thieved. I just cannot come to terms with the notion that one of the brotherhood could have taken it from a rider who, demonstrably, was far from home, so needing it. Anyway, this gizmo was such a good idea, I later bought another one, which I still have, though take care of it better.

Our road remained as straight as a railway line, stretching into the distance traversing a virtually treeless landscape of dry brown and blowing dust. Unimpeded by any barrier for miles that might dissipate its effects, this hot westerly was hitting us in the flank and hammered us so severely that I couldn't make the most of the easy road by increasing our speeds as it would have normally allowed. Often, particularly intense gusts meant I had to drop down to 40 mph just to keep us relatively upright as we were frequently battered violently to port.

Patsie had tucked herself tightly behind me, so as not to be knocked about too excessively and remained more or less uncommunicative. Readers should not have the impression that was normally the case. I received regular route and safety comments from her, when she thought they would assist and a more or less constant stream of observations on any topic that arose about us from architecture to flora and fauna. She was particularly interested in the proliferation of mistletoe among the deciduous trees of Northern France compared to its relative paucity in Yorkshire, for example. There was some talk of a future commercial venture involving us and mistletoe farming which, perhaps fortuitously, went nowhere.

Whatever crop had been growing in the fields on either side of this road had been harvested and cut down to stubble, though there also remained expanses of standing blackened sunflowers. After surveying this bleak landscape, Patsie's voice in my ear-piece commented that it was only a few weeks previously that this road would have offered an entirely different and more cheerful aspect, because then we would have been riding between fields of tall, yellow waving blooms. Now the countryside was positively post-apocalyptic and that, combined with the searing, hard buffeting wind, meant she, 'wasn't having a very nice time'. That ostensibly innocuous observation bothered me more than one might expect, because I know that phrase is 'Patsie-speak' for being miserably unhappy.

One comes to interpret these codes over time, as anyone who has been married for some time knows. So for the uninitiated, Attila the Hun, for example, would be, 'probably not a very nice person'. The 'probably' would be in there to give him some benefit of the doubt, in case he transpired to be an absolute charmer after all, but was the victim of unfounded malicious rumours circulated by someone who was probably not a very nice person. That second person's 'probably'—I expect you get the idea. So far as I am aware, there is but one unambiguous, irredeemable and dyed-in-the-wool stinker in Patsie's world and there are no prizes for guessing who that is.

As the sun climbed higher, the day became hotter and time was slipping away. It looked as though this was going to be yet another very long day and possibly an even later night-stop arrival.

15. Fifth and Sixth Gear:
In which we hang around where the hanging houses are

Eventually we needed to refuel 'Madam', so we pulled into a filling station which had an unprepossessing *cantina* behind it. Lunch and toilet time had come around, so agreeing to 'kill three birds with one stone' our duty done as regarded the bike's needs, we walked through its door. We then metamorphosed into two of those fly-blown drifters in the Wild West films who part the swinging doors of saloons to be transfixed by the hostile glares of townsfolk. All eyes turned towards us, several necks twisted or craned and silence fell upon the place. We sat down self-consciously at a table, but the woman behind the bar eyed us narrowly and lips turned downwards, shook her head in refusal. We hadn't even got as far as 'What ya having, stranger?', so we stood up again.

Patsie whispered she thought we should have a quick coffee and leave, but I was disinclined to be driven away, so gestured with a shrug and a gaze about the place (that had empty tables aplenty), so someone would tell us where we could sit. Fortunately, they had a tight corner reserved for British motorcyclists and, presumably, other unwelcome, non-local interlopers. It was entirely possible that we had unwittingly encroached on the reservation of the Camioneros (truck drivers) which must remain off-limits, notwithstanding it was a huge area filled with tables that had no one but us within it. When in Rome etc. I can't remember what we ate. Nothing very inspiring, therefore, and I suppose our hostess was as happy to see us leave, as we were to go. This was possibly the only inhospitable reception we ever received in Spain, so on balance should not make much of it.

We continued our ride south-westwards. By this point I was certain that we would be arriving at our night stop after dark, when we found ourselves, quite unexpectedly, riding on an auto-route that neither we nor our Sat Nav (which was having a bionic hysterical fit over this unheralded development) knew existed. As I have previously commented, the Spaniards do not 'hang about' in building a new road, so the event in itself was not especially remarkable. This outstanding Spanish industry can take some assimilating for UK travellers until they become used to the occurrence. I suppose that is because when we ride the A1 (still, without irony, known as 'The Great North Road' which goes from London to Edinburgh), we know that once, long ago, a Roman drove a chariot along it, Dick Turpin, the highwayman (in romantic fiction, at least) galloped along it on his own Black Bess and many of its two hundred year old coaching inns still exist. In Spain, it seems to me, one can ride upon what appears to be a comparatively new dual carriageway by our standards, whilst half a mile distant and parallel to it, a newer one, almost inexplicably to us, is being laid.

It was apparent from the piles of building materials scattered about and unfinished exits and lay-bys along this road that it was not only new but, despite being partially open for traffic, some construction remained underway. Spanish auto-routes, even when fully operational, can be notable for having very little traffic moving along them compared to similar roads in the UK. Let's put it this way, in Spain one could sometimes play the, 'Guess the colour of the next car we are going to see' game. This one had practically nothing moving along it at all, so Patsie had no issues with our taking it, given we had some distance yet to cover to reach our destination.

Our Sat Nav, unfortunately, didn't feel the same way about its current predicament and was going doolally in that 'does not compute' way that digital brains sometimes do, crashing and rebooting, spinning its maps around, reaching out to nearby roads it recognised as existing, suggesting we turn around at the earliest opportunity to take the first exit so we could follow these ever changing instructions. These included taking non-existent junctions which we could not have accessed, even had they still existed, because there was now a central reservation barrier in place.

I knew this road was unlikely to be the one leading directly to our destination, so once or twice I came off it to take my bearings, only to return to it again when I discovered nothing by way of signposts that immediately assisted us. I suspect Patsie could sense my growing exasperation and had decided not to endure a repeat of the previous day's frustrations and frayed tempers, because I abruptly felt a *'clonk'* on the back of my helmet, which could only have come from a sharp rap delivered by my sweetheart's armoured gloved knuckles. Other punctuating *'clonks'* soon followed.

'Don't', CLONK, 'look at that', CLONK, *'blanky* thing,' she demanded, (meaning the Sat Nav, of course, in ongoing identity crisis) 'just listen to me!'

Now there may be husbands out there who would be inclined to go their own way notwithstanding that kind of definitive intercession from their nearest and dearest or even protest at this novel method of punctuation, but I am not one of them, because I knew (following the previous day's *contretemps*) this was not merely an issue of navigation methodology. This was something far more important. This was husband and wife politics. This was, 'Am I an equal partner on this venture or something less?' Not something 'else' let it be noted, but something 'less'. So I said, because I occasionally know when it matters to say the right thing at the right time, 'OK, you call the shots'.

'Right, first turn off the 'thing'. How far from Madrid is Cuenca?' she asked tersely, clearly becoming a little 'miffed' herself.

'Not that far', I responded, silencing the 'thing' as instructed, 'I don't know exactly'.

'Well', she said, 'this road doesn't say it's going anywhere but Madrid,(which was true enough—thus far the capital city was the only name displayed, so far as I could tell) but at least it's going there quickly, so just keep going on it until we are about 30 or so miles away from the capital and then take whatever exit that comes next. Cuenca cannot be far away by then, whether it's the first correct exit or not, then switch the 'thing' back on—it will be bound to find Cuenca on normal roads and there you are—done—without all this performance'

So that's what we did. I opened 'Madam's' throttle and we ran down the remaining miles like they were easy prey. An exit offered itself at about the distance that Patsie had suggested, so I took it and though I then had planned to reset the Sat Nav there was no need to do so, because at the top of the slip-way a signpost indicated Cuenca before any other destination. The lady did not withhold declaring, 'I told you so—listen to me more often in future'.

The tedium of the plain gradually transformed into more inspiring undulating folds and dusty browns gradually burgeoned into fresh greens. Our rigid road loosened its girdle and shook itself free to become the long lovely curves best beloved of the motorised two-wheeled. We were somewhat saddle-sore, it was true, but a change really can be as good as a rest and we began to enjoy ourselves, instead of simply wishing the journey would quickly end. Well, I did anyway, for what it's worth. There is no point in not admitting we pilots have the better part of the arrangement. I assume Patsie's feelings at the time on the basis that there were no complaints.

The landscape became forested with fresh scented pine trees and the roads beyond Duron followed the shores of beautiful lakes of almost impossibly bright, turquoise-blue water. We paused for rest in an idyllic lake-side picnic spot which we had to ourselves. Rising from the waters like a skeletal arm, near to the shore, was a leafless tree which was entirely stark, bright white, so I had it in mind that some chemical might be responsible for the extraordinary colour of the water. However, when I wandered close to the shore-line to make a picture, given the effect was so colourfully dramatic, I noticed a couple of good sized fish swimming around which looked healthy enough, so have no explanation for this phenomenon. Refreshed by this welcome break, we continued riding towards our hotel, situated on the outskirts of Cuenca, arriving at about 6pm in the evening.

Cuenca can trace its origins to the 8th century when Muslim forces swept through the region and realised the strategic value of a fortress built across a steep spur, between the gorges of the Jucar and smaller Huecar rivers. They called the fortress Kunka (I don't know why, but it stuck, more or less) and it was surrounded by a long defensive wall. Places built for trouble are often fated see their fair share of it, so over the centuries there were several assaults upon the city that failed and as many that succeeded. The deprivations of Napoleon's invading army drove away most of its early 19th century population. It was sacked during the Third Carlist War of 1874 (a civil conflict, the details of which this account and its readers can live without) and as recently as 1938 it was held by the Republicans, until it fell to Franco's Nationalist troops during the Spanish Civil War.

In fact, Cuenca only recovered its fortunes during the later 20th century with the growth of Spanish tourism and a cessation of strife that had ravaged it for a thousand years. It is, indisputably, a distinctive city in a unique and dramatic location and has become, justifiably, a UNESCO World Heritage site. We saw Cuenca for the first time on this journey and at night, which imposes its own perspectives on how one views anywhere, but we returned to stay in later years to do proper justice to the place on a couple of occasions.

When I initially researched hotels for our Cuenca visit, I concentrated on reviewing those within the old city, but could not find any that offered their own parking facilities. As a rule I am reluctant to leave 'Madam' on her own in the street at night in an unknown urban area, since she presents a tempting prize, but in Cuenca I may have been persuaded that it was safe to do so had I realised that there is a well-lit motorcycle parking corral near to the cathedral, which is used extensively by the locals. One more bike among the many has the advantage of safety in numbers combined with the added security of regular police patrols. As it was, I chose a little hotel for us outside the city, because it was really good value for money and apparently offered parking. This latter transpired not to be quite as secure as I would have preferred it to be, since it turned out to be outside the hotel's compound, but the overall location was comparatively remote which counter-balanced those concerns. That, or we just got away with it—who knows?

We checked in, moved into our room, had a wash, a change of clothes and a short rest before hiring a taxi, (so I could have an alcoholic drink or two), to take us into the old town for the evening, arranging with the driver to pick us up again at midnight. Less than ten minutes' drive dropped us in the Plaza Mayor. We wandered around the old stone-walled streets for a time, peering into courtyards and down alleyways. The principal problem for us as regarded seeing Cuenca's most notable features—the hanging houses—was that it was now dark, but more importantly, to view them hanging to best effect one must be behind them and on the other side of the gorge. From the front elevation they look like any other houses built 'cheek by jowl' in cities of this vintage.

So, we returned to the Plaza Mayor by the cathedral of Santa Maria and San Julian (this latter sainted individual a former archbishop of the city) which was where the night-life of the place was principally happening. The cathedral, which is the *plaza's* dominant feature, is fronted by a deep flight of steps and these had a Bohemian looking crowd scattered over them animatedly chatting, debating and drinking beer. That potential irreverence didn't seem to bother any of the relaxed policemen or clerics in the vicinity, so far as we could tell. In daylight on another visit, we have seen a band of Spanish gypsies on these steps playing their guitars, singing their songs and putting away a fair amount of beer from the bottle-neck. That didn't seem to bother anyone either.

The area contained several bars which were packed with patrons who spilled onto the pavement or sat at tables, eating and drinking wine, beer or coffee. Every so often some young blade would cruise down the square displaying his ride, often cruising away again with a female passenger on board. We found ourselves a free table and settled down to 'watch the world go by'. An efficient young staff was collecting food and drink orders, then delivering plates and glasses passed through a large sash-window into the street. So, when a young waitress came our way, we opted to join in with the local crowd and eat. The menu consisted of two or three *menu del dia* options and, since we didn't really understand what it all said and not much English was being spoken to ask, we picked the cheapest one with items we more or less recognised at just 10 Euros each (the Sterling exchange rate was pretty good in those days), to keep the price of a mistake to the minimum.

A veritable avalanche of food shortly arrived accompanied by beers, that I definitely had not ordered. Two huge plates of different pasta dishes (which alone were enough to satisfy our appetites) were then followed by an enormous salad which was hotly pursued by croquettes and fried calamari in industrial portions. We looked at each other uncertainly. This had looked like a desirable '*café* society' scene to us and too nice a spot to be dishing out this kind of meal for just 10 euros a pop. But hey ho, we were hungry so tucked into it with gusto.

Eventually, Patsie leaned towards me and hissed, 'We have a problem!'

'Well, you've picked a fine time to come out with this,' I said, 'I tell you what, if I can keep the bike, you can have the cat and half the house'.

'Not that, you fool,' she whispered, 'besides I would get both anyway and more besides.'

'You would—would you? We'll jolly well see about that. Let me. . . .'

'Ssshhhh,' she shut me down and leaning towards me conspiratorially expressed a concern that I had been silently cultivating myself from the moment the dinner began to be delivered, 'something, went wrong when we ordered. We can't be getting all this food for just 10 euros each'.

'Oh, that. I think you be might be right,' I mumbled, 'I wasn't going to mention it. Perhaps we have someone else's dinner. I mean, we wouldn't know one way or the other, because we don't really know for certain what we have ordered, do we?'

'Well, just don't make a fuss,' she said, peering about like a pantomime spy, which would have been almost certain to draw attention to both of us among a more sober gathering, 'because if you do everyone will think we are absolute piglets for ordering so much to eat, but then we are causing trouble, just because we can't pay for it.'

'What are we going to do with it all then?' I pleaded, surveying an embarrassing volume of uneaten provender before us.

'We can spread what we have left around all the plates, so it doesn't look quite so much. Then, if it doesn't stop coming,' she said, setting to work industriously with a spoon, 'I will open a napkin on my lap and you can casually shovel all the left-over food onto it. Then, you quickly pay whatever it turns out to be without passing any comment about what we expected it to cost and I will hold the napkin close to me, so no one will notice.'

'Oh, Lord,' I groaned, visualising myself casually pouring volumes of wet, sticky food over her or the napkin's over-burdened contents flopping loudly onto the *plaza* like something falling casually from the south end of a north facing cow, 'then what?'

'Then we will stand up together, you stand right in front of me and we will casually walk together into that dark patch, away from the lights, where I will surreptitiously slide all the food into a rubbish-bin'.

'Is there a rubbish-bin in that dark patch, then?' I queried, squinting into the night, 'I can't tell, because it's a dark patch'. There was no point in mentioning that soft-shoeing across the Plaza Mayor like Flanagan and Allen performing 'Underneath the Arches' would be hardly inconspicuous, even though nobody watching us would have ever heard of Flanagan and Allen. Any reader who has no idea (and cares) what I am talking about can find out with an online search.

So it was a simple plan—doomed to disaster in several casual ways—but the best we had. Digging an escape tunnel was out of the question, because the Plaza Mayor is mostly stone or cobbled. Out of options, I simply called for *la quenta*. When it came it was for 20 Euros 'on the button' and though I was at pains to point out we also had been drinking beer, was told that too was included in the price of the meal. All of which was a massive relief to both of us, though it remains an abiding wonderment. The air was by this time of the evening becoming slightly chilly, so we decided to adjourn indoors to the bar, which was one of those modern beer emporiums full of friendly younger folk, drinking a variety of interesting ales and generally having a good time.

The Spanish motorcycle Grand Prix appeared on a giant T.V and was greeted with unanimous enthusiasm since everyone in the know was apparently waiting to watch it, so more beer was ordered and drunk and we shouted and groaned at the action along with everybody else. I can't remember who won. I'm not sure anyone cared very much, because it was a recording, the actual event raced months previously, though I didn't realise that myself until fairly late on in the proceedings. I did wonder how it was broad daylight on the screen, yet pitch black outside at a certain point, but only momentarily because it wasn't concerning anyone else.

'Another one? Well, just one more then. Does Lars want one? Sven, is it? Fair play, well, does Sven want one?'

Our taxi arrived at the stroke of midnight, as reliable as Cinderella's pumpkin coach, except we were ready to meet it and in possession of all our own footwear, a triumph in itself given how full our tanks were. The following morning our hotel hostess treated us to a really superb and lavish breakfast complete with her own home baking. I wish we could have done better justice to it, but we were still a bit tight around the waist-band.

We had just one more night on the road before we arrived at the Mediterranean shore at Mojacar. Just two more days or less. What could possibly go wrong?

16. Third Gear again:
In which we enter Andalucia and encounter several of its wonders

My chosen destination for this day's riding was a village in north-eastern Andalucia, I had never heard of nor had any particular wish to visit. The reader would be absolutely forgiven for asking, 'Why does everything have to be so complicated with this bloke? Why can't he just get on the bike and go?' Well, you see, it's not always that straightforward.

I knew very well we could be in Mojacar that evening, if we really wanted to be. We had driven there from the ferry ports on the northern Spanish coast at Santander and Bilbao in the past. The route from Santander will take one close to the west of Madrid (which is in the middle of Spain—more or less) and from Bilbao, to the capital's east. As a matter of fact, one could also go (and we have) through the middle of Madrid via a tunnel or use its ring-road, but let's not get into that, because large cities (whilst not impossible) are to be avoided on journeys in my view, unless one is specifically visiting them. If truth be told, I think the best way to arrive in a metropolitan area is by train.

Neither one of Madrid's close contact passages compares to the *Périphérique* around Paris in my experience, it's fair to say, but there are a number of easier and more enjoyable ways to move beyond Madrid, in my opinion. Furthermore, we had driven from the Atlantic ports to Mojacar in one uninterrupted journey and also, more frequently, with halfway overnight stops in towns more or less level with Madrid—at Aranjuez on the western route, for example.

So, from Cuenca we could head south on a main eastern route before much time had elapsed. We would have by-passed Teruel, famous for its Serrano ham and distinctive Mudejar architecture,(though once dismissed by Ian Robertson to me, thus, 'Ah, Teruel-bricky!') and once we struck the Mediterranean coast road, we could then take a right turn at Murcia and *'Roberto es tu Tio'*, readily thence to Mojacar—dual carriageway all the way.

I didn't want to do that,however, because that would be about expeditiously reaching a destination using direct routes we knew, as opposed to riding over country we didn't know, for the sake of adventurous riding. In any case, that direct route would still have involved a minimum of seven hours in the saddle and we knew from experience how that worked. We would, all being well, though for no particular dividend, finally arrive late and be absolutely jiggered and good for nothing the following day. 'Been there and have the T-shirt', as the saying goes.

So I looked for a town on a cross-country route that fitted the bill for one final single night stay. That town—whatever and wherever it was—had to offer us a reasonable day of riding to reach it and then a little over half a day following to take us to Mojacar. However, that idea didn't work out as I had hoped. Simply put, I couldn't find a town to ride to. So, putting aside the search for towns, I then began looking for suitable hostelries that might stand isolated in the *campo* or be situated in villages on an arc at about the right distance and in the right direction, irrespective of where they were. I found one of those that looked promising at somewhere called Segura de la Sierra.

As a night-stop, this place offered us a comparatively straightforward ride from Cuenca. The following morning there would be a short cross country jaunt before we reached Velez Rubio (a place we knew) and then on to Huercal Overa (another familiar place on the coastal autoroute) and then a very simple run into Mojacar arriving in the middle of the afternoon at a time when, if we ate something, we would be legitimately able to call the meal, 'lunch'. So, on the face of it, a perfect solution.

The photographs of the general location and the accommodation we chose both looked very pleasant. The views from the bedrooms were beautiful and suggested the village was in an elevated location. That was not particularly surprising given the village had the word, 'Sierra' in its name. Nor yet was that a particularly alarming signal. The Sierra Cabrera rises behind Mojacar and that is quite an accessible little range, whilst, a little farther away, tourists enjoy skiing on the Sierra Nevada. I am not a complete fool. Had the place been called something foreboding like 'The Mountain of Horror' or 'The Gorge of Stranglers', I obviously wouldn't have countenanced going anywhere near the place. What are you saying, reader? You can hear the sound of distant disembodied laughter? Yes, well, that will probably be the Olympian gods making merry at the expense of some poor mortal. I wonder who that might transpire to be.

 Although the final stretch of road riding into Cuenca was, as I have explained, very enjoyable through attractive countryside, the road onwards to the south-west bore a similarity to those interminable plains we had traversed for most of the previous day. The road was ram-rod straight ahead of us and the parched air blowing with brown dust as we rode through a monotonous flat expanse of stubble, maize stalks and dead sunflowers. At one point we crossed a terrain of huge fields planted with thousands of cabbages. The sun was high in the sky and making its presence felt by generating a familiar, though overwhelming, foetid aroma of boiled cabbage which seemed quite peculiar in the absence of an essential cooking pot. 'Madam', need it be said, will, all things being equal, make as short work of this kind of terrain as I ask of her.

 I had, on several occasions during this journey, been guilty of imposing my expectations on yet to be revealed realities and this bad habit had, as you have discovered, invariably set me on the wrong track. So, one would have imagined that by this point in the journey I would have learned my lesson. I had not. When one is aiming for somewhere called 'Sierra something' or even 'Something sierra' one may reasonably expect, it seemed to me, to see a mountain range in the distance which will make some sense of the name. So far as I know, mountains never skulk in the undergrowth, when viewed from a level landscape. They are reliable that way and where they differ most markedly from large holes in the ground which can be clandestine to the disadvantage of the incautious.

The country was gradually becoming undulating and the field crops of the flat-lands gave way to rows of hundreds of olive trees. Nevertheless, despite the Sat Nav reporting that we were, once again, not so very far from our destination, I could see no mountains. Then, in the distance, I noticed a solitary conical protuberance, as though a Titan had emptied a giant sack of rocks into a heap. As we came closer, I could see that this feature had a fortification upon its summit and frothing around its curtain walls like a garland, the buildings of a white *pueblo*. We were too far distant to have seen a signpost, but there was no doubt in my mind, in the absence of any sensible alternative, that this was Segura de la Sierra. So, I assumed the name indicated the village was on a little mountain, as opposed to laying within mountains.

Actually, the prospect of spending the evening and night on the top of a rocky cone was quite a novelty and appealed to both of us. We had been frying for hours as we crossed the griddle of the plain. This destination suggested something of the Indian hill station, wherein the broiled *sahibs* and *memsahibs* of the *Raj* took refuge in cooler elevations during the sub-continent's hot season.

Whilst I can find no record of it in my notes, I have it in mind there was a filling station nearby the foot of this protuberance and since the bike needed a refill, we attended to her before we began to climb. In fact, I recall standing next to the bike, noting the name of the village and being surprised that following 'Segura de la Sierra', was written, '5km'. I had already thought this place was pushing its luck to call itself a mountain and 5km seemed improbably far by road, given that when we looked up the pine covered slopes, we could quite clearly discern details in the buildings of the village. I knew very well that we were not going to ascend that elevation, 'as the crow flies', but that taken into account, 5km still seemed a long way to cover a distance that didn't seem that far to me.

Concluding that none of that mattered very much given we were on the start line of the last stretch before a waiting welcome shower and ready for 'the off', we climbed back aboard the bike. I gunned her engine to bring her 'revs' up, let out the clutch and we began to climb. As the reader is aware, we had already ridden over the Pyrenees and by comparison this climb was no more than a pimple of an obstacle. That said, I hadn't been expecting a steep climb at this stage in the proceedings and what made this one different was we were on the outside of the road, closest to the edge, immediately off our right side. The promising security of the cliff face was not so far across the width of that narrow road, but it seemed a very long way away to me. Moreover, there was no safety barrier that I can recall to separate us from the drop, which was no distance away from us at all.

How can I describe that climb for us? I cannot say I enjoyed it, so it couldn't have been much fun for Patsie who had to just sit there with time enough to look around and, indeed, to look down. Fortunately, she doesn't have any greater aversion to heights beyond that which is sensible for most people. Nothing about that rising was gradual. It was steep and it was winding. If that climb was 5km long, then it was the longest 5km of my life thus far—though that record would be broken soon enough. But we rode it successfully, of course, because here I am to tell you about it.

We arrived at the top, at the entrance to the village, which one entered by passing through an impressive Moorish style gateway. It was 4pm in the afternoon. There had been no name to this singular road at the bottom, for some reason, but there was a signpost at one point along it and it was called, if my memory serves me correctly, '*El Gordo Garotte*'—'The Fat Strangler' or something along those lines. Not 'Daffodil Lane', anyway, nor any appellation possessed of a similarly comforting sentiment.

I don't want to make more of this than it was. Segura de la Sierra was a vibrant, living village; a beautiful place in a fabulous location and probably, I suspect, a popular tourist destination these days. It was a busy village when we saw it. We saw traffic buzzing up and down this road from postal vehicles to food trucks, as though they drove it every day and they probably did. We rode it just twice—once up and once down, as usual two-up, fully laden. As I have emphasised before—those considerations do make a difference and I can only report anything as we found it from our own fleeting perspectives.

I suppose it is worth mentioning that when we have travelled abroad, we have, of course, seen all manner of different bikes on similar tours, but perhaps a preponderance of tall machines. Their riders, invariably identifiable by their peaked helmets, 'bum-freezer' jackets and side clasped boots, seemed to know their business and, for all I know, these kinds of machines are best suited for some of the situations we experienced in difficult country. Their pillions, when they had one, were often lithe young women, tall enough to be able to ascend and descend from their rides with the grace of ballet dancers. I have never ridden that kind of motorbike—not even for a test ride—so know little to nothing about them, though at time of writing practically every rider coming on or off the ferry to Spain is riding one. So, they are clearly very popular, which means I definitely don't want one, because I am perverse! Pillions, I have noticed, seem to have diminished in numbers.

The style of these bikes, demonstrably, does not particularly appeal to me, but there is another consideration. My pillion rider has a small leg issue, which means tall bikes are impractical for her convenience. Heading southward from the knees, my wife's legs perform as well as any—reaching towards the ground infallibly, but in the opposite direction they run out of steam fairly quickly. So, Patsie is happiest if she can climb aboard from an elevated position, like a fuel-pump platform at a filling station, for example, to give her an extra four or five inches 'from the get-go'. Further elaboration on this subject is surely unnecessary, though good things actually do come in small packages, so you will hear no complaints from me.

As one might expect, this *pueblo* boasted just one main thoroughfare that would support traffic, so it came as something of a surprise to us that we couldn't find our accommodation.

After abortively cruising backwards and forwards a few times, I telephoned the contact number on our reservation document and connected to a lady who was transparently very ready to assist us. We spoke together fluently for a time in the spirit of cooperation, though regrettably, in two different and incompatible languages.

Improbable as it may seem, I possessed slightly more Spanish than she had English. In a village of this modest size, we surely must pass by her, if she simply stood on her own doorstep, so I repeated, *'Buscar moto grande negro'* a couple of times (the second time possibly slightly louder, on the off chance she was deaf. I have no idea why.) It was clear, volume notwithstanding, she understood the essence of that message well enough. On that day if a *moto grande* cruised down the street in that village we both knew it would have to be ours, because there certainly wasn't another *moto grande* in evidence, irrespective of what colour it might have been. That was, on the face of it, a perfect plan so, of course, it failed comprehensively and though we continued to promenade at snail-speed, there remained no sign of anyone inclined to flag us down: One more lesson on the distinction between a plan and a solution.

Eventually, Patsie decided to climb off the bike to see what she could discover on foot. I elected to ride up towards the castle to see if there were any clues in that direction, though I didn't really expect there would be. To my surprise I came across a tiny bull-ring and just beyond it the road doubled back on a sharp hair-pin bend. Just then I spotted the name of the street we were looking for, so I quickly turned the bike around and sounded the horn (as previously agreed) so Patsie would know I had found what we were seeking and was coming back for her. I picked her up and we had just turned the hair-pin again when we encountered our hostess who was walking in search of us. She guided us back to our accommodation which was a delightful little single level, self-contained dwelling with its own compact kitchen. The views across the landscape from the windows of our eyrie were even more remarkable than its photographs had suggested. Breakfast, our hostess told us, would be served at a nearby location and after giving us directions where to find it, she left us so we could enjoy the evening.

We went through the usual procedure of peeling off our motorcycling clothes, washing, resting and changing into something lighter and cooler before we wandered out to explore. This was the south of Spain. The north of the south of Spain to be sure, but Andalucia nevertheless. Magnificent Andalucia—the region of Spain most exotic, most foreign, where the spirit of Africa and Islamic culture established itself most deeply and abided the longest. We loved it and still do. Segura de la Sierra may have been a tiny village, but it was rich in the artefacts of both European and Moorish cultures which are so diverse they always seem to me to collide rather than exist in harmony, though that combination typifies the region and has a character of its own.

As we walked into the village, a fiesta of the *Virgen del Rosario* was being prepared with coloured bunting and banners displaying Mary, Mother of Christ and the rosary together with market stalls offering everything from souvenirs to cooked food, though since we were leaving the following morning we would see nothing of it when it was in full swing. However, a small travelling funfair, erected on a recreation ground at a lower level was already open and, judging by the excited squeals of children's pleasure that floated up to us, was being enjoyed in full measure.

We then came across two local men sitting in the sunshine, drinking beers outside a small tavern from the open door of which came the most astonishing Spanish music. We stopped to listen in the street, because we thought this must be a private affair, but the men smiled at us, indicating that we were welcome to enter. We were ushered into the bar to be greeted warmly by its patrons who were gathered around three musicians, all guitarists, one of whom was a senior *virtuoso* on a twelve string instrument, who were improvising *flamenco* for the pleasure it gave them.

Patsie and I were completely entranced by the sight and sound of this intimate tableau and sat in its heart; an experience that money can't buy and of a kind that happens so rarely. There was a short break in musical proceedings, when the lady who had been serving drinks behind the bar wiped her hands on her apron and came over to accompany the guitar players with staccato hand-clapping, before spontaneously bursting into song with a fine, mature, urgent and plaintive voice. When she finished her impromptu performance and after the last *'Ole!'* and the enthusiastic applause (including our own contribution) had subsided, she simply went back to work behind the bar: Absolutely priceless.

I recall, though made no note of it, that there was a Spanish family there who had with them a charming girl child, whose long hair was untypically blonde, and being reminded of Velázquez's painting of the *Infanta* (without the distinctive Habsburg jaw, fortunately for her) and what a fascinating melting pot Spain can be. We saw the beer drinkers several times as we wandered around the village, each time drinking other beers and happy to see us again. Segura de la Sierra certainly packed a great deal into its small footprint.

The village was, in fact, once the seat of a minor Moorish potentate and still possessed a well preserved example of the traditional long Moorish *fuente* and baths. These fountains were so efficient that many of them have survived in working order—access to good water being an essential practicality, pragmatically elevated above matters of political power or faith. Segura de la Sierra's Christian architecture dated from the 15th and 16th centuries.

One house, which if my memory serves, was for sale at the time, belonged to Jorge Manrique (circa 1440-79) who had been both a soldier and a revered poet and whose works remain the subject of academic study. The reader may be relieved that I am not going to include an extract of Manrique's poetry here. Firstly, in recognition that this book must steadfastly maintain a motorcycling thread (and he didn't have one) and secondly because his verses are a bit heavy going in translation—with a fair amount devoted to how fleeting life is and how soon we are all going to be dead and so forth. They make Patsie's, Ottoman sea-battle verses sound like positively cheery affairs, if you ask me, though admittedly I know less about late-medieval Spanish poetry than practically any other subject, including the wine of Navarra, which, at least I can confirm—is 'alright'.

Anyway, a statue of Manrique stands on a *mirador* near the gate of the village, gazing into the hazy distance, enjoying a first-rate elevated view of the surrounding countryside, attired in armour, a sword at his hip, studiously reading a *tome*—implicitly, I suppose—of his own material. Hard on him for eternity, if that is the case, because I could have told him, from personal experience, the more often he reads that stuff—the more readily he will come to thoroughly dislike it.

Manrique was a supporter of Queen Isabella of Castile. She and her husband, Ferdinand of Aragon were known as 'The Catholic Monarchs', (*Los Reyes Catolicos*) and were responsible for the completing of 'The *Reconquista*' which defeated and expelled the last Muslim forces from Spain in 1492, amongst other things including sending Christopher Columbus off to discover America again.

All of that is too much to dump on little Segura de la Sierra at this point in our tale, especially since we shall be in Andalucia for some time in these pages, so there will be opportunity and space enough for a bit more on the subject later. Manrique died in battle comparatively young, aged 38 years, in 1479, not fighting against the Moors, but in a minor civil bust-up of succession, storming the castle of Garcimunoz near Cuenca. We have been to Garcimunoz since this trip, by the way. Considered from the perspective of everything that has happened to Spain in the intervening years, it is, inevitably, worth getting killed over about as much as most piles of rocks are. Another poet gone down to war.

Our day ended in the usual way—in search of somewhere to eat dinner. Presumably in preparation for the coming festivities, not much was open in the village by way of eating establishments, so we returned to the bar of the musicians and made a simple, but satisfying supper of locally baked bread, La Mancha's famous Manchego cheese and Serrano ham washed down with a bottle of a white wine from Cadiz—each!

The white wine of Cadiz, incidentally, for all you wine enthusiasts and aficionados who are not familiar with it, is 'alright' in my considered opinion, (on the nose it smells reassuringly of wine and on the palate, that's wine too) though I appreciate so much is obvious, given we cheerfully saw off two bottles of the stuff.

I know some readers are going to consider me an absolute philistine on this subject, but I remain unrepentant. Quite recently I was selecting a bottle of wine in a supermarket and above the shelf was one of those little cards that described its attributes. On the 'Taste' line following the usual implausible flavours it also allegedly tasted of 'ethereal'. I had a possibly jaundiced view of that claim, but of course purchased a bottle anyway since the potential of having that flavour on one's tongue is, however improbable, irresistible. 'Hope springs eternal in the human breast' and so forth. I couldn't taste anything beyond wine, so perhaps it did taste of 'ethereal' after all and so worth every penny.

Incidentally, I would not wish readers to have the impression that Patsie and I habitually sank a bottle of wine each. Singular circumstances provoke singular celebrations and we thought this was one of them. In any event, on this journey, we were usually abed by 10.30 p.m. and soon fast asleep, so it was routinely twelve hours before we were once more in the saddle.

17. Second Gear:
In which we ride into a mountain range I didn't know was there

To be fair to the day, it started well enough. As a matter of fact, we were both feeling quite chipper, because the previous day had eventually been enjoyable and we knew this day's ride would be a short one and then there would be some days of rest by the Mediterranean shore before we set out on the return leg of our journey, which would be by a different route, and included some promising destinations along the way.

We left 'Madam' parked outside the door of our little *casa* and strolled the short distance to where our hostess waited to serve us breakfast. *Desayuno* is not the same all over Spain and in Andalucia it is so distinctive that if one constructs one at a hotel breakfast buffet elsewhere in Iberia, staff are likely to say, 'Oh, you are from Andalucia—what place?' This one was as good as it gets being, she told us, home-made and by our own lady hostess.

Firstly, of course, freshly squeezed *naranja* (orange) juice, natural yoghurt (sometimes with honey) and newly baked and toasted *tostadas*. These shallow lenticular loaves are crunchy crusted, but when split in half, soft under a toasted top. Upon each half (for those who can manage a whole one) one pours virgin olive oil, salt and a cold condiment of tomatoes. Then one mashes it all together with the back of a fork, so it sits in the shell of the crust.

Our hostess made a particular point of telling us she had made this *tomate* herself. That is always a good augury. On the face of it, this seems to be just pulverised tomatoes, but there must be more to it than that because sometimes, like this time, it is fabulous. Some people add cheese and or thinly sliced ham on top of the *tomate,* but this one definitely didn't need embellishing. To finish the meal, she produced her own home-made egg biscuits and the essential gorgeous coffee, taken black.

As a matter of fact, if the bread is good and warm, the olive oil, emerald green with a slight taste of apples and the salt, coarse from the sea, we can really enjoy that too: As simple as a meal can be imagined with a few thousand years of heritage as its credentials. Add a little (or better yet, 'a lot') of *Alioli*—Heaven!

By the time we had undertaken a modicum of repacking and fitted the hard luggage back onto the bike, there appeared to be more people milling around our end of the village. Certainly, the area was considerably more busy than it had been on the previous day which made sense since the festival had begun, though that was concentrated on the main street so far as we could tell.

The actual reason for the congregation became apparent soon enough. This was also the first day of a two-day bull fighting event and the people of the surrounding countryside were flocking into the village to see the spectacle. That tiny bull-ring was a curiosity in itself, since it is rectangular—not round as usual. It was easy to understand—if any sense could be made of having a functioning bull-ring at the top of a cone of rock within small village—why it would be of necessity diminutive.

I know nothing about the finer details of fighting bulls, but this 'ring' demonstrably came with its own issues. For man or beast there was nowhere to go. The *matadors* must presumably be in almost perpetual close contact with the bulls. Whatever was going to happen in the centre of that arena would occur with the minimum of time between cause and effect, leaving little to no room or time for error. However, such potential discouragements notwithstanding, I recall being told that the most renowned *matadors* in Spain have willingly performed there. Having witnessed, even to a small degree, how *matadors* are apparently wired, for all I know it is possible these additional hazards were why this place held attractions.

Candidly, though I didn't discuss it with Patsie, who may well have felt differently about it, I wouldn't have objected to witnessing the spectacle, which promised to be an intimate, if gruesome, affair. Though we had never seen the real event, we had watched bull-fights on Spanish television several times. This kind of book is not the right place to enter into the debate on morality that surrounds bull fighting. I am not, for example, advocating we convert Rugby League pitches in Yorkshire into bull-rings. This was Spain, though, where they fight bulls. There was the bull-ring and there we were, so one must say something.

I am not a vegetarian, nor yet a particularly enthusiastic carnivore as it happens, but I know enough about slaughtering animals for meat to confirm that it is not a more palatable execution—if one has genuine principles on the subject—because it is not generally open to numbers of paying spectators. Furthermore, I live in a household where we routinely spend 20 minutes attempting to liberate a solitary trapped, daft bumblebee.

All that having been said, we have watched a slender, young *matador* mockingly wag his finger an inch away from the steaming nostrils of one of those ill-tempered, big black bulls, which had been doing its best to impale him, and then turn his back on it and walk slowly away. I cannot say, to be honest, I am capable of rationalising—by culture or courage—that kind of behaviour. However, since I have enjoyed, on more than one occasion, the distant relatives of one of the protagonists with thick, double-fried potato chips, onion rings and a blob of English mustard, I am disinclined to be hypocritical on the subject just now. So, if I absolutely must pick a side—arm twisted up my back—then it is going to be with the *matadors*.

The bull-ring audience may well have seen their share of big, black bull action in that arena, but it was soon evident they had not seen many big, black motorcycles and their riders in its vicinity before. That crowd was milling about the road demonstrably convinced that it was, temporarily at least, a pedestrian precinct, so when a purring 'Madam' nosed through them their reactions were quite amusing. We were positively crawling along, of course, and then that wonderful engine barely makes a sound.

I didn't want to be rude, since we were guests, by sounding the horn, so when several people first saw us we were right next to them and the sight of us made them positively leap skywards. I wonder if they caught a glimpse of a large black moving object and—given their reason for being there drew—for a split-second—the obvious, though mistaken, conclusions. Most, once they realised what we were, laughed and waved good-naturedly to us afterwards, anyway.

So we ambled through the village and passed through the Moorish gate again, leaving behind us Manrique on his *mirador*, predictably forever scrutinising his open page, perhaps thinking to himself, *'Why on earth did I write that? Never mind, I will change that clunky line to something better, after I have given that Garcimunoz shower the sound thrashing they transparently deserve. They are bound to be a push over, anyway. Paco says they couldn't fight their way out of a reed basket, so it should be a short campaign and back home in no time. Hmmmm, now I think on it, maybe I should slip in a few chuckles here and there'*

Gravity (or levity) aside, riding the road downwards was easier than riding up, because, having already ridden it, I had some idea of where the road went and this time the cliff face was reassuringly huggable by our right shoulders. We were alone leaving the village on that morning for obvious reasons. 'Her Ladyship' was on good form as usual, bless her, and was, I thought, likely to have some roads to run where she could lift her skirts and really go for it. I am, naturally, referring to the bike on this occasion.

The reader will recall that we arrived at Segura de la Sierra from level ground and I thought, since we were now back to that level, that constituted part of the coastal hinterland. It didn't though and from this promising beginning, the terrain began to inexorably rise and become progressively more rugged. In fact, mountains were rising in front of us, which came as something of a surprise to me, because I had no idea this high, wild country existed, notwithstanding it was quite close to a region we believed we knew comparatively well.

Before I continue, I need to clarify that whilst I have a shrewd idea where we went during the following hours, I am not absolutely 100% positive. I have pored over maps and it seems to me there are a couple of alternative routes between points I can identify—one of them looking as though it might be easier going than the other. However, that was not the way we tackled that ride, because I didn't think it would be in any way exceptional. So, I had simply set the Sat Nav to our final destination—barring any other considerations—and simply followed where the instrument told me to go, by whatever inscrutable criteria it was employing.

There came a point when I stopped looking at the 'thing' (as Pastsie called it) anyway, because there was nowhere else to go and I had more pressing issues that demanded my attention at that moment and the next moment and, indeed, the ones after that. We were in for an 'interesting' time and, after the fact, we were genuinely glad we experienced it. We would probably go into this region again, because it's stunningly beautiful country, though unless there have been some changes to the condition of the road, possibly walking next time, with stout sticks, a light rucksack and ideally accompanied by an elderly, short-legged dog to set the pace.

So further into that high, wild country we rode. It occurred to me fairly quickly that this was not the kind of terrain which offered quick passage to anywhere, so I apologised to Patsie for misleading her, confessing that I thought this wouldn't transpire to be a short run after all. Segura de la Sierra was evidently part of a mountain range after all. It was its first mountain. The first mountain of the Sierra Segura, or the last one, dependent on which direction one was travelling. Neither of us were especially downhearted by this development. We had come to ride for the fun of it. Patsie said that all was well. We would arrive in Mojacar sooner or later and in the meantime we had been given a surprise of adventurous riding in the clean, warm air among dramatic scenery. Still, the Sierra Segura—who knew? Flat road maps again, you see. You may say it, reader. I will understand. This was, as you gather, some time ago.

The first thirty miles or so took us up to Hornos, a village dating from the Moorish period, set on a cliff edge in a spectacular setting overlooked by a castle. We rode by it in an instant and though I have seen attractive recent photographs—at the time—what I saw of it as we rode by it, didn't seem in such good condition to me. A fairly good rising road took us by a pine forest on our left, which was positively bursting with the fragrances of resin and needles, whilst away to our right and far below us was a large, long lake of brightly coloured water, overlooked on its farther shore by another ridge and mountains. This was Embalse del Tranco and since a handy pull-in presented itself we climbed off the bike to take in the view and snap a few photographs.

We could barely believe our luck and the ride, though demanding, improved with every mile we rode. That road, in my memory and according to my notes made shortly afterwards, was narrow, twisting and progressing through scenery ever more imposing as we climbed and climbed until it seemed we must level out, until we climbed even higher. Thank goodness, we never saw another vehicle in either direction. At some particularly high point, I stole a glance through the tops of thin pines to my right and there was a vista of layered mountain ridges like long edges of torn paper, their blue to grey hues becoming paler by increments as they slipped away into the distant heat haze.

Things change and sometimes they change quicker than we imagine. Possibly, the older we become time condenses faster and it seems incredible that so much can change in a little over a decade. So having researched recent photographs of the region I am describing, I can only report that this is not how we remembered it or how I reported it in my notes made shortly after the event. Either matters have much improved regarding the conditions of the road, possibly including new sections of road laid, or our memories are considerably at fault.

We saw no other road traffic in the most demanding parts of this ride and there were places where the prospect of any vehicle coming in the opposite direction and meeting us as I was accelerating into a rising blind hairpin (not very far beyond the previous rising hairpin bend) had me in paroxysms of terror at the time, because the road was sometimes so narrow that a collision would surely have been inevitable.

This route was either absolutely not in a time and place for tourist recreation on four or two wheels or it was, despite our impressions of it. That consideration notwithstanding, it was indisputably fortunate nobody was travelling it at the time apart from us! So proceed reader, if you will, on that not particularly satisfactory basis. As I have admitted I have struggled to square our memories with maps. I recall that we rode by a small village which seemed almost a hamlet to me at the time, though on this road it might have been Santiago-Pontones which appears to be larger, so maybe it wasn't. Shortly afterwards Patsie tapped me on the shoulder.

'So', she said quietly, 'have you found this ride exhilarating?'

I had definitely found the ride exhilarating, but I was thinking to myself, I would not object if it was a little less exhilarating for the time being. What I replied, however, was, 'Yes, have you?'

'Yes', she said, 'but I wouldn't mind if it was a little less exhilarating for the time being.' And that raised a laugh from both of us, because I knew that she knew what I had been thinking. She knows me, you see—just a little. The prospect of less exhilaration seemed promising for a few minutes, but then we entered a sharp drop which led to a small bridge over a deep gorge and thereafter the road rose so quickly that I had to pour on the revolutions to ensure we didn't stall, disregarding the indications from the soaring temperature gauge. The first hairpin with an obscured exit came very quickly. It seemed to me that these hairpin bends came very closely one after the other. The road was steep and narrow with no possible chance of pulling over for whatever reason, so I just kept going.

Sometimes we were crawling along and the combined weight of machine, luggage and riders was palpable and dragging. Patsie urgently appealed to me (and that is definitely the polite version) not to stall the bike. The road became not only narrow, but I noticed its edges were crumbling away and so there was no way we could know how much beneath the surface was firm enough to support us. Beyond this frayed, unguarded rim, the land seemed to drop away immediately into a void. I remember thinking to myself, 'If I make a mistake and we go over the edge, there will be no rolling over for a few meters until we are stopped by some obstacle'. That was no flight of fancy. We had seen the remains of vehicles that had plummeted to the bottom of high places from the High Atlas to the Himalayas. So I pulled into the centre of the road, irrespective of its narrow confines, aware that now we risked a head-on disaster, if anything came in the opposite direction.

Patsie leaned into me and whispered, 'I am just saying hello to God'.

I replied, 'Not yet, love'. She knew what was happening. I knew she was attempting to be light-hearted; trying to reassure me that she was bearing up, bless her, but I thought, 'I've put us into a jolly serious predicament this time' or words more or less to that effect.

Every now and then shale or gravel spread across the cracked road surface and since I had taken a low-speed spill on the like of those little loose stones in the past, was as wary of them as it was possible to be. Worst of all were occasional very steep counter-cambers, materialising on hairpins, which inevitably always also seemed to be blind turns. Of course, I could feel their twisting effect pulling us in precisely the direction we must not, at all perils, go. That precarious development, which required pressuring the bike against its inclinations, combined with everything else I have described, was having its inevitable debilitating effects.

My hands were becoming painful, because I had been gripping the bars fiercely and going through low-end gear changes, braking, accelerating and decelerating over again without remission. The temperature gauge was indicating higher than I had ever seen it. This procedure seemed to continue interminably and I remember thinking that our luck could not hold indefinitely; eventually my limited riding abilities or strength in my arms would fail us and, out of my depth, I would make a mistake which would be the end of us. I have no memory of guard barriers (or low walls) anywhere by the roadside and, though Patsie has since confirmed my impression, accept that does not mean there were none. There remained, again so far as I could judge, no place to stop or pull over on this roller-coaster.

Patsie leaned forward again and whispered, 'I am about ready to cry. Are you?'

Reader, I was by this time very anxious for our safety and especially concerned for my wife. 'Madam's' big heart was still pulling us along gamely and my own options were down to none. Frankly, irrespective of her last comment, Patsie wasn't actually going to cry, because this was not our first tight spot and she never deals with them with tears. We both knew that for a fact without making more of it. So, as I put the bike into yet another sharp climbing turn, I just silently nodded, did the best I could and wondered how many times I had gone through the same procedure and how many turns were yet to be made.

I have no idea how long this state of affairs lasted. Almost certainly nowhere near as long as I thought it did, but abruptly we came upon a short, level, tree-lined stretch and ahead was a shallow scoop of ground, off-road, though no more than two bikes long, that appeared to be secure. I headed for it like a drowning man to a floating coffin. Having quickly braked to a halt, I put the bike on its side stand and we gratefully, though stiffly, climbed off.

Patsie and I stood limply, looking at each other through our visors like a couple of exhausted pugilists separating after a hard-fought bout. It is, apparently, possible to be both stiff and limp simultaneously. Patsie took off her helmet and reader, if you think I would concoct what came next, that is up to you, because I am disinclined to be persuasive on this subject or about that moment. For reasons that should require no elaboration, this vignette has its very own page in 'The Bumper Book of John & Patsie's Marriage'.

She looked up at me in the eye and quietly said, 'I'm not going to complain, dear'.

I smiled at her, because she is a fine, rare gem and said, 'I know you are not, love'.

'How do you know?' she asked *coquettishly*, (Yes! Even then!) knowing very well how I knew. I knew—and I really did know—because she was mine and I was hers and we had put in approaching thirty solid years together already. These are rare moments, devoid of politics or anything extraneous, when two people are right down to the essence of monogamy, which unapologetically actually is enduring love, if you need it spelling out.

She is a 'steel bonnet' on her mother's line—a Hetherington from the Northumbria west border marches, by the way. So, I know the stuff she is made of, when 'the pushing comes to shoving'. Fey as Queen Mab, friend to the birds of the air and the little creatures of hedgerow. All of that and tough as a pike underneath—predator fish or weapon both—pick your pike. I would marry her again tomorrow, if she would have me.

So I gave her the bald truth, as much as I could see of it at the time, leaving out the most important part, that did not require saying and would have earned me an admonishment for being 'soppy' when action was needed:

'Because you know we are in trouble, don't you?'

'Yes', she said quite simply, 'so that wouldn't help. But we must rest now for half an hour if there is going to be more of 'this' ahead'.

It wouldn't help, it was true and she wasn't going to put any more burden on me that might take my focus away from getting us out of this mess. There you go. Chips down. Close ranks. Totally reliable when it absolutely matters and her respite conclusion was exactly what I was thinking myself. Apart from all else it would give the bike time to cool down, because this was no place for her to give up on us.

My hands were really aching, so I pulled off my gloves. Both of them were completely black and for a moment I thought it was bruising, until Patsie peered at them and said, 'Don't be such a daft ha'porth. You have been sweating and the dye has come out of the leather'. She gave them a brisk dismissive swat to punctuate that she was done considering them. I felt a bit disappointed myself—they deserved to be bruised or have some wound to show after what they had been through! The reader will note how quickly we can step away from the romantic stuff. Ha'porth, for those who justifiably might not know, is old English—a half-penny, so little value—or colloquially, a foolish person.

I took the opportunity to check the Sat Nav, because I had not examined it for some time. There had been no alternative route on offer to make that necessary and, more importantly, I had been far too busy trying not to kill us to look at it anyway.

'Are we nearly there?' Patsie asked as I checked the figures on the instrument's screen, which were not very encouraging.

'Well, no,' I replied, 'I'm afraid we're not'.

'Really,' she said, genuinely surprised, 'how long have we been travelling, then?'

'Apparently, just over four and some hours.'

'Well, we *must* be nearly there, surely', she said with emphasis, 'How far have we come?'

'According to this,' I said, thumbing at the Sat Nav, though I could barely believe it myself, 'Fifty-one miles.'

'Is that all? Are you sure that's right? So, how far have we left to go?'

'About 115 miles,' I replied, 'but it's not all going to be like this, because we know what it's like from Mojacar up to Velez Blanco which can't be that far away now. Anyway, first of all we have to get out of these mountains'.

18. Fifth & Sixth Gear:
In which we come down from the mountain and reach the blue sea

Despite our recent passage through a stressful and physically demanding wringer we were, as we stood together regaining our composure, gradually feeling more positive about our prospects. We had a plan for moving onwards that we both agreed upon and that put us back in control of events, instead of being driven by them. So we rested for a time to put our equilibrium and our kit in order. We attempted to telephone ahead to let it be known we would be arriving later than forecast, but, perhaps predictably, there was no signal in the high boonies. I tried to send a text too, but it never arrived.

After a few minutes had elapsed, a small cream or white vehicle passed by us heading in the direction from which we had recently come. This was the first traffic we had seen, thank goodness, throughout the crossing. It was my impression the two men inside it were wearing uniforms and this vehicle had (I think) green text on the side which gave me the impression it belonged to a regional natural reserve service. It occurred to me that their job might be to patrol this stretch of road to provide assistance (if 'assistance' was, for whatever they came across, by that point applicable) in the event of incidents.

On the positive side, we could at least, once again, be grateful that we had been blessed with yet another beautiful day, so there had been no adverse weather conditions to compound our problems. I am conscious I might have given the impression we had crossed some trackless waste. There were some scattered buildings along the way, of course, so to put all of this in perspective, people must have come and gone about their lives inevitably and presumably without so much drama.

I struggle with my recollections of this episode, I really do. There is no doubt in my mind that there are riders and bikes which could have romped through our difficulties. Conversely I know there are some riders who wouldn't ride the motorcycle we were upon at all—far less over those mountains, 'two-up' and laden. Believe it or not, someone actually went so far as to refer to 'Madam' as, 'that monstrosity'! As usual the hard truth of the challenge will lie in some equation drawn from the road, its condition, the terrain, the rider, the bike and her burdens. I am, need it be said, the wrong person to give an objective view on the percentages of each consideration. I am minded, though have no evidence to support the claim, that a really experienced long distance rider would have some sympathy for us.

'Right lad, let's get going', Patsie announced eventually, decisively putting her helmet back on her head, 'but I'll tell you this. The first place we ride into that has a bar—I want a stiff drink. A BIG one!'

I am not certain how far it was that we rode along that straight section of road with the pines falling behind on our right, but if it was much more than a mile I would be surprised. When we cleared the end of the stand of trees, there before us was a completely open panorama-horizons to big open sky stretching in three directions. The expanse below us contained nothing more daunting than the occasional green hummock, and through its centre our homeward road could be seen running and bending in long lazy curves into the distance. So by the time we had stopped, though we had no way of knowing it, we were already through the worst the Sierra Segura had to throw at us. Need it be said, we were elated.

'That's it!' I announced (with some relief, I don't mind confessing), 'we're out!'

'Good', said Patsie, 'Drink!' Not one to mince her words, our Patsie. We didn't 'whoop', call for 'high fives' or anything like that. We hadn't won anything—we had simply managed to endure intact. The observant reader, additionally, may have noted that whilst my wife had not complained, that didn't mean she didn't hold me responsible for our predicament. So, I didn't merit a kiss, not even a chaste peck, in its most poignant moment. It was my fault, of course. When is it not? I was at the front end. Still, the worst was over and we like long lazy curves. Oh yes, we do, especially when we don't have to worry about going off a mountain.

I let 'Madam' have her head, so she could blow out her tubes, and it was an easy run down to the village of Puebla de Don Fadrique, though we didn't stop there for Patsie's promised stiff drink, which suggests there wasn't a bar by the roadside—or one that was open anyway. Mrs. Lewis would, I am sure, have made her feelings known had I swanned past one of those regardless. The place was named, incidentally, for a Toledo bigwig in the early 16th century who had control of the place, though there appears to have been human settlement there since forever.

The road then became level and straight across familiar flat, dry, farmland and we made short work of that too, because the bike was in its element. In these conditions the burden of two passengers and all that luggage melted away—not quite to a point of perfection—but very nearly. Patsie was and is a good pillion rider, delivering as near to 'two-up' Nirvana as it's possible to get, because much of the time I don't actually feel that she is there and that is good riding. In the middle of this stretch of road we entered a small village, which I am fairly certain was Canadas de Canepla, because I have examined photographs of it since that day and think I recognise the bar we went into where I ordered a large, though not especially expensive brandy.

'I deserve this', declared Patsie, as she took a gulp. I think that brandy was taken neat, its quality notwithstanding, which spoke to her frame of mind (or put upon nerves) because normally she cannot manage to drink spirits of any description without drowning them in volumes of a diluting mixer with bubbles—not excluding in some of my own fine malts.

'Yes, you do', I affirmed as her tumbler drained. I meant it, too. She might have had another, I can't remember and don't care. Lord above knows what that ride would have been like on the pillion seat. I wouldn't have wanted to do it, irrespective of whose hands were on the bars. Verily, though they had been those of 'The Motorcycling Sadhu' himself. She can pour dry ginger ale by the bucket-full onto single malt whisky forever for all I care and has earned the right, so I will cheerfully pick up the tab. I downed a coffee myself for reasons previously explained, despite my inclinations. The tough riding maybe have been over, but I never forget that no one is truly home until they take their boots off, so steer clear of the 'Who-Hit-John' completely until then.

And so that was that. Now we could make some progress, it was not long before we had passed through the farmland and ran onwards and beyond Velez Blanco. There is a well preserved castle that is worth a look, though, of course, this part of the world, its history perpetually turbulent, is hardly lacking in castles, as you may have gathered. This one is Spanish, built in the early 16th century, though as it happens, over the top of an older Moorish one, demonstrating that the right spot for a castle remains a constant. The place was comprehensively looted during the Peninsular War, though it has clearly been used for military purposes in comparatively modern times, because some of the walls have had narrow horizontal firing positions cut into them; during the Spanish Civil War, probably. Needless to say, we were not very interested in sightseeing ourselves on this particular afternoon.

We rode onwards to Velez Rubio—where I think I can recall young people under a red awning drinking in the sunshine—and then to Puerto-Lumbreras (which isn't a sea-port at all), where we joined the autoroute that more or less follows the Mediterranean coastline. On this road one could ride from Lisbon in Portugal to Palermo in Sicily—2,500 miles—rarely losing sight of the ocean and then the sea. For our part, all being well, we were not much more than an hour away from Mojacar. Normally, when one is riding one of these bikes on a not especially busy Spanish autoroute there is not much to say beyond, *'Te Estare Viendo'*, *(I'll be seeing you)* but we had not been going for long when Patsie's voice (sounding clearly in pain) demanded in my ear, 'I've got to get off! Pull-over'.

'What's up?' I responded.

'Cramp in my leg'. That was not good. Hardly surprising though, given what we had been through most recently. Well, we all know what that is like, so I told her I would get us off the road at the earliest opportunity and opened the throttle wider, so that time came along sooner rather than later. Put that fact in the back pocket of your memory for later in this tale, reader, when the cramp tables were turned.

So, we hurtled westwards, in my case with the words, 'Let me off, Let me off, Ahhhhh! Let me off', urgently resonating in my ear. I pulled into a service road and Patsie scrambled off, stamping her feet and rubbing her calf furiously. It was a good twenty minutes before she felt inclined to climb aboard the bike again. By that time the first striations of a pink and violet dusk were beginning to tint the sky

From this direction the first sight of the old Mojacar *pueblo* (as opposed to the *playa,* where we were headed) appears in the distance as an incongruous pale torn, eastern end to a little range of blue-grey mountains which is the Sierra Cabrera. Most of the *pueblo,* facing out to sea, is hidden against the mountain from this perspective. Our familiar exit was at Los Gallardos and from there, turning towards the sea, by-passing Turre and round the foot of the hill upon which the *pueblo* stands. Seen fully from a distance, the old village resembles a pile of tumbling white sugar cubes.

Mojacar may have its foundations planted in Europe, but immediately beyond its south eastern precincts Europe ends and there is only open sea. So its flat-roofed, rectangular dwellings could stand harmoniously on the farther shore in any of the countries and cultures of North Africa. Possessed of an almost magical allure, within its narrow white alleyways, over hung with vivid bougainvillea, its heritage is undeniable and the visitor may readily imagine that Mojacar remains a Moorish settlement, part of the lost Kingdom of Granada.

A short descending stretch of rose-bush lined road (black

cinder when we first came to stay) carries one down to the promenade echoing a strand of light sand, caressed by the shifting hem of the Mediterranean Sea—a sight, fragrance and sound that never palls for those who return to it. We turned right at the Commercial Centre roundabout and cruised slowly along the beach front, as the last mile or so of our outward journey disappeared beneath the bike's tyres.

All seemed in slow motion and quiet, beyond the time of the daily Levanter wind, which comes hard and hot as passion here in the mid-afternoon. I recall the strangest sensation; as though we were within a calm, special bubble and this was an honour lap that required some acknowledgement from those we rode past. Here we were at last. Did they not appreciate that not so long ago we had been sitting on our own driveway in northern England? Yet now we were at an ending of sorts—having come so far, through all those experiences. For them, of course, we had no story; just another motorcycle rolling along, gone in a moment. So, they ignored us, if they noticed us at all, as everyone does passing traffic. A lifetime allegory for practically all of us, I suppose, if ever there was one.

Our accommodation was within a small community, high upon a hill overlooking the bay. It was here that we would rest and spend the following three days unwinding.

Before we turn to the unwinding and before we began the next stage of our journey, heading—after a westward interlude—more or less northwards, there is an interesting postscript to our ride from Segura de la Sierra. I will remind the reader about our association at the time with the Hispanophile, the late Ian Robertson. He had been party to the planning of the route we had taken and as I have explained as an historian and former author of a highly regarded and internationally renowned guide book to Spain (among others actually, but he was particularly well regarded for the Spanish one) knew the country intimately.

He also wrote a seminal work on the English travellers in Spain during the 18th and 19th centuries and was an authority on the traveller and author, Richard Ford (1796-1858), whose works on Spain he greatly admired. I can't say I knew anything about this particular Ford myself, until Ian spoke to me about him. It is possible in his way, and with some justification, Ian saw himself in same mould as Ford and he was certainly one who, among very few others in the modern period, could have claimed to have walked in Ford's footsteps, by practically every definition of the term. We spoke together quite frequently, mostly about the Peninsular War as a starting topic, about which he was a principal authority among living historians and he regularly sent me his most recently published material on various subjects—including art criticisms—to read. Beyond that we chatted, as people who like each other do, about anything and everything.

Anyway, given all of that, it was not surprising that our motorcycle adventure appealed to him. He had, as I have said, some input in its planning, was following our progress and passing interesting and useful information over to us. The reader will remember that shocking image of the Pyrenees 'white-out', for example. Of course, after we had established ourselves in Mojacar we informed him we had arrived safely.

We had some email from him I think, but I have it in mind I spoke to him on the telephone about this last day of riding in the Sierra Segura, because I can hear the conversation in my head and Ian's voice and delivery was very distinctive. That voice was a version of what is sometimes referred to as 'RP diction', so unmistakeable. On occasion, when he called, he would say no more than, 'Hello' and when I answered, 'Hello, Ian' he would reply, 'How on earth did you know it was me?' as if it could be anyone other. So, he had me laughing from his first sentence. The reader should bear in mind we were on quite familiar terms with each other. As near as I can recall it, the interchange went along these lines.

Him: 'I must say this last part of your journey was most interesting. It had me reaching for my Atlas'; it was, predictably, the one produced by the same company that produced the guide books he wrote. 'By my reckoning you went. . . .' (and then he proceeded to name roads and villages sequentially defining a route which was, so far as I could tell, our route).

Me: 'Yes, I think you have it about right there'.
Him: 'And how did it go?'
Me: 'That was tough country, I wasn't expecting. It frightened us to death, to tell you the truth, Ian.'
Him: 'Yes, I am sure it did'. *(I know he said this following verbatim, because I wrote it down at the time)* 'You have, after all, crossed what is regarded as one of the last wild fastnesses of Spain.'
Me—in jest: 'Well, if you knew that, it might have been useful if you had mentioned it before we actually went into it! How did you get on yourself?'
Him: 'Good Lord! You don't imagine I would go in THERE, do you?'

I found that succinct rejoinder, coming from a man with Ian's well-known credentials when it came to Spain and guide books, highly amusing. In one of his obituaries, the author commented that Ian had a 'waspish wit'. Did he ever, as evidenced! He made me laugh every time we spoke—absolutely including on this occasion.

When I announced I had written a military history book (to be published under my own name—rather than a pseudonym), he greeted the news with a sepulchral and theatrical, 'Oh, dear'. I don't know to this day whether he was teasing me or not, so didn't dare send him a copy. I acknowledged him in the book I next wrote, but didn't send him that one either, not least because I was in awe of his scholarship and anxious about his acerbic verdicts, many of them voiced to me in caustic detail, on the efforts of those he felt fell short of the mark academically or in their command of language. There were quite a number of those actually, and I was in no hurry to be included in their ranks. I felt guilty about that, because he always sent me copies of his own books and credited me in them too, which I thought was more than I deserved.

So, though he admitted to me he had been 'in the area' (which could have meant as far away as Jaen, for all I know), I am not entirely sure if he was candid about his avoidance of the Sierra Segura. He seemed to have been everywhere in Spain, even if it was no larger than a broom cupboard, but I didn't press him at the time because, as per, the interchange was light-hearted as they always were.

I do miss him, though bizarrely although we spoke and communicated over approaching 15 years, we never actually met in person, because for most of that time we lived a thousand miles apart. Ian, though incorporeal as usual, does reappear again later in this tale.

19. Ignition Temporarily off:
In which we rest before turning to the west

The reader will recall that earlier in this book I spoke of a husband and wife couple with whom we rode motorcycles for a period of time. It was that relationship that brought us to Spain in the first place, because once they owned an apartment near Malaga—and they invited us to join them there for a short break. Up to that time the Spanish *costas* had not, by reputation as British holiday destinations, particularly appealed to us, but having discovered the ease in which we could fly out to the sunshine and in short order be relaxed, drinking good wine and eating grilled, salt encrusted sardines on a beach, we became converts. Foolishly, we had never hitherto considered that an actual Spain existed—and by far the majority of it—wrapped closely around the larger and better known resort areas.

We spent a year or so flying out to Malaga airport, hiring a small car and thereafter exploring the coastline eastwards, looking for a place that would suit us as a base, before we discovered Mojacar. If my memory serves me well, we were about to visit its area when our friend, knowing of our search and having recently visited the village himself, told me that he was certain it was the right fit for us, because it had a laid-back atmosphere and was devoid of high-rise buildings.

On the first day we saw the village we had driven the dramatic coastal road from San Jose and Carboneras. Having come through the natural cleft that gives egress from the Cabo de Gata, *(Cape of the Cat)* natural park (part of Europe's only desert region) we saw the white buildings of the Mojacar *playa* before us and, upon a *penon,* the minaret-like structure that is its defining feature. Patsie, at first sight, simply and decisively declared, 'This is it!' We had seen our fair share of villages along that coastline by this point, but in any event, I never demure when Patsie makes a statement in that manner. Mojacar is a holiday resort of course, because it is ideally situated by the sea—it's just not a very big one.

The windows from our little retreat offered panoramic views on three sides. One unimpeded aspect looked towards the Sierra Cabrera, where shepherds trailing flocks of goats could regularly be seen wandering on its lower slopes and where occasionally wild pigs could be spotted rooting in the scrub of its ravines and gullies. In the opposite direction was both coast and seascape. To the north, the farthest seawards protruding white buildings of the *playa* comprised the foreground and beyond them, lay the working fishing port at Garrucha. Far beyond that, though sometimes invisible in the haze rose the mauve-grey heights above Cartagena and the lagoon of the Mar Menor.

Directly before the terrace, lay an expanse of open sea where, beyond the skyline, as the migrating swallow flies, the first landfall would be Africa in Algeria, somewhere near Oran, ninety miles distant. On an exceptionally good day, across the bay we might see a ragged file of low-flying pink flamingos, their long legs trailing, skimming the swell, passing from one salt pan to another. In the season of the bait-fish shoals, very occasionally, cavorting dolphins could be seen in pursuit of them. More dependably, every working day little fishing boats would trundle by slowly—left to right—as we drank our morning coffee and we would watch them chug back home again at the close of the day, as we sipped our cocktails. The sun might not have been quite over the yard-arm by that time, but as I reassured Patsie, who occasionally queried the propriety of the hour for a gin and tonic, it was certainly over the horizon.

To our right the beach and sea view was shortly blocked by a final wedge of high ground before it dropped into the sea, though just beyond and out of our view stood an *atalaya*. These old watchtowers were once employed to guard against the predations of raiding pirates whose objective, among other rapacity, was to capture the young to be sold into slavery. If a raid occurred in daylight, smoke would be sent skywards and at night a signal flame would be lit to be seen by settlements and other *atalayas*. There remain *atalayas* both inland on high vantage points and all along the Spanish coast—rectangular ones, Moorish, round ones, Christian. Traders in human flesh, then as now a blight on civilisation, were not overly concerned about the religion or ethnicity of their victims.

Through these heights via a narrow gap, already mentioned, ran the road to Carboneras where we would go (and probably went during this sojourn) to eat a really well-prepared *paella de Marisco* at a popular restaurant renowned for making them on the beach front. This *paella* only includes seafood as opposed to the *mixta* style which can also include chicken and rabbit. The trick was to order your *paella* for a non-existent extra diner, so everyone had a share of the crunchy *soccarat* at the bottom of the pan.

Despite our initial intention to use Mojacar as an exploration base, very few of those plans were ever realised in practice. The place induced an uncanny soporific effect upon those—including us—who came to stay. So, one surrendered to its spell and days drifted by. The sea sparkled azure in sunshine or blue-black ink in moonlight. We dozed on the terrace during the day as warbling, brilliantly plumaged, bee-eaters flew by and were lulled into sleep at night, listening to the waves rasping idly back and forth on the sand of the beach below us. If I have made the place appear exotically idyllic, I can only confess that is the way it pleased us to see it. I know there were people who lived there as they lived habitually far further north, but in more sunshine, and that was their immutable prerogative. However, we were not ones to pass up a fantasy when one was presented to us on a platter, so we lived in *al-Andalus,* (as Moorish occupied Iberia was known), as much as modern times allowed. Ways of seeing can, thankfully, be readily extended into ways of being with a little imagination; in Mojacar we were happy.

It was a magical place, hanging by its fingernails on a farthest extremity of Europe whilst its connections to North Africa were ever present. The Spanish people we met there were invariably kind and it was a privilege to be welcome among them as guests in their community.

If I was asked what we did during those days of rest, though I would have no genuine memory, I could invent it all and be confident I would not be far wide of the mark. Most other lotus-eaters of our acquaintance there would summarise it as, 'Not very much'. I did take a solo ride to Garrucha to motorcycle mechanics there to see if they could help me with the broken connection to the Sat Nav but, of course, they couldn't. In those days Mojacar was not the kind of place where one could have readily purchased a motorcycle Sat Nav 'off the shelf'. These days the area appears to be better known to motorcyclists. I have noticed groups (predictably of the Adventure variety) regularly passing through and nearby—though I have never been to one—are a couple of race tracks.

I slept longer and more deeply than my conscience should have allowed. I did spend some time staring into the dark, re-living that ride across the Sierra Segura and had a shudder or two at the 'might have been' of it all. Patsie and I discussed whether we should speak about our experiences to friends in Spain and, at the time, we decided that we would not. We did not want to feel even notionally responsible if anyone we knew headed off to see the region, and then found themselves in trouble or worse.

There is much more that could be told of Mojacar, but to be true to this book's intentions I must keep its narrative on mission—which is to describe the motorcycle journey. To that end I must put us on the road again as quickly as is practical. Speaking for myself, I began to wish we had elected to stay longer in the south, though by the same token I knew we should not lose the momentum of the journey and when the time came to leave, I was ready to go. I do not remember Patsie saying anything to the contrary, which suggests she knew we had a plan and was content to abide by it.

Our decision to ride over the Pyrenees entirely influenced our route from the time we landed on the continental shore in Belgium. The Roncesvalles (Ronceveaux) pass is the most significant passage nearest to the western reaches of the mountain range, though there are a number of road crossings (some of them through stunningly beautiful scenery) and several tunnels. Irrespective of which Pyrenees crossing we had selected, our route to Mojacar would be and remain necessarily east of Madrid. Given we intended to return to the UK by leaving Spain at the port of Santander, we would pass to the west of the capital. Mojacar is on Spain's eastern coast, so our first direction had to be directly westwards—more or less riding across the length of Andalucia.

Need it be said, I spent some time reviewing our journey thus far, for lessons had definitely been learned, especially regarding the actual time taken to complete a daily ride compared to that forecast. Originally, for no better reason than to try something different, I had planned to begin the journey from Mojacar with a ride through the Alpujarras. This valley route runs along the southern foot of the Sierra Nevada range which runs parallel to the Mediterranean coastline. The main east to west autoroute runs along the same line closer to the sea, but we had driven along that on several occasions. The Alpujarras are ruggedly beautiful with a unique eco-system, watered by snow melt. We could access the eastern end of them readily upon leaving Mojacar, but I came to the conclusion that we probably risked a compromising start before we had made any headway, so abandoned the idea.

There is little doubt in my mind that the ideal; some might say 'essential' destination for our first night would have been Granada. Indeed, who could go to Granada, but elect not to do so? The answer to that question was, of course,on this occasion, us. Granada is comparatively close to Mojacar and so we had been regular visitors. I would take any opportunity to visit it again,with the exception of this one, because this was to be a simple night stop and the first after a comparatively long break. So with that in mind we were heading to Antequera—which is not so far distant beyond Granada, but is smaller and was somewhere we had never before visited.

It crossed my mind to write a fictitious visit to Granada into this book, as though we had stopped there on this journey, but could not make sense of the idea given Antequera's close proximity. However, since we certainly rode past Granada and since it is, in our opinion, one of the most notable cities in Europe, I will not permit us to pass by without some attention at the appropriate point in these pages.

So, the moment came when it was time to leave. We said our goodbyes, rolled down the hill onto the coastal road before heading back towards the Los Gallardos junction—this time turning west towards Almeria. We slid down onto the autoroute and 'Madam' swept us away like the wind. We whipped by the prison on our left and the exit to the craft village of Nijar. As we came level with Almeria, we took a right turn beyond the dusty hill that bears the huge symbol of 'La Legion', the Spanish version of the more widely known French Foreign Legion. The Legion remain an elite force and have been active in the most recent conflicts of the 21st century.

This road would take us around the northern foot-hills of the Sierra Nevada and we knew it well. Even those who did not know it would have been forgiven for imagining the surrounding terrain was familiar. Whilst that memory was being explored, that most memorable and iconic of Western movies musical soundtracks may unbidden come to mind. This was a location where 'Spaghetti Westerns' of the 1960's were made. These days tourists can relive the western experience in theme parks, though these old film sets and locations, left behind in time and relevance, had eventually assumed an almost authentic atmosphere of western ghost towns.

A bit further down the road, over to the left, upon rising ground is the peculiarly foreboding and sombre castle of Calahorra. It has odd shaped towers at its corners, reminiscent of giant salt and pepper pots, though apparently its claim to fame is actually that it was the first Renaissance fortress to be built in Spain in the early years of the 16th century. The place is undeniably dramatic, particularly viewed against a back-drop of the Sierra Nevada's peaks when they are snow covered and under a rising full moon. Apparently, though we have never been able to confirm the matter, it's jollier inside than out. Well, it would have to be.

The next town we by-passed was Guadix, a site of human habitation since time immemorial. The Romans called it Acci and the Moors, Wadi Ashi. I assure the reader that in researching these details I had no idea that it was also the home of the pre-eminent female poet of the *al-Andalus* period, whose name was Hama bint Ziyad. Poetry seems to keep cropping up in this journey, despite my best efforts to exclude it. I shall not be offering a taste of Hama's verse however, because in English translation it possibly remains in copyright, though I have dipped into it myself and it is finely crafted and delicate, bringing to mind a place and time that is irresistibly alluring.

Unsurprisingly, Guadix is not most notable for passing motorcyclists for its poetry, nor yet the battle that was fought there in the 14th century between the Moors of Granada and a Castilian Army. The Moors won that time, though a hundred years later gave the place up without a struggle during the final stages on the '*Reconquista*' when it was apparent the cause was lost and the glory days of *al-Andalus* were forever in the past.

Most notable for traffic of all types and clearly visible from the road are its troglodyte dwellings. These cave houses are quite common around Guadix, but exist widely over the region. Many who live within them affirm their comfort and convenience, especially their coolness in hot weather and warmth in winter. Nearby to Mojacar is Cuevas (caves) de Almanzora and whilst we were visiting on this occasion a huge section of rock over the cave-house settlement slipped, obliterating some homes with loss of life among the inhabitants. I believe I can recall the television coverage of the incident in which a journalist interviewed a survivor touching on the wisdom of troglodyte living. The response he received was quite poignant since the cave dweller philosophically commented that these occurrences were very rare and that, in any event, they had nowhere to go if they abandoned them.

An easy hour or so of riding farther on will bring one to Granada. I am conscious that I could write reams on that subject, but absolutely must not do so, for every good reason, so far as this book is concerned. Patsie and I have always viewed Granada as though it remained Moorish and recommend that perspective, because then it was at its most magnificent. To achieve this effect, imagine your view as though it was a photograph. The photographer selectively chooses what is included within the parameters of the frame, but equally that which is excluded and so, in effect, does not exist at all. It is a subjective position as far as considering Granada is concerned, suggested by a hopeless romantic, as you will have long ago gathered. Anyway, let's run with it.

Having taken over the North African shore, the Muslim invasion of Iberia took place in 711 AD and since the invaders had come from the south, the first area to fall under their influence was what became Andalucia. Their armies quickly destroyed the ruling Germanic Visigoths (who had occupied the territory for 200 years) and by 717 AD had spread over Hispania, crossing the Pyrenees into what is now the French Riviera. The Umayyad Caliphate (Moors—as they became to be known) colonised Spain, ruling until they were finally defeated by the Christian armies of the *Reconquista* under the Catholic Monarchs; the Nasrid Kingdom of Granada, being the most southerly and last to fall, after centuries of uneasy peace and periods of strife, in 1492.

The Moors lived in Spain for approaching 800 years—a time equal from the present day to the Middle Ages, Magna Carta, and the Crusades to the Holy Land and so forth: Robin Hood too, if that helps. Many modern nations are unable to come close to a comparable claim of sovereignty regarding their homelands, yet the disenfranchisement of their populations as interlopers would be considered totally outrageous. Ultimately there is no wrong nor right in matters that can be determined by might and the longer the outcome abides, the righter it becomes in the minds of the invested, until there are no influential detractors remaining.

Despite a fundamental irreconcilable issue of religion, the victorious Catholic Monarchs appreciated many of the benefits the Moors had introduced into their world and embraced several of them. Well they might, for they had inherited the rewards from a period which brought forth advances in governance, the sciences, philosophy, architecture, agriculture and art. In the end, perhaps predictably, the victors didn't take care for several of them quite as well as they should have done for their own good or ours, though they retained a fair number of wonderful recipes, thank goodness. That is enough history from me, though. The rest must be seen and felt by those with the inclination to experience it.

In Granada—to appreciate it from a Moorish perspective—there is merit in establishing oneself on the plateau in one of the hostelries adjacent to the Alhambra, because that will probably be where most time will be spent. Rise before the crowds have gathered and be among the first to enter the site. Visit the Alcazabar citadel and the beautiful pleasure gardens of the Generalife. Accompanied by Washington Irving's, medley of fantasy and travelogue, 'Tales from the Alhambra', explore exquisite courtyards and chambers decorated with the colourful geometric tiles of Islam. Linger by fountains, rills and pools. In the gathering dusk, liberated of one's own transport, descend to the Albaicin below. Take in a spectacular view of the Alhambra from the *mirador* at San Nicolas.

The labyrinthine sprawl of the old city will be familiar in form and spirit to anyone who has visited the cities of Morocco and Tunisia. Arabs and North Africans still live there and one may wander its more regularly visited streets with its tea-shops where *hookah* water-pipes are smoked, and where *cafés* and restaurants serve the spiced flavours of the desert lands and the Levant. Yet all of this unique experience, of course, remains within Europe. I can think of nowhere that wears its lost past so lightly, intentionally or otherwise, as Spain.

There are several famous paintings titled. 'The Moor's Last Sigh'. They all portray Boabdil, the last Muslim ruler of Granada, ousted from his kingdom and homeland, entering into banishment, sighing wistfully, as he took one last look at his beloved Granada before he left it behind forever. The story goes that his mother—who had been kicked out of the country with him—told him *'not to weep like a woman over something he had been unable to keep as man'*. This incident is usually taken as illustrative of the poor man's weakness, but I think it just demonstrates that 'Mummy' had been screwing his confidence down from the get-go, so have every sympathy for him. In any case, practically every Moor in Spain had been defeated by that time, so his chances of turning the tide in their favour were negligible to non-existent. Be that as it may, five hundred and more years have passed since that moment occurred, if it ever actually ever did happen in reality, but I could wistfully sigh for the passing of the very best of Granada and *al-Andalus* myself. To be fair, since this was the 15th century, I expect the worst of the place was fairly grim, though that said, the opposition was rocking up with the Inquisition in tow.

When all immersion in the Granada of the Moors is finished and night has fallen, the visitor may return to the present, head towards the banks of the slender Darro, at the foot of the illuminated walls of the Alhambra. Find a good bar, where the corners are dark, the drinks are ice cold, the music hopefully educational (sticky table-tops are optional—that's just me) and where they will order a taxi for patrons, because it's some climb back up to the top, as we know. That said, there were several fabulous small hotels in the *riad* (Moresco) style, originally built in the late 15th century on the outskirts of the Albaicin that have wonderful views of the Alhambra above, and to reach one's bed—from the nearest drained glass or coffee cup—requires hardly any climbing at all.

20. Fourth Gear:
In which we ride north of the Sierra Nevada across Andalucia

Once we had by-passed Granada, Antequera was an easy ride of about an hour or so further westwards. There was, in fact, a practical reason for terminating the days riding there, because in that direction the city was a logical terminus of our journey. From here we could conveniently turn northwards, heading towards Cordoba—another jewel of Andalucia.

I can recall nothing significant about that short ride between Granada and Antequera, so I will touch on another aspect of the total ride that does not bear on terrain, weather or national borders and that is rider to pillion communication which also provided the Sat Nav voice to the rider.

In the time that has elapsed between this journey and the writing of these pages, the reliability and technology of these instruments has almost certainly improved. I cannot claim, furthermore, that any issues we may have experienced in those days were entirely the fault of the equipment without the influence of my own ham-fisted interventions. I can only report that pairing them was regularly a hit and miss affair, requiring multiple attempts, if it ultimately worked at all. One function or another would suddenly cut out as we were riding and quite regularly we gave up on sound altogether as being too unreliable and time-consuming to perpetually resolve. At least extended silences when riding meant we had something to chat about when we stopped. That having been said, I preferred to be in contact with Patsie, because four eyes are indisputably better than two in the interests of our safety.

Sometimes Patsie and I could communicate with each other, but I had lost the Sat Nav voice, sometimes I could hear the Sat Nav, but not Patsie. If I had to choose one or the other and then I favoured—usually out of necessity—the Sat Nav. The problem, of course, was that one never really knew what function was working. So, the simplest way to find out was to say something that would elicit a response. On one memorable occasion as we were riding, rather than saying a formal 'Testing, Testing', I opted for what I thought was a more familiar, 'Are you there, love?'

The reply I received in my ear-piece (one must, for full effect, imagine this delivered in the mannered outrage of Lady Bracknell from Oscar Wilde's, 'The Importance of Being Ernest' as portrayed by Dame Edith Evans) was, 'Of course, I am. Who do you imagine is sitting here behind you?' Ah, that's my Patsie—never a dull moment!

I tried many instruments with varying degrees of sophistication or lack thereof in those days, never really finding a totally reliable solution. Finally, we fitted a robust wired system, but that was later and on another touring motorcycle. Whether we had sound on this occasion, I really couldn't say at this distance in time. Throughout this narrative I am aware I have given the impression we were in continuous headset communication, but that was not the case. We were in communication continually when we needed to be however, because where there is a will, there is invariably a way.

My own motorcycling, in my opinion, including on this journey, has not been forgiving of errors caused by technical failings or anything else. Straightforwardly, when riding a motorcycle, I do not want or need distractions of any kind. That's it. I am certainly a purist. I might be reactionary. I am very likely a curmudgeon, but in the middle of a difficult bend or an occurrence unforeseen, I don't want my telephone to ring, receive a text or email and I don't want to listen to music either. Furthermore, everything that is supposed to work should work simply and reliably. Too much is at stake for me to be considering anything, but that which is essential. Is not riding a motorbike at its most fundamental so wonderful, that it is 'enough'? It is for me anyway. In the vernacular, I like to 'keep it real'. That's my flag, so I will run it up the staff for all to see. Reviews of motorcycles that contain appraisals of their degree of 'tech' make me shudder. Each to their own, though, as always.

I had booked a room for this night in one of the well regarded government managed hotels that are to be found all over Spain and are noteworthy because they are often situated within historic buildings or are architecturally modern in notable locations, often with outstanding views. They are invariably exceptional in one way or another and often command, in consequence, something of a price premium. However, though we have stayed in them before, on this occasion I booked us into the Antequera one, because it offered a tempting price deal at the time. The building was contemporary and minimalist. We rolled into its car park (occupied as usual by top-end vehicles) and parked under its portico, in front of its enormous glass entrance doors.

Ours was the only motorcycle in evidence and most readers of these pages will understand there are few opportunities open to motorcyclists quite like that one to give one the sensation of superiority! A trivial, simple and possibly delusional pleasure, I know. I hope it's not my imagination, but sometimes it has seemed to me that I have pulled up next to the driver of a very expensive motorcar and when our eyes met, I knew that he knew I didn't envy him. He would be able to buy six of what we were sitting on for what he was sitting in—but then, he didn't did he? He was on his bottom in a 'box', whilst we were out in the world. I cannot explain this sensation more comprehensively or convincingly to the general reader, but can only confess that it makes some kind of sense to me—even if it transpires to be nonsense.

We made our entrance, *sans* options, like a couple of interstellar storm-troopers and predictably were greeted and welcomed professionally by friendly and efficient reception staff who, 'had seen it all before'. We should have expected nothing less! Our room was chic and spacious with an enormous bed: A far cry from that tiny green tent of days gone by we once happily shared, sleeping on an inflatable mattress between two zipped together sleeping-bags. It is odd, really, that one's fondest memories derive from simple things and times when one didn't have much money to spend, whereas the time spent in 'posh' hotels, for all their benefits, coalesces almost without distinction. We refreshed ourselves as usual and headed into the town on foot to investigate.

Antequera has an imposing Moorish citadel and its history is a typical one in Andalucia. It rose, prospered, endured decades of strife—since it was a border town during the conflicts with the Catholic powers—and, after a four-month siege, eventually fell in 1410. The inhabitants, though expelled, were permitted to sell their property, so egregious as their lot was, they fared better than many Moorish people during the *Reconquista* who were either brutally dispossessed of practically everything they owned or put to the sword.

That having been said, on first impressions Antequera could not be more different to its more exotic neighbour, Granada, because its atmosphere was, it seemed to us, decidedly Spanish. We wandered by a bull-ring where the resident band was bashing its way through a cacophonous rehearsal. Oddly, that dissonance sounded more appropriate in its place than if that music had been harmonious. On the pavement of the principal commercial street, outside its numerous *cafés*, comfortably proportioned *señoras* sat, sipped coffee, gossiped and, in the heat of the late afternoon, worked dainty fans which blurred at top speed, driven by seemingly motorised wrists.

The distant past is, however, never so far away in Andalucia. The slab-sided, stone curtains of the early Christian-era buildings occasionally parted to reveal elegantly arched courtyards, reminding us that this also indelibly remained *al-Andalus*. We strolled onwards until the street entered a square dominated by a church. Beyond it we could see the beginnings of a tangle of alleyways that constituted the old quarter, which would, true to form, rise to join the walls of the castle. We both knew that to proceed any farther would mean a climb for us as the sun reached its zenith. Though no words were spoken, we turned about by common consent to discover somewhere to sit in the shade.

According to Patsie there are two kinds of 'people watching'. There is the kind that everyone (including her) apparently does, which is to inoffensively 'watch the world go by' and then there is the kind that I can be guilty of doing, which is to encourage someone to punch me. I can assure the reader that, so far as I am concerned, I am also just blamelessly gazing about. However, I cannot see myself doing, whatever it is, according to her, that distinguishes me so unfortunately, so am in no position to dispute what she has to say on the matter. I can happily report, her auguries notwithstanding, no one has thus far taken issue with me on the subject of gazing.

I am indisputably a keen observer, and what I have seen was vital for the creation of words and images which were components of how I have made a living. That is the best I have by way of a defence, bar re-emphasising my innocence. I hesitate to mention the injury I suffered as a result of that previously mentioned orc attack in France, though that is surely reason enough to dissuade anyone from physically abusing an incapacitated senior citizen.

★★★★★★★★★★★★★★★★

'You stare John, that's the problem', 'Could we not say—I gaze intensely?', 'That's what I said, you stare, John and one day someone will punch you on the nose for it'. 'Could we not say then, that I gaze for a long time on one subject?', 'You can say what you like, so long as you don't say I haven't told you so, when someone punches you', 'You will beat him off for me—come the day though, won't you, my love?', 'Of course, I will. Since I don't punch you, I'm certainly not going to allow anyone else to do it!'

★★★★★★★★★★★★★★★★

There is a sweetness in there—somewhere.

I am fairly sure we didn't pick our place to 'watch the world go by' based on the likelihood of the afore written, but had that been the reason we probably couldn't have chosen a better one. A very small digression follows. Whilst there are a few subjects upon which I could confidently bore the reader at length, the development of arts and crafts in post-Moorish Spain—fortunately for everyone—is not one of them.

So as usual I will just give my own uneducated impression, which is mercifully short. Putting aside the ancient and Dark Ages, there are remnants of Spain's distinctive Moorish past, originating as it does, in faraway cultures and continents, practically everywhere. Less common is a similar style, almost entirely Moorish, though combined with European tropes. This occurred immediately after or possibly during, the *Reconquista*—presumably since artisans and Moorish style preferences still existed among the living. Thereafter, European influences from northern lands seem to have been embraced whole-heartedly. Of these, Spain appears to have adopted the most darkly ponderous, so far away from that of the Moors that their incongruity was pointedly political. The ethereal and exuberant had apparently fallen to earth and obsessions with sin.

Catholic Spain, as it first stood upon its own southern shoreline, its heels in the surf, had simply turned its cultural back to the sea. It was as though the banishment of the Moors had expunged Africa, Arabia and its own past from memory. Instead, it proclaimed to the north, over thousands of miles of Europe, *'This is who we are—not only in faith, but in every way'*. And, until comparatively modern times, the heaviest examples of the Gothic, Renaissance, Baroque and their gloomiest progeny proliferated, as one can still see in many Spanish homes and public places. That's it. Done; it's just a personal impression, of course.

All of which brings us to this particular bar, which was typically Spanish and of a kind we had seen before and since in Spain from Jaca to Tarifa. It sat on a corner, its brown exterior beckoning the potential customer into a sepia complexioned room with dark wooden fittings and furniture. A simple creamy-brown walled dining area lay at the back. Peering inside it looked like the kind of place that local life happened, so we entered and ordered coffee with brandy on the side, to see what transpired.

'Front of house' was being effortlessly handled by three men, several years beyond middle-age, who gave the impression they had been doing this job, in this place, for decades. In a corner, a vigorous conversation was taking place between a huddle of male customers and a single formidable, mature, raven-haired lady. Alcohol had been imbibed and its influence was possibly escalating both volumes and strengths of convictions. All the men combined were giving nearly as good as they got from the lady, though if I was a betting man my money wouldn't have been on them. One of the men, a dapper bantam elevated on Cuban heels, expressed himself with the gestures of a *matador* and occasionally took a step towards the lady to make a point, before immediately taking a prudent, tactical one-step retreat. The barman, leaning upon one elbow, shoved a thick digit deep into his ear and, looking in my direction, slowly shook his head in resignation which brought to mind an animated cartoon guard-dog. So, I assumed these were most likely 'regulars' and this was a performance he had seen before and more than once.

At a certain point the bantam left this group and, with a sharply folded newspaper under his arm like a swagger stick, marched up to a door, stood to attention before it, made another expansive *matador*-like gesture, took a deep breath, opened the door and walked out of view. Five or ten minutes later he reappeared, stood to attention, made another gesture to no one in particular that I could see and marched away.

I admit it—I was paying attention. Nobody tried to punch me on the nose at the time, though in my opinion, had the 'pushing come to shoving', Patsie could have seen off the bantam easily, because although they would have been ostensibly evenly matched, his progenitors were not 'Border Reivers' or maybe they were, now I think about it. Different troubled borderlands—same principle. So 'fur might have flown' after all. Had trouble come from the raven-haired lady, I would have run away without hesitation, dragging my wife with me.

****

Were you aware, dear, that the artist, the late Howard Hodgkin, would gaze at a subject for a very long time until he, as he put it, 'could feel a painting coming on'?', 'Hmmmmmm. Did anyone punch him for it?', 'So far as I am aware, they did not'. 'Well, he didn't do it like you, then'.

★★★★★★★★★★★★★★★★★

We ate in this place because it was inexpensive apparently, but my notes have left no clue as to what we ordered or whether, having eaten, we decided it was any good or not. With a performance that was worth risking nasal and olfactory damages to witness to its credit, that didn't seem to matter very much. When we left I took a quick look at the door the bantam had entered and noticed that written upon it was the word, '*Servicios*'. As the reader knows, my Spanish is not that good, but he didn't come out again holding a draught beer, that's for sure.

★★★★★★★★★★★★★★★★★

'Perhaps if I slowly blinked every so often, that might help', 'Why would you do that?', 'I do it to Rani and she seems to like it. It's a non-threatening indicator, apparently', 'That's because she is a cat and our cat, if you do it to people you don't know, you will be even more likely to get punched'. 'It might be worth a try, though', 'Yes, well do it when you are not sitting next to me'.

★★★★★★★★★★★★★★★★★

The following morning came around and we were bound for Cordoba. I have nothing remarkable to say about breakfast at our hotel, except we have eaten breakfasts at other hotels in this group and they have never been less than comprehensively excellent—some might describe them as lavish.

Having spent a fair amount of this book describing journeys which took far longer than expected, it seems something of an anti-climax to admit that this one was bound to be unexceptional, because it was deliberately only 80 miles long on a good road. Once again, we were no strangers to this part of Spain and so to Cordoba. As a birthday experience for Patsie, we had once flown into Malaga, stayed overnight in its own example of this same hotel group (which is delightful, set high on a hill with spectacular city and sea views) and then took the really excellent train—indulgent, though inexpensive first-class—to Cordoba where we stayed for a week in an hotel by the walls of the Mezquita. It will come as no surprise to the reader that our feelings about Cordoba are similar to those regarding Granada. We wanted to arrive comparatively early so we could enjoy—once again—what it had to offer.

I would feel no reason to apologise for any of the foregoing except to any reader of this book, who signed on for a motorcycle journey and latterly has not had much of one in these pages nor one to look forward to imminently. Which leaves me in something of a quandary. Should I sketch Cordoba and move us along on or describe it at the risk of succumbing to travelogue which might lose the readers interest? Lest, anyone thinks I am over-reacting, I shall explain my concerns with, fortunately for me at this juncture, a motorcycling anecdote. What happened was this.

We were returning from the continent, boarding a ferry at Zeebrugge to sail back to Hull. As usual we were waiting among a loose queue of other motorbikes and their riders when a man and his female pillion pulled alongside of us on a sports-tourer. He started a conversation. It could have been me, but it was him. We motorcyclists speak to each other very readily, as you don't need telling.

'So', he said 'did you have a good time?' I replied that we had, indeed, had a very good time. 'Yes, so did we. We rode down to *somewhere*' (please reader, forgive my memory lapse on the details), *very many miles* in one day and then we blasted around the *'something racetrack'* (and so forth in the same vein). So, what did you do?'

And I said, because it was true, 'Well, initially I wanted to explore the battlefields of the Waterloo Campaign of 1815 and a motorcycle is really useful for that because you can....' I petered out. His face became suddenly wooden. I could see I had disappointed him. That wasn't what he wanted to hear. He wanted to talk motorbikes and I should have known that. I felt he was thinking he had made a mistake in getting stuck next to me and was wondering how he could edge away, which, unfortunately, just then in that wedge, he couldn't. Some uncomfortable moments for both of us ensued. So that is why I don't want to make the same mistake too often in writing this book, though I probably have. Ironically, we had been on a racetrack ourselves, as it happens, at Spa I think on that occasion, though I never had the opportunity to tell him. That might have redeemed me a little.

I know what the problem was, of course. I was a big man, dressed as a biker, suitably sitting astride a large motorcycle. I looked like a biker, I am a biker, but then I open my mouth and all that other 'stuff' comes out. I can't help it sometimes, because that's me too.

I am unrepentant on the subject of visiting the 1815 battlefields, incidentally. Waterloo was a particularly significant historical event and the visitor centres are exceptionally well presented and interesting. The reason they are worth touring on a motorcycle is the usual one—one can go nearly everywhere on them without much hindrance and park readily. They offer a great short trip from the UK (for anyone with an interest in history) and the food and beer in Belgium are excellent for anyone interested in eating and beer. In nearby Brussels, among other things, there is not only a Rene Magritte gallery, but also a gallery within an interesting building, designed by Victor Horta, one of the founders of the Art Nouveau movement, dedicated to Belgian comic books and their art. So, a brilliant city for those, like us, who not only compulsively ride motorcycles, but whose diverse tastes also embrace exceptionally fine beer, Surrealism, interesting architecture and tiny blue people in funny hats.

As I have disclosed, we had previously spent a week exploring Cordoba, so we knew that the old city is another labyrinth potentially problematic for vehicles and for hotels that had secure parking. Some of those hotels have underground car parks that are several levels deep and feature ramps steep enough to be daunting for some—by which I mean me. It's the last ramp—coming out —that frightens me most. One has to be 'gunning it' in a car or on two wheels to avoid stalling and then one 'pops' out at the top, often crossing a footpath. So, I am always afraid I am going to collide with an innocent passing pedestrian or even find ourselves blundering into a previously obscured llama.

★★★★★★★★★★★★★★★★★

The reader may think I am just being fanciful with the hidden llama allusion. I'm not as it happens. Readers may be relieved to know that no llamas or authors were injured during that encounter, though it didn't occur in Cordoba. We may attribute that outcome to a motorcyclist's timely reactions, with no credit at all due to the llama which just stood there looking gormless as they usually do. It didn't spit on me though, for which at least, one must be grateful.

★★★★★★★★★★★★★★★★★

However, that problem was not an issue on this occasion, because just across the impressive Roman bridge on the other side of the Guadalquiver River was a modern hotel that was easy to reach and leave by road and had its own straightforward to access secure parking. So that was where we were headed. All went well and we arrived in good time and checked in. It was lunchtime when we wandered over the bridge into the old town.

One first passed by a small museum at the bridge's end within an outwork known as the Torre de la Calahorra. It holds a modest, but fascinating introduction to the city and its history and shouldn't be missed. Cordoba was remarkable in that during its golden age it was a paradigm of intercultural coexistence. Christians, Jews and Muslims once lived there in tolerance and harmony. The University taught in the most spoken languages of the region and so forth. Inside the *torre,* through a personal audio headset, the visitor could hear the voices of the great Cordovan writers and philosophers—each from a different faith — speaking in concert of enlightenment, emancipation, tolerance and kindness. What they had to say, given how long ago and where they said it, was quite remarkable.

My abiding memory on that subject is of a casual conversation we had with an Australian couple we briefly met, who asked us if the *torre* was worth visiting. We confirmed that it was and not to miss listening to the philosophers. By chance we saw these folks again on the Roman bridge, just after they had made their own visit to the *torre.* The young woman spotted me and, as they passed by, wistfully asked, 'Where did it all go wrong?' I knew what she meant. Unfortunately, I had, and still have, nothing more reassuring to send her on her way than a shrug.

On reflection, I recall we have been in the *torre* when several people have walked out on the philosophers as being too irksome to listen to—on one occasion dragging away their children, who had been inclined to listen, with them. So perhaps that is the tragic foundation of the answer to her question.

We should be consoled, perhaps, that since the future indisputably belongs to the young, that which has happened before can one day happen again. That would be a fine thing, indeed.

21. Still in Fourth Gear:
In which we visit a wonder of the world and ride the road to Rome

This lunchtime—as with most lunchtimes when we were afoot, we had more temporal matters in mind. Besides, the sun was blisteringly hot, so we ducked into a *tapas* joint for cold beers and something light to eat.

Cordoba has its own distinctive cuisine and I am very fond of its famous cold soup, *Salmorejo*. I confess I harboured a prejudice against cold soups for years. The idea of them seemed just wrong. Soup, surely, was restricted to cold days that necessitated inner warmth and so would only be consumed cold if one was so impoverished as to be in want of a flame. By this point though, Patsie and I would cheerfully eat/drink another one, *Gazpacho*, every day of the week in hot weather. She didn't quite share my enthusiasm for *Salmorejo* which combines bread, tomatoes, olive oil and garlic often garnished with chopped Serrano ham pieces and a quail's egg, probably because it is marginally heavier than *Gazpacho*. Both soups are available practically everywhere, though rarely made in exactly the same way. This one was alright and Patsie and I shared a bowl. We also had fried aubergine chips covered with dark honey, which were better than they sound they might be, though destined to be a novelty for us.

There is no way I can do justice to the principal reason for visiting Cordoba in a paragraph or two within a motorcycle journey book. The Mezquita is unavoidable and dominates the old city. If readers can be impressed by works of great historical significance, human endeavour, architectural vision and faith, then the Mezquita in Cordoba will stay with them forever. It is that impressive and I have seen my share of those kinds of places, including magnificent mosques in Istanbul, Damascus and other places. When we saw this one for the first time, we were astonished and, in my opinion, it qualifies as one of the wonders of the human world. That said, I am no expert on any of those subjects and my view of the Mezquita is one confined to an unacademic impression of its aesthetics, devoid of any doctrinal considerations.

Readers will appreciate (possibly in more than one sense) that in the interests of brevity I cannot describe the entire site. From the outside the building, though monumental, presents a largely blank facade in the manner of much Islamic architecture, but once inside the space can take the breath away. The roof is supported by numerous slim pillars, each one marginally different to the next because they have been re-purposed and originate from different periods of time and cultures. So, one has the sensation of standing within a cultivated forest of stone that sweeps away, out of concluding sight, in every direction. Above are tiers of Moorish banded terracotta and cream double arches, that confuse the eye with the effect of their multiplicity. The visual experience is amazing today. One may only imagine how it must have appeared, in centuries past, to those who had only known comparatively humble buildings and for whom the sacred permeated their lives. If the architects' intention was to awe; to create an impression of infinity and the eternal—then they succeeded.

To see the best of the detail of the Islamic building one must walk to the end farthest from the main entrance, where the craftsmanship is exquisite, the decorative gold copious and colours dazzling. After Cordoba fell to Christian armies in the 13th century, it was determined to convert this building to a place of Christian worship; a new cathedral. The hand of history falls most heavily upon the defeated. There are churches throughout Spain that were once mosques and in Istanbul there are mosques that were once, before the fall of Byzantium, churches—most notably the incomparable cathedral of the Eastern Roman Empire at Constantinople, the Hagia Sophia. In fact, it is believed there was an early Christian church upon the site in Cordoba, before construction on the mosque began in 785 AD.

It is not difficult to understand why the conversion of large buildings was seen by the victors as a more practical option than creating entirely new ones and why the converters would be disinclined to accommodate the original works sympathetically. The footprint of the mosque was presumably too expansive to be adapted in its entirety, so the Roman Catholic cathedral sits in its centre, completely embraced by the architecture of Islam. Integration of design (as I have mentioned) was impossible, since contrasts in style are irreconcilable. Perhaps, concordance was never intended, because the political statement—as emphatic and uncompromising as the landing of a gigantic spacecraft—would have been plain enough for all to understand. If there is a single place where one can grasp the story of *al-Andalus* and the *Reconquista* it is surely here. Did we visit the Mezquita again on this visit? Of course we did.

Cordoba has much more to offer. One can enjoy some spectacular *flamenco* performances by accomplished artists (enthralling even for those who might imagine they are unlikely to be impressed) and the Royal Stables of Cordoba offers an excellent equitation display, including an interesting interlude wherein a female *flamenco* dancer performs with a horse and rider. Everywhere in Cordoba postcards featuring the work of a local artist, Julio Romero de Torres are for sale and his actual work can be seen in a gallery that bears his name. They are evocative paintings of their era, many of them featuring ladies—some carrying the oranges that are emblematic of the city, because citrus trees actually do line the streets. A few miles outside the city is Medina Azahara which is a ruined Umayyad fortified palace city built in 929 AD by the *caliph* of Cordoba, Abd ar-Rahman. It's a UNESCO World Heritage site, so worth a visit.

In the late afternoon we returned to our room for a *siesta*. The hotel had a rooftop bar which is a good place to sip a cocktail and watch a sunset over the city, but I cannot remember if we went up to it on this visit. On this evening, however, we certainly (because I made a note of it) wandered back over the bridge into the maze of the old Juderia, drank wine and snacked on one of Patsie's favourite tapas dishes—broad beans and bacon—in the relaxing atmosphere of a typical Moorish period courtyard *café*, its walls hung with terracotta pots, overflowing with flaming red poinsettias and geraniums.

The following morning, we rode out of Cordoba as easily as we had ridden in to it, heading northwards to our next night stop which was to be in Merida. The distance was about 200 miles, but so far as I was aware (not that this meant very much on the wisdom scale, as the reader has discovered) we had no reason to expect anything dramatic along the way. We rejected the hotel breakfast, because we had long ago discovered the rewards of *desayuno* at Spanish petrol stations. We pulled into one not far from the city limits, parked the bike, settled ourselves at a table next to her in the morning sunshine and enjoyed orange juices, *tostada* and fabulous coffee, for which we paid just three euros.

Back on the bike the morning was cool and the countryside rolling, green and easy on the eye. It was not very difficult to understand why the Moors didn't want to give it up. As we entered Estramadura, the landscape reverted to more unremitting miles of hot, dry agricultural plain which would have been tolerable on a good road, but at the time the surface was rough and on occasions uncomfortable to ride upon. Lunchtime rolled around with no likely prospects for a break in view, until we passed an Iberico pork factory, which quite unusually had a restaurant nearby, so we pulled in for a light bite. Iberico pork comes from pigs indigenous to Iberia which graze in wild areas on natural foods and is considered a delicacy, so were not expecting to be served it.

Given the choice between riding the bike on an empty stomach or a full one, we opt for an empty one every time. So, lunches, whilst on a ride, were always required to be light. Unfortunately, we were greeted by the kind staff at this establishment as something of a novelty. We certainly ordered a couple of *tapas*, but what arrived at our table was a volume of food that possibly would have provisioned us back to the UK. We eventually resorted to our futile tactic of attempting to hide uneaten dishes, but that only seemed to encourage our friendly hosts to bring more. And more. Finally, we had to go through an embarrassing and difficult performance to refuse it. And the bill was inconsequential, of course. One meets some very nice people on one's travels.

So, we set off again, considerably more replete than we had intended to be. The road continued to be unrewarding and offered little to report, so once again I will touch upon aspects of the ride that applied irrespective of where we were.

Most readers know that the motorcycle we were riding featured linked brakes. There were riders, at the time, who promptly declared this was a step too far from what riding a motorcycle should be about. I thought this was a logical evolution myself, especially applied to a bike with the weight, dimensions and potentials of ours and the more so for a vehicle transparently designed to comfortably accommodate two people and their luggage.

Linked brakes never bothered me, because brakes are principally concerned with not crashing into something and I have no problem with anything that assists with the effectiveness of that. 'The Motorcycling Sadhu' once said—and this was probably the only time I didn't really understand his subliminal message—'Do motorcycles actually have rear brakes?' It may be that one can become so proficient a rider that they are rarely employed, but if that is what he meant, he was seriously overestimating my riding abilities and it is not a view I would subscribe to, nor one I would promote. I have every reason to believe motorbikes do have rear brakes, having in my distant past applied mine incorrectly, so experienced the disconcerting sensation of the rear end of my motorcycle passing on my right—determined to achieve the impossible—which was to sit beside the front end of my motorcycle. I still ride motorcycles with conventional brakes—front and back, though, tellingly, those bikes rarely carry a pillion these days.

That issue brings me to the second of these motorcycling interludes which is about speed and danger. Once again, this anecdote came from one of those occasions when we motorcyclists were congregated to board a ship. Patsie had wandered off to purchase some coffee, I think. A sports bike rider in a one-piece leather suit came by and looked 'Madam' over, commenting, 'I bet you get up to some speeds on that!'.

I knew what he meant, which was 'three figures and then some' speed, but I said, because it was true, 'To be honest, I don't,' and there was that disappointed look again, but I ploughed on, 'It seems to me that most roads pretty much dictate the speed I can ride on them and when I get a free-run, which isn't that often really, I will cruise along at between 60-70 mph and very rarely exceed that on the continent when it's allowed, even when overtaking on a dual carriageway. You see, I have the wife on the back'.

'Oh', he said smiling, and it was my impression, recovering some lost respect for me, 'I get it now,' and he leaned closer, and said confidentially, in case he had a solution I had not been smart enough to think of for myself, but wouldn't want anyone to know I was missing a trick, 'I leave mine at home'.

Of course, he was not alone in employing that methodology, as any biker headcount on a dockside could reveal. Actually, I know for a fact that some of those ladies are not so much abandoned as liberated to enjoy themselves elsewhere, doing something more to their taste. I do not see that solution, in candour, as much assistance for us, because for all our ups and downs on the road, we enjoyed being together on the bike, as we did travelling by any means. However, I am naturally haunted by the prospect of a nightmare telephone call made by me to the kids which would probably run along the lines of, 'The bad news is I have accidentally killed your mother, but the good news is I have an extremely plausible explanation as to why it wasn't really my fault'.

The reader may be tempted to observe, if I was so concerned, I had best not encourage her near a motorcycle at all. Nor yet in that case, into that canoe on the night when the jungle river was in spate at the Long-necks village or on that bush football pitch the day that bad tempered, one-tusked rogue came over from Kilimanjaro and so on. The list is a long one and sometimes I was following her, let it be noted—not the other way about. Patsie would possibly offer, 'venture forth into life, but 'keep your cough-drops about you'. Good advice without doubt, especially for those (presumably including most of the people who might read this book) who actually are going to venture forth irrespective of anything I might write, because you never know when you might develop a cough—literal or figurative. Eyes like gimlets, too. Don't ever forget about those, whatever you do.

So back to our ride, because we were nearing our destination—Merida or as it was once known, for good reason, Emerita Augusta. It is said that 'all roads lead to Rome' and that is probably true in Europe, because the Roman Empire has made it's presence felt practically everywhere. We Brits know that Julius Caesar showed up at our own door, one bright morning in 55 BC, but the weather predictably turned nasty, so he forthwith departed. The following year he gave it another go, but 'rain stopped play' that time too. In 43 BC the Romans returned and stayed in Britain, probably wet, cold and miserable the entire time, for over 400 years. They eventually went home, pining for pizza that didn't have pineapple on it, leaving remnants of themselves lying about, including some straight roads and a wall in the North that goes, coast to coast, from one side of the country to the other.

So, we think we know a thing or two about Romans. I am not sure many of us gave much consideration to the idea that Spain is some distance nearer to Rome than Britain. It is, which is why by the time the Romans looked covetously in our direction, they had been living well in Spain for 200 years, not least, I expect, because the climate suited them better. Incidentally, riding the country around Hadrian's Wall in northern England, close by the Scottish border is recommended. On the way one will see remnants of Rome more than usually intact for the UK, and be rightly impressed by them. That is, until the day one first rides into Merida.

The reader has by this point gathered that Patsie and I have been interested, by degrees, in practically anything that can be classified as interesting, whether we had previously given much thought to the subject or not. That consideration included Roman buildings and engineering, specifically in this case, the Roman bridge at Merida across the River Guadiana. This is the world's longest surviving ancient bridge at 790 metres (865 yards—just shy of half a mile) comprising 62 spans, which has been standing for two thousand years. For anyone possessing any imagination at all, it is an incredibly impressive and evocative sight. There can be few things that bridge the lives of people across the centuries like a really big bridge, because the traffic it has seen during its existence is irresistibly fascinating to contemplate. The massive Roman viaduct at Segovia will 'knock your socks off' too, incidentally, should you find yourself that way.

The ancient town of Merida was founded in 25 BC under the orders of the Emperor Augustus to serve as a retreat for the veteran soldiers of two of his legions, V Alaudae (Gallica) and X Gemina—a reward for meritorious service, in fact, hence the name. It became one of the most important cities in Hispania and the capital of Lusitania. So it hardly needs saying that the place once contained examples of every type of Roman building and engineering work. Whilst the same could be said of many Roman towns and cities, what makes Merida exceptional is that the vestiges of the theatre, amphitheatre, aqueducts, Temple of Diana and the bridge among many other sites, rather than ruins in the form of the usual metre high, stone floor plans, remain incredibly well preserved. The theatre still possesses some of its upper levels with statuary in place and is really impressive. There is an accompanying museum of Roman art and artefacts which is also excellent.

Roman remains are scattered throughout the attractive modern town including in the walls and along the corridors of our hotel for the night. This time it was another government managed hotel within a converted convent which offered secure parking for the motorcycle. The town had a bookish, cultured atmosphere which supported a lively *café* and *tapas* scene. The action, as usual, was focussed around the main square which was full of families enjoying themselves and I have a memory of children playing football there, as their parents chatted in the surrounding *cafés*, until quite late in the evening. We had another belt-straining lesson in 'one man's *tapas* is another's half-*racione*' before heading back to our bed for the night. Our room was in a former cell fitted with a large comfortable bed, wide-screen T.V, and mini-bar, and in the bathroom, several little bottles of indulgent toiletries. All of which was a very nice surprise, because I thought monastic types traditionally lived quite austerely.

22. Fifth Gear:
In which we ride over the hills and far away

Venimus, vidimus, ivimus. We came, we saw, we hit the road. There was much to see in Merida that we could not see in one afternoon and evening. So, we vowed to return to spend more time in the town to do it justice. We did return on two or three occasions, as it happens, and that is why I have been able to describe it in a little more detail based on our personal experiences. Since we are on the subject of visiting Merida on other occasions, it is probably worth mentioning that one of them was in early January—the 6th to be infallibly accurate—because that is 'Three Kings Day'. In Spain this festival is often regarded as the most important one of the year, because Christmas Day itself is not celebrated so enthusiastically as it is in the UK and other parts of the world. Gift giving—quite logically if one considers the Christmas story—takes place on 'Three Kings Day'.

The Spanish also celebrate the coming of the new year and one has to be a guest at a large Spanish New Year party to witness how this usually quite diffident people can really 'let rip' and have a good time. At the stroke of midnight in the Almeria region and others—one is required to cram twelve grapes into the mouth—presumably for good luck. This custom, whilst ostensibly possessed of quaint antiquity, is comparatively recent, originating in 1909 when there was a bumper grape crop and so a surplus. Fortunately, the apricot harvest, so far as I am aware, has thus far been unexceptional.

We have been in several different cities for the 'Three Kings' festival over the years and they always include a carnival procession that has numerous floats including three notable ones, each carrying one of the Magi. We saw the Merida event and it was a good one; a wholeheartedly family affair involving the community of all ages dressed in costume and having a grand time. Those on the floats hurl *caramelos* (little wrapped sweets) in huge quantities into crowds that align the route, where excited children scramble or catch them—sometimes novelly in quantity, employing upturned umbrellas! We caught our share of sweets and forthwith handed them over to the nearest family possessed of the smallest child who could safely suck a *caramelo*, but who was not that proficient at competing for them. The interesting variant of this festival near Mojacar took place in Garrucha. Since it is a working fishing port, the three kings come ashore from the sea in small boats, before mounting their floats in the procession.

Whilst on the subject of Spanish festivals—of which there are many—it would be remiss not to mention, 'Moros y Cristianos'—'Moors and Christians', which particularly takes place in the south of the country and in Mojacar in June. It, of course, celebrates the *Reconquista* though in a fashion far less celebratory historical re-enactment than colourful, good-time carnival of the Rio de Janeiro variety. The participants are divided into themed clubs, each belonging to one of the two principal factions. The costumes are spectacular and the entire ensemble, interspersed by walking bands, processes sedately with pauses for dancing from the top of the *pueblo* to the bottom at the *fuente* of the old village. The festival is three days in duration and includes street markets and large outside night-time parties in the *pueblo* with show-bands and dancing for everyone.

Our next destination was Ciudad Rodrigo. From Merida our road ran northwards, more or less parallel to the border between Spain and Portugal to the west. The riding was easy going across undemanding terrain as we left Estramadura and entered Castille and Leon. As usual we stopped for a morning coffee break in small village *café* where we were greeted with the usual reserved curiosity, until the owner's son wandered in wearing a T-shirt that announced his appreciation of a well known British rock band. So, I gave him an extemporised rendition of a few lines of one its best known songs which raised a laugh and proved to be an ice-breaker. Before long more family members arrived, customers gathered around and our coffee stop turned into a minor social event. For the following half an hour we conversed in a melange of Spanish, English, drawings on napkins and sign language, which works fairly well if everyone involved is determined that it should. Well, you can sit on the shore and look at the lake or you can jump in and get wet—your choice.

★★★★★★★★★★★★★★★★★

We Brits are accused of being rather lazy when it comes to speaking other languages. That might be true, though we have travelled globally and practically everywhere we went someone spoke English which, let's face it, is not much of an incentive to try harder to be a multi-linguist. I am not sure those speaking English as a second language were intrinsically more considerate. They spoke English out of necessity, because English was the most widely employed *lingua franca*. Only the Brits would consistently beat themselves up over that good fortune, in my view.

This state of affairs was surely brought about by a conflict in the middle of the 18th century which to this day pays dividends. It decided whether the French or the British would colour the global map their own way. So, 'The Seven Years' War' is recognised by historians as the first true, 'world war', not the one from 1914-18. What went wrong for the French? They were brilliant at marching, but we, being islanders, whilst no slouches in boots ourselves, were also brilliant at sailing—which is useful when one lives somewhere that is 71% covered in water and when aeroplanes have not been invented yet. So, the French lost. Had they won, it would have been their language that was comprehensively broadcast across the planet by trade and colonisation and we would now all be speaking French as a first or second language. That would mean, a couple of centuries and change later, they would have been the ones feeling guilty about it, instead of us. Possibly.

Of course, since we have spent so much time in Spain, I know I should rightly have made more effort with the lingo. The fact was, where we usually stayed, one could not get a couple of

Spanish words out one's mouth before someone picked you up in English and carried the conversation forward. *'They like it when you make the effort'*. No, *they* don't, in my experience. Most of the time, *they* just want to hone their own language skills and make no bones about it. I try to be a considerate person, so I don't impede them. Conversations about quantum mechanics and astrophysics are problematic it's fair to say which, as one might readily imagine, has frequently been particularly frustrating for me. Getting fed and watered, though—not so much of an issue—usually. There are exceptions to the rule, as the reader has discovered and will hear more about in due course.

★★★★★★★★★★★★★★★★★

One of the valuable pieces of information we were told during our coffee break was that we had made a mistake in our intention to by-pass the town of Caceres, which was actually on our road. Our new chums told us that Caceres was for the later medieval period what Merida was to the Roman period and so was essential to visit. Given how impressive Merida is, that was some accolade, though there was nothing we could do about it immediately. Rooms were booked and I had my own reasons for visiting Ciudad Rodrigo, so Caceres would have to wait for another time.

That time did come around eventually and so we can confirm it is absolutely worth a visit. It is also great favourite—though one among several others—of the migrating white stork population which can be seen (and heard by their unmistakable loud, rapid bill-clacking) on the high buildings of many towns and cities in Spain during the nesting season. Caceres' typical high stone renaissance towers built by the town's wealthy merchants for vanity and status still make for perfect stork roosts.

For those travellers who simply must own a cuddly toy white *ciguena,* but have never seen one, there are quantities of them available in various sizes to be purchased in Caceres. That undeniable attraction aside, it is fair to say that a newcomer to this part of Spain, coming and going from the northern Spanish ferry ports, time permitting, could do worse than spending a full day in Granada, Cordoba, Merida, Caceres and Ciudad Rodrigo.

Ciudad Rodrigo is situated very close to the Portuguese border, so we left the main highway and cut across country to reach it. To my amazement the road began to twist and climb. By this point in my mountain riding career I didn't need a picture drawing for me to know what this boded, which was shortly confirmed by a signpost which declared we were entering the Sierra de Gata—The Mountains of the Cat, I suppose, though there is, within the region, a village actually called Gata. I know what the reader may be thinking. How on earth was I caught out again by yet another mountain range? I have, I think, this time a plausible enough explanation. One may examine several maps of this part of Spain and not see that title appear upon them or to put it another way—it didn't appear on the ones I had scrutinised. Believe me, after the fright of the Sierra Segura, for the return leg of this journey, I was actively on the lookout for them, so it wasn't there.

As usual, it was too late to worry about any of that now that we had arrived on the starting grid, so I settled myself into position on the bike and thought, 'Here we go again. For what we are about to receive etc'. Patsie took the news remarkably and fatalistically well, as I recall. As it transpired the rising curves we encountered were comparatively long and the road was wide enough not to concern me about the dangers of oncoming traffic. Had this been our first mountain road there is no doubt I would have been impressed by it, but after tackling the Pyrenees and the Sierra Segura, I thought it tame enough to offer some potentials for riding enjoyment. Every motorcyclist is going to grasp those, whenever they present themselves. At a certain point I recall passing a poster nailed to a stake left by a Spanish motorcycling club that made it clear they regularly used the road for pleasure which was reassuring. In fact, a local solo rider on a red and black sports bike at one point whipped by us, suggesting tempting options. On the other hand I could feel my wife's body pressed against my back as a constant reminder of my own perpetual priorities.

Somewhere near the highest point we came upon a *mirador*, so I pulled in so we could climb off the bike to enjoy the view.

Very impressive it was too, for a mountain range that didn't appear on maps. I made a photograph or two which predictably didn't make the view seem that impressive at all, though that was par for the course.

There is no more detail, in my notes, to elaborate on the remainder of that ride over the Sierra de Gata. Furthermore, whilst I can remember some horrors and high points of our travels clearly without referencing my notes, I cannot bring anything significant to mind about this episode, which rather suggests we simply enjoyed our time and it was not especially demanding. Perhaps I was becoming *blasé* about motorbikes and mountains, but if that was so, I absolutely should not have been, because there were more mountains ahead and they would not, for several reasons, prove to be so accommodating. One can never afford to take one's eye off the game on a motorcycle.

Since the ride described in these pages, we have passed through the Sierra de Gata on the road from Ciudad Rodrigo to Badajoz. That road, in more recent times, was certainly wider and better maintained than the one we rode on this trip. That consideration notwithstanding, it was still beloved by the local two-wheeled fraternity, because we saw a solo rider, on the rising side, leaning way over, 'giving it beans' on a big, naked muscle bike. The bends naturally demand focus, but were comparatively open so possible for a careful, experienced rider and there were plenty of them passing through a fabulous terrain of slab-sided rock faces and fresh fragrant pine forests. The wider vista, when one has leave to safely snatch a quick look at it, is stunning.

During our original ride, Patsie, always interested in wildlife, scanned the sky and pointed out some raptors riding the thermals, but they were so high above us that we couldn't really identify them at the time other that they were very large—so according to my notes—they could have been eagles or vultures. These days I am fairly sure we would be able to identify them that basically, because we have seen both on numerous occasions.

That recollection brings to mind another incident of mountains and birds in Spain that I have not thought about for some years. It was not on this trip, but later when we were riding another sports-tourer. We were moving northwards through Andalucia, not over mountains, but along a narrow valley threading through them which had high, raw cliffs on either side. If my memory serves me well, there was some on-going consternation (*only on my part, as Patsie has reminded me.*) concerning an extraordinarily large bee (*I have been informed it was merely a bee-sized bee*) which was climbing over my shoulder with the imminent danger that it might also find its way down my collar. That last consideration, in my view, does influence one's impression of the size of the interloper, which was conservatively, in this instance, no smaller than the size of a golf ball.

Anyway, 'imminent danger' or not, I eased off the throttle, but before I could pull over to decisively deal with this pest, I spotted a large (enough) dark winged raptor flying low to the ground, through the tops of the tall meadow grass, across our route to the left. Abruptly, it changed direction and rising, flew straight at me, head-on, and in less time than it takes to tell the tale, it spread its wings wide filling my vision, threw forward its legs and talons, aiming to hit me in the chest or face. I was quite surprised by this development, I don't mind admitting. The bird apparently thought the better of this manoeuvre at the last half-second and it flapped its wings crazily, appearing to furiously back-pedal in the air, before it sheared off and flew away. I know that sounds an absolutely terrifying experience to have on a moving motorcycle, so I am aware how implausible it may seem that Patsie and I dealt with it in fits of laughter.

The situation was so ludicrous. This creature had presumably confused us for prey and, despite our significant disparity in size, had decided to take us on as though we were a stray, ailing goat. I suppose the fact that this event happened so quickly from beginning to end prevented us from being alarmed, though had it hit me we certainly would have taken a bad 'off', because I have known a rider knocked off his bike by a paltry pigeon which struck him in the head: Combined speeds of opposing forces and all that. Think what you will about the size of our raptor—it was certainly no pigeon. Actually, once a duck attempted to fly through the front wheel of one of my motorcycles. Fortunately,

I didn't fall off that time either, though the duck fared rather poorly. The bee? When I recovered myself, I realised it was still sitting—if momentarily—upon my shoulder. There was no way one could train it to say, 'Shiver me timbers' or 'Pieces of eight', so it had to go.

★★★★★★★★★★★★★★★★★

'You are being a bit hard on me about that bee, if you ask me. You wouldn't have liked it crawling down your collar.', 'Huh! I wouldn't have made the fuss you do. You can't handle creepy crawlies'. 'Nobody likes them, that's why they have two names—one, 'Creepy', the other, 'Crawlie', and neither of them flattering', 'Why you don't you just pick them up and put them somewhere else, as I do?' 'Who does that apart from you?', 'Everybody. Other wives' husbands', 'Here we go again, other wives' husbands do everything I don't do', 'Well, they do, don't they?', 'Yes well, if that's true, I do all the things other wives' husbands don't do. Did you ever think about that?', 'Since we are on that subject, I wouldn't mind choosing the duvet covers sometimes, you know!'

★★★★★★★★★★★★★★★★★

Talk is cheap, if you ask me. If one has a gashed leg or need a vacuum cleaner repairing then Patsie (since—in the latter case—it's her toolbox) is your 'go to' girl and no one will hear a dissenting word from me, but if you want a meaningful conversation on the subject of interior fabrics, I would advise giving her a wide berth: Just saying.

23. Neutral:
In which we go back in time for walls and invisible balls

In the middle of the afternoon, we first saw the defensive walls of old Ciudad Rodrigo on their elevated position upon the horizon. As I have already indicated I had particularly wanted to visit this place, because it featured significantly in the history of the Peninsular War. I am very well aware that the number of readers who are likely to share our interest in this early 19th century conflict, who also gravitate towards continental motorcycle touring, is likely to be comparatively small. So, on the one hand I shall attempt not to be boring on the subject, whilst doing some kind of justice to the fact that we had come to this part of Spain precisely for that reason.

There are many places in the world where it is not difficult to visualise events that occurred there in times past. Battlegrounds have, sometimes, the potential to be problematic in that respect, especially when they have taken place in open country when, unless one is an expert, it is difficult to know whether one is actually in the correct location or even looking in the right direction. There are places, possibly smaller in size and made singular by buildings or distinctive topographical features that make the task much easier. I suppose sites of assaults and defences are the easiest to grasp, especially when they have been well preserved.

During the Peninsular War, Wellington had to assault three formidable fortifications in Spain. One, towards the closing stages of the war that readers will recall I have already mentioned when I described our passage through St Jean Pied le Port. That siege was at San Sebastian, (1813) on the northern coast of the Spanish border with France. There were two others. Badajoz, (1812-March) which is not too far distant westwards from Merida close to the border with Portugal and prior to that, Ciudad Rodrigo, (1812-January) which was to the north and our destination. Strictly speaking, there was another assault at Burgos, but Wellington had to march away from that one. The reader has no doubt gathered we were visiting, for obvious reasons, the locations of actions of the Peninsular War in reverse chronological order.

The old walled city of Ciudad Rodrigo is positioned upon a bluff, one flank of it protected by the River Agueda. Around the outside of the landward walls, true to pattern, the modern city had spread incrementally and, as is also often the case, had been built over sites which would have been noteworthy on the battlefield. The historical walls and the small city (it has a cathedral) within are in good order and fundamentally as they were in 1812. So interested visitors can understand those by-gone events from the perspective of the French defenders and Anglo-Portuguese besiegers quite readily.

We rode around the walls and up the gently sloping modern road which gave access to the principal gate through them. Irrespective of its brief moment of bloody history Ciudad Rodrigo was a delightful and attractive place. I had booked us into a small hotel within the old city and had set the Sat Nav with the address so we arrived at its front door without difficulty. This hotel was a real find, being small, friendly and despite the antiquity of its surroundings offering an underground car park that featured a lift that brought one into the reception area. As I have explained, I tended to remove the hard luggage from the bike at this time to be on the safe side. That continued to be a heavy task for me irrespective of how often I had lifted it all, so any assistance I could obtain for getting everything into and away from our room—human or mechanical—was always welcome.

I cannot remember why, (because there had been no particularly taxing event to motivate us) but we decided that the first order of the day, after changing into our walking-out clothes—

had to be a drink, so we asked our young hostess for two glasses of *tinto*. She asked us if we would prefer Rioja or Ribera. We asked her to choose for us and if you have arrived with us at this point in the book, reader, you know why that was. She told us she must choose Ribera for us, because she hailed from that region and to do less would be disloyal and we said that was quite right (quick decision—quick arrival of wine) and Ribera it should be.

She served us two very respectably sized glasses. We drank them and they were, perhaps predictably, 'alright' and possibly a bit better than that. So, once again, it paid dividends to put ourselves in the hands of people who knew about subjects of which we knew little to nothing. We were also given a snack we had never seen before, which was possibly a hybrid concoction of pork scratchings and musket-balls which we attempted, but failed, to eat, and secreted in our pockets so as not to cause offence. I don't remember being told what this piggy ammunition was called, but if I came across a homicidal colossus and had a sling-shot about my person, he would have been (given my aim was true) a 'gone goose'.

Warmed internally by our generous serving of red wine we went out into the street to explore. The city has a museum dedicated to a collection of chamber pots for some reason, but fascinating as they might be to some people (particularly urinal enthusiasts, I imagine), I had a more war-like subject in mind. Without bragging, it may be no surprise to the reader that I know how the assault on Ciudad Rodrigo featured in the Peninsular War: what came before it, why it was necessary for Arthur Wellesley, who ultimately became known as the Duke of Wellington, and what came afterwards and after that and so on to the muddy farm land outside Brussels three years later where the Emperor Napoleon was finally brought to ruin. To bring that context to life would require many more pages than can be devoted to it in this book. So, it's impractical, quite apart from the fact that very few motorcyclist readers would potentially want to read it. I will just very briefly describe what happened at Ciudad Rodrigo which will give readers an idea of what an assault on a fortified position was like, a little over 200 years ago, for the men of the British, Portuguese and French armies.

Before I come to that, Patsie and I did what any tourists do and that was go for a stroll to find out what there was to see. We climbed up on to the walkway that ran next to the battlements (the terreplein) to the citadel and back and then to the Plaza Mayor which gave a nod to the siege, because a period cannon stood there, its impotent barrel stuffed with empty crisp (Chips) packets. Then we wandered over to the cathedral and back to our hotel. All this was very pleasant, but at the same time frustrating to me because I couldn't immediately find evidence of the historical assault that, for me at least, made the place particularly interesting. I possessed maps which would have illuminated the matter. Unfortunately, they were in England.

By the time of the Napoleonic Wars the fortifications familiar to knights in armour were a thing of the past. Defensive works in later centuries were built lower and wider to withstand the certainty of concentrated artillery fire upon them. Nevertheless, old defensive walls still existed, combined when possible, with newer works, especially when they encircled a town or city. No general relished breaking into these places when defended by a determined enemy, because it was certain to be a costly business in time, materiel and lives.

The method employed before the days of aerial bombing involved the making of a 'breach' (in the case of Ciudad Rodrigo two breaches—the 'greater' and the 'lesser') which was created by concertedly pummelling the wall with artillery until sections fell into the surrounding ditches, creating a scree slope leading to a vulnerable gap. At the appointed hour a storming party of volunteers, for very good reason known as, 'The Forlorn Hope' would rush this weak point and (hopefully) the survivors would break through into the interior, hotly followed by the main force tasked with taking the town. The process, as one may imagine, was far more straightforward in the description than in the application.

I ran up to our room and brought down our mini lap-top PC. It was the work of moments to send an email to Ian Robertson, who was fortunately at his desk in Arles at the time. Where was the illusive breach? Ian asked if we could see the cathedral. See it? I could hit it without the slightest effort by flinging one of the pork musket-balls I had in my pocket. Ian replied. We would see, he wrote, that the wall of the cathedral's tower was pockmarked with the indentations of British cannon balls and the spatter of shell bursts. How exciting, we thought, and how novel to be in communication for the exploration of a site in real time with a leading historian on the subject. Historical discovery in action. We rushed outside to look. There was the stonework of the cathedral's tower as smooth as the day it was erected.

I suppose it would have helped had we been on the correct side of the building. We skittered round the block to a place where, looking about us, everything now made immediate sense. There was the damage made to the cathedral frontage that faced the walls, caused without doubt, by artillery over-shots fired from outside. I have seen no reference in my notes, made at the time, whether I confessed to Ian Robertson that my orienteering wasn't up to elementary boy scout standard, but if I did, he must have passed on his usual witticisms which, given I would have presented him with an opportunity to make merry on a plate, seems unlikely. Maybe Patsie counselled one of her favourite English idioms, 'Least said, soonest mended'

★★★★★★★★★★★★★★★★★

That is good Patsie homespun advice I should have adhered to (but didn't) on many occasions. Like that time in a Sardinian beach resort, when we gathered for a drinking session, with a group of Swiss bikers whose respect for us knew no bounds, when they discovered we had come from England 'on the bike'. Then I opened my big mouth and told them we had put it on a train in Holland which took us and it across Europe (as we ate, slept and drank 'fizz' with our feet up) to Livorno in Italy, before we climbed on her again, very briefly, prior to taking the ferry to Corsica. Having buzzed round that island, yet another short ferry sailing delivered us to Sardinia and so eventually to their company. This place had a tourist trolley-train which trundled back and forth along the promenade, heralding its arrival with the opening notes (forever now etched upon my soul) of, '*La Cucaracha*'. Whenever that tune sounded, the Swiss bikers called out in English, 'Whoa! Get ready, Johnny. Your ride home is here', followed by hoots of laughter. That was a jolly enough jape at my expense, it's fair to say, the enthusiasm for which, for some incomprehensible reason, they never seemed to tire. Least said—soonest mended, indeed.

★★★★★★★★★★★★★★★★★

So, the site of the breaches at Ciudad Rodrigo had been discovered. As a matter of fact, had I examined the wall more closely, their position was obvious because one could clearly discern the repaired area which had been patched with red brickwork. We climbed up to the wall and stood in what would have been the heart of the assault.

★★★★★★★★★★★★★★★★★

Winter was hard upon Spain in the middle of January, 1812. Snow lay on the ground and the temperature plummeted as darkness fell. The allies had been battering at the walls for days and much damage had been done. The Frenchmen within the walls would know that an assault was coming at night and at this very point. So as more wall was eroded they would have attempted to fill the gaps with masonry, gabions and barrels filled with rubbish. Lethal obstacles would have been fabricated, like wooden beams with sword blades and bayonets driven into them, which the attackers would be compelled to negotiate as they climbed. The British artillery would have been firing cannon balls and grape shot up at the defenders and the French artillery would have been shooting into the entrenchments of the besiegers.

As the British infantry rushed forward with ladders to negotiate outer defences and ditches, the defenders would be shooting down upon them, hurling hissing grenades and rocks onto the mass of struggling climbing red-jacketed men. That slope would have been a scene like the torments of Hell, filled with scrambling, cursing and screaming, pain-racked men surrounded by the flashes of explosions, thick acrid battle smoke and the stink of evisceration and expelled bowels. The living clawed their way upwards over the wounded, dead and dying to come to grips with their enemy, whereupon struggles of the most primitive kind ensued with blades, bayonets, skull-crushing musket butts, bare fists and anything that came to hand that could destroy another man. Over 1,000 British troops—including a general—were killed or wounded in this small space, notwithstanding enemy casualties which were a further 530—the so called 'Butchers Bill', as usual always most severe among the stormers.

The British Army of the day, though usually held in order by severe discipline, expected that any town taken by storm would be temporarily turned over to the soldiery to despoil as a tacit reward for their sacrifices. So the attacking troops would run amok in an orgy of drunkenness and rapine that took no account of the fact that whilst the city was occupied by an enemy, it was populated by the citizens of an ally. Officers of all ranks, whilst generally finding this behaviour repugnant, did nothing before the fact to prevent these excesses and could only restore order after an expected and accepted period of time by the erection of a gallows and the application of the lash.

★★★★★★★★★★★★★★★★★

We ate a simple but satisfying meal in the town square that evening, sitting outside a restaurant we had been tempted to eat at because it belonged to the same folks who owned our hotel and we had been given a discount voucher as an incentive. We slept and breakfasted well, packed our gear and rode out of the walls of Ciudad Rodrigo the following morning in need of petrol. According to our friendly hotel receptionist, the nearest filling station was coincidentally situated in a place that enabled us to easily examine the greater breach in the city wall from the perspective of Wellington's assaulting troops. A modern authoritative cross-section illustration, puts the height at approximately 50ft from the ditch bottom and that seemed about right to us.

In fact, we have also circumnavigated the fortified walls of

Badajoz which was the next French held town to be assaulted by Wellington's army. That place epitomised the horrors of this kind of warfare. In places the walls of Badajoz are so high (especially since many of them stand on formidably high rising ground to begin with) that the prospect of fighting one's way through them seems inconceivable. The British Army lost over 4,600 men, of which over 3,700 of them fell in the storming of the breaches alone.

There is one more incident about the breaches at Ciudad Rodrigo that I have deliberately left until the last in this chapter, because it segues nicely with the following chapter of this book. As we were wandering around during the previous evening, I made a few photographs. At the time, the light of the day was falling into mauve twilight, so I had no great expectations of them other than as *aide-memoires* of our visit. They portrayed, after all, nothing more exciting than rather uninteresting sections of anonymous wall devoid of context unless one was 'in the know'.

As I examined my efforts, some of those digital images were absolutely covered with what appeared to spherical bubbles of various sizes in the air. Need it be emphasised, there were no 'bubbles' at all visible to the human eye. Annoyed, I deleted them from the camera as useless. Sometime later, I saw a television programme that claimed this phenomena, recorded digitally, was sometimes attributed to supernatural manifestations. Need it be said, I was not ready then or now to subscribe to that theory without question. Firstly, there is an explanation for practically everything that is more pragmatic than the other worldly and secondly, photography is something I know a little about. So, I know that light can create all manner of effects (including spheres) especially when it hits dust particles and the like. All that having been said, I did think the effect was peculiar, because I had never seen so many of these spheres or orbs before on a single image and I would not expect there to be much dust or other particulates suspended in the air outside, high in a light breeze.

All that taken into account, these photographs were indisputably taken on the site of human trauma and slaughter. So the location, the unlikelihood of inexplicable phenomena aside, held a verifiable potential for the extraordinary. If anyone is curious whether I felt something unusual in the atmosphere at the time, the answer is 'not a thing', but I suspect the palate of my psychic sensitivity is as blunted as the one in my mouth, so that doesn't surprise me.

Those who know anything about the literature of the supernatural will recall that in times past larger works of fiction sometimes included a self-contained ghost story. Ghost stories were once very popular among an audience whose principal entertainment was reading, so I imagine these inclusions were intended as diversionary interludes. I have what may possibly be a ghost story for the reader that concerns Patsie and I. Our tale took place as we were wandering around Spain, though not at the time of this journey. It didn't happen in Ciudad Rodrigo, but in a town that was not too far distant from it as the raven flies, though considerably farther away for flitting bats, which can be easily distracted and then forget where they were going. Where was I? Oh, yes. Non-disclosure.

I am not going to name that town or the house specifically because it is, or was at the time, commercial premises. In my opinion it would be inappropriate to draw attention to such a place when, for all I know, there is a perfectly rational and reasonable explanation for an experience that only we can report as having taken place at all or consider inexplicable. So why include it here? I doubt that I will be writing another book concerning our Spanish travels, two wheeled or otherwise, so if the story didn't appear in this one, it would not appear in print at all, which would be a shame, in my view, since it's the only uncanny story entirely based on my personal experience that I have.

Oh, come on! Who doesn't like a ghost story—even if it's only a ghost story—maybe?

24. Another Interlude:
In which there are definitely things that go bump in the night

What happened was this. It was winter. Believe it or not, during the final days of December, when the white-walled streets of the town remained festooned with hanging baskets of poinsettias. Red bunting and banners featuring a rosy complexioned, though otherwise naked and pallid Christ child underwritten by, *'Feliz Navidad'* completed the festive scene. So, credit me with this at least, one could hardly give a tale an earlier self-inflicted dent in its credibility; a ghost story—perhaps—that actually did take place at Christmas time.

We had selected somewhere for a single night stay in a bed and breakfast establishment within a very old and historic building—16th century, I wouldn't be surprised to learn. The house was typically wide and low, standing directly on to the street, with a single upper floor level, a heavy, studded timber front door and redoubtable metal *rejas* at the windows, which would have kept practically anything unwelcome outside.

Once inside, (where the *rejas,* possibly disconcertingly, if one dwelt upon them, would do much the same job for whoever or whatever was within) the rooms had the quality of a dimly lit regional museum. I suppose it was very typical of many traditional Spanish town houses of that kind, because the furniture was dark and heavy, the ceilings were low with massive exposed beams and opposite the main door rose a substantial sombre wooden staircase which would have accommodated two or three *caballero*s wearing *cuirasses* and *morions* tramping up or down it. I know I am setting the scene in a manner that suggests *cliché*, but that was genuinely what the place appeared like to us.

We did not see over the entire building during our brief stay, but I believe it was divided into two parts separated by a central courtyard where breakfast was served in good weather. It was the front part that contained the rooms for guests. The rear section, as I understand it, was occupied by our hostess and presumably her family, though we did not see any permanent resident, other than her, during our time there. She was a friendly, accommodating lady and we had no complaints of her attention or service. Our room was to the right of the front door on, of course, the ground level. Our travelling companion (for there were three of us in our party) had a room on the left, also on the ground floor, though further from the street, adjacent to the courtyard. I am sure we were told there was only one other guest when we checked in, but at that point we had not seen who it was.

Our room was large and, quite typically for Spanish dwellings of this vintage, filled with antique furniture, interesting old prints on the walls and ornaments scattered around as though it was someone's home—which essentially was what it was. The large double bedstead had a magnificent ornate brass head and foot.

I suppose there would be some people—especially those more familiar with contemporary living—who might have found these surroundings oppressive, but that never occurred to us, because we have slept in everything from a medieval castle to a reed *basha* on a raft in our time and, in any event, live in a period property ourselves. Several visitors have enquired, upon their first visit to our English mid-Victorian period home whether it was haunted and I have told them that it wasn't or (at the other end of a scale of possible options) a tale of a translucent lady, who we had Christened, Mrs. Laxative (because she materialised wringing her hands when one was seated on the lavatory), dependent on what I calculated they were gullible enough to believe. So, we considered our room for the night on this occasion to be both characterful and comfortable.

We spent the evening in a local restaurant as usual before returning to our hostelry for bed. As we came into the place that evening our companion said his 'goodnights' without delay and wandered down the corridor to his own room. Our hostess was in the entrance area at the time having been in discussion with the other guest. I do not remember seeing his face, but as she turned to speak to us, I could see him over her shoulder as he began to climb the staircase. So, his room was somewhere on that first floor, but we didn't know where and we had no reason to enquire.

My impression was he must have been an elderly person, because he was quite small and as he slowly climbed his body was bent forward, so I could not see much of his head, though I am not suggesting, for a moment, that he didn't have one. He was wearing a pale blue sweater, slacks and trainers, because I recall a band of white rubber—visible at the heels—on the dividing line between the soles and the uppers. Odd how tiny details stick in the memory. We exchanged a few pleasantries with our hostess, who locked the building for the night, and then, bidding her a *buenas noches*, went to our room to prepare for bed.

There was nothing remarkable about that, except that when we shut off the main room lighting a small amount of dirty, sodium yellow light crept into the room through the slats of the window shutters from the street lights outside. That wasn't much of an issue, though it meant that the room was never in complete darkness. Nevertheless, we settled ourselves down to sleep and since the mattress was deep and soft, it was not long, I suppose, before we both fell asleep. We hadn't heard the guest who occupied an upstairs room moving about, so we didn't think he must be somewhere else on that floor—we just didn't consider him at all.

Then I awoke. I don't know why and wasn't drowsy, but instantly wide awake. I had been sleeping as usual on my right side and I recall turning halfway over and seeing the yellow light still filtering through the shutters and beside me, of course, Patsie's sleeping form under the sheets. I had a sense (maybe I checked my watch—I can't remember) that it was after two thirty in the morning. Everywhere, as one might expect, was completely quiet.

Then the noises began. They were extraordinarily loud as they broke the silence and were coming from the room above ours and so made upon the wooden floor of that room which was, of course, also the ceiling of our room. First came five or six brisk steps, made it seemed to me, by someone wearing hard 'Cuban', wide-heeled shoes. It struck me straight away that these steps seemed to start nowhere in particular in relation to the walls of our room and ceased abruptly somewhere just beyond the end of our bed. In other words, whoever it was had not just come through the door, if the upper room corresponded with our own. I didn't really have the time to think whether this was someone suffering from insomnia or in the process of leaving or arriving at an unorthodox hour, because then the next noise began.

This was the sound of a ball—a very hard ball being rolled diagonally across the wooden floor. My sense was it was like a Petanque *boule* or a small metal cannon-shot. That noise stopped, also abruptly, at a distance more or less, halfway up our bed, but over in the right side of the room. Most notably, that noise didn't start from the place the steps had finished. I thought all this must surely have awakened Patsie, so I levered myself onto my elbow to look, but she had not moved a muscle and was apparently sleeping soundly, lying, as usual, on her left side. Next and directly above my head came the sound of a large chest or some other piece of heavy furniture, which was standing against the wall, being dragged about creating very loud hollow, scraping noises. Patsie still didn't move. Then everything fell quiet again.

I lay down on my pillow to think. That was very peculiar, I thought, not least because the person upstairs must have put on the boots before the short walk and then removed them afterwards to tackle the chest. Unless there were two people up there—one stomping about like a *flamenco* dancer and the other as silently stealthy as an Apache, until he began rolling cannon-balls and moving furniture around. Furthermore, it was difficult to reconcile any of these antics with the figure of the small man

I had seen climbing the stairs to his own bedroom, given he was, allegedly, the only person occupying a room on the upper floor. Surely there had been no late arrival after we had retired for bed. The place had been locked in our presence, our hostess had returned to her rear wing and in any event our room was adjacent to the front door, so one would have expected to have heard someone attempting to gain entrance. I suppose my deliberations lasted for no more than two minutes, because then the noises began again.

I am fairly certain that the noises were not merely similar the second time, but were identical as they would have been if an audio tape was being replayed. I may as well confess that it is—at this distance in time—not entirely clear in my memory whether I heard this sequence twice or three times. I can definitely claim that I had enough time to consider that these sounds had a quality to them that resonated on the floor/ceiling in a way that I thought the playing of an audio tape *within the space* of the upper room would not have done. To clarify that impression, I decided that when it came time—by that point reliably—that the chest was being moved, I would try to find out one way or the other.

Anyway, as the scraping noises reached their loudest, I reached behind me, over my head and lightly pressed my finger tips on to the plaster of the wall. Tremors of movement ran down the wall, through my fingers and into my hand. So, I thought, 'Oh, this is really happening, then'. I looked over at Patsie again. She still had not stirred and I was considering I was experiencing a haunting—on my own.

So, what to do? There was no one to inform near at hand and we had nowhere to go in the middle of the night. I could see no point in waking Patsie. She would be grumpy and upon being disturbed, she would have listened to me as I recounted what I had heard and then, without doubt, she would have asked me what I would like her to do about it. When I inevitably said, 'Nothing', she would then have asked, 'Then why did you wake me up?' I know her. What could I say, 'To share it all with you.' or, 'To frighten you?' Neither answer would have gone down well with her, especially the second option which would have been viewed as adding insult to injury, since she knew that I knew she wouldn't be frightened.

Had there been a howling Banshee flying about our room that would have been an acceptable reason to disturb her night, but if it had already flown out the window to howl somewhere else before she woke, then troubling her would have been reckoned selfish on my part. No blame would have been ascribed to the Banshee (the presence of which wouldn't have been queried, by the way) which she would have considered was only doing what came supernaturally, but which, in departing, would be credited with having more consideration for her nightly repose than I could be depended upon to ensure.

I know what you are thinking, reader. How could there possibly be a scenario in this poor man's life that involved a Banshee, but could still result in it being his fault? Fairly easily, actually, because I'm married. So, concluding that my best course of action was the proactivity of a pupating caterpillar, I settled myself down with a determination to ignore our neighbour's shenanigans—phantasmagorical or otherwise—and go to sleep. I don't think I was very long dropping off either.

Morning came around as it invariably does. I didn't mention the night bumps and we went into the sunlit courtyard for our breakfast. When we had finished eating, I took my wife gently by the elbow to guide her to a quiet corner and once there said, 'Can I have a word with you about something, please love?'

You have a fair idea, by now, what is coming next, don't you, reader?

She replied, cool and innocent as you like, 'Is it about the haunting?'

'No, No,' I responded, 'I was just wondering if you would like to borrow a clean pair of my socks'.

'No thanks. I'm alright for socks at the moment', she said, turning away as though we were done.

'Hang on a minute,' I said, 'Yes, of course it's about the flipping haunting. What else would it be about? Were you awake the whole time it was going on?'

'Of course, I was,' she replied with theatrical sigh, as though it was a ludicrous question, 'who could sleep through that racket?'

'Well, I rather had the impression you could—you didn't move, anyway—I checked.' There was no point whatsoever in making any more of that when she was being inscrutable, so I said, 'Was it a haunting, then, do you think?'

'To be honest', she replied, 'my first thought was the man in the upstairs room was doing a 'moonlight flit'; clearing off in the middle of the night without paying his bill. But then I realised it was something else. So, yes, I do think it was possibly a haunting. I didn't sense it meant any harm though, did you?'

'No, not really,' I said, since that was true. To me it wasn't an 'it', but rather a series of noises, though made by something, not an instrumental recording of something. So, I was more puzzled than fearful. Nothing had walked moaning through a wall, pointing an accusatory skeletal finger in my direction. I wouldn't have liked that very much, though I'm not prejudiced against the translucent community. That said, Patsie is the fey one; my usual criteria for determining whether something doesn't mean us harm is when it stops twitching or is a dot receding into the distance as we flee. I believed her, though. I always do when it comes to this kind of other worldly stuff. I am not claiming that the problematic to explain comes along regularly; just sometimes and this wasn't the first time. I wouldn't be surprised if she attracts it.

'No, well, in that case', she said, 'the simplest thing to do was go back to sleep, so that's what I did. No point in making a fuss about it and, as it turned out, you didn't need your little hand holding'.

'I suppose not' I said. I can't say I would have objected to a little hand-holding actually, had I been asked, but as usual, I wasn't. After all these years I remain bewildered at the ease with which my wife can discuss a potentially supernatural event in the same manner as she would the arrival or otherwise of a No.10 omnibus.

Did we ask our hostess if she knew her house was possibly haunted? No, we didn't. In any case, we might have been the first and only people ever to hear those noises. Did we ask her which first floor room her other guest occupied? No, again. Well, we wouldn't want to cause a fuss, would we? What can I say.? There is something about us that's compulsively undemonstrative. I have often wondered what is bad enough to warrant a fuss for my wife (a favourite word for any unwarranted disturbance in the requisite ripple-free waters of her life), though oddly, before the journey principally described in this book had concluded, I would find out. That eruption wouldn't be motivated by a vampire or a werewolf, but by a creature far less sensational.

That was the end of it, so I'm sorry it's rather tame as ghost stories go and not a yarn M.R. James would have been particularly proud of writing. I am, incidentally, aware of the 'stone tape' theory regarding manifestations of this kind and, improbable as that sounds, can also see how our own experience might qualify for that classification. That explanation—since it suggests a recording (though of a kind for which science has no explanation, so far as I am aware)—would be quite a relief to me. I then would not have anxieties about the plight of the sentient shade of Juan, the furniture removal man, doomed to unhappily roll his cannon-ball for eternity as punishment for some long ago and forgotten indiscretion, until released by 'someone' who would do the essential 'something' that would guide him into 'the light'. Unless that 'something' was eating a good breakfast and drinking coffee in the winter sunshine, that 'someone' wouldn't be me and so he might be rolling his ball in the night-time yet. Ah, how easy it is to be flippant much later, far away and in broad daylight!

I can reconstruct this episode, please do not doubt it, in a manner that has no element of the Spanish phantasm about it at all and with an explanation that would satisfy the peerless logic of the famous fictional detective of Baker Street. To do that, however, I have to accept there was a person or persons unknown in the room above ours that night, inclined to behave so bizarrely that on balance and given the choice, I would have preferred to be sharing those early hours moments with a harmless, if noisy, wraith.

Alternatively, that ostensibly inoffensive small man we saw

climbing the stairs may once have been in reality, 'The Great Alfonso—Magician and Practical Joker' who, bored with his retirement, had decided it would be a giggle to 'put the breeze up' the Brits downstairs. Perhaps, he never travelled anywhere without slipping a small cannon-ball into his overnight bag in the hope of such an opportunity arising. I know that sounds absurd, even from someone who demonstrably has a taste for the absurd, but the question is surely, 'Is it more absurd than that we were disturbed by a ghost?' How he managed to replicate those sounds so realistically several times over—well, you've got me there!

Sherlock would say, 'When you have eliminated all which is impossible, then whatever remains, however improbable, must be the truth'. In my experience practically everything we have to seriously fear is not supernatural. We have (and have always had) monsters of our own kind in abundance, without ever having to turn to that recourse. In fact, all the monsters are usually our own kind and we have had some real shockers. All the other terrifying things that are not erupting volcanoes, earthquakes, typhoons, tidal waves and the like are mostly just hungry, afraid or legitimately protecting their offspring.

You reader, are of course, at liberty to believe this tale or consider it as a work of fiction. I cannot say I am concerned which you choose, one way or the other. Go with whatever leaves your mind untroubled and your nights (hopefully) perpetually peaceful. I know that's what I am going to do, especially since there is every likelihood that I have written an elaborate and fanciful description of the resonance of housekeeping.

On the other hand, if you are ever in Spain and wake in the middle of the night to a spectral voice saying, '*Disculpe, Senor, Per favor, podemos recuperar nuestra pelota?*'—you may possibly be in the vicinity of where we were. How one gives a ghost ball back to a ghost (other than with minimum delay, I expect) is a puzzle I shall have to leave with the reader to resolve, come the time.

25. First Gear:
In which we visit a battlefield of the Peninsular War and its postman

Back in the main narrative of this story, the following morning we were on the bike again about to leave Ciudad Rodrigo behind us and deliberately heading away from our direct route to the northern coast to visit another notable site of the Peninsular War where a battle was fought—Fuentes d'Onoro (sometimes written as 'Onore' or 'Onor'). In fact the place we had booked for the night was only two hours away to the north from Ciudad Rodrigo, but this day was to include a couple of interesting stops and, additionally, a brief excursion into Portugal.

Before long, following the city walls, we arrived at the principal modern bridge across the River Agueda with the original bridge—the Puente Romano (not much doubt who built that one then) on our left. The Sat Nav indicated this was the way to Portugal so we crossed over. Before we rode away from Ciudad Rodrigo's environs I wanted to see its fortifications from the other side of the river.

The old bridge featured in the assault because British and Portuguese troops were ordered to make a diversionary demonstration over it whilst the main attacks went in on the breaches 'around the corner'. This original bridge leads to the most imposing feature on the city walls which is the 14th century Castillo de Enrique II. It houses a hotel, these days. There would be a good view, with the possibility of a decent photograph from the tiny settlement suburb of La Marina on the river bank of the Agueda, so we rode through it and climbed off the bike. Ian

Robertson had been kind enough to send us a copy of his 'An Atlas of the Peninsular War' and subsequent examination of the map of this action revealed that the suburb had changed little in size during the intervening two centuries.

We made some photographs which drew the attention of some elderly local gentlemen who were taking their ease and chatting with each other in the sunshine. Limitations in language in both directions required the usual patience and imagination. Did we agree, one *viejo* asked, that their city was very beautiful. We did agree, of course. Then one of them asked me why we had come to Ciudad Rodrigo at all. I told them it was because of 'Lord Wellington'. This intelligence instantly animated them and they launched into a rapidly delivered dialogue that was unfortunately beyond our linguistic talents to follow very well. I regret that shortcoming on my part on this occasion, because I am certain that perspective would have been fascinating to hear.

Mounted again, we turned our backs to Ciudad Rodrigo and followed the signpost that had, 'Portugal' written large upon it. Fuentes d'Onoro is a village situated only about 20 miles west of Ciudad Rodrigo so the plan was to visit it, see what we could make of it from the perspective of the battle fought there, then cross the Portuguese border riding northwards to visit the fortified town of Almeida, about which there will be more later in these pages.

I would like to be able to report that very little happened in that short ride and I suppose, judged by the standards of what happens to most motorcyclists quite often, nothing much did. However, I was left with one of those abiding memories—still fresh after these years gone by—so I will tell you what it was. That first section of road must have been undergoing some work, because I can recall passing through recently excavated cuttings of dry earth and pale stone. The road was good enough, but it wasn't particularly wide nor straight for very long stretches. So all things equal we rode along at an unspectacular cruising speed, which was what I thought it warranted.

The moment came when—as one must—I took a look in the mirrors and there behind us was a large white lorry or 'truck', if that suits the reader better. When I say it was behind us, I mean it was virtually on the end of our exhaust pipes, filling my vision completely. We were not crawling along, but clearly, we were going too slow for this *camionero*. He couldn't overtake us because the road didn't allow that for a vehicle of its bulk—he just wanted me to go faster. He gave me a fright because, of course, I knew very well that if I made the least mistake or if anything occurred on the road beyond my control that slowed me down precipitately he would be over us in a heartbeat. Equally, if he made a mistake, breaking too late or whatever, he would be over us in a similar heartbeat.

I increased our speed a fraction. He predictably closed up behind us. I accelerated again. He moved up. We could not carry on in that fashion, so I reluctantly told Patsie what was going on and to prepare for what was coming next. Then, much against my better judgement, I opened the throttle and employed my road craft. There was just no equable way out. It's very unpleasant to be bullied in that manner, as most of us know from experience. I suppose we all think we should be able to expect more consideration from other folks on the road given our obvious vulnerabilities as the two-wheeled, but need it be said, we also know that sometimes we are just not going to get it. We have had worse situations to contend with, of course. Some much worse. Anyway, it would be a poor thing if a rider on a 1137 cc motorbike, having put his mind to the necessity, could not at least put some distance between himself and a lorry. The exit to our first stop came soon enough which drew a veil over our (and his) problem.

I am fairly confident that Fuentes d'Onoro is larger today than it was in 1811, but suspect most of that development has taken place beyond the site of the original village and so furthest away from where we entered it. I do not believe that we expected the place to be markedly different from many Spanish small towns and villages with their low buildings and dry stone walls and so we were not disappointed in that regard. Furthermore, there were plenty of old and crumbling stone buildings and corrals that could have been built and fallen into disrepair over time without being of a vintage which meant they would have been standing at the time of the battle. The streets remained narrow and winding and occasionally, on a corner here and there, were placed cruciforms, floral wreaths or flower vases. We looked out over the empty fields to the east from where, long ago, they would have been packed by five divisions of the French Army as they made their attack. Then we wandered about, eventually strolling around the walls of the Church of the Assumption of Mary which featured prominently in descriptions of the battle. A simple commemoration stone stands before it.

Of the present day local population there was nothing to be seen with the exception of a lone postman on his delivery rounds. As usual, anyone who didn't know the history of the place and who hadn't bothered to read the inscription on the memorial would never guess what had once happened there. In fact, it would be very easy to suppose nothing ever happened in Fuentes d'Onoro.

To give the reader some idea of what these sleepy inconspicuous streets were like, not so very long ago, during the battle fought among them in early May, 1811, I have taken the liberty of reproducing a short description of the fighting penned by a subaltern of the 1st battalion, 88th Regiment of Foot, 'The Connaught Rangers' who was present and has left posterity with an interesting account of the war in Spain from his personal perspective.

His name was William Grattan, a young Irishman from a well-known Dublin family, who had joined his regiment as an ensign—the most junior officer's rank in the British Army—in 1809. Fuentes d'Onoro was his second battle and he would go on to fight in another four engagements (including Ciudad Rodrigo), serving, 'with the colours' continually for four years. His Irish regiment had a reputation of some notoriety for being troublesome, though this aspect of its character transformed into an asset, for obvious reasons, when there was a battle to be fought.

I have edited this piece slightly to make it more accessible for the modern casual reader. The style of speech is somewhat old-fashioned as one may expect, but no less emotive for that and remains an evocative portrayal of the brutality of close contact European infantry warfare during the first years of the 19th century. Readers might note that although we were visiting this village after visiting Ciudad Rodrigo, historically speaking these notable events were in reverse order.

Allow young Will Grattan, reader if you will for a short while, to carry you there:

> All the roads leading to the town of Fuentes d'Onore were quickly filled with French troops. The town itself was occupied by our kilted Highlanders, the light companies of two British divisions together with those from some German and Portuguese battalions, supported by five regular British and two Portuguese regiments.
>
> The French Army, advanced on the buildings with the characteristic impetuosity of their nation, forcing down the barriers, which we had hastily constructed as a temporary defence and came rushing on in a torrent, threatening to overwhelm all that opposed them. Every street and every angle of a street became a battleground where inch by inch was gained and lost in turn.
>
> Whenever the enemy were forced back, fresh troops motivated by their energetic officers impelled them on again, and towards midday, the town presented a shocking sight. Our Highlanders lay dead in heaps, while the other regiments, though less remarkable in their dress, were scarcely so in the numbers of their slain. The French grenadiers, with their immense caps and gaudy plumes, were in piles of twenty and thirty together—some dead, others wounded. The exhausted state of many of the wounded, and the weight of their cumbersome equipment, made it impossible for them to crawl out of the range of the dreadful fire of grapeshot *(a number of small metal balls within a canvas bag fired from a cannon)* and round shot *(large cannon-balls)* which their countrymen poured into the town. Great numbers perished in this way and many more were

crushed to death in the streets.

It was now half-past twelve o'clock, and although the French troops which formed this attack had been several times reinforced, our forces never had. Nevertheless, ownership of the town was still in dispute. The French Marshal, Massena, aware of the importance of the town, and frustrated by the tenacity with which it was defended, ordered a fresh column of troops to reinforce those already engaged. These attacks, constantly supported by new troops, required super human exertions to withstand them. Every effort was made to sustain the post, but efforts no matter how great, must have their limits. Our soldiers had been engaged in this unequal contest for upwards of eight hours, the heat was excessive, and their ammunition was nearly expended.

The Highlanders were driven to the churchyard at the top of the village, and were fighting with the French grenadiers across the tombstones and graves; while the French Light Infantry had penetrated as far as the chapel, distant but a few yards from our line, and were preparing to assault our centre.

Colonel Wallace with his regiment, the 88th *(Connaught Rangers)*, was in reserve on the high ground which overlooked the churchyard, and he was attentively looking on at the combat which raged below, when Sir Edward Pakenham *(the adjutant-general)* galloped up to him, and said, "Do you see that, Wallace?"

"I do," replied the colonel, "and I would rather drive the French out of the town, than cover a retreat across the River Coa." *(Roughly 10 miles to the west, towards Portugal. By this Wallace meant if the town was lost.)*

"Perhaps," said Sir Edward, "His Lordship don't think it tenable."

Wallace answering said, "I shall take it with my regiment, and keep it too."

"Will you?" was the reply, "I'll go and tell Lord Wellington so; see here he comes."

In a moment or two Pakenham returned at a gallop, and, waving his hat, called out, "He says you may go—come along, Wallace."

At this moment General Mackinnon *(the Brigade commander)*, came up, and placing himself beside Wallace and Pakenham, led the attack of the 88th Regiment, which soon changed the state of affairs. Our battalion advanced with fixed bayonets in column of sections in double quick time, their firelocks at the trail. As it passed down the road leading to the chapel, it was warmly cheered by the troops that lay at each side of the wall, but the soldiers made no reply to this greeting. Not one hurrah responded to the shouts that welcomed their advance—there was no noise or talking in the ranks, the men stepped together at a smart trot, as if on a parade.

It so happened that the command of the company which led this attack devolved upon me. When we came within sight of the French 9th Regiment, which was drawn up at the corner of the chapel, waiting for us, I turned round to look at the men of my company, they gave me a cheer and I thought that moment was the proudest of my life. The soldiers did not look pale as men usually do going into close fight; the trot down the road had heightened their complexions.

The enemy were not idle spectators of this movement; they witnessed its commencement, and the regularity with which the advance was conducted made them fearful of the result. An artillery battery of eight-pounder guns advanced at a gallop to an olive-grove on the opposite bank of the river, (*Rivera del Campo O del Berrocal as it is today or Dos Casos stream then which ran just beyond the precincts, parallel to the length of the village to the east*) hoping by the effects of its fire to annihilate our regiment; but we continued to press on, joined by our exhausted comrades, and the battery did little execution.

On reaching the head of the village, we were vigorously opposed by the French infantry, supported by some hundred other troops, but it soon closed in with them, and, aided by the brave fellows that had so gallantly fought in the town all the morning, drove the enemy through the different streets at the point of the bayonet, and at length forced them into the river that separated the two armies. Several of our men fell, killed on the French side of the water.

About one hundred and fifty French grenadiers in their flight, ran down a street that had been barricaded by us the day before, and which was one of the few that escaped the fury of the morning's assault; but their disappointment was great, upon arriving at the bottom, to find themselves shut in; every man of them was put to death, but our soldiers, when they had leisure, paid the enemy that respect which is due to brave men.

As soon as the town of Fuentes d'Onore was completely cleared of the enemy, we sheltered ourselves in the best manner we could behind the walls, and at the angles of the different streets; but this was a task not easy to be accomplished, the French batteries continued to fire with such effect: nevertheless, Sir Edward Pakenham remained on horseback, riding through the streets with that daring bravery for which he was remarkable. If he stood still for a moment the ground about him was ploughed up with round shot.

(Pakenham's luck in this respect did not hold indefinitely. He was killed far away from Spain by American fire at the Battle of New Orleans, in January, 1815. His death was the more tragic because that battle was fought after the peace treaty had been signed which terminated 'The War of 1812'. He was, incidentally, Wellington's brother-in-law and 36 years old.)

About this time, Colonel Cameron, of the 79th (*Cameron*) Highlanders, fell, as did also Captain Irwin, of our regiment; whose death was singular. He had been many years in the army, but this was his first appearance in action. He was short-sighted, and the firing having in some degree slackened, he was anxious to take a view of the scene that was passing. He put his head above the wall behind which his men were stationed, but had scarcely placed his glass *(telescope)* to his eye, when a bullet struck him in the forehead—he sprang from the earth and fell dead.

General Mackinnon and a group of mounted officers were behind the chapel wall, which was the highest point in the village, and consequently much exposed to the enemy's view. This ill-built wall was a feeble defence against round shot, and it was knocked down in several places, and some wide gaps were made in it. The general stood at one of these breaches giving his directions; he attracted the enemy's notice, and they redoubled their fire on this point. Salvoes of artillery astounded our ears, at each of which some part of the old wall was knocked about us; at one of these discharges, five or six feet of it was beaten down, and several men were crushed. Colonel Wallace was covered with the rubbish, his hat was knocked off, and we thought he was killed, but fortunately he escaped unhurt. By two o'clock the town was comparatively tranquil. The cannonading on the right of the line had ceased, but the enemy continued to fire on the town; this proceeding was attended with little loss to us, and was fatal to many of their wounded, who lay in a helpless state in the different streets, and could not be moved from their situation without great peril to our men—and they were torn to pieces by the shot of their own army. Several of these poor wretches were saved by the humane exertions of our soldiers, but still it was not possible to attend to all; and, consequently, the havoc made was great.

Towards evening the firing ceased altogether, and it was a gratifying sight to behold the soldiers of both armies, who but a few hours before were massacring each other, mutually assisting to remove the wounded to their respective sides of the river.

We had now leisure to walk through the town, and observe the effects of the morning's affray. The two armies lost about eight thousand men *(it was something shy of 5,000 in reality)*, and as the chief of this loss was sustained by the troops engaged in the town, the streets were much crowded with the dead and wounded. French and British lay in heaps together, and it would be difficult to say which were most numerous; some of the houses were also crowded with dead Frenchmen, who either crawled there after being wounded, in order to escape the incessant fire which cleared the streets, or who, in a vain effort to save their lives, were overpowered by our men in their last place of refuge; and several were thrust halfway up the large Spanish chimneys.'

Fuentes d'Onoro, as the reader will have gathered, was a particularly hard fought affair that could have gone either way. Wellington certainly thought the outcome was in question at one point and thanked his stars that Napoleon had not been in command of the French Army. No side had much to celebrate at the end of it, but Massena was the commander who disengaged and withdrew. According to the protocols of warfare, the 'victory' goes to the army that remains in possession of the field of battle once the killing has come to an end. That was the British and their allies on this occasion, which makes a difference when it comes to battle honours on regimental flags. The regiments that carry that honour on their colours amply deserved it, for the hard slog of Fuentes d'Onoro was won by soldiers who were possibly unsurpassed at holding onto a position they had been ordered to defend.

✯✯✯✯✯✯✯✯✯✯✯✯✯✯✯✯✯

I have previously explained, Patsie and I have done our best to visit the war cemeteries of our service personnel and their allies who have fallen in our nation's causes. One cannot do that in Spain and Portugal for long ago conflicts. There are no neat rows of white headstones in manicured lawns for the soldiers of the Peninsular War. In those days the dead were stripped of anything useful and buried in pits; unnamed and so mostly forgotten by later generations. So, it occurred to me to offer respects to them with an extract of representative verse as Patsie would do since, though I honestly didn't plan it, poetry has inveigled itself into this narrative. I initially thought the Duoro, given that river was a relevant confluence of nations, men and events for the war, would make an appropriate subject. I undertook some research and, it transpires, there is a poem about the Duoro which would have worked nicely. I then noticed, to my astonishment, another poem written by the same poet and an extract of it is this:

They shall not grow old, as we that are left grow old:
Age shall not weary them, nor the years condemn.
At the going down of the sun and in the morning
We will remember them.

One could barely invent such a coincidence, so I shall accept the intercession of whatever guiding hand brought me to it. This then in remembrance, is for the men of the 'old Peninsular Army that could go anywhere and do anything', according to its own famous commander. The entire poem, of course, is the very well-known and regularly recited, 'For the Fallen', by Laurence Binyon. (1869-1943). He was principally writing about the soldiers of the Great War, 1914-18, but that matters not at all for they were all and continue to be for all time, lest we forget, our own.

★★★★★★★★★★★★★★★★★

As we were about to leave the village a tourist coach pulled into the area and stopped. Its passengers climbed out and were instantly recognisable to us as British men in their middle years, attired for hot weather. It was a battlefield tour group who had come to Fuentes d'Onoro for the same reason that had brought us there that day. They were led by a well-known British author and broadcaster on the history of the Peninsular War. We briefly passed the time of day with some of them and to our pleasant surprise discovered that a few of them had purchased our books on the subject. We could not linger in the village for as long as we may have liked, because we had the rest of the day's schedule before us. So, we climbed aboard the motorcycle again and headed for the Portuguese border.

26. Definitely still First Gear:
In which we are outsmarted by a 'burro'

For those readers that might justifiably feel they have had their fill of Peninsular War battle sites, the news that we were headed for another one might be viewed with some misgivings. Those readers may put their minds at rest. Our destination had a comparatively short war and our own association with it was considerably shorter. That said, our experiences had something in common—both were destined not only to be short, but fraught.

We had hardly settled ourselves for a ride before we arrived at the Portuguese frontier. We have not crossed that border since the UK parted company from the EU, so have no current knowledge to impart, but in those days the traffic moved freely and, unless there were extenuating circumstances, motorcycles like ours only stopped if their riders wanted to do so. In common with several other European border zones, we had crossed, this one contained restaurants, shops and supermarkets selling goods that were more typical to one region or country than they were to the other and presumably better priced as a further attraction.

There are few things like a fully laden motorcycle that offer the discouragement to spend the contents of one's wallet. It didn't matter how appealing anything for sale was—we had nowhere to put it. The hard luggage was full to the brim and the magnetic tank bag in front of me and between my arms was so deeply packed that I had to periodically pull it into my chest so that I could peer over the top of it to see the dials on the bike. So we rode straight through the border-post into Portugal with barely a sideways glance at its many temptations.

Our first destination was, as I have explained, Almeida—a little over 10 miles from Fuentes d'Onoro and following the line of the River Coa, which ran a couple of miles to the west. In this gap of land was fought, 'The Combat on the Coa' in late July, 1810, wherein the famous British Light Division (which included the green-jacketed riflemen, made popular in fiction) under its martinet commander, Craufurd (later killed at Ciudad Rodrigo) had a hard scrap with the French Army. The British withdrew, crossed the Coa and held their line in defiance among the steep-sided rocks along the river's edge—compelling the French Army to remain on the opposite bank.

Almeida was surrounded by the French. It was (and is) a formidable star-fortress (not in the outer space sense—it's more or less shaped like a star) and was strongly garrisoned at the time by Portuguese and British infantry, well supported by cavalry and artillery. The fortress stood ready for a siege and its commander, Brigadier-General Cox had every confidence he could, given his ample reserves of munitions, hold out until relieved. Not to spin the story out unnecessarily, someone left a trail of gunpowder from a broken barrel lying in the open, which led through the open door of the principal powder magazine. A freak French shell struck nearby igniting the exposed powder. The magazine forthwith erupted like a volcano, blowing the place with its reserves of ammunition to smithereens. Six hundred defenders were instantly killed in the blast and three hundred more were wounded. No doubt, everyone else still living within the walls was stupefied, temporarily deafened and wondering what day of the week it was. The defences were extensively damaged leaving a huge crater and rendering the place indefensible. Cox capitulated the following day. The French had lost just 58 men killed in the affair.

I knew something of this extraordinary event, but in fact, that was not the principal reason I thought Almeida was worth visiting. It is, based on aerial photographs I had seen of it, a very interesting example of military architecture. The construction of the defences dates from the 17th century by which time, as

I have explained previously, it was clear the tall curtain walls of medieval castles, that had foiled some besieging armies in the previous centuries, would not survive for long bombarded by modern heavy artillery. In fact, during his early career in India, Wellesley (as Wellington then was) would arrive to reduce a fort which had been impregnable for centuries and have its wall down, to the astonishment of its defenders, in an afternoon. So, Almeida was another example of a fortress with low, but very deep walls. The star shape provided defence against infantry attackers by ensuring there were no blind spots which could not be reached by fire from the defenders, even when the enemy was very close to walls which were, in a star fort, not so problematic to scale as once they were.

We arrived outside Almeida's principal gate with every intention of passing immediately through it, until I suspected that access (which was extraordinarily narrow, I thought) would only be permitted for pedestrians. Confounded for the moment, we climbed off the bike and since we were parked right next to a *café*, sat down in the shade, ordered a cold drink and deliberated what we should do next. This was the first time, incidentally, we had heard the distinctive and softer than Spanish, 'oosh-itsh-shoo' of Portuguese spoken by local folks going about their business.

We were not particularly comfortable with the idea of leaving the bike outside the walls to explore within on foot and in any event, as pedestrians ourselves, we would be lugging our helmets and, in my case, also the magnetic tank bag which contained all our essentials and so was no light weight. The day, need it be said, was typically hot, so the prospect of tramping around for long thus burdened in our riding kit did not seem likely to be very enjoyable or practical for that matter. I was rescued from my indecision when a vehicle, my concerns notwithstanding, trundled by us, crossed over the narrow entrance causeway and passed through the covered gate into the fortress interior beyond. I suppose I am compelled to reveal that 'vehicle' was a cart drawn by a donkey, but I reasoned that a donkey cart was still larger than a motorcycle, so we would be bound to be 'good to go' on the bike.

Readers will no doubt have heard the old idiom that 'size isn't everything'. I can confirm that is true, as it happens. Sometimes what matters is how many feet one has. I made this noteworthy discovery immediately after we followed 'Senhor Burro' into Almeida and shall not soon forget it. The entire area—well, so far as we could see anyway—was paved with cobblestones. Now, there are cobblestones and then there are cobblestones. Your common (or garden) cobblestone can be a tolerable surface in dry conditions, though potentially lethal for two-wheeled transport in the wet. We have many such roads in the UK, particularly within parts of our older towns and cities, so we were no stranger to them. I try never to treat them with anything less than respect.

These Portuguese cobbles, however, were, it seemed to me, of an entirely different order. I know—in common with the little boy who cried, 'Wolf!' too frequently—I am guilty of the occasional exaggeration, but reader, to me each one of these cobbles was the size of a small bread loaf (not a bun, mind, but a loaf!) and each featured a shiny domed top. There were also, it seemed to me at the time, huge declivities between each one and to make matters worse down the centre of the road were stones approaching twice the size of those around them. I put the bike momentarily upon this centre line to see if they offered any better purchase, but they didn't so came off them again. Once again, I must admit I have checked recent photographs of this place and the cobbles in them do not appear—on the face of it—to be as bad as I remember them or have described. Why that is—your guess, reader, is as good as mine.

I shuddered to a halt. Just to our right was the donkey in his traces, standing sure-footedly at ease in the confident manner of his tribe, the broad wheels of the cart taking the weight of his burden. Donkeys are not llamas by any benchmark and this one was looking at me with an unsympathetic, expression on his long face that said (though in Portuguese, obviously), '*You humans think you are so smart compared to us, but the hoof is on the other leg now and you are in a pickle, whereas I can plod around this place all day long without a care in the world. Bikers, eh—I blank 'em'.*

An unfair admonishment, if you ask me, since neither Patsie nor I would ever countenance being unkind to a donkey. Perhaps donkeys are species bigots. Irrespective of how individually reasonable we are, we all bear responsibility for millennia of imposed servitude and beastliness. I don't suppose we can blame them.

I knew very well that this surface held every potential for a spill and if that occurred it would inevitably be a hard one with unpleasant consequences for rider, pillion and the poor bike. The donkey wouldn't have cared less, of course. It may be, for all I know, had we been riding an adventure style of motorcycle I might have been pleased to have found us on these stones given some of those riders attempt riding dry water-courses but that, at the time, was academic.

'That's torn it', I said to Patsie as we disconsolately peered about at the sea of stone bumps that surrounded us. 'We have to get out of here *pronto* and that's the only item on the agenda'.

'Well, take it really steady,' she replied examining the boulders beneath her, not that there was any latitude available on that subject. She did forebear from concluding, 'or you will have us off—YET AGAIN!', but I heard it anyway, because in my mind, I was saying that for her.

I looked about for the quickest *volte-face* out of our situation, only to discover the tunnel we had employed to enter the fortress was understandably available only for one-way traffic. Had it not been so narrow and through the entire width of the fortress defensive wall, combined with the long narrow causeway thereafter, I might have risked it anyway just to get us out. As it was, that would have been asking for head-on trouble, to say nothing of a potential encounter with the Portuguese *policia*. So there was nothing for it but to carefully thread our way through the streets at snail-speed until we eventually discovered an exit. I didn't have any high hopes there would be many of those, because the place was a fortress, the principal function of which was to keep unfriendly people outside. Achieving that objective inevitably had its consequences for those within the walls. Few ways *'dentro'* meant few ways *'fora'*.

I was obliged to ask Patsie climb off the bike to walk, both for her safety and to lighten our load and assist my balance. I had no idea how far we would have to go before a gateway appeared. Furthermore, not only was the day hot, but it was becoming hotter the longer we stayed more or less immobile attired in our full riding kit. It seemed to me that the usual balancing act that we all take for granted on the bike would not work. The amount of tyre in contact with the surface of the road is neither long nor wide and wobbling along at a crawl with heavy luggage attached to the sides on such an unreliable surface only made matters worse.

I have no idea whether what I elected to do would have actually worked if it was required to do so, because it was never put to the test. Had that been the case I might have gone over anyway, because I may not have been strong enough to prevent it. I might have come away with a broken limb—another reason why Patsie was better off on her feet.

Essentially, I positioned my legs outstretched on either side of the bike, the soles of my boots barely skimming across the tops of the cobbles to create a kind of stabilising outrigger. If I cockled over, my hope was I could brace the bike with one leg or the other before it went too far beyond vertical. I was continually slightly lifting my legs and lowering them under tension and so it wasn't long before I could feel muscles in my legs and especially my inner thighs protesting. In fact, I was feeling pain in muscles I didn't know I had.

Was that what 'The Motorcycling Sadhu' would have done in my place? Probably not. He almost certainly wouldn't have been riding a substantial sports-tourer in the first place. He would have possibly stood on the pegs of whatever more appropriate *moto* he was on, riding along at a steady lick and would have been out of trouble in minutes. For all I know, he might not have thought he was in any trouble anyway, so he might have stood on just one peg and sailed along whistling, 'Lillibullero'. Actually, on reflection, I suspect even he would have been in trouble had he tried that last nonsense.

The mid-day sun was relentless with no chance of the usual cooling breeze that forward propulsion provides as a bonus. We were both stewing in our own juices, but fortunately Patsie was able to remove her helmet. I couldn't and was, all things considered I admit, feeling pretty sorry for myself as I crept along passing by some really interesting sites, including an exhibition centre, featuring the Peninsular War episode, that I had been looking forward to visiting and now no longer cared 'two hoots' about.

Deliverance came eventually, of course, in the form of a gate from which egress was allowed. I sighed with relief, glad to be still upright. Patsie put her helmet back on, gratefully climbed back on board and we rolled through the tunnel in the defences. The tension came out of my leg and thigh muscles as I relieved them, but even then I was left in no doubt what I had put them through. Though I didn't know or suspect it at the time, the incident had not finished with me yet, as the reader will discover later in these pages. So much for Almeida. *Adeus bebe e amem.* I opened the throttle and away we went, a little regretfully to be honest, but instantly cooled and heading northwards.

✶✶✶✶✶✶✶✶✶✶✶✶✶✶✶✶✶

Irrespective of whether it's going to be a relief or disappointment to the reader, we had, by this point, just about ridden out of the countryside which was notable for events which took place during the Peninsular War. So, we must take our leave of the Duke of Wellington, because he will not appear again significantly in these pages. The man was indisputably one of the most capable military commanders that Britain produced. In fact, he never definitively lost a battle. The last battle he ever fought in 1815, terminated the career of another great military commander, Napoleon Bonaparte. That defeat (or victory dependent on which team one supports) finally ended 'The First Empire of the French', and concluded the Revolutionary and Napoleonic Wars which had ravaged Europe for almost two decades. Over five million people have been estimated to have died as a consequence of those wars. So, a result, because had Napoleon prevailed he assuredly would have instigated yet more bloodshed.

In the event the reader believes I am simply wasting ink eulogising Wellington within a motorcycling journey book, I shall terminate his tenure by quoting one of his most notable maxims.

'All the business of war,' he said, *'indeed all the business of life, is to endeavour to find out what you don't know from what you do: that is what is called, 'guessing what's on the other side of the hill."*

Wise words—an encouragement, in effect, to continually engage in tactical thinking—from one who indisputably knew what he was talking about; someone who, if he got it wrong, would be responsible for the loss of thousands of lives and the fall of kingdoms and empires. Most people, in my opinion, do not think tactically that much, but almost exclusively reactively, though the principle differs not one jot, irrespective of scale.

As far as we bikers are concerned this consideration surely covers everything from 'crown of the road and cutting daisies' and one's particular vigilance at T-junctions to finding out whether a fortress interior is carpeted with giant cobblestones, before you actually ride into it and more besides. Our decisions also inevitably bear on success or failure, but even, in extreme circumstances, also upon life and death. No small matter, especially since that life or death might be one's own. It might also (or instead) belong to someone else: Possibly to someone known very well, who is both near and dear. That merits a ponder, in my opinion, before twisting the wrist to 'pin' or 'gas' it.

I will conclude this topic with one of my own noteworthy experiences from, as I write, not that long ago. I was riding solo on a clear English country road (on a vintage British machine as it happened) when I spotted, some way ahead, a very large farm vehicle standing in a field (it might have been a combine harvester—something like, anyway), though very close to a wide entrance gate. The nearer I came to it, I could see there were people milling around and I thought to myself—all in an instant—there is something going on there, so it's possible—just possible—the driver could reverse straight out onto the road, which would block it. I slowed down steadily—so far as any bystander would have momentarily seen—for no apparent reason.

That would have been tactically astute action, I think in the circumstances, even if that vehicle had not almost simultaneously moved backwards, halfway across the road in front of me. It did though, as it happens.

I cannot remember what I ate for dinner that night, but, more significantly, I was definitely able to eat dinner. 'Old Mr. Scratch' had to go elsewhere to find someone to drag down. I don't suppose he had to travel far. Cough drops and gimlets, reader, cough drops and gimlets.

★★★★★★★★★★★★★★★★

The plan, having engaged with some historical sites with debatable success, was to enjoy and ride through some beautiful scenery. Immediately beyond Almeida was open countryside that was level enough, though distinguished, on either side of the road, if my memory serves me correctly, by scatterings of boulders and enormous standing stones.

As we rode further north our road fringed on the Parque Natural de Arribes del Duero which promised to be dramatic. It was, particularly in its later stages. It seems a shame to report that the riding was good, the scenery outstanding and so we stopped at a *mirador* at a dramatically high place where we made a photograph of the ribbon of the River Duoro as it threaded through pale grey hills below us, and that two dimensional image, as usual, did no justice whatsoever to our experience. Oh well, it is what it is. We were on the bike together and that was what mattered.

27. Fifth Gear:
In which we ride to somewhere quiet in hopes of a nice dinner

The River Duoro, at the bridge of Barca de Alva, joins the Atlantic Ocean 140 miles or so to the west at Porto, but also marks the border between Portugal and Spain for some miles to the east. Crossing that bridge would take us back into Spain. Barca de Alva is a particularly attractive riverside spot with quays employed by the Duoro river cruise boats, a couple of which were tied up along the opposite bank. It is, I think, far more developed—based on some photographs—these days than it was when we were there. There was a small open *café* on the Portuguese side of the river and so we pulled in for a cup of coffee.

Our arrival provoked the interest of three or four local ladies, or more accurately, it was Patsie who most interested them. I do not think they had seen many lady motorcyclists before and everything about Patsie's riding kit fascinated them. She took off her jacket as she sat in the sunshine and they marvelled at her reticulated 'turtle shell', spine protector, rapping it with their knuckles, but they were particularly taken by the pillion belt with its two stirrup-like handles that I wore around my waist. They demanded, by mime, a demonstration of how it worked, which we provided and which they found hilarious. I suspect that mirth had something to do with having one's husband in a harness, not dissimilar to that worn by 'Senhor Burro'.

Having crossed the Duoro we intended to take a straight ride to our accommodation for the night which was in a place called Penausende. There was nothing notable about that place, so far as I was aware. This was one of those occasions when we needed a place to sleep that was required to be more or less as far from the Duoro crossing as we were prepared to ride before we wanted to get off the bike for the day. So, I searched several suitable locations on an arc of about the right distance from Barca before I found a small country hotel that had good reviews for its accommodation and really excellent reviews for its restaurant, which reportedly served regional specialities.

I am aware that the last time I employed that methodology we ended up in Sierra de la Segura, on top of a cone of rock which led to all that came afterwards. I know what the reader may be thinking, but, 'I am not as green as I am cabbage looking' as we say in our parts. So, I was 100% certain this next stop would be surrounded by miles of very flat and unthreatening countryside: A reliably nice rest, good food and no—absolutely no—dramas. What could possibly go wrong?

The first part of the ride took us through another section of the natural reserve so was particularly picturesque. About an hour and a quarter of almost good straight road (useful because I could turn the Sat Nav off to save the battery) took us to Ledesma which sits upon the River Tormes. We rode straight by this small town which may well have been a mistake, because I have undertaken a little research about it for these pages and it contains some interesting buildings including a castle, which I can't recall seeing at all. We surely must have noticed it at the time, because it dominates the landscape.

I did note the bridge over the Tormes with its tall arches at the time, because I commented to Patsie that it looked as though it was Roman and it was. As the reader is aware we had seen our share of Roman bridges by this point in the journey, so could spot them. In Roman times the town itself was called Bletisa, apparently, named after the tribe that lived in the region, who were the Bletonesii. They were, perhaps surprisingly, Celts. It certainly came as some surprise to me—having Celtic ancestry myself—that there were Celts in parts of both France and Northern Spain. We Brits tend to consider that the Celts were entirely our own—concentrated in Scotland and Wales. Not so though.

The Romans apparently severely punished the Bletonesii for their anti-social habit of practising human sacrifice, which does admittedly seem a bit extreme compared to our Anglican, Harvest Festival, 'All Things Bright and Beautiful' and so forth, though some might say somewhat hypocritical on the part of the Romans, given they routinely threw folks to lions and organised other horrific spectacles in the name of 'reality show' entertainment.

Anyway, our journey was progressing satisfactorily with only thirty miles left to go for the day, so as usual we were contemplating ice cold beers served in frosted glasses in our not too distant futures. We took a left turn onto a smooth road which indicated our destination and so I opened 'Madam's' throttle so she could run. For about 500 yards everything went along a treat, until the road surface turned into something like king-sized granola. I killed the throttle immediately and soon discovered that any speed above 15 mph shook the bike and its riders intolerably. Suddenly, thirty miles seemed like a very long way indeed.

Need it be emphasised that I didn't really think this terrible road surface would continue until our destination and it did not. After two or three miles of shaking, the road returned to a respectably even surface so I opened the throttle again and, with a joint sigh of relief, away we went. Unfortunately, 5 minutes later we were back on bone-rattling granola again. This time there was no imminent relief and mile followed tortuous mile and now it did seem probable we would have to endure those conditions to the bitter end of the day's ride. Furthermore, that end would be later than predicted—once again. In my notes I have written that the road did eventually change back to a well maintained surface when we crossed into another province, but some years later I cannot confirm whether that was the case or not. In any event—as I have repeatedly emphasised—many things will have changed in the intervening years and that especially applies to Spanish roads. Nevertheless, Ledesma is in the Salamanca region of Castile and Leon, whilst Penausende belongs to Zamora.

We were now passing through black bull breeding country

and in the fields as we passed they could be seen quietly grazing whilst elsewhere paddocks of saddle horses were also in evidence. Eventually Penausende hove into sight and our hearts sank a little, because to us, in those days, the place appeared somewhat run down. Such concerns were laid to rest when we found the hotel we had booked for the night, because was a nice looking modern building, almost at odds, it seemed to us, with its surroundings.

We were greeted in reception upon our arrival by a young woman who was friendly and helpful and who seemed to have a broad job portfolio, because whilst we were there, she popped up performing several different tasks. Firstly, however, she guided us to our room, which was very pleasant and included a sizeable terrace which looked out over the surrounding countryside. I was extremely pleased with that myself, because there wasn't a mountain nor yet anything one might reasonably describe as a substantial hill anywhere in sight. There was a huge, lonesome hunk of rock out there, that was once the site of a fortress, but that didn't count, since there could be no compulsion to go near it, far less up it. The view was otherwise the epitome of Spanish pastoral quietude and though I gave the landscape a thorough going over (just to make sure), I couldn't detect any Celts preparing to sacrifice anyone or indeed, engaging in any other unpleasant ritual that might transpire to demand our unwilling participation.

Our hostess then escorted me to a garage that was beneath the hotel. That area was so large and so clean that it could have been employed as a motorcycle retail showroom. So, need it be said, I was pleased with that too and happily left 'Madam' there for the night. She was in better accommodation than she had at home in our own garage, so should have no complaints.

Before returning to join Patsie I ordered some liquid refreshment in the form of a chilled bottle of local white wine that was incredibly reasonably priced. Then I wandered up to our room, where we stripped ourselves down for some sunbathing on our terrace and contentedly relaxed, glasses in hands, as the sun slowly set. Everything was going absolutely splendidly and

I could see no dark cloud on our horizon—literal or figurative. In fact, the only issue on our minds was that we were especially looking forward to an exceptionally good dinner.

Later that evening we wandered down to the restaurant which was decorated in a familiar Spanish rustic style that left little doubt that most main courses would involve generous portions of grilled, fried or possibly braised cuts of expired mammal; not that this was a problem for us, because we were hungry. Our waitress appeared with the menus and we were not particularly surprised to note she was the same young woman who had been facilitating our stay since the moment we had arrived: That, or she had an identical twin.

As we had guessed, the main courses were specifically catering for carnivores. *Postre* decisions could be shelved for the time being, especially for Patsie, whose savoury-toothed idea of a chocolate muffin is a packet of crisps ('chips' for the trans-Atlantic reader) and who can rarely manage to eat more than two courses anyway. That left us with the first course—*primer plato*—to contemplate.

The reader will not be surprised to learn that our menus were entirely written in Spanish and, as is now well known, our Spanish was rudimentary. Unhappily, the same could be said for our hostess (or any other diner present) as far as English was concerned, though they all had the legitimate excuse that we were seated in rural Spain and not in an English public house. That left us trying to decipher what was on offer and we were not making much progress. I am, of course, aware that I have previously claimed that ordering food was never a problem in Spain; nor is it in Mojacar or most of Andalucia, because the local economy depends so heavily upon British tourism. In Penausende in those days, one had the impression that visitors from Mars were potentially equal in number to those hailing from English shires.

Anyway, we soldiered on and eventually found a dish that we believed to be a Spanish equivalent of *foie gras,* which sounded promising. Our waitress returned to take our order and we pointed to the menu and asked if it was good. Well, we could manage that, even without rubbing our stomachs. We were told it was very good indeed and we understood that response very well (because it was a nod), so we ordered two. This, I now realise, was the tipping point. We could have made what happened next perfectly straightforward by agreeing to go along with everything, but for some reason we didn't do that.

It all began when our waitress emphatically shook her head. We were made to understand that this particular starter course was so substantial that one serving was enough for two people. Why did we not say, '*Bueno, uno*' and leave it at that, I have no idea. What we did instead was squint at the description and attempt to discover what had brought about this unusual phenomenon in a first course. Our eyes alighted on one component word that we realised was the key to the whole conundrum, but I am not going to reveal right now what it was. The reason for temporarily withholding that word is because there will be, without doubt, some readers who are far more gastronomically savvy than we were then and that will, for them, spoil what came next and also reveal what duffers we were. If at the end of this anecdote—when that word is revealed—the reader does not know what it is either, then at least our confusion will be understood, if not the reason why we didn't let the issue go as totally unimportant and just eat it.

Patsie put her small forefinger on 'the word' and held out her menu for the young woman to see. That message was plain enough. 'What was it?' A stream of Spanish followed which predictably meant nothing to us. Patsie was determined not to be beaten. She raised her hands to the side of her head, extended her fingers and gave a jolly convincing, 'Moooo'. Our waitress solemnly shook her head. Nothing cow-like then.

Next came more horns, this time made with curled fingers accompanied by a quite realistic, 'Baaa'. No: A slow shake of the head revealed 'the word' had nothing to do with sheep, lamb nor mutton. Patsie got into her stride, determined, I suppose, to nail the matter without further delay. A sound effect that was probably goat followed by a mime that could have been practically anything, nevertheless received a shake of the head.

'Oink,oink,oink' was likewise rejected as was some frenzied palm flapping accompanied by some 'cluck,cluck,clucking'. I am fairly sure had we come that close to some game bird—because the Spanish go for red-legged partridges and so forth—we would have made some progress. So, it wasn't one of those either. Patsie paused for some thought, then raised her hands high beside her head and coupled that with some really endearing nose twitching, but that also earned her a sombre head shake. I thought it was cute, though confess to a bias. No, though, not rabbit.

'Goodness,' whispered my wife to me desperately, 'you don't think it's horse, do you?'

'No, it's not horse. I know that word', I replied, so there was no 'clippety-clopping' forthcoming.

Practically anyone would have thrown in the towel by this point, but not my Patsie. She and her sisters have always given me the impression they live in a world that doesn't have 'defeat' (or any synonym that a Thesaurus might offer) in their dictionaries.

Patsie mused for more moments, then I saw the light-bulb of inspiration spark into life above her head. She joined her arms at the elbows and placed her flattened palms together to make an arrow-head shape. Then she began sinuously swaying her hips one way, whilst moving her joined arms in the other direction and so it went, side to side like an exotic dancer. It really was (though performed seated) a very good performance. I could see that trout making its way upstream, then precipitately leaping to snatch an unwary passing mayfly. I swear one could almost see the droplets of water coming off its rainbow scaled flank. She stopped. We both turned expectantly, breath bated, towards our waitress, who remained silently gripping her pad and pencil. With no change in facial expression, she shook her head and said, 'No'. We expelled a joint sigh of disappointment. Not a fish.

I know the reader probably won't believe me, but I can't say I was surprised to see those mimes. It's legendary in our family that if her hands were tied, Patsie could be rendered entirely mute. Anyway, presumably realising we were going nowhere with our investigation, our young waitress decided to assist by pitching in with some miming of her own. She gave us a stream of totally incomprehensible Spanish as she stooped low and in the air, just above the floor tiles, with her hands crafted a globular shape about the size of a child's small football.

'Ooo,' Patsie's brow furrowed, 'it's nowhere near the size of a chicken, then. Whatever can it be?'

I was trying to imagine a creature indigenous to Iberia which was so diminutive that it could, under any circumstances, be round, but which would, nevertheless, necessarily have legs. It was my fault, as usual. It was me that did it, your honour and I knew I shouldn't have done it in the nanosecond following the last utterance of the next thing that came off my tongue, which was:

'Maybe it's a hedgehog?'

Patsie's head snapped up like a hunting tigress. Her cheeks flushed. Those lovely cobalt blue eyes had, in an instant, turned hard-sharp with ice-cold, sapphire battle-fire and (horror of horrors!) her hands went to her hips. A cold shiver ran down my back as I thought, 'Oh, *blank*, I have put the Hetheringtons in the saddle, out on the moss, fire-brands in their fists and someone's barn is going to be burned to the ground'.

Roast Mrs. Tiggywinkle? Fry Mr. Pricky Ho'shun? (Our local dialect version of the same thing); she was never going to stand for that: Never in a million years, as I very well knew. She would put up with the antics of any variety of ghostie, ghoulie, faerie-folk or boggart, so long as it kept to its own side of the line and didn't take even a teeny-tiny step towards the little ones, but she absolutely, positively would not tolerate that.

'I AM NOT GOING TO EAT A HEDGEHOG!' she asserted stridently in a voice barely recognisable as her own and the forks of diners behind her froze on their way to their owner's mouths. Our waitress simply stood impassively, still gripping her pencil and pad.

Matters, I thought frantically, are getting out of hand here. I needed to get the Hetheringtons safely home to a warm hearth *pronto*, before any more damage was done. This had all been going so well and now we were heading for wild-haired, good-wives running about in their nightgowns, screaming in the dark. My mind raced, mental gears grinding and cogs spinning. What if this item is something else entirely? Think, John think. And then, believe it or not, as though the thought was placed into my head by my better angel or possibly the guidance of dear, long-passed, Grandfather Goodman, who was looking out for me yet, there came a ray of hope and not only that, but against all the odds I actually knew the Spanish word for it, because it's not so very far from the French word for the exactly the same thing.

'*Es*,' I tentatively stuttered, '*Es, um, er, champinones?*'

'*Si!*', replied our waitress decisively with a curt nod. Puzzled, Patsie cocked her head in my direction for enlightenment.

'It's a mushroom, dear', I told her.

Well, reader, you probably do not need to be told that Patsie knows how to laugh and now she laughed until the tears came and her sides ached and she almost slipped off her chair. I took a quick glance at our waitress—who, to be fair to her did have other orders to take—and she simply stood there, pad and pencil in hand, waiting for the moment when that might happen, so far as we were concerned. So that kind of comedy doesn't necessarily cross frontiers. All the world is a stage though, you were right about that, Billy. I stepped in—since I know very well Patsie is especially fond of mushrooms—and said, 'OK, *uno*'. The dish came and very good it was, as was the rest of the meal and the wine that went with it all.

So that was that and all about it, bar the reveal. What was 'the word'? Draw back the curtains and drum-roll! It was '*boletus*'. And what—unless you are in the know—is English for '*boletus*'? Well, it is '*boletus*', to be sure. It's apparently derived, (who would ever suspect?) from the Latin word: *Boletus*. That is a demonstration of complete ignorance for you—front to back. So, we could have spoken Spanish like grandees and still, initially at least, not have known what it was.

I suspect, reader, you would feel entirely justified in not believing any part of this anecdote and that is quite funny too though, as usual, not obligatory. We have seen '*boletus*' many times on Spanish menus since that day, need it be said, but now we handle its presence as though it's the sort of thing everyone knows about from the cradle.

Did the evening qualify as one without drama? I think so, on the whole, by our standards. In all candour, it wasn't all exactly plain sailing, but a full-scale Border Reiver event had been averted and we left the table with full stomachs and happy. So, we couldn't complain and wended our way up to our bedroom to sleep. I am not sure I can imagine what impression we left on our young hostess. I have no idea what her subsequent opinions of English tourists on motorcycles were and on reflection, I don't think I want to know.

28. More Fifth Gear:
In which, after a bumpy start, we follow the Camino route

Not one to fall at the last, through careless inattention to detail, I nipped outside onto our bedroom's terrace and gave the countryside another quick scan, looking out for no good Celtic boys inclined to be up to no good. There were none. Then I checked out that lonesome hunk of rock, on the off chance there were Druids up there intending to fabricate a cane human effigy in which to immolate someone. They would have to get a wriggle on if we featured in their designs, because they hadn't started making it yet and, come the morn, we would be over the horizon—gone but for a whiff of exhaust fumes.

So, all was well in our world. The night was particularly warm so we stripped off, Adam and Eve fashion, and employing just a cotton sheet to cover ourselves, settled down to sleep. Now we were safely in bed we had nothing to worry about but *desayuno* the following morning, which based on what we had been offered to eat thus far, was no worry worthy of the name. We could even—if the fancy took us—confidently request a *boletus* omelette and expect to be served with one.

Then, at some point in the early hours, I think it was about 3 a.m., I woke with a start. No reader, it wasn't another haunting, totally implausible though that would have been. Oh, how I wish it had been a haunting! How I wish it had been the *Danse Macabre*—a whole troupe of gambolling, grave-stained skeletons, dripping corpse-cloth, blowing pipes, beating on drums whilst one of them demonically scratched away on a busted fiddle. Because it was worse than all of that. Much worse. It was cramp in its most horrific form. It was cramp as I had never experienced it before or since.

I had, I confess to that moment, never given a great deal of thought to my own inner-thighs. I will refrain from claiming I had never given a thought to thighs generally—just not mine. I definitely had never experienced cramp in them and in consequence I had always considered them—when I thought about them at all—as merely buffers which prevented my buttocks from crashing down onto my knee caps. Now I was experiencing the hardest re-evaluating education on the subject.

I was not a complete fool. I knew I had muscles in my inner-thighs, even before they made their presence felt by delivering incomparable agony. As I knew them now, they were like taut inflexible bands under my skin, possessed by an intrusive alien life-form, which had disconnected them from my leg bones. I saw them in my mind like strips of rolled hide of the kind one gives to large dogs for their amusement and mine had the crocodilian jaws of a couple of invisible Dobermann Pinschers gnawing upon them.

The pain was excruciating and I had no idea (nor could care less) what the occupants of other bedrooms might be thinking about what was going on in our room. I was sobbing like an infant as I begged Patsie (who was obviously wide awake by this point) for assistance. It has to be revealed she began to laugh, though insisted, at my understandable outrage at this arguably inappropriate response to my agonies, that this was merely a nervous reaction that had plagued her since childhood. It just sounded like uncharitable laughter to me, for the record. I can just see how that would have gone down for me—nervous reaction or not—had I laughed when she was cramped on the autoroute outside Mojacar. I wouldn't have eaten a wife-cooked dinner for a month, irrespective of how imaginative my excuse might have been.

Anyway, to her wifely credit, Patsie then attempted to fiercely massage my legs and thighs, but that brought me no relief whatsoever, just more pain. Then she unceremoniously hauled me off the bed, on to my feet to induce me to move around in the hope that walking on the cool tiled floor would eventually bring about some respite. My legs straight away involuntarily buckled, but she pulled me up, so I was staggering around, supported by my occasionally chortling wife, like a saddle-sore, drunken cowpoke. We were both as naked as the day we were born, so the scene, to any observer familiar with art history, was a vignette from the Bosch school painting, 'The Harrowing of Hell'. If you are not one of those persons, just check it out. That's what it was like, enhanced by pain, groaning and laughter. Hellish!

Patsie continued to slow march me whimpering around the room until, after what seemed like an age, the pain gradually began to subside, though I lived with deep, nagging aches for days afterwards and feared a relapse. I know how I did this to myself, need it be emphasised. I did it by transforming myself into a human outrigger in Almeida fortress. And there was I wondering if that was what, 'The Motorcycling Sadhu' would have done in my place. Of course, he wouldn't! Every day is a school day. If I ever find myself on giant cobbles again, whilst astride a motorbike, I will take the shortest route off them, even if that involves pushing the bike all the way to an even-textured surface. Fortunately, thus far we never again have been in the same situation we were in Almeida, irrespective of the fact that I shall be ready for it.

Breakfast over, later that morning I gingerly made my way to the garage to collect our motorcycle, no doubt looking as though I had been 'riding the range' for too long or had just suffered an unfortunate incident of the bowels. Possibly both. Frankly, I didn't care what I looked like, one way or the other. Pain can empower one with a mighty indifference to almost everything else and besides we were, once again, about to be on our way.

When I first planned this trip, I always had it in mind that we would ride through and possibly over some mountains. More accurately, I planned for two mountain ranges: The Pyrenees and The Picos de Europa. The other ones that flung themselves in our path just came about by accident or my carelessness, if the reader is of a mind to be unkind. So, I deliberately made this day of riding a comparatively short and easy one, because I knew that the day afterwards would be spent in the Picos and I didn't want us to be on anything less than top form when we tackled them. That having been said, I was initially planning a cross-country route to our next destination, which was Astorga, for the sake of riding interest. For reasons explained I didn't want to push my luck, when it wasn't absolutely necessary, given we could do nothing about the ensuing mountain climb. So I decided on this day, in case I cramped again, we would opt for the most direct route to our destination.

Recently I have checked to see what that route was specifically and once again that road does not square with my notes. There is not much doubt that the distance is just over 100 miles, so a less than a two hour ride even with a break, but these days that direct route appears to be on perfectly serviceable A-grade roads, whereas my notes make it clear we rode on a motorway or dual-carriageway (or autoroute, if the reader prefers).

The reason I am quite certain about that detail is my notes contain more motorcyclist's ranting about the behaviour of our fellow road users. Reading my entry now, for some reason and somewhat out of sequence it is fair to say—I was initially musing on the behaviour of several drivers of small hatchbacks in France who had bullied us into the gutter by their inability to stay on their own side of the white centre line. I am aware I have already touched on that subject, but in Spain I was contemplating that this proclivity could not solely be directed at us, but must be habitual and since it would be happening when small French hatchback drivers were travelling in both directions, passing each other, there had to come a time when they would inevitably bring about their mutual extinction. Either that or their rate of replenishment must be astonishing.

I note I was also moaning about some motorists' habit of sounding their horns to 'alert' us that they were overtaking. To be fair, an alerting beep is not such a bad idea if they had done it when they were 10 meters away, but frequently it happened after they had seemingly crept alongside the bike before letting loose a long blast which was so alarming as to cause both rider and pillion to have borderline out of the body experiences. This rather suggested to me that, 'alerting' was not their foremost motivation.

These observations are, of course, subjective. It is so easy to blindly attribute generalisations to other people one has decided are not one's own people. For that to have any credence there would have to be French and Spanish people returning home after driving in the UK, reporting, '*You know, Maria, those drivers in England are absolutely marvellous: Princes and princesses of the road, every one of them and not at all awful like us*'. Well, I wouldn't suggest any such thing, so it is a racing certainty they would not.

That having been said, now back to Spain where we had to contend with a Spanish driver's particular *peccadillo* so far as we were concerned. That was the unpleasant activity commonly known in our part of the world as the 'cut up'.

★★★★★★★★★★★★★★★★★★

Have I been 'cut up' on the bike in the UK? I have, but infrequently. Actually, I remember the last time and it must have been more than twenty years ago, at time of writing. I was riding 'Madam' on a dual-carriageway road, heading for treatment with a dentist whose practise was about thirty miles from our home. A speeding SUV sliced right across me to take what was, coincidentally, my own exit and later to my astonishment that same vehicle was parked on the forecourt of the clinic I was visiting.

I well recall the expression on the face of the person (who was the only occupant of the waiting room) when I walked in. As a large, darkly clad motorcyclist, to a guilty eye, I possibly resembled a space-opera villain.

'Did I cut you up?', this person asked, understandably sheepishly: A peculiar thing to say as an *entre,* if one is in a state of bliss on the subject, if you ask me. The admission of responsibility transparently lies within the enquiry. Most people open with, 'Nice weather for the bike', or something like it.

'You know very well that you did,' I replied, as I shed my

helmet and jacket and settled into my own chair. I may have deepened the natural tone of my voice to enhance the 'Nemesis' effect. I can't remember.

I wasn't the 'ship in the night' that had been expected when the deed of shame was wrought and so I was definitely not expected to turn up in the same dentist's waiting-room minutes afterwards. Some period of embarrassed discomfort followed, though I said no more about the matter or any other. Well, I hadn't taken 'an off', so no actual harm was done. Perhaps a lesson in Karma was learned by the guilty party—perhaps not.

★★★★★★★★★★★★★★★★★

Needless to say I have been 'cut up' considerably more regularly in Spain, though I have no idea why it has been a Spanish driver's habit, if indeed, it actually was one. It has occurred to me the practice might be cultural, having something to do with bull-fighting and if one considers it as a component of the, presumably male, national psyche—that might make some kind of sense.

What happens is that instead of passing on a parallel course, drivers take a diagonal one. So the motorcar shaves across one's front end at high speed, narrowly missing the tyre of the bike with its rear bumper. Being on the receiving end can be a very unsettling experience to say the least and we must have had a particularly taxing ride on our way to Astorga because my notes reveal the same thing happened to us on several occasions. I can't remember them individually, probably because this was an occurrence not confined to this road, this day nor yet to this journey. I am not, of course, suggesting that all Spanish drivers are guilty of 'cutting up' any more than am I suggesting that all Spanish people are bull-fighters or even enjoy or approve of bull-fighting as a spectacle.

I also noted on this occasion, and well recall, that a white sports car came by us travelling so fast that it was on top of us as though it had been beamed down from outer space. As it passed we heard (and virtually felt) a short, sharp, '*VAP*' air-displacement sound and it was a disappearing dot in moments.

It is those kinds of experiences that make one shudder at the memory, because one knows that one is impotent at the time. If you are cruising along minding your own business in the inside lane it doesn't affect you that directly, but if you are making a sensible manoeuvre in the outside lane when it happens, there is every likelihood that you could be shattered to atoms. This is, of course, one of the reasons I don't overtake on the continent, riding on a multi or dual lane road with light traffic, unless I can see nothing behind me and don't hang about when I go either. Make no mistake, that driver was moving at speeds that should only be employed on salt flats devoid of all other life. Instead, he was risking everything on dumb luck.

Need it be said, we arrived in Astorga possessed of most of our atoms, arranged in something like a familiar order. Why Astorga?; the usual reason that I did not want to ride into the much larger, nearby Leon for just one night. As usual I had undertaken a little research to see if there was anything notable, we should take in whilst we were in the city and was interested to note that the place possessed an example of Antoni Gaudi's architecture. His most famous and outstanding creation is the idiosyncratically unique, yet to be completed, world famous, *La Sagrada Familia* church in Barcelona. Astorga's principal claim to fame, however, is probably its place on the pilgrim route, the 'Camino' on the way to Santiago de Compostela.

I have not made much of the Camino in these pages thus far, principally because I knew that sooner or later we would be arriving at one of its well-known way stations and one which is, of course, not too far from journey's end, if one is a pilgrim. It is almost impossible to travel on the roads of the French Pyrenees region or in most of Spain without finding oneself, for a while at least, on a Camino route. There is no doubt on the subject, because by the roadside are plaques bearing a symbol rather like a sunburst, yellow on a blue ground, presumably referencing the badge of the pilgrims which is a scallop shell. The nearer one comes to the north-western corner of Spain, the more likely one will come across the symbol and the pilgrims themselves in often surprisingly large numbers.

Any reader who has travelled with us this far knows there was a point when I reluctantly commented on the business of bull fighting. In Astorga we came up with the subject of religion, which is also not a topic for a book like this one. So, I would rather not get too far into it, especially since we were more concerned with motorcycling with the wind in our faces or at our backs for that matter. We still hadn't had a drop of rain since we left home in the UK, by the way. Anyway, on the subject of pilgrimages and pilgrims—here we were and here they were so, once again, one must say something. I will report what we saw, therefore, and how it struck us.

Neither Patsie nor I are Roman Catholics so ours was bound to be an 'outsider's' view. My father's Welsh roots brought Methodism my way and Patsie's grandfather was a Baptist lay minister. We had both served our time at 'Sunday School' in rooms where *décor* meant white paint. Organised religion of any stripe plays little part in our lives these days however, compared to the simple uncontroversial tenet of 'do as you would be done by'. I assume that principle to be uncontroversial, though accept there is probably someone out there looking forward to something most of us would think was quite horrible. It takes all sorts.

My wife read Charles Kingsley's book for children, 'The Water Babies', when she was a child herself. Within its pages appears 'Mrs. Do-as-you-would-be-done-by', whose philosophy needs no elaboration. Patsie adopted that simple model for living and gently converted me. Fortunately, upon consideration, I suppose most people actually do follow this principle, by that name or any other. I try to do my best, repeatedly sub-standard as that inevitably tends to be.

Christians have been making the pilgrimage to Santiago de Compostela in Galicia, just inland from the Atlantic Ocean coastline, since the turbulent 10th century. However, the journey really gained momentum after the *Reconquista* in the 15th century, though it remained a formidable, perilous endeavour and one only to be embarked upon by those motivated by ardent spiritual conviction. According to legend, the body of the apostle, St. James, was brought to Galicia for burial, hence the pilgrimage.

There is a bronze statue of a pilgrim of the old days before the cathedral of Burgos and he appears to be about right, 'out on his (bare) feet' with exhaustion and dressed in rags, so in need of some good kit to spare him from the elements and a decent meal to fortify him within. Compostela, incidentally, refers to the certificate that the pilgrim receives as evidence that the Camino—(the 'Way')—of Santiago (St. James)—has been completed. Originally, this was an important document for pilgrims, because it proved that those of them who were penitents had fulfilled their obligations.

The Camino Santiago is not what it once was, inevitably. These days one can book a Camino walking holiday which means, directly or indirectly, there are numbers of folks with mortgages to pay and children to feed making their livings out of it—so no bad thing. Some pilgrims roll up in coaches to walk a while and then climb back on board them again. That said we have seen our share of pilgrims who were closer to the 'real thing' as much as modern life would allow. On the roads we saw men and women of every nationality and virtually every age group. We have seen them singly, in pairs, in groups of four or a dozen striking through farm land, striding down footpaths, struggling over hard ground or practically collapsed, boots off, revealing bloody socks or massaging swaddled, blistered feet. One cannot fail to admire their conviction and fortitude, so we don't knock them.

In the funnelling point of Astorga all manner of pilgrims gathered together like starlings in a murmuration. So some serious pilgrim watching can be done and almost certainly with no danger of an altercation caused by 'staring', because they have all arrived there employing a moral compass. There were young folk in bib-fronted dungarees with guitars on their backs; the smiles of perpetually glad hearts on their fresh faces. There were retired folk studiously making notes and poring over reference books. There were virtual beggars resembling old school penitents, taking the business very seriously and who would, of necessity, be using whatever money they received for sustenance.

There was one enthusiastic fellow, thrilled with his recent acquisition, which was a shepherd's crook decorated with scallop shells and a couple of small gourds dangling from it by a cord. There were walkers, ('fit as lops', as we say in our part of the world★) who were equipped like serious walkers and who arguably didn't need a pretext to be there, because they were having a good time. Notably, one lone ancient gentleman appeared to be decidedly ill and unlikely to make it through the night, far less the walk of 160 miles that lay ahead of him to the finish line. To be honest, I was really rooting for him and didn't much care what his motivation was, because he was game for a monumental challenge.

Almost everyone had a rucksack, outdoor clothing and walking boots and so if it wasn't for the distinguishing scallop shell they displayed, they looked like a ramblers' club out on a hike, which I suppose, on one level, was what they were. As to what prompted each of them to walk the Camino—I am sure their reasons were as varied as they were many and what they took away from their experiences afterwards (apart from their own *compostela,*) equally numerous and varied. So, we wished them well, every one of them, and we hope it benefited them, whatever that was. I especially hope the old gentleman made it and found what he was seeking, because he deserved a medal the size of a dustbin lid in my view.

★*The Vikings were responsible for this phrase—it comes from 'hloppa'—a flea!*

29. Third Gear:
In which we see fantasy palaces and high peaks

So far as I know there are hostels that specifically cater for pilgrims, but how they operate and whether they are comfortable, offer good food or are reasonably priced we, from experience, don't know. Mrs. Lewis, at that point in her career, would have taken a dim view of a dormitory in a European city like Astorga, if those were the sleeping arrangements on offer. She would sleep (and has slept) without a murmur of complaint, mind you, on the teak-planked floor of an elevated jungle hut, *sans* better options being available.

From my own perspective, those kids with guitars were undoubtedly credits to their parents, but I, (a curmudgeon), harboured apprehensions as to what was lurking in their musical repertoires and didn't want to discover the hard way that my forebodings were well-founded. So I booked us, instead, into an ultra-modern boutique hotel that had private parking for 'Madam' in a yard secured behind a giant metal gate which would have been an effective deterrent against all comers had they been motorbike thieves or well-intentioned troubadours singing, 'Kum-by-yah'. I confessed to a sub-standard best, remember. I never claimed to be a paragon.

Our room for the night was huge, containing a bed massive enough to discourage intimacy even among couples who were not staggering about, bemoaning aches and pains in every limb, muscle and bone and who did not fall into a horizontal position with a groan to immediately succumb to oblivion in less than a minute. Because we too, in the name of no higher or spiritual pursuit whatsoever, had suffered physical rigours on our own journey.

Had we achieved any enlightenment as a consequence? It is a fact we had none in mind when we started out and certainly, by this late point, we hadn't come to any conclusions we had shared with each other. Possibly, I am too insensitive for spiritual revelations and on occasion not even bright enough to appreciate every minute of the good fortunes that have come my way. I have actually travelled the road to Damascus several times, incidentally, without experiencing any manner of epiphany, notwithstanding that it can sometimes be the place for them.

There were unanswered questions, as there always are. Why did we go through all these trials, yet continue to ride motorcycles? Why was it, indeed, that in spite of everything, we really looked forward to slinging our legs over the bike each morning and doing it all again? For me, the overarching consideration was what made the courage, tolerance, companionship, faith, solidarity and support which induced my wife to uncomplainingly climb up behind me day after day? I suspect I may know the answer to that one, as will most readers who have stuck with us to this point in our story and especially if they are also tribe.

For reasons I have explained, we had made good time—better than expected, which was a first—on our way to Astorga, so we had plenty of time thereafter as pedestrians to enjoy the place while the sun remained shining. There was a museum of the Roman period in the region very close to our hotel, so, time on our hands, we visited it. There was a video presentation of Roman life from the perspective of a female slave accompanied by her actual gravestone which was interesting.

Then we wandered to see Gaudi's episcopal palace. Cards down, I at least know my Frank Lloyd Wright from my Walter Gropius, because I am interested in architecture, but that doesn't mean I know much about it. We have seen Gaudi's masterpiece in Barcelona and it defies comparison, so it is almost impossible, in my view, to have an objective opinion about it. That said, it is also impossible not to be taken by *La Segrada Familia's* scale and complexity or fail to be impressed by Gaudi's imaginative vision and the commitment to bring such magnificent organic weirdness into being.

Gaudi commendably ploughed his own furrow and when anyone creative does that they invariably have to work their way to their most distinguished efforts. Often, they leave behind the evidence of their progress. We recognised that the palace's angle-sided portico bore similarities to the one on the *Segrada Familia* and its conical tower roofs paid homage to the style we have seen on the palaces of Olite and probably other grand Spanish buildings of that period.

Gaudi's stature as an architect notwithstanding, the episcopal palace, a comparatively modern building constructed between 1889-1913, rather resembles a fairy tale castle in a theme park; the kind of place before which a songstress might induce the local wildlife to assist with the household chores. I know no one could have made those connections when the place was built, so it probably wasn't intended to appear whimsical. Philistines that we are—we probably just missed the entire point of it. I snapped a few photographs for the record, then we wandered off to find a bar which offered cold brews, a white wine for the lady and more pilgrim watching.

'It's odd that it's designed by Gaudi,' mused Patsie over her wine glass, 'because it's—you know—a bit gaudy. I suppose that has nothing to do with it, though'.

'No', I replied, 'I don't suppose it does' It doesn't, in Spanish—not that I knew—it would be *llamativo,* apparently.

'Ah, oh, well, no, er, hum' she replied. I agreed with her summation on that score, though the place clearly would have appeared differently—possibly radical—when considered through the lens of a *fin de siecle* eye.

Astorga, naturally, has its own Plaza Mayor, but next to it is a more modern looking open-space called the Plaza del General Santocildes, which features a large fountain surmounted by a sculpture of a lion stamping the living daylights out of a sprawling eagle in symbolic commemoration,(just when we thought we had done with the subject) of the defeat of Napoleon's

French Army during the Peninsular War. The Spanish general was responsible for the unsuccessful defence of Astorga in 1810. He didn't have much of a chance to be fair to him, because he had practically no ammunition at his disposal.

★★★★★★★★★★★★★★★★★

During the early stages of the war in Iberia, the British Army was commanded by Sir John Moore. His campaign didn't go to plan, so he was forced to retreat northwards through the gruelling winter of 1808-9 to the port of Corunna—just 160 miles from Astorga and 40 miles north of Santiago de Compostela—from where the army was to be evacuated by the Royal Navy. For much of that march he was pursued by Napoleon, but the emperor relinquished command to a subordinate, when Moore was almost within his grasp. Napoleon had learned a political crisis was brewing in Paris that demanded his attention and that the Austrians were preparing to fight him again. Moore was killed in the final battle outside Corunna (now La Coruña), creating the vacancy notably filled by Wellington. The French Army was, nevertheless, defeated and the British Army escaped to fight again.

Napoleon never returned to Spain, so he never fought an experienced British Army led by a talented commander until June 18th, 1815; the day of Waterloo. On that fateful morning the emperor elected, against the advice of his generals, who knew better from bitter experience, to underestimate Wellington and his men. Possibly, had he not turned away from chasing Moore, he would have made more informed choices later and that might have changed the course of global events. There you go again: History—dots that connect and those that fail to connect by mere hours.

Apparently, Napoleon briefly occupied an aristocrat's house in Astorga, possibly on his way home, though I don't know that for certain, and the place is now a hotel.

★★★★★★★★★★★★★★★★★

As the evening drew on the crowd began to change in character. Among the pilgrims there were now numbers of Spanish families. Their children were enthusiastically enjoying the modern interpretation of the All Hallows Eve festival—Halloween—which we had entirely forgotten was almost upon us. For us—in the north of England—Halloween is always dark and cold and the 'spookier' for it. On this decidedly balmy evening, the face-painted little ones were wearing their 'scary' fancy dress costumes and running, laughing and squealing around the *plaza* brandishing luminous witches and black plastic bats swinging from strings on sticks. There was even the occasional illuminated pumpkin which assisted in turning our minds towards dinner. We couldn't manage much volume in our stomachs following the previous evening's flesh feast, so we ate a light pasta meal in an Italian joint in preparation for our penultimate day in Spain, traversing the mountains of the Picos de Europa.

The following morning I told Patsie that before we tackled the day I wanted to re-fill our fuel tank, so we didn't have to worry about fuel when we were travelling through remote country where filling stations would be necessarily few and far between. I told her that I would attend to that before we checked out of our hotel and before we re-fitted the hard luggage, so she could spend a little more time resting with her feet up, before we embarked on what would almost certainly be a demanding day. Little did I know how prophetic that forecast would transpire to be. We had taken the panniers and the back box to our room because the bike, though in itself secure, was parked outside and there was a convenient lift in which to readily transport the luggage.

So I went down to an unencumbered, 'Madam', alone, slung my leg over her and fired her engine. Oh reader, what can I say? I love my wife, but it had been quite some time since I had ridden that motorcycle with no luggage attached to it and no pillion rider sitting behind me. The hotel, it transpired, was actually built on high ground, but one had no sense of that from its front entrance. From the back of the building the road swept downwards and away in a series of long sweeping curves. We went down and through them like a swift flying for the joy of simply being alive and just kept going. I will not deceive anyone.

It took quite a long time for me to 'find' that filling station and return to Patsie again.

Astorga was an easy town to leave (again), though we somehow missed its *muralla* (city walls) which I would have found interesting—even as a 'ride-by'—had I known the city still had some. I am not sure how we managed to overlook them when we were pedestrians, because there is a good length of them nearby the palace. We exited the city by a main road, but soon turned off it to ride across country. I must have planned that ride specifically, but can't remember, because the most direct route will take one through or near to Leon and we definitely went nowhere near that city, but rode north of it by some distance. Our destination, Potes, had been chosen as an 'overnighter' because it is just sixty-six miles from the ferry terminal at Santander. So I was hoping for a comparatively short, pressure-free ride on the following morning. As a bonus, Potes appeared to be an attractive town with a river running through it and set among stunning mountain scenery.

These days most continental touring motorcyclists know about the Picos de Europa, but it wasn't an especially popular destination for bikers—judged by how many of them we had seen—during the time covered by this book. Unhelpfully, I have discovered that my old notes do not go into much detail about the early stages of our ride from Astorga to Potes, though I am certain that there came a point along the way when options on that score are whittled down to one.

The distant peaks of the Picos de Europa soon appeared before us as we rode and I am conscious, at this point in this narrative, that it is quite difficult to make the fifth mountain range we have encountered appear exceptional. So, the road climbed, gradually rising through alpine meadowland often bordered by streams of fresh running water that foamed over boulders and gravel beds. The terrain was initially quite gently reminiscent of the uplands leading to the western French side of the Pyrenees, though the roads were considerably wider and far better maintained than those we had experienced in the Sierra Segura. The day was once again warm and the sky clear and bright blue.

Notably, though the year was becoming elderly, we still were wearing our cool, warm weather gear. We stopped along the way, climbing off the bike nearby a small hump-backed Roman bridge with a view of the mountains in the background and made a few photographs, because we knew that once the serious mountain climbing began, in those days before helmet cameras were widespread, that would be impossible.

When we arrived within the mountains themselves it was evident these peaks were of an entirely different kind to any we had experienced before. Where the previous mountains we had traversed were mostly gently folding ridges or rotund heights partially covered with trees and scrub, the dramatic rock formations of the Picos appeared to have been aggressively thrust from the earth to create high, sharp edged, raw sided crags like the broken teeth of gigantic, monstrous creatures. Rock face seemingly clashed and collided with rock face, some of which were covered with vibrant green lichen which made the landscape appear even more other worldly.

Reader, I am going to have to do my best to accurately remember what came next in detail and I confess some of my memories may be at fault. Beyond debate, however, the vistas from these high peaks were simply stunning and the view as we passed the signpost that declared we were entering Cantabria, nothing less than breathtaking. In the San Glorio Pass at a point where the road turned to begin a descent there stood a statue of a deer. Once again, the roads appear wider now in recent photographs than they are in my memory of them. So the fact of the matter is I cannot say, with any certainty, where we were specifically when the incident I will recount occurred, except it was on this road and beyond the deer statue to the north. Anyway, it was on this day and coming down from the Picos, where we were so high that the landscape below almost appeared to be a map, that we came closest to destruction. Ultimately, I was to blame, as usual.

So, as I have mentioned we were now on the downward stage of the mountain ride. I could see the landscape for miles into the distance and our road twisting, bending and turning, growing narrower in perspective as it descended to the valley far below. It really was an eagle's eye view, but as usual I was less concerned about that, than aware we had arrived at a point where not only gears and brakes were a consideration, but also the inexorable pull of gravity. So it was time to be especially careful as it always is when one combines great heights, precipitate drops, two wheels, big engines, heavy weights, downward gradients, other traffic and one's wife. In short, I had but one job in hand which, once again, was to bring Patsie safely down to level ground.

On this occasion there was four-wheeled traffic on the road going our way and even if I needed it to set my pace—which I didn't—it was going to do exactly that, if the drivers took the descent steadily and they were. There was a small white motorcar in front of us with a single occupant taking the conditions very carefully as he should, so I held back from him, as I should, to allow him make his way without having undue concerns about us. On our immediate right there was, according to my notes, a low, wide wall, six to eight courses high and beyond that, the drop; down, down, then more down. There was no metal barrier on top of that wall, I can recall. Next to the opposite side of the road was the flat cliff face. The afternoon was in its last quarter and the low sun was bright, throwing a sharp, black shape of the bike on to the flat screen of cliff like a shadow puppet.

There reliably was our motorcycle, there was John, her rider, there was Patsie, his pillion rider and wife, there was the back-box and there, between the shadow of the back-box and Patsie's shadow was the shadow of another human head and shoulders.

'Hang on', I thought, 'that can't be right, can it?'

30. Several Low Gears:
In which we have a most peculiar experience up a mountain

I have known people, men mostly, though it has nothing to do with gender, who have reliably kept their heads, never rattled by any crisis that came their way. Men whose voices were never raised or changed in tone, who were perpetually composed and effectively dealt with what came first or must come next, irrespective of its magnitude, as though it was no more important than flicking a fleck off their cuff. I know that there are institutions from public schools to military academies which train young people to conduct themselves in a like manner; calm, capable, decisive and authoritative, irrespective of the circumstances. I genuinely don't begrudge any of those people their advantages, howsoever they came by them, but simply wish I had been in a position to learn the invaluable lessons they were taught.

I possess none of those attributes or abilities—whether learned or as a consequence of natural talent—and now never will have them. I have, since my teenage years, compulsively put myself, 'out in the world', in one sense or another, trusting that I was tactically astute. Despite my vigilance, I have then found myself precipitately falling into 'sink-holes', that have opened at my feet, and down I have gone into them, jangling with terror until the 'brown and foaming' has all but closed in over my head. Not a very commendable record, I know, but there it is. Perhaps it's my fate, unwillingly shared with those closest to me. I did reveal all this early in the pages of this book, to be fair, whether the reader has been inclined to believe me or not. That is not the end of it all, of course. Nor has it been, thus far, the end of me, but that is how it always begins and *quelle surprise*—here we were again—right in the 'you know what'.

Words, predictably, since they take so long to write and read, cannot do justice to the following incident, which went by like a flash of lightning or possibly two or three flashes of lightning. That having been said, this was not my first potential disaster, so it was not a total surprise to me, in retrospect, that I was able to connive survival in 'fight or flight' mode. It's almost always in 'flight mode', if I'm honest. Anyway, everything that happened from this point onwards, until I say it's over, happened very, very quickly indeed.

I would not wish to give the reader the impression that we were riding along on a twisting mountain road on the edge of a precipice, whilst I was engaged in reveries, gazing at shadows on cliff faces. I caught the 'third rider on the bike', image I have described out of the corner of my eye, momentarily didn't understand it, nor was able to immediately process it, so glanced again to try to make some sense of it.

As I then turned my head to the left, I found I was looking directly into the elongated face of a woman, so close she was almost at my own shoulder, wild-eyed, her mouth wide open, teeth bared in a rictus of fierce excitement, howling a scream of exultation directly into my face like a Valkyrie. My heart lurched, my stomach flipped over and a shudder hammered through me from the top of my head, down my spine and into my fingertips. Bluntly, she frightened the life out of me and, disorientated, I hadn't a clue what was happening. So, I instinctively grabbed hard on the brakes.

I am aware, reader, I have failed to adequately portray just how traumatic that moment was. Allow me to put it this way—it was the kind of 'shock moment' one only usually sees contrived in horror movies. Let's face it, most people would 'jump out of their skins', if such a thing happened to them, had they been leaning against the bar of a cosy pub, drinking a pint at the time. Our situation, by contrast, was about as much contrast as it is possible to have.

In the next less-than-a-second she had passed us whooping wildly. How could any of this possibly be happening? She was riding a light-weight racing bicycle, hurtling down the gradient, peddling like a fiend. A bicycle? That revelation alone covered me in a cold sweat. Now I could see she was wearing the usual 'banana bunch' helmet and distinctive colourful cyclist's outfit.

In far less time than I can relate it, she was beside the poor man in the white motorcar in front of us. She actually bent down, so she could give him the same treatment she had given me, through his side window—bearing in mind he was driving a left-hand drive car—so was also right next to her. I could see, through his motorcar's rear window, his silhouette visibly jump upwards, then shy away and his vehicle brake lights flashed red as his motorcar momentarily slewed to the right, though to his credit, he got a grip of it before it struck the wall.

Reader, remember you are receiving all this information sequentially when, of course, these events were happening simultaneously. So back inside my swirling mind two things were happening. The first was straightforward unfettered panic and the second, which made the first worse, was, 'road cyclist's peloton-pack'. When are they ever alone? How many? Ten? Fifty? Like a swarm of wasps behaving in the same fashion? Sure enough, another female cyclist immediately shot past us and now there was traffic coming up the mountain towards us—a quartet of motorbikes with other vehicles coming into view behind them. Was this second rider merely the next of those shortly to arrive? Would there be other cyclists racing by on the right or left? This was surely a serious accident unfolding on this cliff edge and we were going to be in the heart of it. I was trying to look everywhere at once. My overarching thought was the necessity to be clear of them. In short, 'flight', though I had just, at that moment, braked.

So what did I do? Forgive me, dear wife, family and all bikers. I should have taken possession of myself with a calm, slow deep breath, but I didn't do that. I yanked open the throttle—just for a second before I closed it down again—but that touch was all it needed and we surged forward. I knew, upon the instant I did it, that it was not only the wrong thing to do, it was a potentially fatal thing to do because this was very far from a straight road. The white motorcar was no longer directly in front of us, it had turned round a comparatively tight left-hand bend and beyond the beginning that bend, beyond that low wall before us was nothing but the clear air on the far side of the precipice. That wall was coming at us very quickly—in fact, too quickly. I thought we were gone, I genuinely did. I can feel sick to my stomach at the memory of it all, even as I write these years later.

 The moment of truth instantly arrived. I hit the brake momentarily again, turning the bike sharply to the left to take the bend, stamping hard on the left peg attempting to force her over, though I have no idea whether that helped or not. I threw myself over to the left, further than I can ever remember doing before and Patsie, bless her heart, remained tightly tucked in behind me. Knee out, over we went.

 How far, I do not know, but far, I think. That 'Empress of Motorcycles' responsively and effortlessly took us round that bend as smoothly as though we were sliding upon a band of silk. To give her the full justice that is due, she performed that turn as though it was nothing at all. I can feel her doing it to this day. I was trembling as we came upright again and remain convinced, she did her job far better than I did mine. Perhaps our overworked guardian angel had also stepped in to assist us—yet again. It was over, the entire episode, beginning to end, lasting less than two hand's full of seconds.

 I know there have been riders of big sports-tourers and sports bikes for whom this manoeuvre would not have been exceptional (all be it not on a cliff-edge road—no place for high jinx for anyone, need it be emphasised), but this had happened to us and I had been given a demonstration that our motorcycle was capable of far more than the demands I habitually put upon her. Had she turned her panther's head around, fixed me with her yellow eye and said, 'There you are, now at last you have really seen me, so think yourself lucky,' I wouldn't have been terribly surprised, because I had and knew we were. I have previously revealed that, for all my shortcomings, I was inexplicably blessed by successful brinkmanship and that the reader should reserve judgement on that dubious claim until near to the conclusion of these pages. Now is that time, though needless to say, my misadventures do not usually take place on an actual brink.

My riding limitations confessed yet again, I would be surprised to discover that this kind of thing, in its entirety, happened to many motorcyclists that frequently or even once in their careers on two wheels. It was certainly a new one for me and one, nor anything like it, that has ever happened since. I was shaken without doubt and I was angry. As I recount this, I cannot remember whether there were any other cyclists present or passing at the time other than the two I have reported. Most of what was in my mind, I kept to myself. It shortly became apparent that whilst Patsie was aware of the incident, such was the speed of its passing, she had no inclination how perilous our situation had momentarily been and had not especially noticed that taking that bend had been extraordinarily dramatic. We were still upon the mountain, furthermore, so we must concentrate on coming down again safely.

I also knew that there was every chance that, before very much time had elapsed, we would be riding on flat or even rising ground which meant 'Madam's' 1137 c.c's would come to bear and we would catch up to those cyclists. I am guilty of many human frailties; thoughts fleetingly came unbidden and a notion of restorative justice briefly entered into my mind, but I suppressed it instantly. Mostly, once again, I felt I had let Patsie down. She put her trust in me during every minute we were on the bike and had every right, having agreed to do so, that I would look after her properly irrespective of the circumstances. So there was no action I could take that would not involve more jeopardy for her. Additionally, there was the far from inconsequential consideration that I didn't want to end our adventure behind the bars of a Spanish prison.

We came down from the mountain, of course, and onto level ground. Sure enough, before too long, we could see a block of cyclists ahead of us. There were not just two of them though, but a solid wedge of possibly a dozen or more. Where the rest of them came from, I have no idea. As we came closer I noticed, recognising the clothing of the female rider, that these were, indeed, at least in part, the same group. Patsie's voice in my ear-piece said, 'Are you going to give them a fright?' I think I have intimated that this lady holds the key to the door of my thoughts and so wanders around inside my mind opening draws and cupboards, peering into them as it pleases her.

'No, I'm not,' I replied, 'we've no excuse for not behaving properly. What they have done is a measure of them, not of us. We don't want to hurt anyone, do we?'

She gave me a silent little squeeze with her arms and knees and I know what that means. By this time, we had come up behind them on a comparatively narrow road and so, by our standards, we were practically crawling along. I don't believe they didn't know we were there, but they showed no inclination to give way a little or ride in any kind of file, but filled the width of the road. I eventually gave them a short blast of the horn. Still, they ignored us. So, refusing provocation, I held back a safe distance for some minutes until the road widened and I could see a good distance ahead, then passed them swiftly and cleanly, leaving them in our wake without regret—gone forever, thank goodness. Was I seething, though? I absolutely was!

In my notes, written that evening, I have entered into a lengthy polemic on the behaviour of those cyclists, but I am not going to repeat that here. What would be the point? Does any reader really need an explanation or verdict on that kind of incomprehensible, contemptible behaviour? The only comment I wrote down at the time, that I will reproduce here, was my final one. It was that some of those people would be unlikely to make 'old bones' and that one would struggle to grieve over them, were it not for the likelihood that some innocents would probably be going down with them. For all I know, by time of writing, that might already have happened. If not, since they would be somewhat older, I hope they are now wiser, kinder and have done no more harm in the interim.

I am aware, that these days, this anecdote can be viewed as

inflammatory, since it concerns bicycle riders and other road users. That issue can be a bone of contention, hotly debated with accusations of bias flying from both factions. I declare I carry no incorporeal baggage on the subject so belong to no faction. I also try, with varying degrees of success, not to be given to generalisations. So, I am minded to simply note that my Rajput friend in Gwalior, when introducing himself to Europeans, would explain the significance of his name thus, 'It is true that all Sikhs are named Singh, but it is not true that everyone named Singh is a Sikh.' Nothing that happened to us that day was instigated by a cyclist. It was brought about by a person.

Shortly afterwards we rode into Potes. Our hotel transpired to be far better than I had imagined it might be, because it was a very spacious, friendly family run enterprise where everyone could not do enough to make us feel welcome and comfortable. I think it may have been apparent to them that we had experienced some kind of mishap on the journey, because I can remember that before we went to our room we sat in the public lounge and sank two stiff drinks each. We then ordered a bottle of wine which was a Rueda-Verdejo. I think this was possibly the first time we had tasted a wine of this type, because we were surprised it wasn't a New World wine, but of course, Spanish. Maybe it wasn't quite as wonderful as we remember it. Most things seem better shortly after one has had an experience which might have been one's last.

This was to be our last night on Spanish soil for the time being so, on several counts, we owed ourselves a good dinner. The light was fading by the time we were ready to set out for our walk, so I decided there was no point in my taking a camera with us to record the town. There was enough light—I was just behaving sulkily. Patsie accused me of being unable to shake off the events of the day and that would, unless I took a hold of myself, spoil the evening which should be a special one. There was an element of truth in that accusation, which I now regret, though I had still not fully explained to her all that had really happened on the mountain; that moment wasn't the time to do it, either.

The town was pretty in an alpine way, though it had become indisputably a tourist resort, full of restaurants, bars, shops offering hiking and ski-wear, thick knitted sweaters and cuddly toys in the shape of Mouflon sheep and other local wildlife. We found ourselves a suitable bar, that I cannot remember much about in detail, though my notes reveal that we fell into conversation with a man and his wife who lived in the region and who had ridden into town that day on a British motorcycle, though I cannot remember which model. We thereafter discovered an appealing restaurant which was very busy and, as most people know, that is always a good indication as to the quality of food and service one might expect.

The dish this establishment was especially promoting and which most diners appeared to be eating was one that—at the time—we believed to be a regional speciality. We ordered it and the meal began with a broth containing noodles, followed by a stew which utilised the identical liquid, but enhanced by the addition of cabbage, beef, chickpeas and *chorizo* sausage; brilliant for a chilly evening. There was no doubt this was hearty, satisfying, homely food, though I suspect we paid enough for its novelty. I made a note of the name of that dish, but it did not occur to me, until I wrote these pages that it wasn't really 'local' at all, because it was called *Cocido Madrileno*, which sounds as though it originates in Madrid and it does.

We wandered back to our hotel. Predictably, I had made a familiar miscalculation about the location of Potes, because I believed it was situated slightly beyond the northern precincts of the Picos towards the ocean coast, whereas it was actually situated within the range. So, I asked our hosts how much of the remaining sixty-six miles of road to Santander remained within the mountains. That was an important consideration, because ideally, we should be upon the dockside, ready to board when called upon, at around an hour or so after midday. If we arrived earlier, then no harm would be done. We were advised that our road ran for eighteen miles across country before the highway began. That, of course, did not seem so very far, but we had never ridden that road, so had no idea what the terrain would be like. Assuredly eighteen miles in the mountains does not equate to the same distance on level ground. So, I suggested to Patsie that it would be best to make an early start.

We were, as needs little emphasis, by this point in the most northern region of Spain and October was marching onwards towards its close. Those considerations combined with mountain altitudes meant the temperature was dropping sharply during the day, unless the sun was performing particularly well at its zenith. That would mean in the morning the sun would not have risen enough to warm the valleys, so our last Spanish ride would be certain, at least at the outset, to be a chilly one. It was time to break out the cold weather clothing again—the first time we would be wearing it since we had desperately peeled it off in the sweltering heat of the day in Limoges.

31. Parked in Gear:
In which we ride to the sea and board ship

The fact was, I persisted in carrying the burden of that afternoon's drama, obsessively running it over and over in my mind. I felt I had to get the full facts off my chest to Patsie, before we turned in to sleep that night. So as we sat together on the bed in our room, I took her through the truth of it—especially confessing my own near fatal error. My wife listened to me quietly and if anything I told her was a cause for alarm, she gave no indication of it. Thereafter, Patsie was supportive to a degree, but I suppose I should have known she would also be single-mindedly pragmatic. In short, she shrugged off the whole business as unworthy of further discussion. Since we were in a position to have this conversation, she reasoned, the disaster which might have happened had not happened; the incident was as much in the past as it could ever be and I should put it behind me forthwith without delay and get on with concentrating on what was to come.

Well, that told me and in a familiar style too. Most solutions boil down to, 'Get on with it' from her sooner or later; usually 'sooner' if truth be told. She had a point of course. Another way of retelling the same event, recounted by someone with more nerve than I possessed, (but possibly with less imagination) might have been, 'a bicycle rider overtook us and other traffic on the mountain and then I rode us round the next bend'. The contents of this book, however, had I adopted that policy throughout (impossible though that would have been with me as its author), could have been better described as 'a pamphlet' and would have been about as engaging to read as a telephone directory.

★★★★★★★★★★★★★★★★★

Our morning came around as no morning at all, because it was pitch black outside. I decided to put on practically everything I had with me that would assist in keeping me warm. I pulled on a full set of thermal underwear—long sleeve vest and long-johns, thick socks and inserted my thermal glove inners which were necessary, because I always wear light-weight gloves. I feel in better direct contact with the bike. It is a personal choice, but I dislike riding in thick gloves. Patsie decided that she would follow suit, but not would not need her lower thermal underwear, because her legs were always protected to a degree by mine.

Our hosts kindly provided us with an excellent early breakfast and by the time we had loaded the motorcycle and were ready to climb aboard her, first light was colouring the sky. The early hour of our departure from Potes meant we practically had the road to ourselves. As expected, the temperature was on the low side, though I felt it was bracing and crisp rather than uncomfortably freezing. That first eighteen miles of mountain road was a fabulous ride through spectacular scenery, more or less following the line of the beautiful River Deva between Cantabria and Asturias as it carved its way through tall, stark rock formations. As the sun rose, it cast the dramatic shadows of the surrounding angular heights across lower ground, sometimes throwing us into a false twilight, before we burst out into full morning sunshine again. We both thoroughly enjoyed ourselves and once the autoroute was reached progress was as swift as it always was.

In those days, though the approach had changed several times by the time these lines were written, to reach the dockside for the ferry from Santander, one literally rode into the city on a road which ran parallel to the harbour which had a green square backed by retail stores on the other side of the road. At first sight, this arrangement—with a ship docked prominently in the city centre-seemed most peculiar to us.

As we rode through the gates of the dockyard, it was apparent on this occasion we would not be alone as the only bikers on the boat. There, across the dock, was a tight crowd of motorcycles comprised of most varieties—sports bikes, cruisers, big tourers, naked muscles and tall, beaked adventurers. Their riders and pillions were companionably chatting with each other beside their rides in the sunshine. Two riders who were on the fringe of the pack were still mounted, so presumably the most recent to arrive. They spotted us heading their way, waved, shouted a welcome and beckoned us over—one of them clearly heard saying to his companion, 'Move over, and let the ———— in!' The reader either knows how heart-warming that kind of greeting feels or is not a motorcycle rider.

 I rode into the gap they made for us and have to admit that as I greeted the two bikers that flanked us with huge smiles on their faces, the thought occurred to me that there had been a time when I would have found these two men, 'hard as nails and big as bears', somewhat intimidating. Now, of course, I had a *bona fide* tribe membership card underneath me, no questions (fortunately) asked. This unexpected fillip tempted me into believing we had earned some bragging rights, all things considered, though fortunately events transpired to save me from making an utter fool of myself. Two other riders nearby also turned to greet us, though only one of them spoke to us because, so far as I can recall, the other one was munching away, I think on an *empanada* (a Spanish pasty), throughout the conversation.

 'Been on the road long?', enquired the man who didn't have his mouth full by way of an *entre*.

 'Yeah, well you know,' I replied nonchalantly, whilst thinking to myself, 'I will let them into this outstanding tale of ours gently,' 'it'll be about a month by the time we get home, I expect'. I didn't want to come across like a 'blow-hard', right out of the box, after all.

 'That's great!', his eyes widened, genuinely impressed, 'you were lucky'. I may have nodded with a firm expression on my face in that way we 'real chaps' do.

 'We', he continued, with a nod towards his pal, 'only had five days for our trip, didn't we Eric?' ('Eric',smiled, nodded his head and offered a genial 'hmm', as he continued masticating his *empanada*). 'Yes, so what we did was—it was Eric's idea—we came over on the boat then we rode the spine of the Pyrenees from the Atlantic coast to the Mediterranean coast on the Spanish side of the border and then we turned around and rode the spine of the Pyrenees back again on the French side. Didn't we Eric?'

Once that revelation had sunk in, it put me on my heels and back into the right-sized boots in short order. Their own concentrated trip, likewise, put our own European riding adventures into some perspective. Suddenly, our efforts didn't seem all that remarkable, after all. 'Eric' nodded, smiled and took another bite of his *empanada* or whatever it was he was justifiably enjoying.

'Eric' wasn't his name, by the way, unless it was, by complete coincidence. I cannot honestly remember his name. I vaguely recall that—as usual—he was one of those quiet, later middle-aged men, wearing metal-rimmed spectacles and a riding jacket that had probably seen better days. Take him away from that machine he was leaning upon, put him in a cardigan, say he was a philatelist and no one would have given you a quarrel about it. When are they are ever seven feet tall, looking or sounding like super-heroes?'

'Good Lord, did you really?', was the best I had, by way of a response. I was mightily impressed, need it be said. Deliberately making a rapid trip of unremitting mountain road riding, day after day, with every hour, no doubt, offering up the kind of challenges that I had found most problematic on the few occasions we encountered them, was beyond countenance for me.

'Oh yes', continued our new friend, as if this last incredible revelation was insufficient, 'Well, that's Eric for you. A couple of years ago, he did a solo ride from the north to the south coast, right through the middle of Australia. He does that sort of thing, you know sleeping next to the bike in the bush, under the stars with all those snakes, spiders and such like creeping about, don't you, Eric?'

'Eric', still smiling companionably, and demonstrably a man few words, but mighty deeds, simply nodded. I, knowing upon the instant that I was in the company of motorcycling giants (yet again), said as little as possible about our, 'nice ride through

France, Spain and a bit of Portugal'. Patsie looked at me from under her eyelashes with a faint smile. She knew in which disastrous direction I had been heading. Of course, she did. Least said—soonest mended. I got the message loud and clear that time, fortunately.

★★★★★★★★★★★★★★★★★

There is no doubt that since those days further experience has tempered my behaviour and possibly enhanced my wisdom in so far as what I say. The leopard never entirely changes its spots, of course. In the Far East I have seen my share of Buddhist monks, but until comparatively recently I had never had a long conversation with one. In Northern Thailand, near the Golden Triangle, I did spend some time speaking to one of them, who spoke faultless English, and who tended an out of the way temple.

At a certain point I asked him if he had always been a monk or if he had once lived a more conventional life, before donning the saffron robes. To my astonishment, he told me that he had, for years, made his living as a motorcycle mechanic. That, as one might expect, changed the course of the conversation for a while. Nevertheless, he did have some insightful things to say to me of a more spiritual and temporal nature and he was such a wise, calm, open-hearted person that he made a lasting impression upon me.

When it was time to say goodbye, he said, 'Perhaps we shall meet again. I would like that very much'.

To which I replied, 'Yes, perhaps in another life, another incarnation, perhaps upon the astral plane'.

I sometimes just can't help myself. He was a Buddhist monk, after all. So I jumped straight to whatever my Ka might get up to, once it was beyond the veil. I mean, who wouldn't? Patsie, unfortunately, wasn't closely at hand at that moment to give me a sharp little kick on the ankle.

Actually,' he said, 'I was just thinking, you know, if you came to Thailand on holiday again—say next year—and you came by, that would be good, because I will still be here.'

★★★★★★★★★★★★★

Pleasant though it was to chat among our fellow bikers on the dockside, the sun had now climbed high in the sky, whilst I was dressed for cold and altitude. One can readily remove one's jacket, but removing one's lower underwear in public is problematic, unless one is a burlesque artiste. Since I have neither the figure or talent to be one of those, I was beginning to cook. It came as some relief, therefore, that motorcyclists were to be boarded first and, upon the welcome signal from the dock marshal, away we went among the usual low revolution babble of variously pitched engines.

Before long we had established 'Madam' securely on the garage deck for the voyage and had hurried off to our cabin to change into more comfortable, cooler, lighter clothes. The cruise would be an overnight one, delivering us to Portsmouth, on the Channel coast of southern England in the late afternoon of the following day. The first order of business was a *de rigueur* adjournment to one of the ship's bars. Patsie ensconced herself in a comfortable seat with a table, by a large picture window which offered a good view of the expansive harbour.

At the bar I initially intended to order a large gin and tonic for my wife, but as I stood waiting my turn to be served, I looked over at her, waiting for my return, and two thoughts came into my mind. The first is nobody's business but hers and my own and the second one was, 'My love, you deserve much better than a G & T.' So I chose a really excellent (by which, as the reader knows, I mean 'more than I would normally spend') bottle of Chablis (since I know Patsie particularly enjoys it) and asked for a proper metal ice-bucket to keep it chilled and proper white napkin to accompany it, so she got the idea this was special—definitely a Category No. 3 wine and not just any old guzzle-juice. When I returned to the table bearing my offering, she looked up at me, eyes smiling in surprise and said;

'Well, this is very nice. Is this because we made it?'

'Absolutely', I confirmed, as I played sommelier for her and filled her glass.

To be honest, had I been as stupid as I can on occasion be,

I would have said, 'Actually, love we haven't strictly speaking 'made it' yet, because there is a long way to go by sea and then another long ride northwards, after we get ashore on Blighty. Only after we have gone through all of that and you are back in your little fluffy mules with your feet up in front of the TV, and the cat curled up next to you, can we truly say we have 'made it''. I said nothing of the kind, of course. There is no point in blowing up a party balloon for someone, only to forthwith burst it in their face.

All that taken as given, whether we had finally, 'made it' or not, the continental part of our journey was indisputably completed, so this was definitely an appropriate moment for celebration. Admittedly, one can make a celebration of the day if it has a 'Y' in, it, but this was more a legitimate reason than that. In my notes, made at the time, I wrote that it had been 'a journey that would live long in our memories'. I suppose this book has ensured it will endure longer than that, because now it will abide as long as anyone cares to read about it.

Though we knew there would be other rides in the future, it was too soon to wonder when and to where they would be or whether they would be as memorable as this one. Those that followed would all have their ups and downs, though the downs became incrementally fewer in number, the wiser we became on the subject of long-distance motorcycling. Bizarrely, that consideration had the effect of making them somewhat less memorable, because they contained fewer noteworthy dramas.

Once on Corsica, for example, we were due on the following morning to ride to a hotel positioned remotely and high in the mountains, that offered a challenging ride through stunning terrain to reach it. On the previous evening, we received a weather warning that severe thunderstorms were forecast over our route and destination. There was a time when we would have set off anyway, simply because we had paid for our room, which wouldn't be refundable at such short notice. What we did instead was book another night at the place we were already staying (which was in Ajaccio, so interesting enough), biting the bullet on our financial loss as a price worth paying to avoid an especially elevated risk: And that was the front and the back of that story.

If we had gone on that ride and *if* we had survived, that would certainly have made a better tale. Someone, I cannot remember who, said 'if', though one of the smallest words in the dictionary was potentially the most hazardous. As usual everything comes down to weighing the options and odds. Whilst those trips to come were enjoyable, including the ones that drenched us in deluges we were unable to dodge, the first big ride would always be a special one. How could it be otherwise?

As we sipped our wine, the ship's engines throbbed into life below us and we began our voyage, nudging our way towards Santander's harbour mouth. Inside the harbour walls the water was calm and blue with little sail boats skittering around its surface for fun. High upon the headland to the west stands an imposing, 'bits-box' of a building, seemingly cobbled together from a number of 19th century architectural styles. It appears as though it might be a hotel, though I speculated it would also make a great location for a 'dark and stormy night' themed motion picture, in which the cast would be whittled down incrementally. The 'distraught lady in the negligee' character could take a header off the conveniently situated cliff edge. In fact, this place is the Palacio de la Magdelena, built during the first decade of the 20th century as a summer residence for the Spanish royal family.

The second we left the protection of the harbour walls into the implacable swells of the Bay of Biscay, the power of the deep ocean hit the ship like a mallet and from even-keeled calm everything began to pitch and roll, taking unwary passengers by surprise. Patsie found thus sudden sea-change quite amusing for the period that we sat polishing off that bottle of Chablis. She could even raise a giggle as we made our way to our cabin, hanging onto rails or anything else permanently fixed that we could use for stability. Unfortunately, in the final corridor, there came a moment when she was putting her foot down to a deck that was suddenly not where she expected it to be and, in that instant, I could see that the lady was no longer amused.

'Right, that's it' she snapped, as she regained her composure, 'I am getting on to my bunk and I am not getting off it again until we are inside the Channel'. As always, the lady was as good as her word.

Fortunately, the following morning the seas were moderate and we could move around comparatively normally. We sat together looking out at the sea-swell, drinking coffee, hoping to see whales breaching or dolphins playing, but didn't catch a glimpse of either doing anything at all. We chugged along, occasionally glimpsing the coast of France off our right (starboard) side and eventually the appearance of our own familiar, pale fringed coastline off the port side. We passed the Isle of Wight, Portsmouth came into view with its sea-fort, coastal defences and, as we slowly progressed towards our dock, rows of resting, grey Royal Navy warships. It was time to don our riding gear again and prepare to rejoin our bike.

32. Headlights on:
In which we disembark, shiver and head back to the North

As usual with long-distance ferry ships, docking time was one thing, whilst disembarking time was quite another. In the meantime, one attempts to patiently wait to ride off the ship, in a reverse of the way one once felt about boarding it. Eventually, upon a signal, invisible to most of those waiting, vehicle engines come to life, red lights appear up the line and everyone creeps forward to the waiting shore. So, we rolled, at last, down the ship's ramps onto England's not very green nor pleasant concrete.

Once we were in the open air again, the early winter weather clenched its cold grip upon the body and spirit. The sky was predictably overcast. We were grateful we had taken the precaution of personal insulation to a degree, but I cannot say I was looking forward to the final stretch of our journey very much, or particularly happy to be back in northern climes generally. Patsie didn't say much at all, so I knew that she was of a similar mind. In fact, I knew that if she could have been instantly transported to her own kitchen that would have suited her very well. Abruptly, after all that good-natured sunshine to which we had become latterly accustomed, everything now appeared to be rather dull and downbeat.

These were days before much very wisdom regarding ship arrivals or road journey times had been acquired, as the reader is by now, very well aware. I was bright enough to realise that this day was an extraordinary one, because we were only beginning our ride towards our home in Yorkshire when the afternoon was already well advanced. That journey, if all goes well, can take five hours by motorcar. Even if all went without a hitch, I was not optimistic enough to believe we would be unlocking our own door at half-past seven in the evening.

So, I decided we should overnight somewhere *en route* and take an easy ride the following morning to arrive home around lunchtime. Actually, that was not much of a decision on my part, because some time had elapsed since Patsie had insisted, for safety reasons, that we didn't ride or drive late into the evening just to save money on an overnight stay. We were on home turf, so I knew, with certainty, that we were not going to be taken by surprise by the delaying barrier of the Rutland Alps. Rutland, for those who may legitimately not know, is an English county that is not only very small, but quite flat. That did not mean, however, I was not about to make another blunder; in fact, several, if the reader can credit that. Whilst the road to Hell is principally paved with giant cobblestones, some sections of it remain paved with good intentions

What we should have done was ride for an hour—possibly two hours at the absolute maximum—and then go into a hotel or better yet, an inn for the evening with pints, wine for Patsie, honest British 'pub grub' and a comfortable bed for the night, irrespective of where that might have been, so long as it was broadly in the right direction. As anyone who has read this book knows, I already knew that was the right way to tackle this kind of problem, because I had applied that methodology on the rides we took to Segura de la Sierra and Penausende and that initially worked well—more or less. Of course, it's fair to say what happened after those stunts didn't go so well, which only goes to underline that if the celestial Lords of Misrule have got it in for you, the chances are they are going to get you one way or another.

Be that as it may, we didn't do that or anything similarly sensible. I knew of a good country hotel in a village just off the A1, a former coaching inn, and about sixty and some miles north of London, that I thought fitted the bill in terms of the onward journey the following day. So, we headed for it. That was, of course, entirely the wrong way round to tackle the problem, because had we hunkered down farther south that final leg of the journey would assuredly have taken place in daylight, hopefully with a little bit of sunshine, and an hour or so on the bike one way or the other would not have made any difference.

Notwithstanding that this fundamental planning flaw would be bound to have eventual consequences on this day, it all went wrong instantly for other reasons. To arrive at the southerly end of the A1 from Portsmouth meant we had to ride the M25, the London Orbital Motorway (ring road). This was my first mistake, because there is a far less pressured way to initially move to the north from Portsmouth (via Oxford), that doesn't entail going anywhere near London or its infamous traffic densities. Harassed afternoon turned into miserable evening as we grappled with heavy traffic, inconsiderate speeding motorcars and bullying commercial vehicles. The congestion we experienced was what I should have expected, had I thought about it in advance. That then turned into rush-hour, gridlock, (which I hadn't crossed my mind to consider at all), so tightly packed, that on occasion, it even brought our motorcycle to a standstill.

Eventually we arrived on the motorway portion of the A1 (The Great North Road which goes from London to Edinburgh)—the A1M. Full darkness had now fallen. Traffic was not so dense, but was moving very quickly. Cold? I was feeling, by this juncture, as though I was stuck rigidly in one position. Patsie was unhappily clinging to my back like a limpet. The reader should not forget that the roads we had been riding in Spain—even the autoroutes—carried nothing like the volume of traffic that was habitual on English roads. Furthermore, we never rode during the hours of darkness and we were never compelled to ride in extremely low temperatures at any time. So, this sudden cold, dark and traffic hassle was taking some assimilating.

Reader, as I clung onto that motorbike, my mind went back to the days when our company employed the services of motorcycle couriers very regularly. We often worked late into the evening on deadlines and our courier was invariably the same rider, whom we got to know quite well. I vividly remember the physical condition he was in sometimes when he arrived in reception after a long ride. He would stagger in carrying his package, gaffer tape round his cuffs and ankles, so cold he had icicles on his hair and beard. We would sit him down and pour hot, sweet tea into him until he thawed and then send him on his way again. Worse even than that, we also sent him off on similar treks in all weathers and seasons, leaving us in the evening with a satchel full of work with many miles to go in front of him. I know it was his job to do, but now—just very briefly—I experienced what he endured on our behalves. Bless him and all his brethren. He earned his living the hard way, was always good humoured and, of course, never once complained.

When the exit eventually came for our destination, I sent a prayer of gratitude heavenwards. We pulled up outside the main entrance of this hotel and though I was heartened by the warm amber lights emanating from within, found I could barely move. It was by now between 8.30 and 9 pm. So, I asked Patsie to climb off the bike and announce our arrival, whilst I unfolded and creaked myself back into working order, freeing my hands from their claw-like grasp on the grips. Besides, I knew the parking spaces of this place were positioned behind the hotel and I would have to move the bike from the roadside, to remove our luggage so I could bring it inside.

As I sat there, the thought did occur to me that our late departure that day from the dockside combined with our *'warmer as we went further south'* theories were now coming home to roost through lack of consideration of the inevitable *'much colder when we came back again, when November was upon us'* consequences. Still, who was I kidding? We would have gone on this ride anyway, in those days: Later was later for us sometimes and, if the prize was worth it, must look after itself. As usual that is not a recommendation for anyone else to follow, because it was irresponsible, though it would have been markedly less so had we been already tucking into beef and ale pie, ensconced in the snug of some comfortable hostelry at the time.

A few minutes afterwards I stumped into the hotel reception, where Patsie stood bearing the glad tidings that the hotel staff had no record of our reservation—through no fault of their own, as it transpired. Well, that was just *blanking* marvellous! However, she did have the presence of mind to order two large warming brandies and was sipping hers as she handed me mine, bless her. I was ready for it. Thank goodness, our unheralded arrival notwithstanding, there was a room available for us. We had missed the last service for dinner, though a sandwich could be rustled together for us. That offer was good enough, as practically anything edible would have been. We went to our room thereafter, stood under a wonderful hot shower for an age and then poured ourselves on to a deep, soft mattress covered by a very comfortable warm duvet.

The following morning opened with bright sunshine creeping though our bedroom curtains, though plainly accompanied by the temperatures one may expect of the season. We were hungry and enjoyed a really excellent full English breakfast, which is particularly welcome when it has been some time since one ate the last one.

Need it be said, we both put on our thermal underwear again for the ride and, in my case, also a lightweight thermal Balaclava helmet, which came out of the luggage for the first time and which I wished I had remembered I carried on the previous day. So, we paid our dues, then set off for the two and something hour journey which would bring us to our home.

We rode up a familiar northbound road and, whilst the temperature made for a crisp morning, it wasn't so low as to be particularly challenging. Our motorcycle, in those conditions, was a mile-eating missile. After we had covered something over half our distance, we noticed that ahead of us heavy cumulus clouds were forming. 'We are are going to have rain', said Patsie's voice in my ear and as we know once that forecast has been given, the fact of it is sure to follow, even in circumstances when the signs were not so evident. The only question in my mind, given we had no rain at all thus far on this entire ride, was whether we would arrive home before it began to fall upon us.

Journey's end is always anticlimactic. Speaking for myself, as I come closer to the little patch of ground where I habitually spend my time, I did not really have that, 'Great to be Back' sensation. In those moments, if the last place I have been has not been demonstrably unpleasant, one place seems to be much the same as another to me. Yet 'returning' involves hours and sometimes days of effort to achieve. 'Arriving' tends to leave me at something of a loss to understand why I have gone to the trouble. It is a temporary state of mind inevitably, because all our connections essentially coalesced in and emanated from this particular English blessed plot.

So, what, that was profound, had this prolonged ride taught us? I cannot speak for Patsie and she, independently minded woman that she is, would not only not wish me to do so, but would object if I tried. Quite right too! Should I say that for all the trials, tribulations, slight disagreements and outright arguments, I knew I was married to the right person? Well, I could say that, but then I knew that, for a fact, before we left, so could hardly claim it as a revelation. So, I suppose it all came down to an affirmation that we both loved the 'Way' as part of our life together on the 'Wheel' regardless of the mode of transport, but if there could also be two wheels and an engine, then so much the better.

Patsie's feelings about her home are somewhat different to mine. Her own affinity with it is irrefutable. Indeed, there occasionally comes a time—and this is a standing joke in our household—that she will close and bar the 'big gates', *'drop the portcullis, flood the moat and let loose the piranhas and alligators into it'*. To be scrupulously fair to Patsie, one of her essential considerations, when she is feeling the need to be the absolute undisturbed mistress of her own domain, is that I, as consort, am required to be behind those walls with her.

So the outskirts of our small market town came into view; the last Autumn leafed, tree-lined avenue passed under our tyres and that sinking feeling I have described dropped by another degree. This was undoubtedly a very good place to live, but even a very good nest can only have so much appeal, after one has experienced the sensation of free flight. Reader, if you have arrived with us at this, the furthest end of our tale, then you are almost certainly one of the last people who needs that perspective explaining to them.

We rode into our courtyard. I stopped the bike and Patsie climbed off, the keys to our door already in her hand. As always, at times like these, a place we had left comparatively recently appeared to be slightly other worldly and unfamiliar, as though it wasn't quite our own and ages—far beyond the fact of it defined by a calendar—had passed since last we had seen it.

'So that's that', I said. Now it could legitimately be said, we really had 'made it', even though I was still wearing my boots. I, wisely for a change, said nothing at all on that subject.

'I will go in', Patsie declared as she departed, 'and put the kettle on', Tea then: Is that not how for Britons absolutely all journeys end? Someone is always drinking tea.

I opened the door to our garage (which was a converted stable) and thereafter slowly rode 'Madam' into it. I put her on her side stand and climbed off; the final act. I believe I sighed—possibly wistfully, like poor hen-pecked, Boabdil, for all that had gone before and had now irredeemably passed into memory. Into history, one might say, at the risk of labouring a point.

Had this ride scratched my motorcycling itch? It had for a little while and I wasn't upset that I would have some time to relieve my aches and pains, but it would be certain to be just for a little while. If someone had said, 'Right, in a couple of weeks we are off again!', I would have signed on without hesitation, so long as we were bound for somewhere warm!

Before I left her, I distinctly remember putting the palm of my hand upon the bike's big tank. What could I possibly say that would be adequate? 'Thank you,' I whispered as I patted her, 'you brought us home'. That, as you now know, reader, was something of an understatement.

Then I closed the door upon our 'Lady in Black', 'Madam', 'Empress of Motorcycles', our outstanding, well reader, you know what she was by now, don't you?.

As I turned towards the house, the first fat raindrop fell, like a tear, onto the back of my glove: And that *is*, if unbelievable, absolutely true.

IGNITION OFF & KEY OUT

Epilogue:
In which we say goodbye and farewell

So that really is it, done and dusted, kind reader. The odyssey of our, in reality, 4,000 (ish) mile little adventure has ended. Admittedly about 1,000 miles of it was by ship, we were asleep some of the time, so that part probably doesn't count. You may metaphorically climb off the metaphorical bike now. That's *the* nod from me. Steady as you go. Don't come a cropper, now of all times. Take a stretch and you are good to go. I trust you enjoyed our journey together and those parts of you that are aching in consequence of your ordeal recover quickly. If you are happy to be seeing the back of me, today is your lucky day. I hadn't forgotten about the cat, incidentally, she was being pampered in a luxury cattery and we collected her on the day following our arrival, prising her reluctantly off her bed which was a miniature brass bedstead for some reason.

Patsie and I remain, 'Lifers', and do you know—we have not had a disagreement—Today! Well, she hasn't spoken to me much today—truth be told. Something to do with digging up a buddleia, apparently. 'Madam' and I are, alas, no longer together. Why is that? Through no fault of her own, need it be said. She was performing as reliably on the day I said goodbye to her as she did on the first day that we met. If I had any more room in the garage, there would still be a 'Madam' in there to this day. I would not (or would I?) be setting off on marathon expeditions upon her, but I would be very happy to occasionally relive the wonderful experience she provided for ride outs and daytrips, because that bike was unforgettably well composed and flew like the wind.

So, what happened? 'Madam' in no way showed her age so far as I was concerned, but unfortunately, we gentlemen are not so inured to the progress of time. Simply put, my poor wrists (never that strong, as it happens, in consequence of an early incident with a rocking horse, that I would prefer not to elaborate upon) found it increasingly difficult to ride on lower bars for longer periods of time. 'Madam' carried her weight well and, I would go far as to say, reassuringly so in certain circumstances, but she was a heavy lump for me to lug about as a dead weight, nevertheless.

We were touring when I decided we must part company with her and the reader has learned what we next purchased for the job, because it was implicitly revealed in these pages. How that came about is moderately interesting.

I knew we had to have a bike where I could sit more upright, but was still comfortable for Patsie and readily carry our usual complement of luggage. Which motorcycle that would be, from my perspective, came down to—as usual—two short-listed options. As it transpired an opportunity arose to privately purchase a recent year, low mileage example of one of them at a fair price, so I grasped it and provisionally did the deal with the owner, who conveniently lived in our county, though about 40 miles distant from our home. Then GB (of course, GB was involved) and I drove off in his van to conclude the purchase if, upon scrutiny, all was considered well. So, GB gave the machine his expert appraisal and then offered his 'thumbs up' verdict of approval. The deal was done; the bike ramped up into his van to be taken directly to his workshop.

At that point I had not ridden the bike. In fact, I had never ridden one of these motorcycles at all. I was not especially concerned on that score. European police services used them and as the reader now knows, we had that conversation with the French motorcycle policeman who rode one; so an affirmation from a professional. I make it a policy not to ride a motorbike that has not been purchased new, before my friend has thoroughly dug into its vitals, instituted any remedial action he thinks it needs, serviced it and test ridden it thereafter, himself. By the time he has presented it to me as OK—I have every confidence the bike is, indeed, entirely good to go.

GB's work completed, I received the telephone call from him to the effect that the time for me to take a test ride had arrived. So I showed up at his place, put my leg over the bike, fired it up and away I went into our local countryside to put it through its paces. No more than five miles had passed under its tyres. I didn't like it! I had spent all that money on a motorcycle without trying it first and now I didn't like it! I returned to my friend's workshop disconsolately.

'So how did you get on?' he cheerfully enquired as I rolled up.

'Oh, dear,' I replied somewhat crestfallen and instantly bringing the mood down, 'I think I have made a terrible mistake. I don't like it.'

'Why ever not?' he responded, demonstrably confused, 'I've been on it and it performs brilliantly. In fact, I really like it and it's just right for you'.

'But, but,' I stammered, 'it's *SO LIGHT!* There is nothing to it! It feels to me as though it's made from kitchen foil!'

It has to be said, he began to laugh, which nonplussed me somewhat. 'Motorcycling technology has moved on some way since you bought your bike. Now they are even using this new stuff. It's called aluminium, you know.'

'Oh, so it is strong enough then, is it?' I replied, 'Because it's a big bike'

'Of course, it is!' he laughed again, 'get yourself out on it again and give it another go'.

So, off I went again. I was suitably reassured, given it was guaranteed not to fold itself up like origami as I rode along upon it. I very quickly discovered, as I became used to the idea, I rather liked the fact that it was so light and biddable. So, when conditions were safe and appropriate, I did some cornering and acceleration tests. To my very pleasant surprise I found this bike was absolutely no slouch and in every respect responsive, comparing favourably with my previous machine (possibly better in several instances—though indisputably different) and it was considerably more comfortable for me with its higher bars into the bargain.

The peculiar thing of it is, my new machine wasn't lighter than the the previous one at all, it's actually heavier, (departing bike—first series 492 lbs-223kg/new machine 582lbs-264 kg,). The deficiency of my technical knowledge has been well established, though I have heard it suggested that this impression of lightness (not entirely confined to me, I have since discovered, thank goodness) could be explained by weight displacement. That proposition suggests that my recent acquisition carried its weight lower in the bike. I just ride one; I have no idea how that works, if it does, which will surprise no one.

As the reader knows from these pages, we toured with this replacement motorcycle frequently. It also never let us down and as I write these lines, that machine sits (among a couple of others) in our garage, though I ride it particularly, practically every day. She is comfortable, handsome, capable and pulls like a train, though perhaps tellingly, I refer to her in my mind, simply by the letters that identify her model. We don't have conversations, because for me it doesn't quite have the *cache* that the 'Empress' had, though that view is admittedly totally personal and subjective.

Strangers, nevertheless, do stroll up to me when I am sitting astride the parked bike and comment that it is a fine-looking machine. I would have no hesitation in recommending one to anyone who was looking for what it can deliver. In fact, I have done so and, as I write, not so long ago to someone of my vintage with similar wrist issues. I didn't ask whether he had been unfortunate whilst riding the purple sage on his own rocking-horse, because some cowboys can be thin-skinned on that subject.

Before we go, Mrs. Lewis has insisted that I make it clear that the portrait of her in this book, whilst she concedes is honestly presented, is merely an impression of a woman as perceived and written by a man. Accordingly, she feels, it is likely to be about as accurate as anything a man can write about a woman; especially, apparently, if that man is me. Whilst that observation is certainly not a compliment, I have no problem in acceding to her wishes, because I have noticed she is preparing one of my favourite dishes for dinner and, when it's ready, I hope to be able to eat it, as opposed, as it is said in our parts, to wearing it!

May I finally leave you, reader, with our thanks and best wishes for happy trails, but also perhaps predictably, with a well-intentioned and extremely short historical vignette—which reassuringly has absolutely nothing to do with the Duke of Wellington.

When a successful ancient Roman general returned to the Eternal City in triumph, as he processed on his chariot through the adoration of the crowd, behind him stood a man (known as the Auriga) who held the laurel crown, symbolic of victory, over his head. That man's task was also to repeatedly whisper a simple sober message into the general's ear. Lest he was tempted to believe himself greater than he truly was, he heard these words, 'Remember, thou art mortal.'

For your own sake, 'Ride Safely'.
For anyone riding with you, 'Ride Safely'.
For everyone who loves you or your pillion, 'Ride Safely'.
For those you meet upon the 'Way' and 'Wheel'
And for all their loved ones,
Rider, please, 'Ride Safely'.

Cough drops and gimlets!
Remember, thou art mortal.

J.H.L.

Acknowledgements

As usual my thanks go out to the members of my family and abiding close friends who have consistently assisted in making these kinds of projects come to fruition. They know who they are, because they remain constantly in my heart and mind.

Special thanks are due to GB who has provided technical advice on motorcycling matters and who has not objected to his appearance in these pages.

Thanks, must be finally given to the people of Spain, especially of the region of Andalucia and most particularly to the residents of Mojacar for their abiding welcome, friendship and open-hearted kindness.

J.H.L.